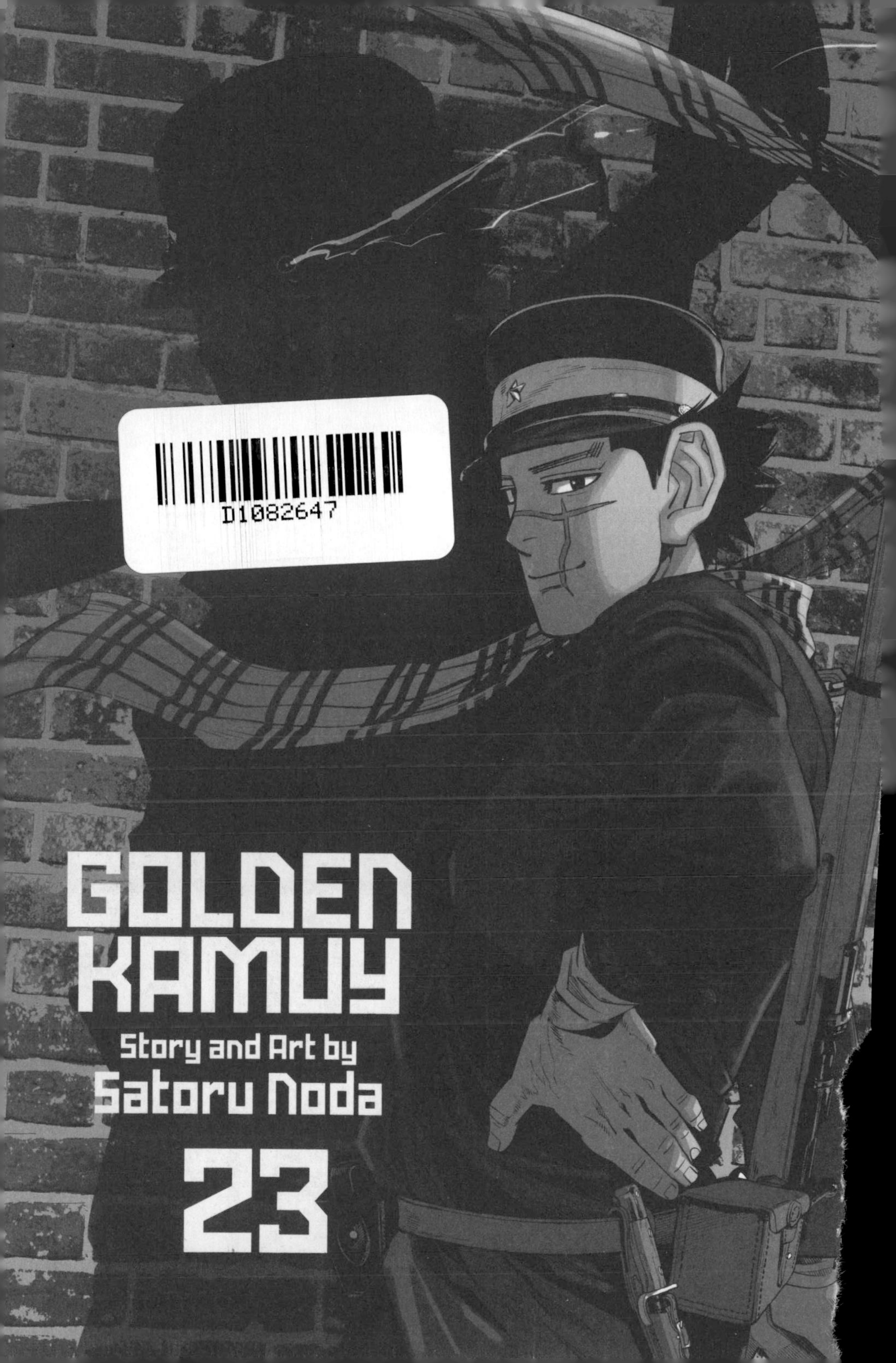
GOLDEN KAMUY
Story and Art by
Satoru Noda
23

The Story So Far

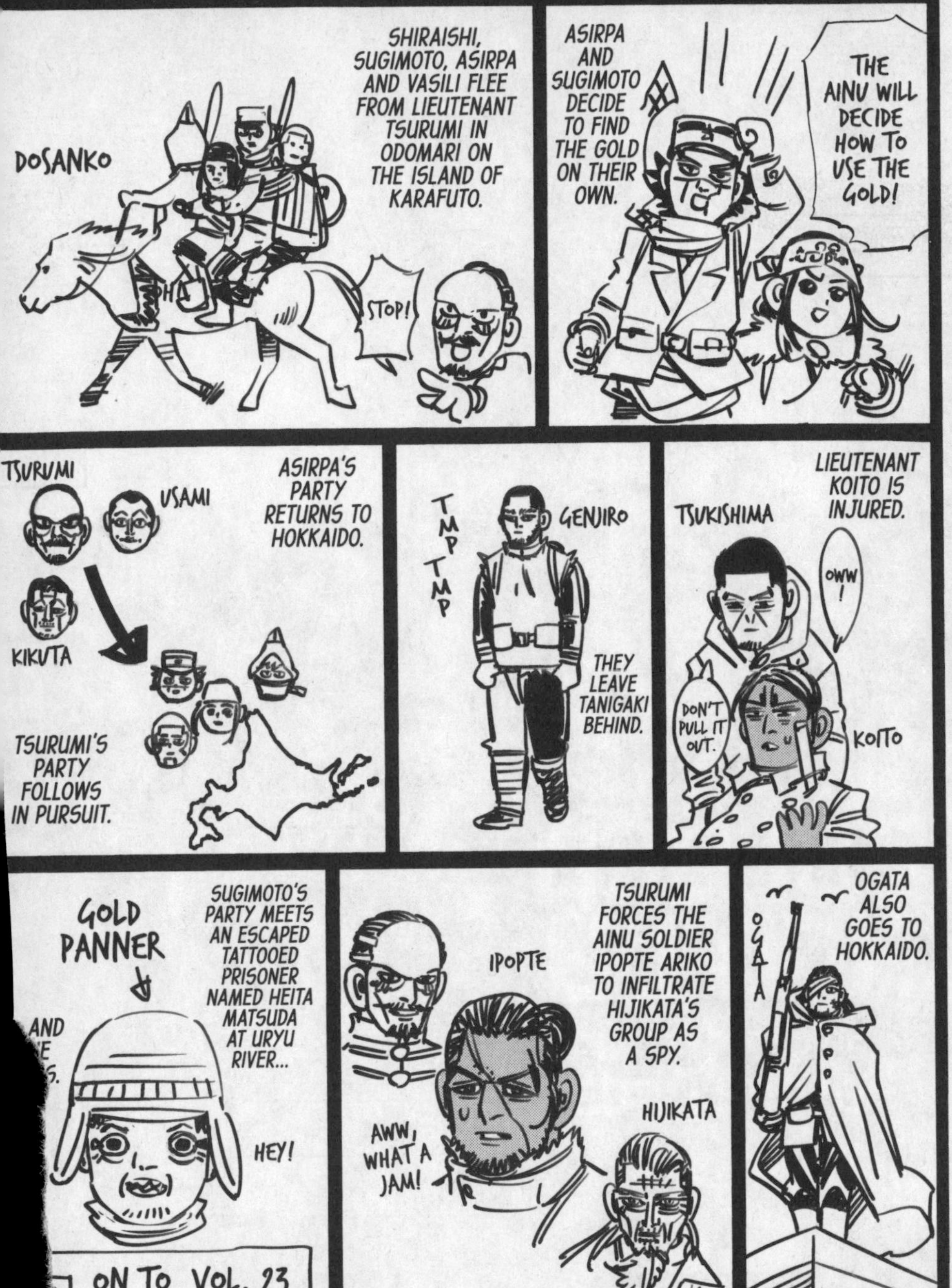

ASIRPA AND SUGIMOTO DECIDE TO FIND THE GOLD ON THEIR OWN.
THE AINU WILL DECIDE HOW TO USE THE GOLD!
SHIRAISHI, SUGIMOTO, ASIRPA AND VASILI FLEE FROM LIEUTENANT TSURUMI IN ODOMARI ON THE ISLAND OF KARAFUTO.
DOSANKO
STOP!
LIEUTENANT KOITO IS INJURED.
TSUKISHIMA
OWW!
DON'T PULL IT OUT.
KOITO
GENJIRO
TMP TMP
THEY LEAVE TANIGAKI BEHIND.
ASIRPA'S PARTY RETURNS TO HOKKAIDO.
TSURUMI
USAMI
KIKUTA
TSURUMI'S PARTY FOLLOWS IN PURSUIT.
OGATA ALSO GOES TO HOKKAIDO.
OGATA
TSURUMI FORCES THE AINU SOLDIER IPOPTE ARIKO TO INFILTRATE HIJIKATA'S GROUP AS A SPY.
IPOPTE
AWW, WHAT A JAM!
HIJIKATA
SUGIMOTO'S PARTY MEETS AN ESCAPED TATTOOED PRISONER NAMED HEITA MATSUDA AT URYU RIVER...
GOLD PANNER
AND
HEY!
ON TO VOL. 23

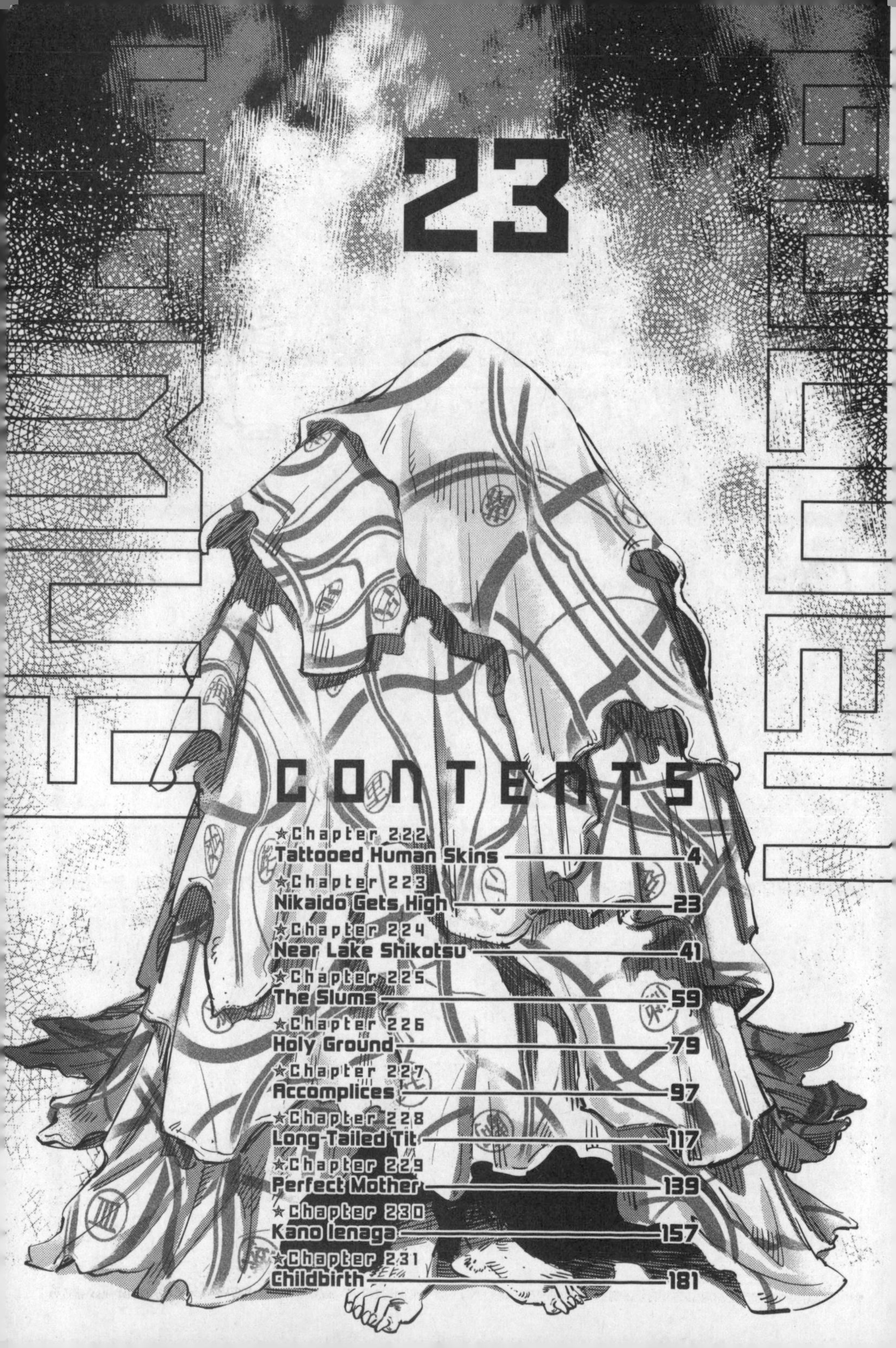

23

CONTENTS

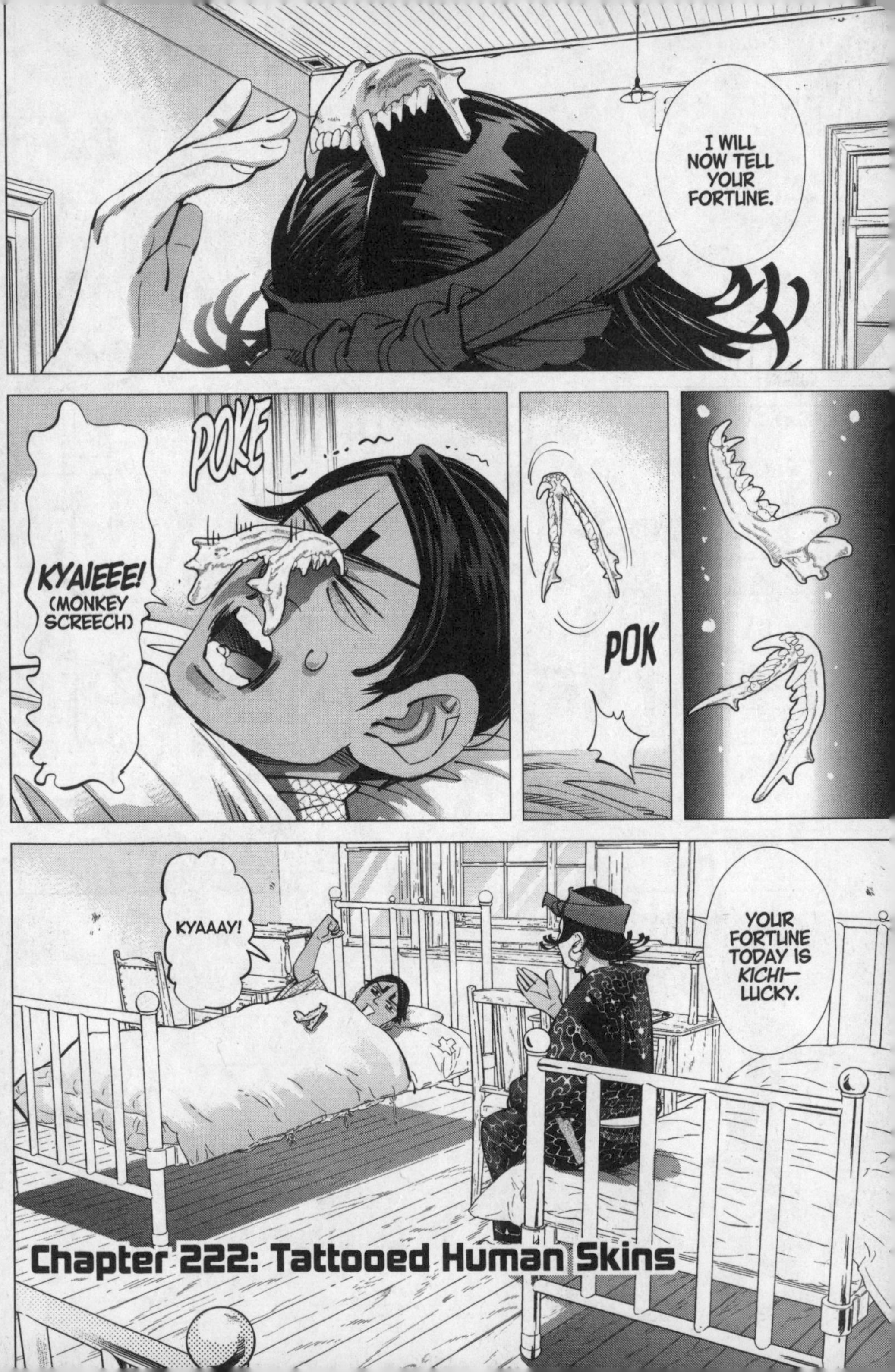
I WILL NOW TELL YOUR FORTUNE.
POK
POKE
KYAIEEE! (MONKEY SCREECH)
YOUR FORTUNE TODAY IS KICHI— LUCKY.
KYAAAY!
Chapter 222: Tattooed Human Skins

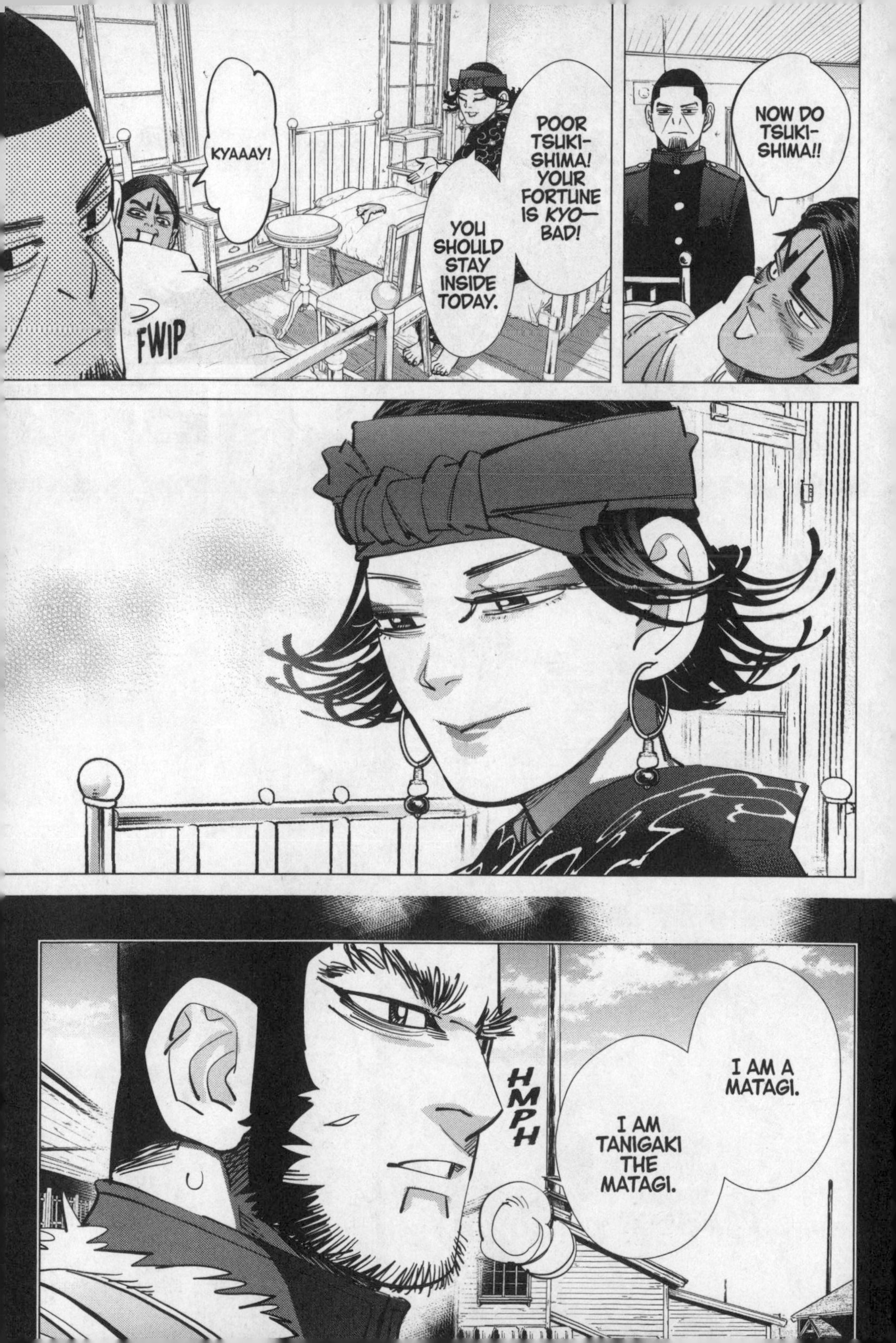
NOW DO TSUKI-SHIMA!!
POOR TSUKI-SHIMA! YOUR FORTUNE IS KYO—BAD!
YOU SHOULD STAY INSIDE TODAY.
KYAAAY!
FWIP
I AM A MATAGI.
I AM TANIGAKI THE MATAGI.
HMPH

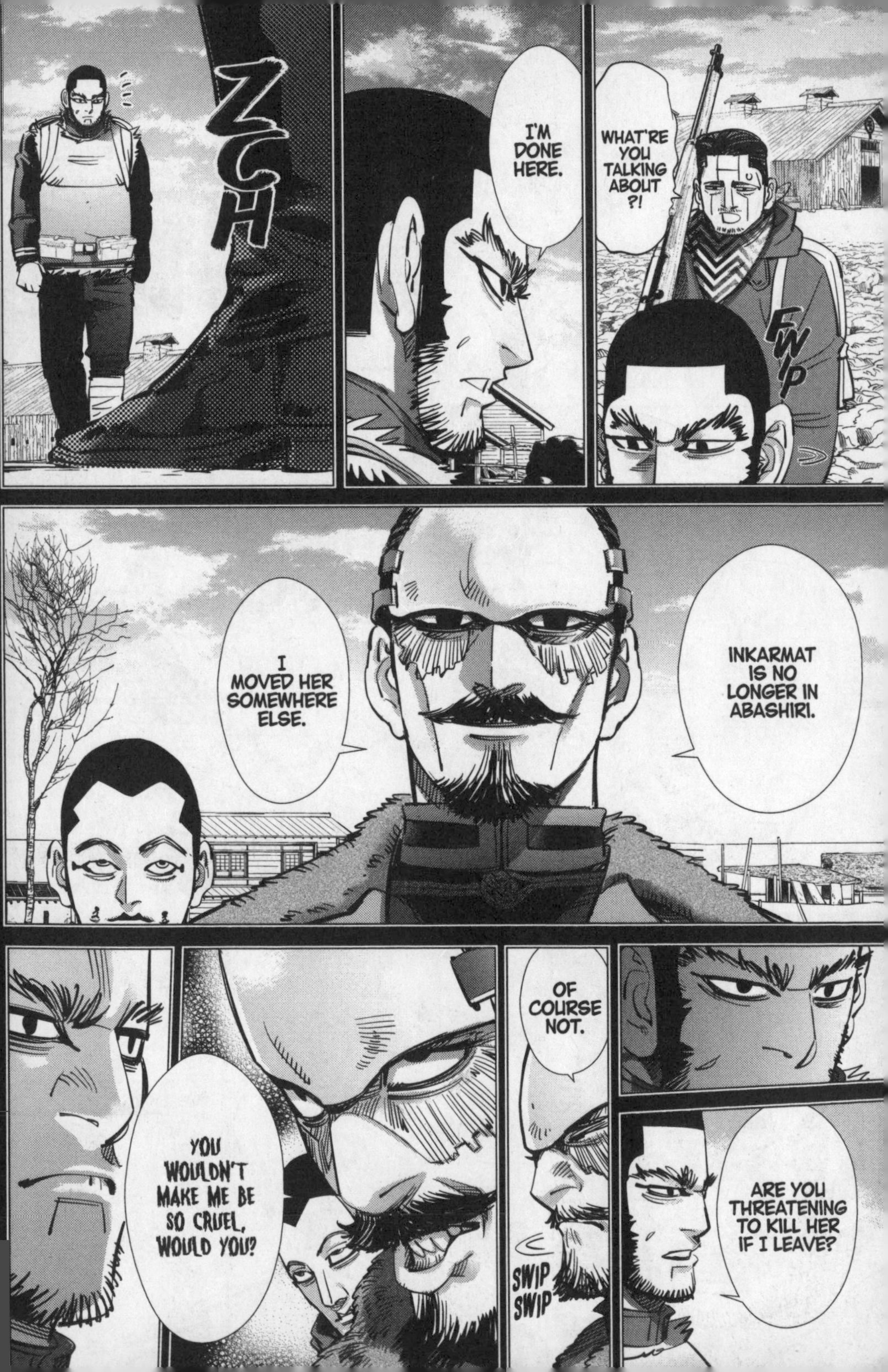
WHAT'RE YOU TALKING ABOUT ?!
FWIP
I'M DONE HERE.
ZCH
INKARMAT IS NO LONGER IN ABASHIRI.
I MOVED HER SOMEWHERE ELSE.
ARE YOU THREATENING TO KILL HER IF I LEAVE?
OF COURSE NOT.
SWIP SWIP
YOU WOULDN'T MAKE ME BE SO CRUEL, WOULD YOU?

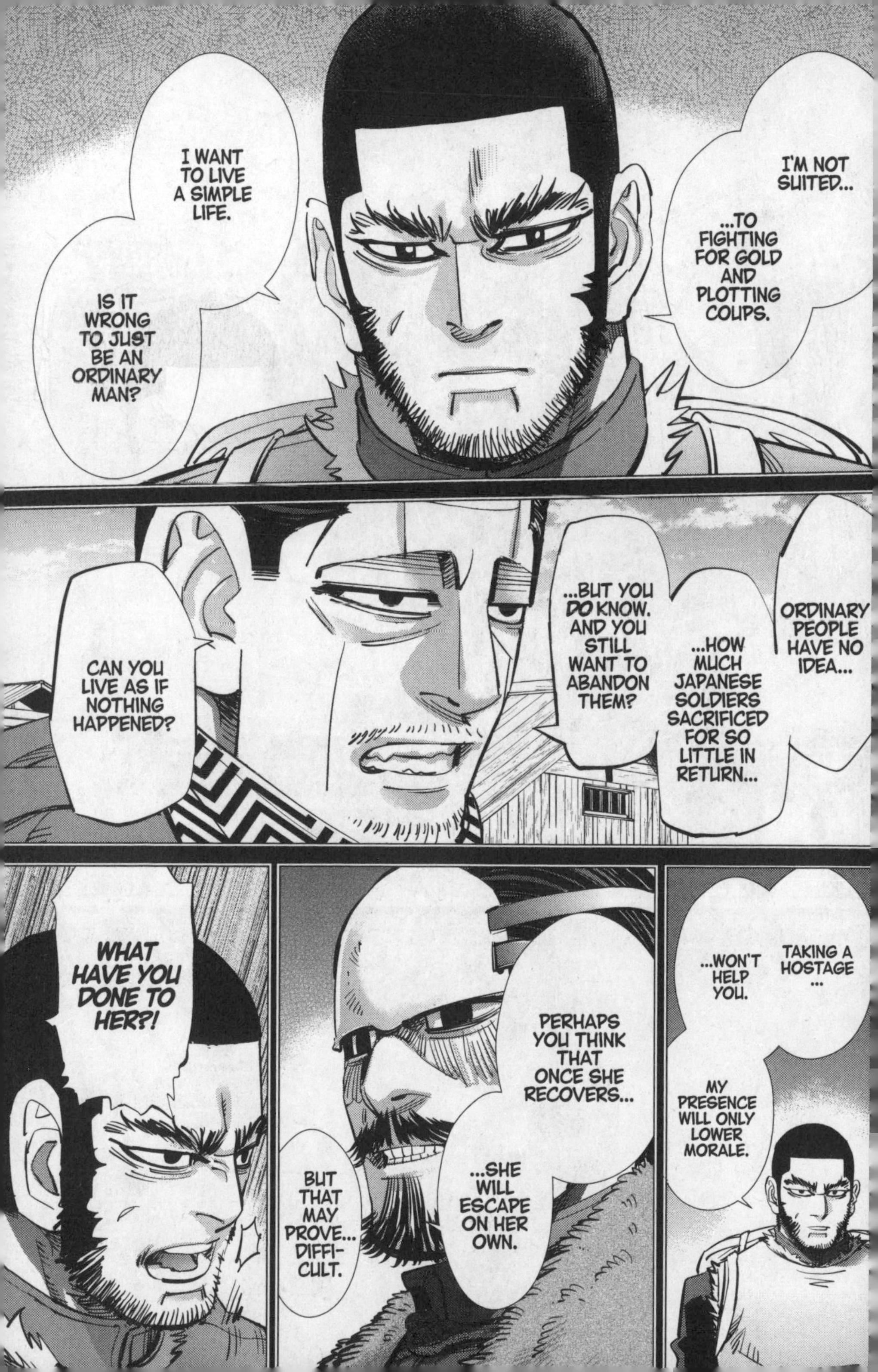
I'M NOT SUITED...
...TO FIGHTING FOR GOLD AND PLOTTING COUPS.
I WANT TO LIVE A SIMPLE LIFE.
IS IT WRONG TO JUST BE AN ORDINARY MAN?
ORDINARY PEOPLE HAVE NO IDEA...
...HOW MUCH JAPANESE SOLDIERS SACRIFICED FOR SO LITTLE IN RETURN...
...BUT YOU DO KNOW. AND YOU STILL WANT TO ABANDON THEM?
CAN YOU LIVE AS IF NOTHING HAPPENED?
TAKING A HOSTAGE ...
...WON'T HELP YOU.
MY PRESENCE WILL ONLY LOWER MORALE.
PERHAPS YOU THINK THAT ONCE SHE RECOVERS...
...SHE WILL ESCAPE ON HER OWN.
BUT THAT MAY PROVE... DIFFI-CULT.
WHAT HAVE YOU DONE TO HER?!

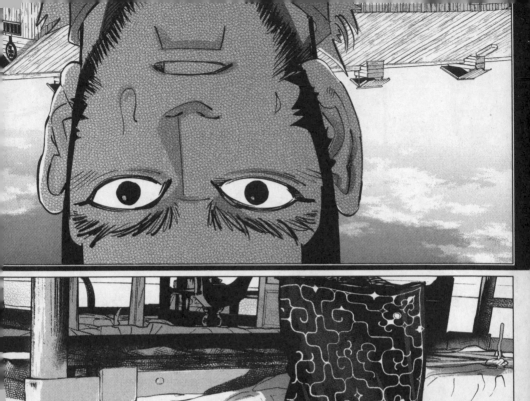

ACTUALLY, SHE'S PREGNANT WITH YOUR CHILD.

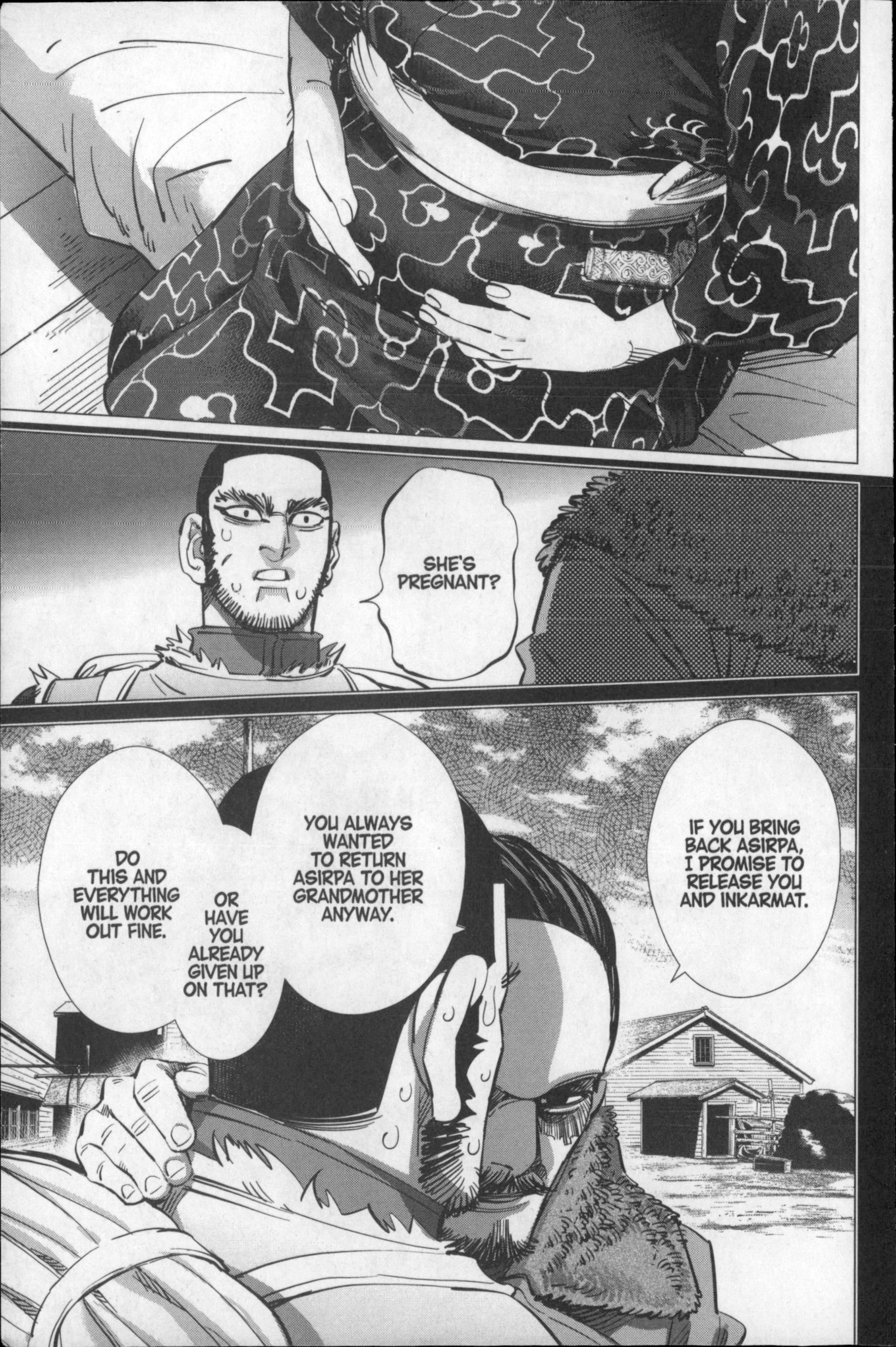
SHE'S PREGNANT?
IF YOU BRING BACK ASIRPA, I PROMISE TO RELEASE YOU AND INKARMAT.
YOU ALWAYS WANTED TO RETURN ASIRPA TO HER GRANDMOTHER ANYWAY.
OR HAVE YOU ALREADY GIVEN UP ON THAT?
DO THIS AND EVERYTHING WILL WORK OUT FINE.

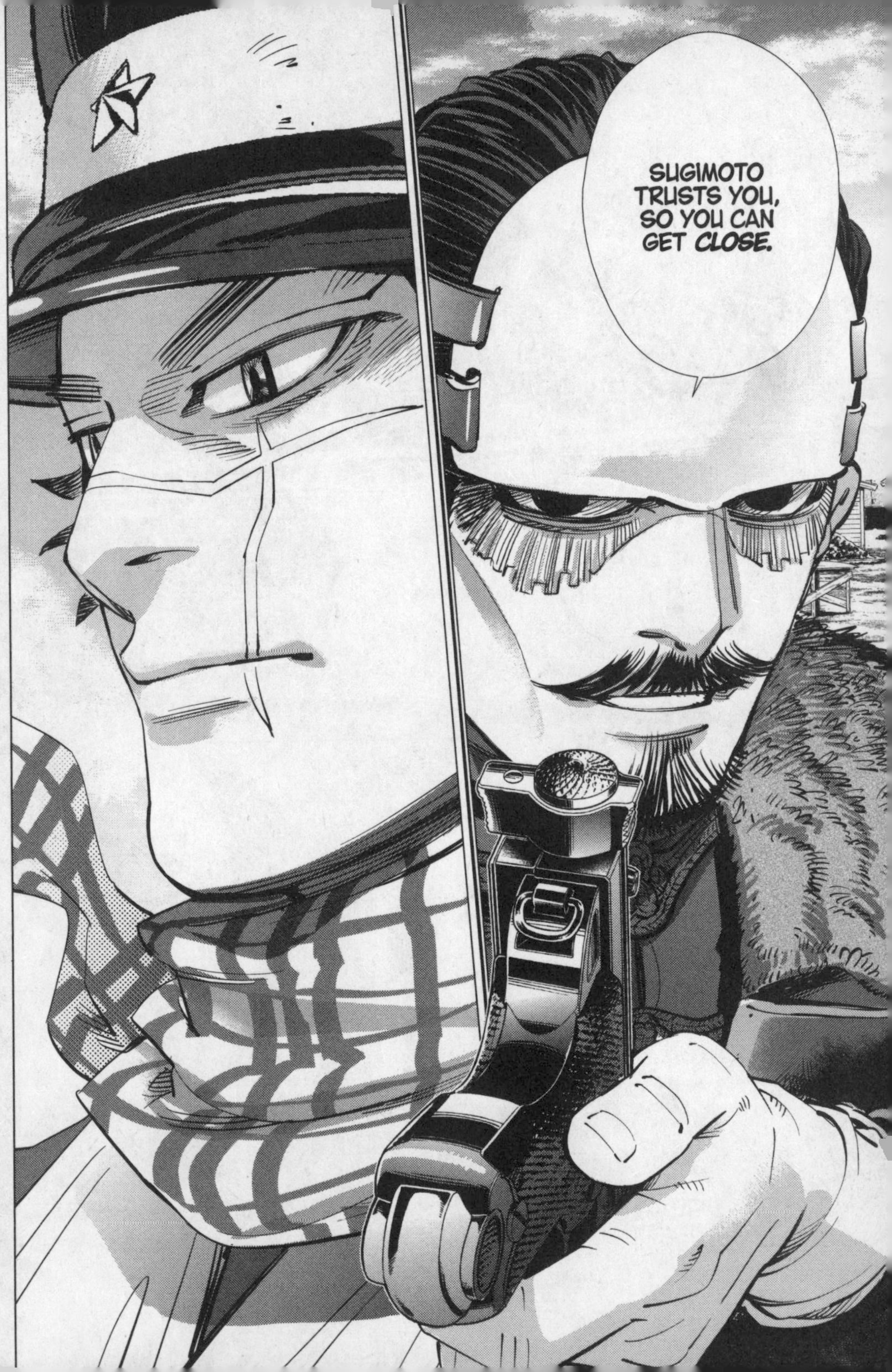
SUGIMOTO TRUSTS YOU, SO YOU CAN GET CLOSE.

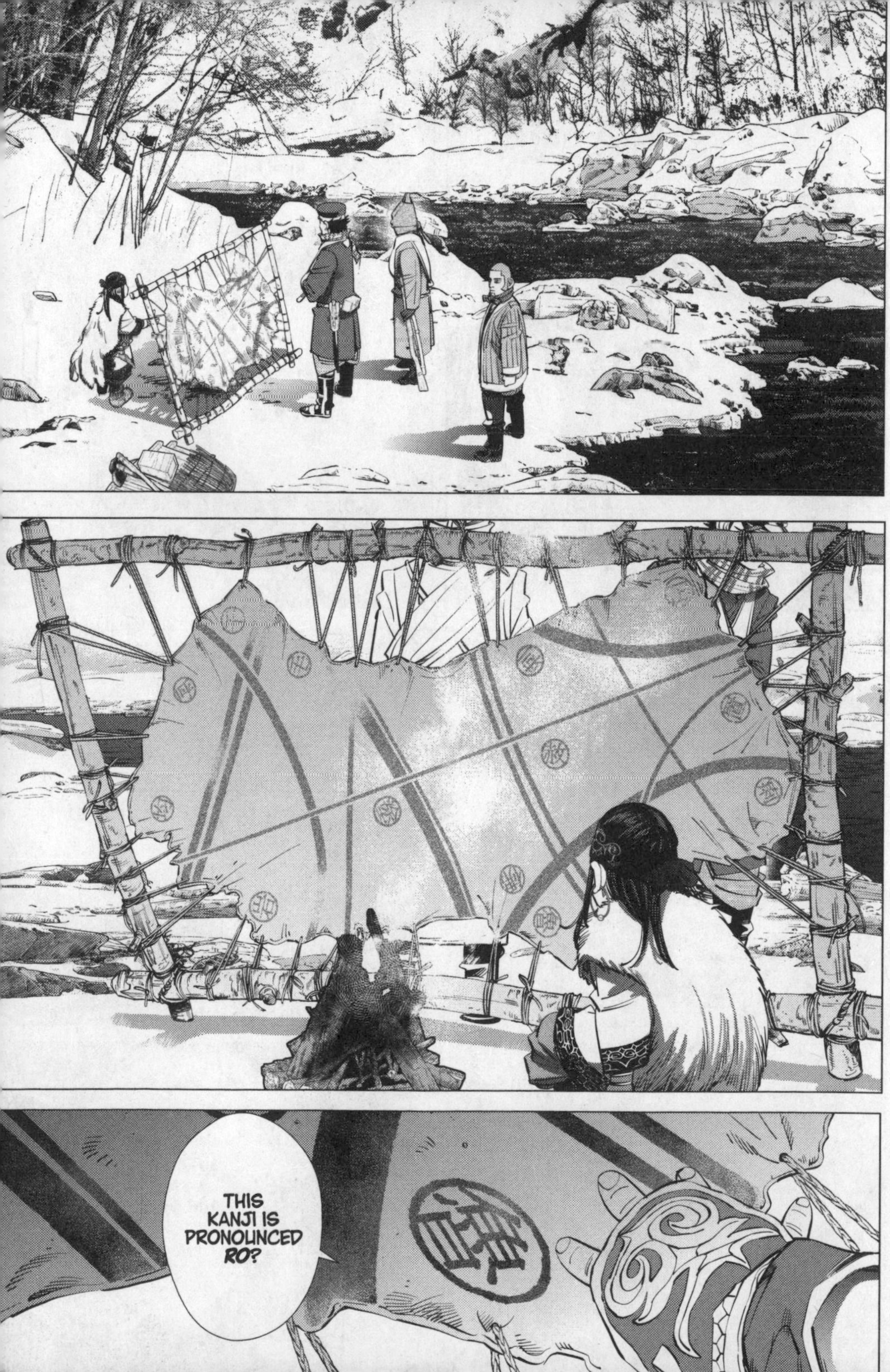
THIS KANJI IS PRONOUNCED RO?

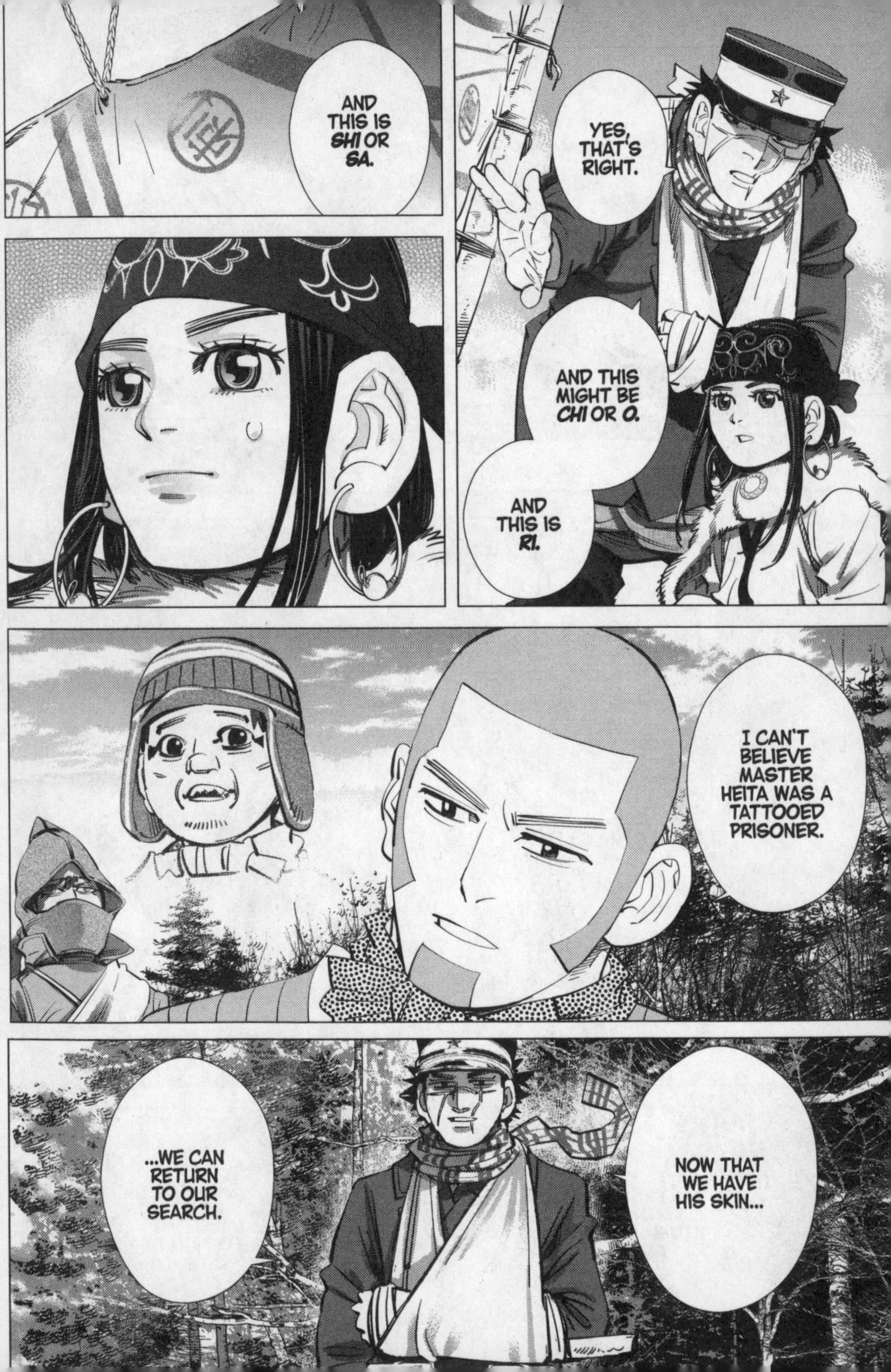
YES, THAT'S RIGHT.
AND THIS MIGHT BE CHI OR O.
AND THIS IS RI.
AND THIS IS SHI OR SA.
I CAN'T BELIEVE MASTER HEITA WAS A TATTOOED PRISONER.
NOW THAT WE HAVE HIS SKIN...
...WE CAN RETURN TO OUR SEARCH.

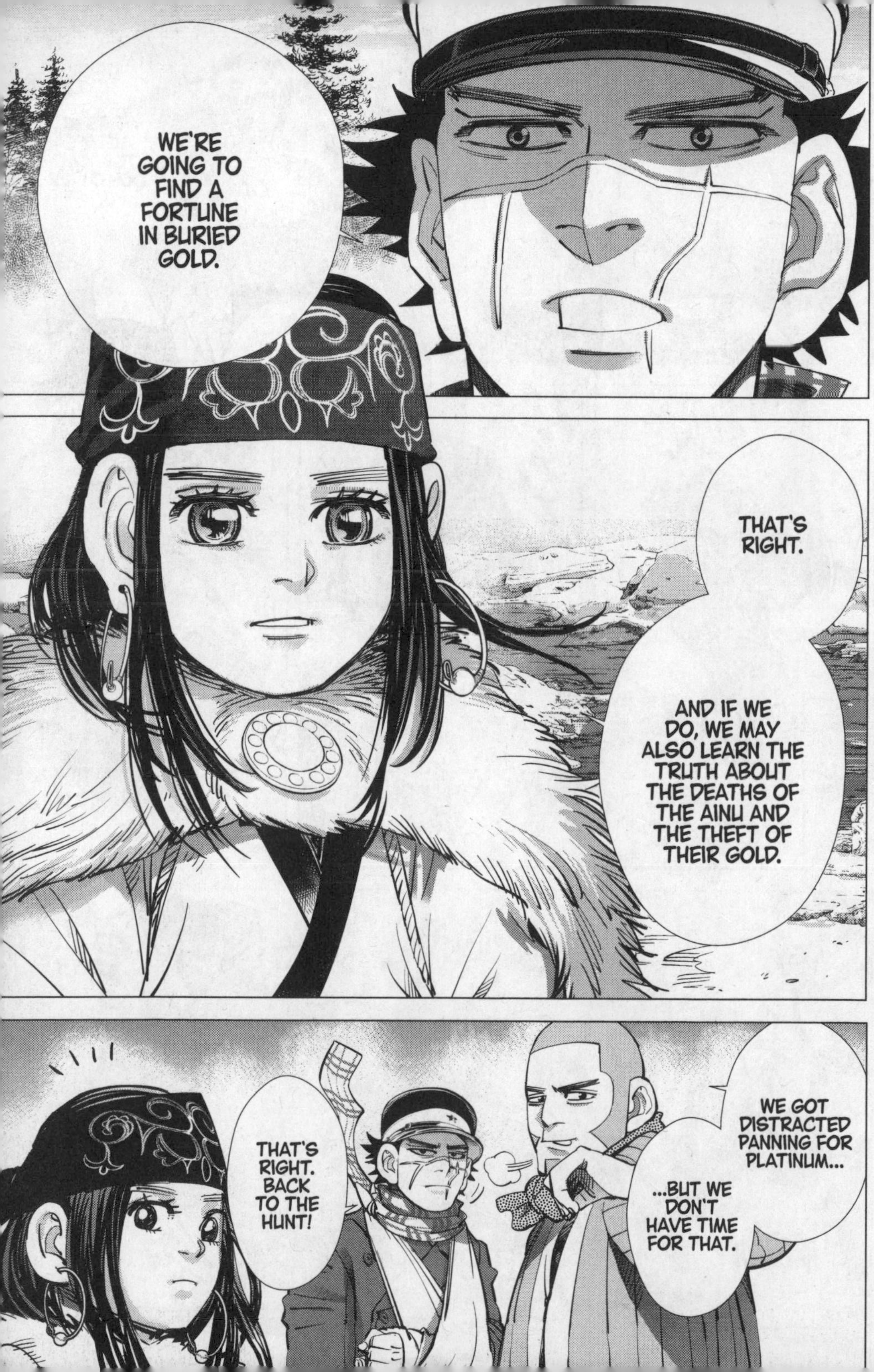
WE'RE GOING TO FIND A FORTUNE IN BURIED GOLD.
THAT'S RIGHT.
AND IF WE DO, WE MAY ALSO LEARN THE TRUTH ABOUT THE DEATHS OF THE AINU AND THE THEFT OF THEIR GOLD.
WE GOT DISTRACTED PANNING FOR PLATINUM...
...BUT WE DON'T HAVE TIME FOR THAT.
THAT'S RIGHT. BACK TO THE HUNT!

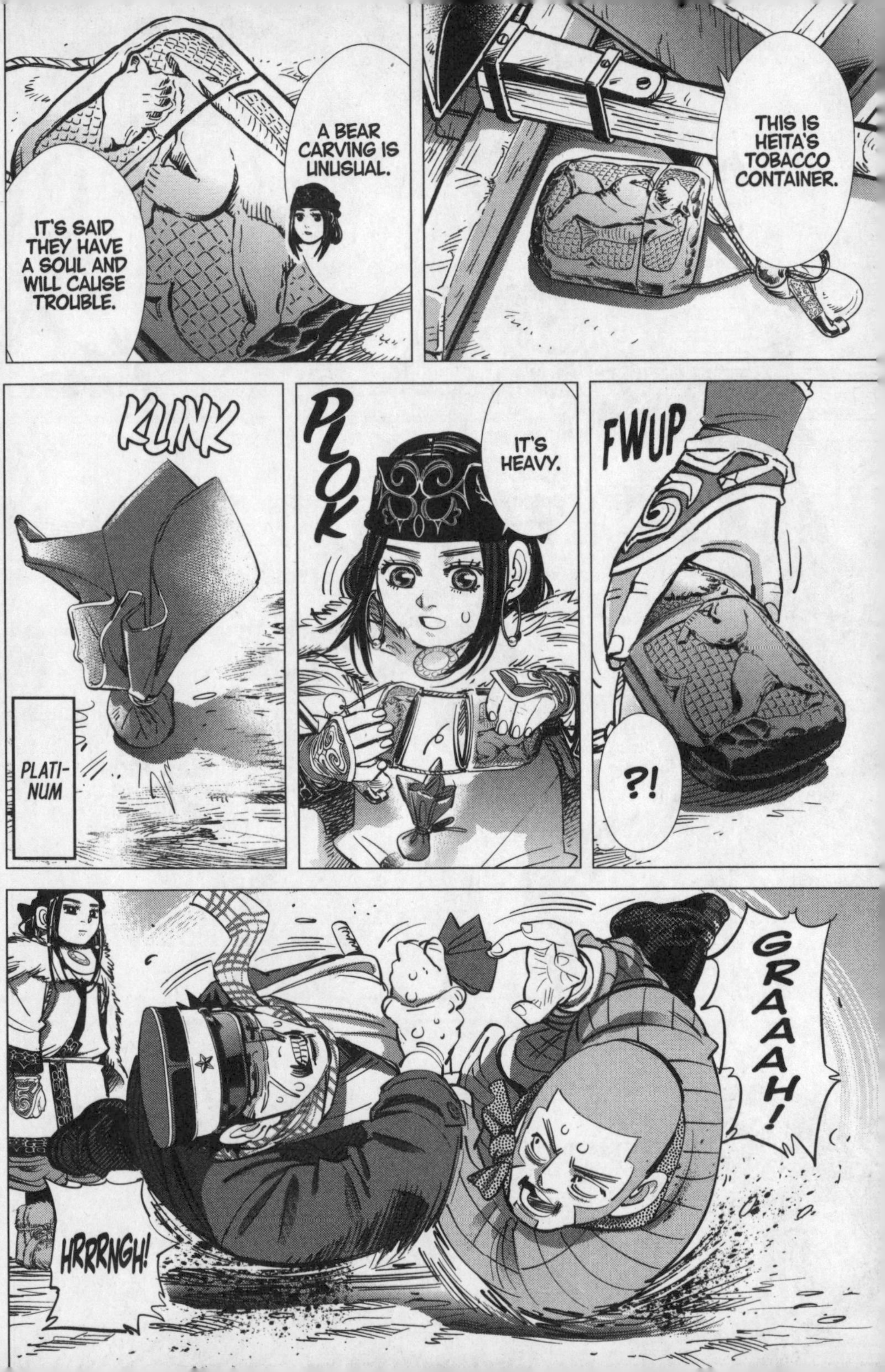
THIS IS HEITA'S TOBACCO CONTAINER.
A BEAR CARVING IS UNUSUAL.
IT'S SAID THEY HAVE A SOUL AND WILL CAUSE TROUBLE.
FWUP
?!
IT'S HEAVY.
PLOK
KLINK
PLATI-NUM
GRAAAH!
HRRRNGH!

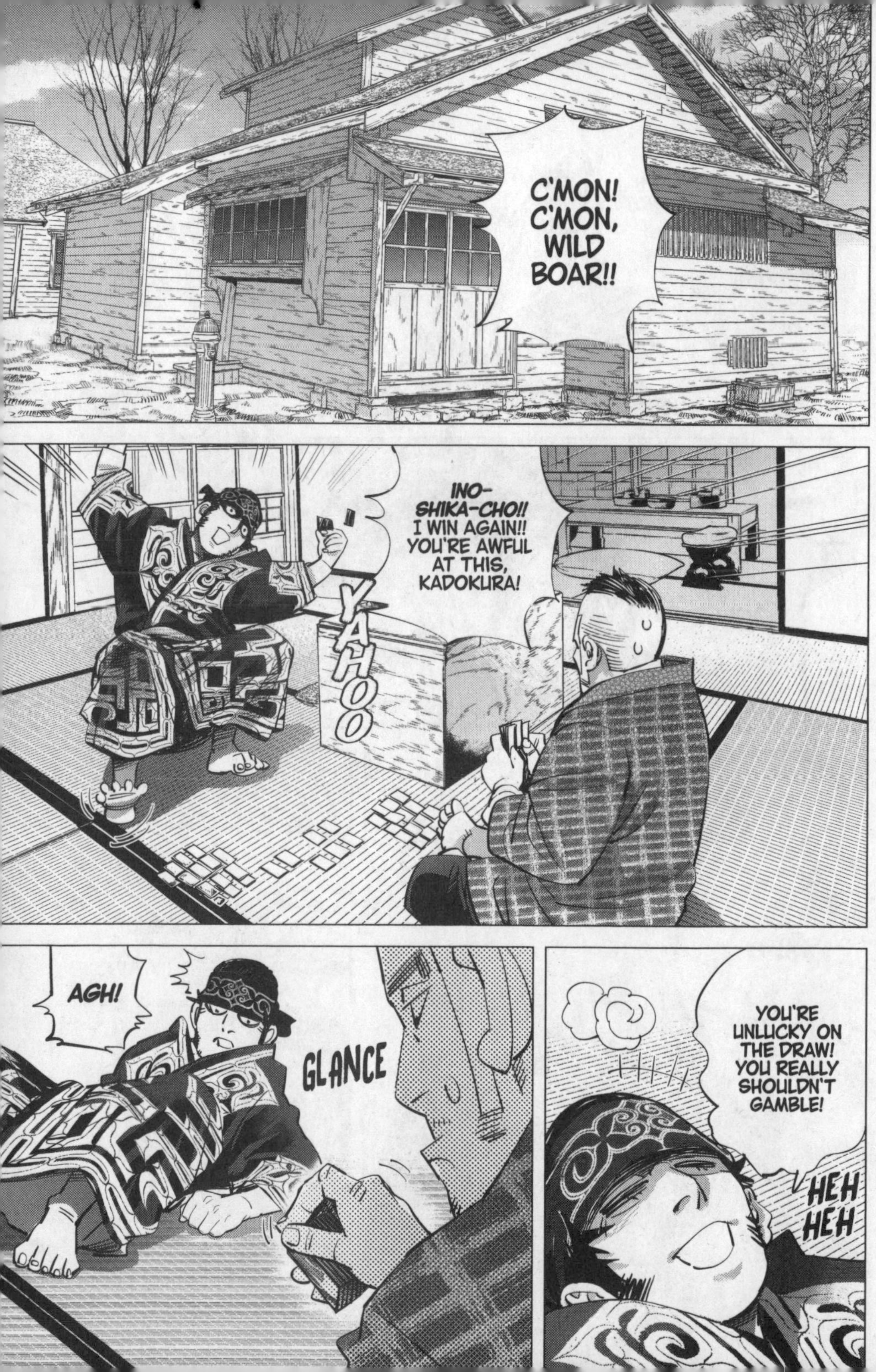
C'MON! C'MON, WILD BOAR!!
INO-SHIKA-CHO!! I WIN AGAIN!! YOU'RE AWFUL AT THIS, KADOKURA!
YAHOO
YOU'RE UNLUCKY ON THE DRAW! YOU REALLY SHOULDN'T GAMBLE!
HEH HEH
GLANCE
AGH!

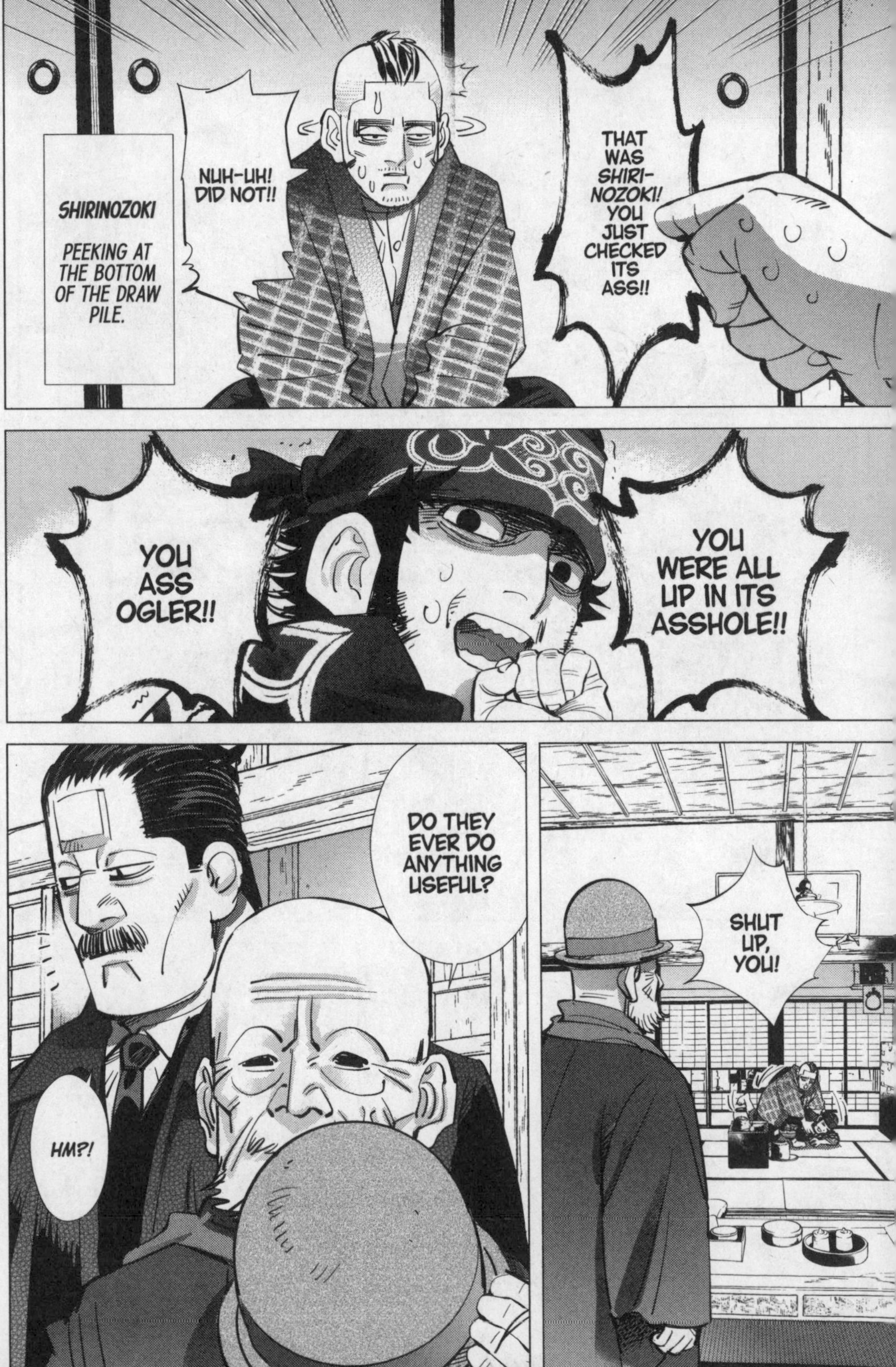
THAT WAS SHIRI-NOZOKI! YOU JUST CHECKED ITS ASS!!
NUH-UH! DID NOT!!
SHIRINOZOKI
PEEKING AT THE BOTTOM OF THE DRAW PILE.
YOU WERE ALL UP IN ITS ASSHOLE!!
YOU ASS OGLER!!
SHUT UP, YOU!
DO THEY EVER DO ANYTHING USEFUL?
HM?!

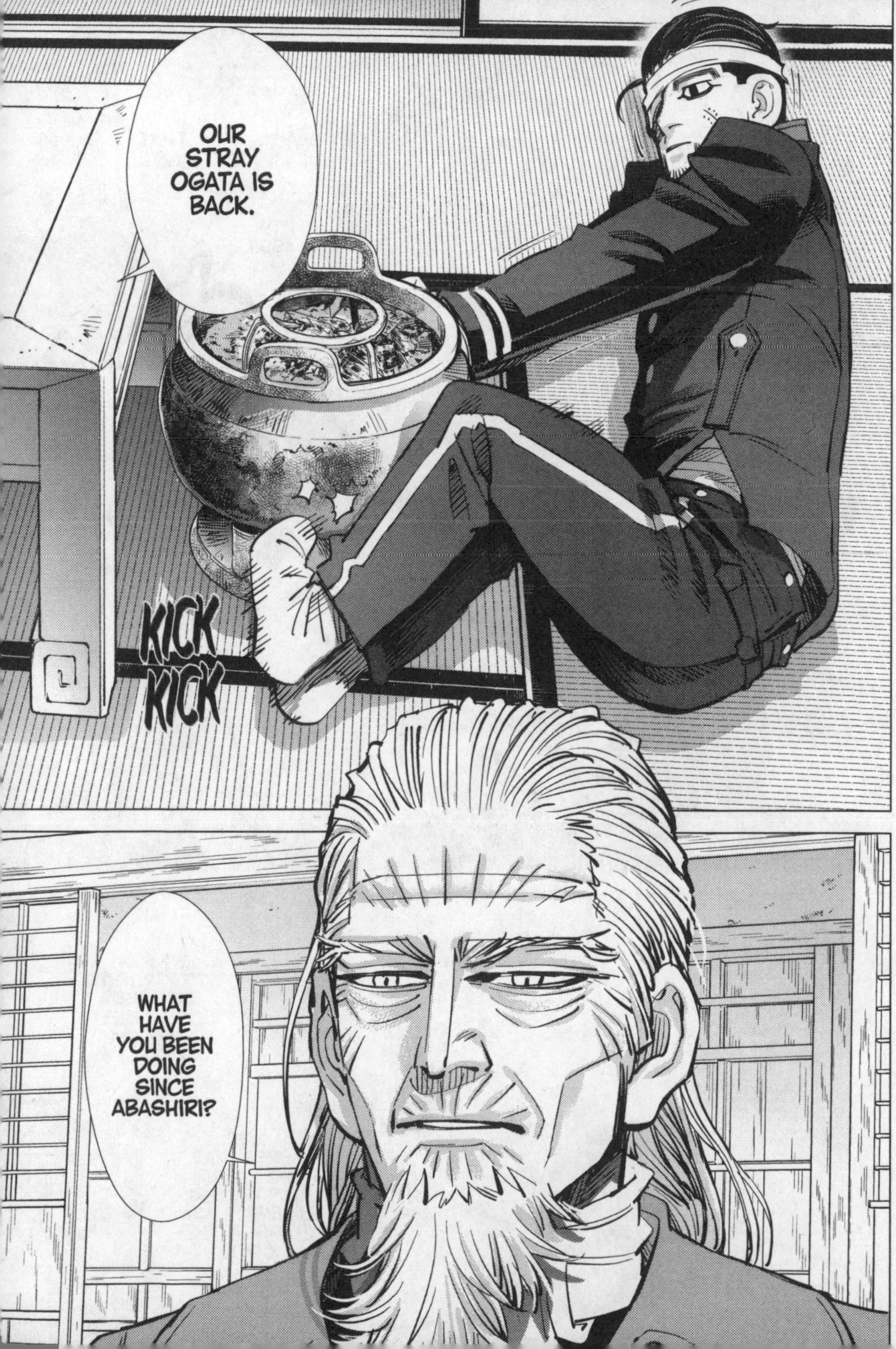
OUR STRAY OGATA IS BACK.
KICK KICK
WHAT HAVE YOU BEEN DOING SINCE ABASHIRI?

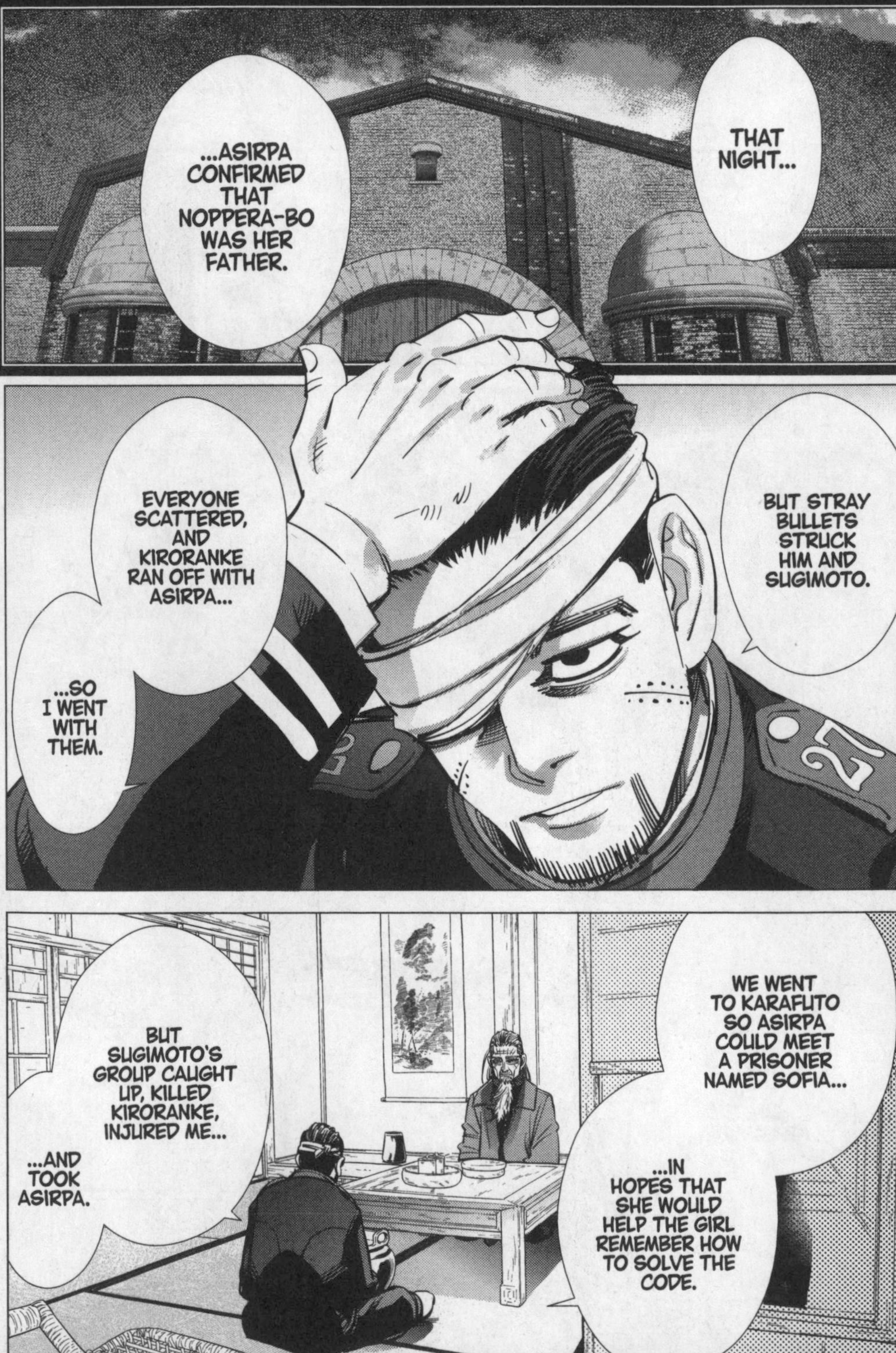
WE WENT TO KARAFUTO SO ASIRPA COULD MEET A PRISONER NAMED SOFIA...
...IN HOPES THAT SHE WOULD HELP THE GIRL REMEMBER HOW TO SOLVE THE CODE.
BUT SUGIMOTO'S GROUP CAUGHT UP, KILLED KIRORANKE, INJURED ME...
...AND TOOK ASIRPA.
THAT NIGHT...
...ASIRPA CONFIRMED THAT NOPPERA-BO WAS HER FATHER.
BUT STRAY BULLETS STRUCK HIM AND SUGIMOTO.
EVERYONE SCATTERED, AND KIRORANKE RAN OFF WITH ASIRPA...
...SO I WENT WITH THEM.

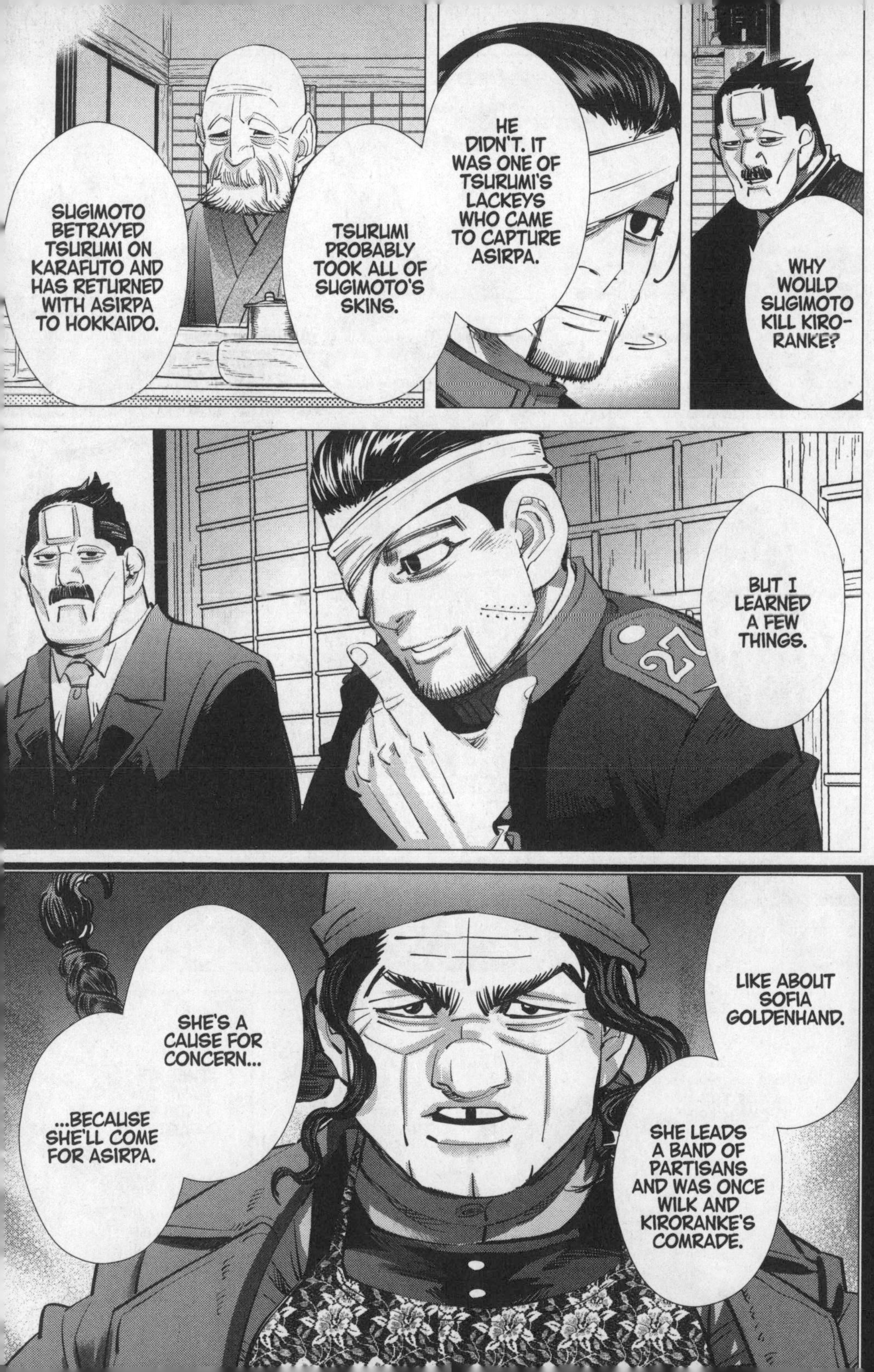
WHY WOULD SUGIMOTO KILL KIRO-RANKE?
HE DIDN'T. IT WAS ONE OF TSURUMI'S LACKEYS WHO CAME TO CAPTURE ASIRPA.
TSURUMI PROBABLY TOOK ALL OF SUGIMOTO'S SKINS.
SUGIMOTO BETRAYED TSURUMI ON KARAFUTO AND HAS RETURNED WITH ASIRPA TO HOKKAIDO.
BUT I LEARNED A FEW THINGS.
LIKE ABOUT SOFIA GOLDENHAND.
SHE LEADS A BAND OF PARTISANS AND WAS ONCE WILK AND KIRORANKE'S COMRADE.
SHE'S A CAUSE FOR CONCERN...
...BECAUSE SHE'LL COME FOR ASIRPA.

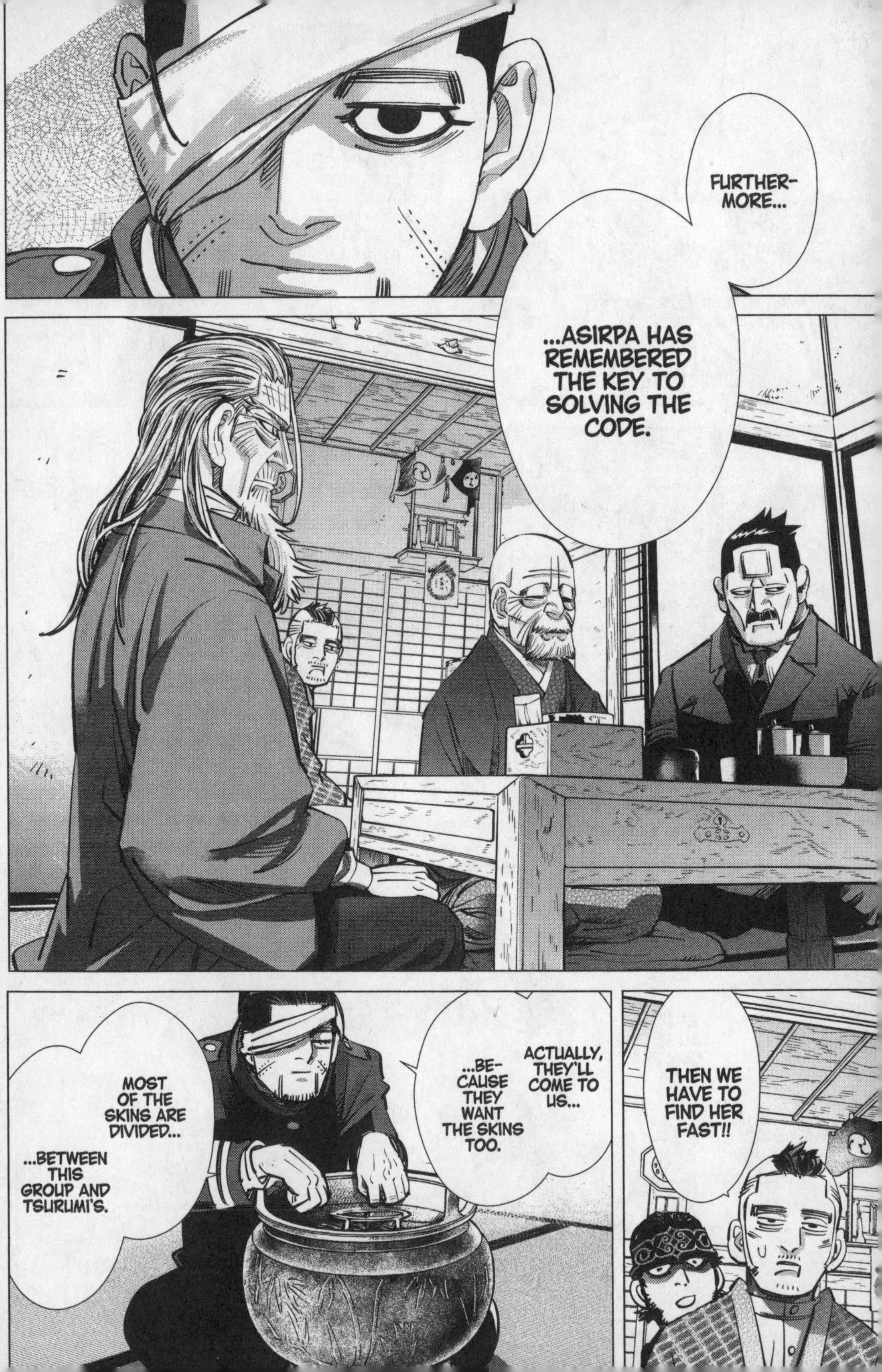
FURTHER-MORE...
...ASIRPA HAS REMEMBERED THE KEY TO SOLVING THE CODE.
THEN WE HAVE TO FIND HER FAST!!
ACTUALLY, THEY'LL COME TO US...
...BE-CAUSE THEY WANT THE SKINS TOO.
MOST OF THE SKINS ARE DIVIDED...
...BETWEEN THIS GROUP AND TSURUMI'S.

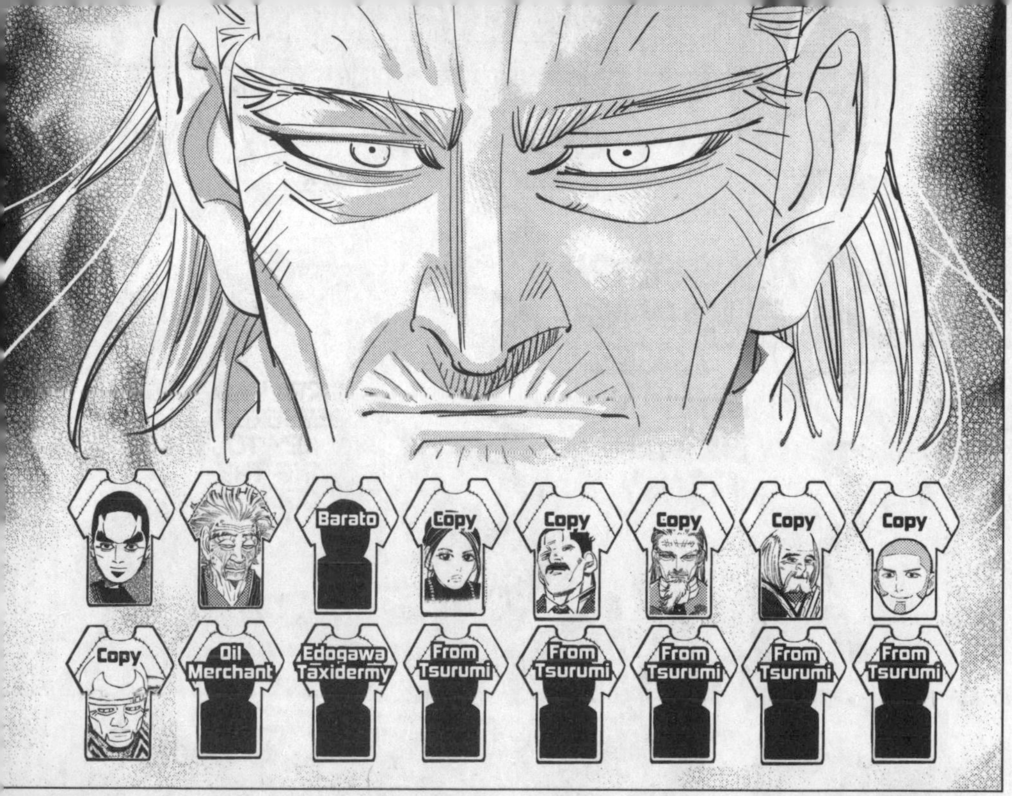
Copy
Copy
Copy
Copy
Copy
Barato
From Tsurumi
From Tsurumi
From Tsurumi
From Tsurumi
From Tsurumi
Edogawa Taxidermy
Oil Merchant
Copy
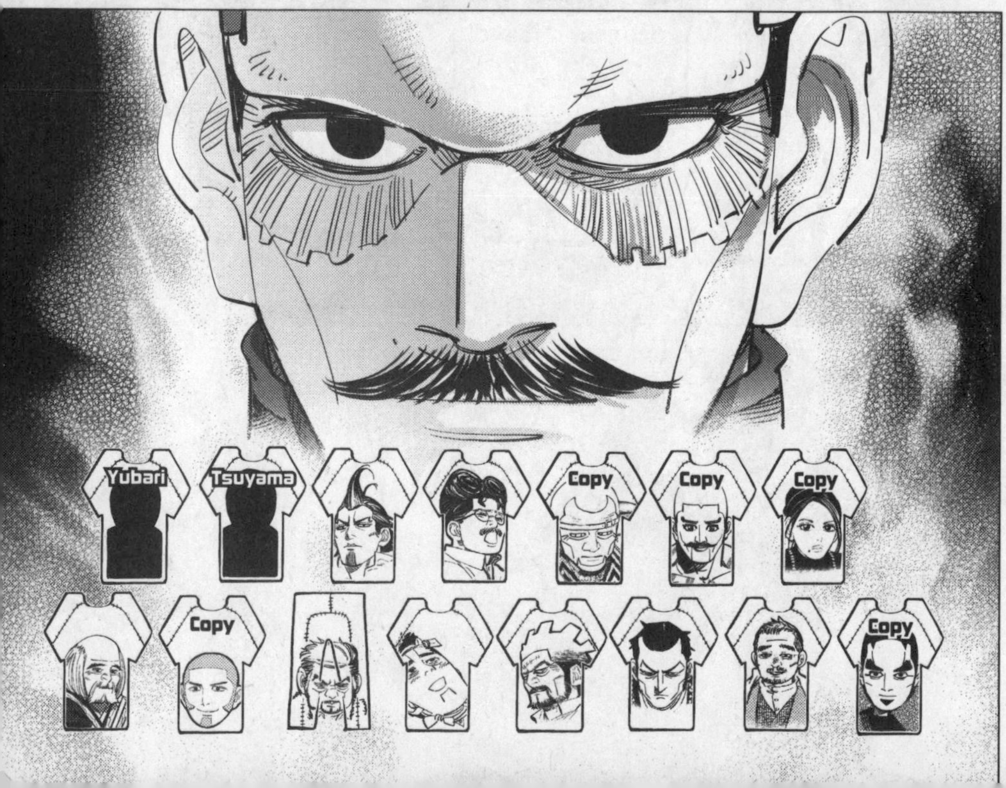
Copy
Copy
Copy
Tsuyama
Yubari
Copy
Copy

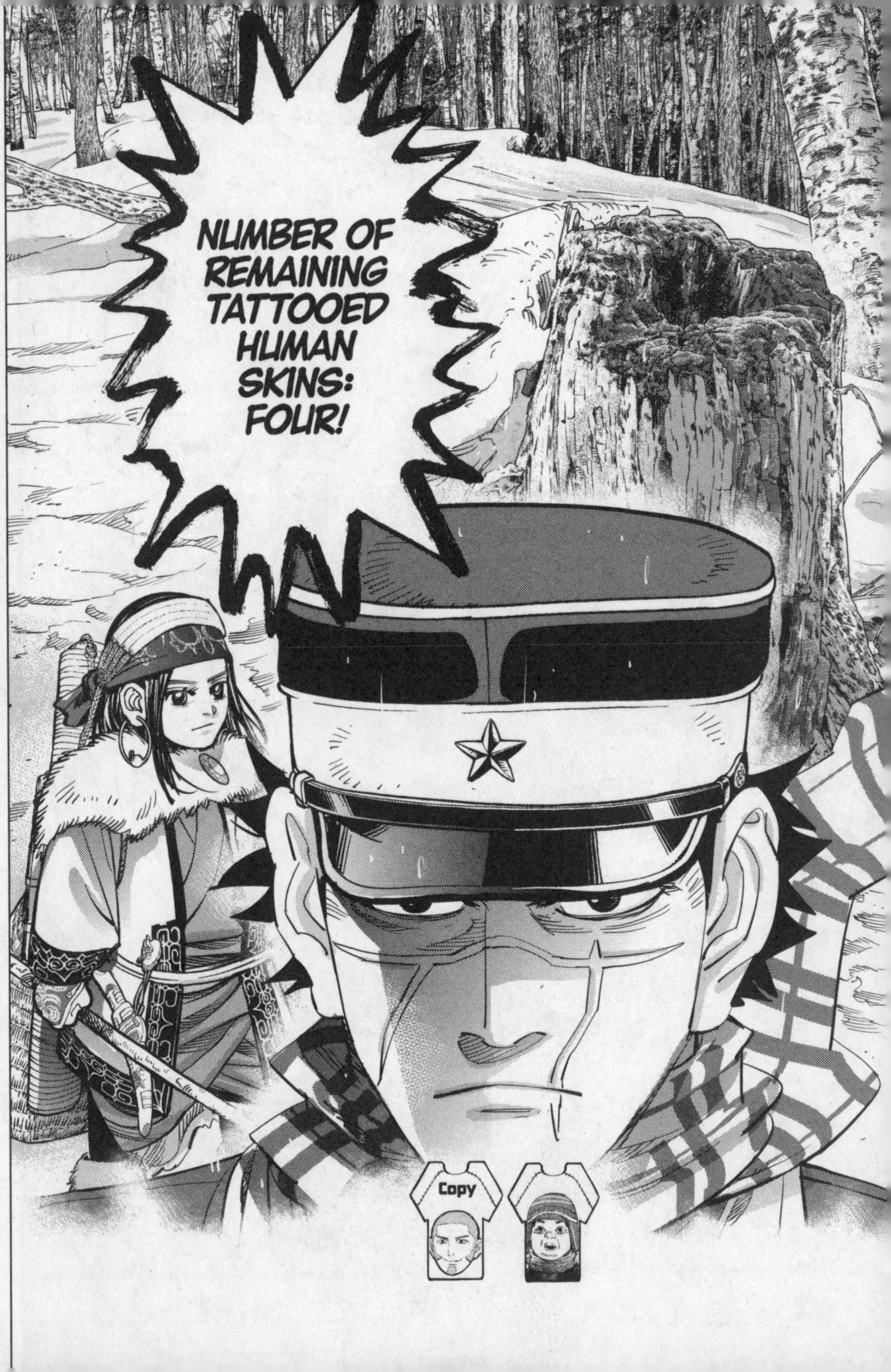
NUMBER OF REMAINING TATTOOED HUMAN SKINS: FOUR!
Copy

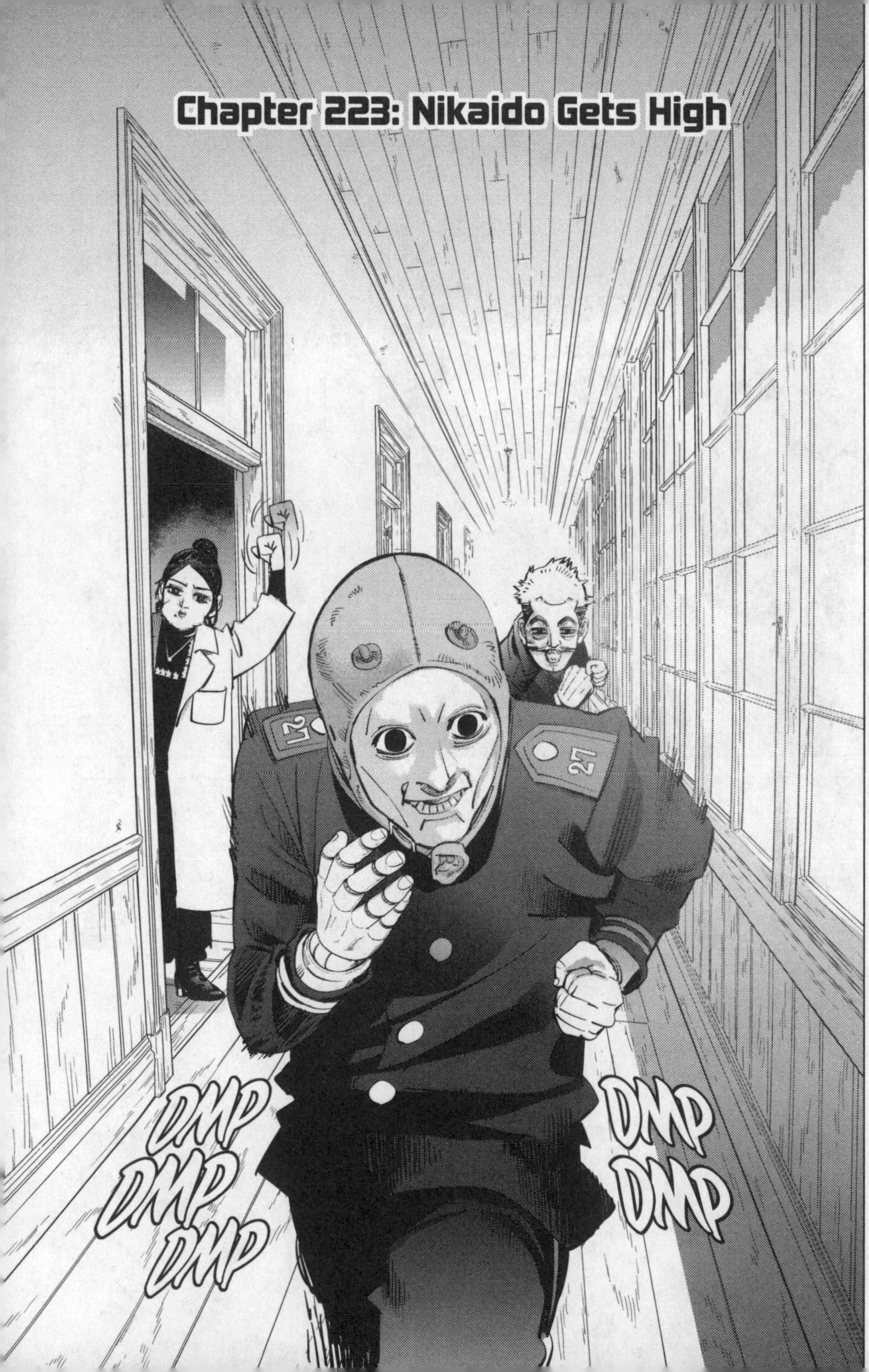
Chapter 223: Nikaido Gets High
DMP DMP
DMP DMP DMP

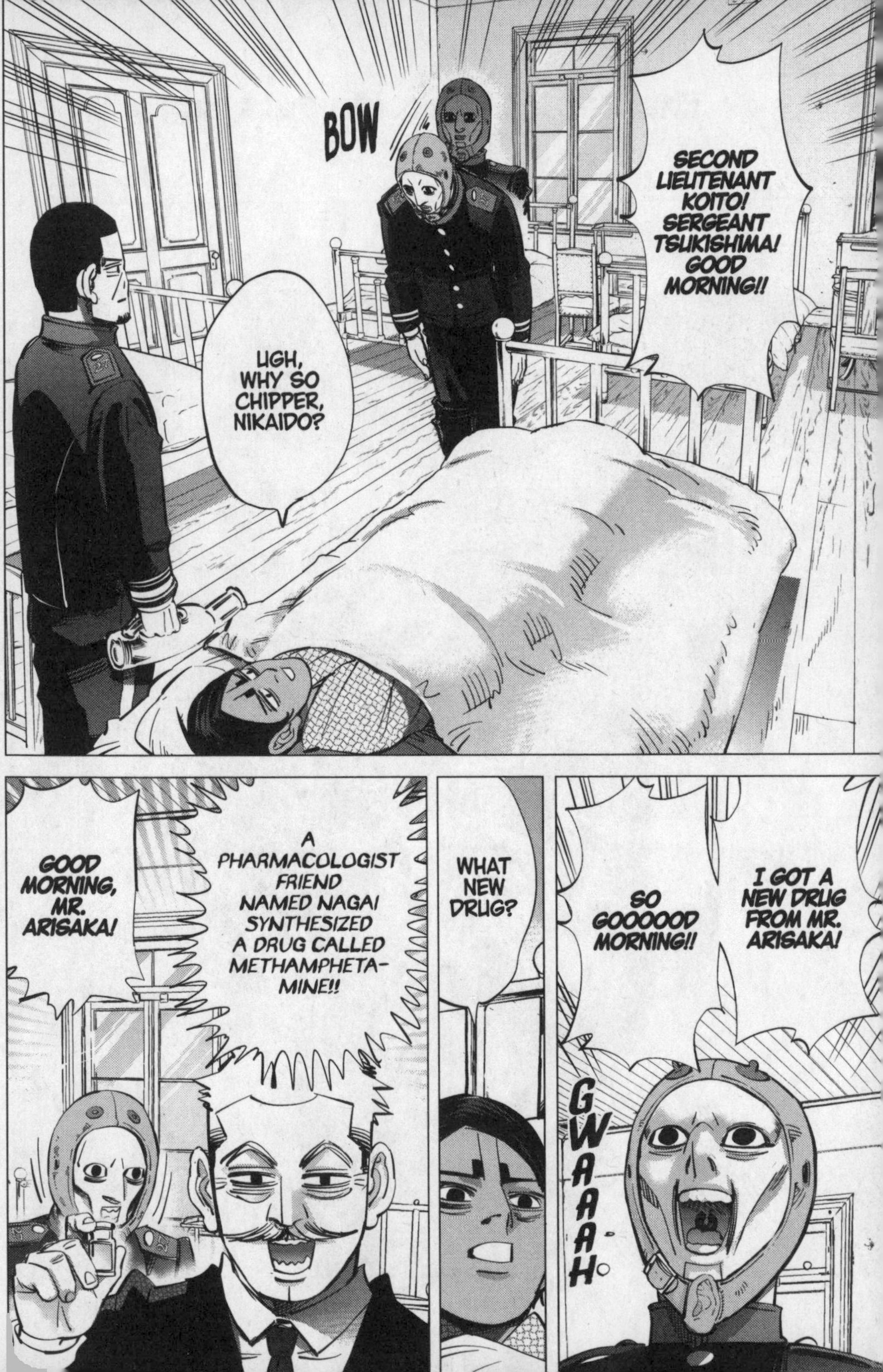
SECOND LIEUTENANT KOITO! SERGEANT TSUKISHIMA! GOOD MORNING!!
BOW
UGH, WHY SO CHIPPER, NIKAIDO?
I GOT A NEW DRUG FROM MR. ARISAKA!
SO GOOOOOD MORNING!!
GWAAAAH
WHAT NEW DRUG?
A PHARMACOLOGIST FRIEND NAMED NAGAI SYNTHESIZED A DRUG CALLED METHAMPHETA-MINE!!
GOOD MORNING, MR. ARISAKA!

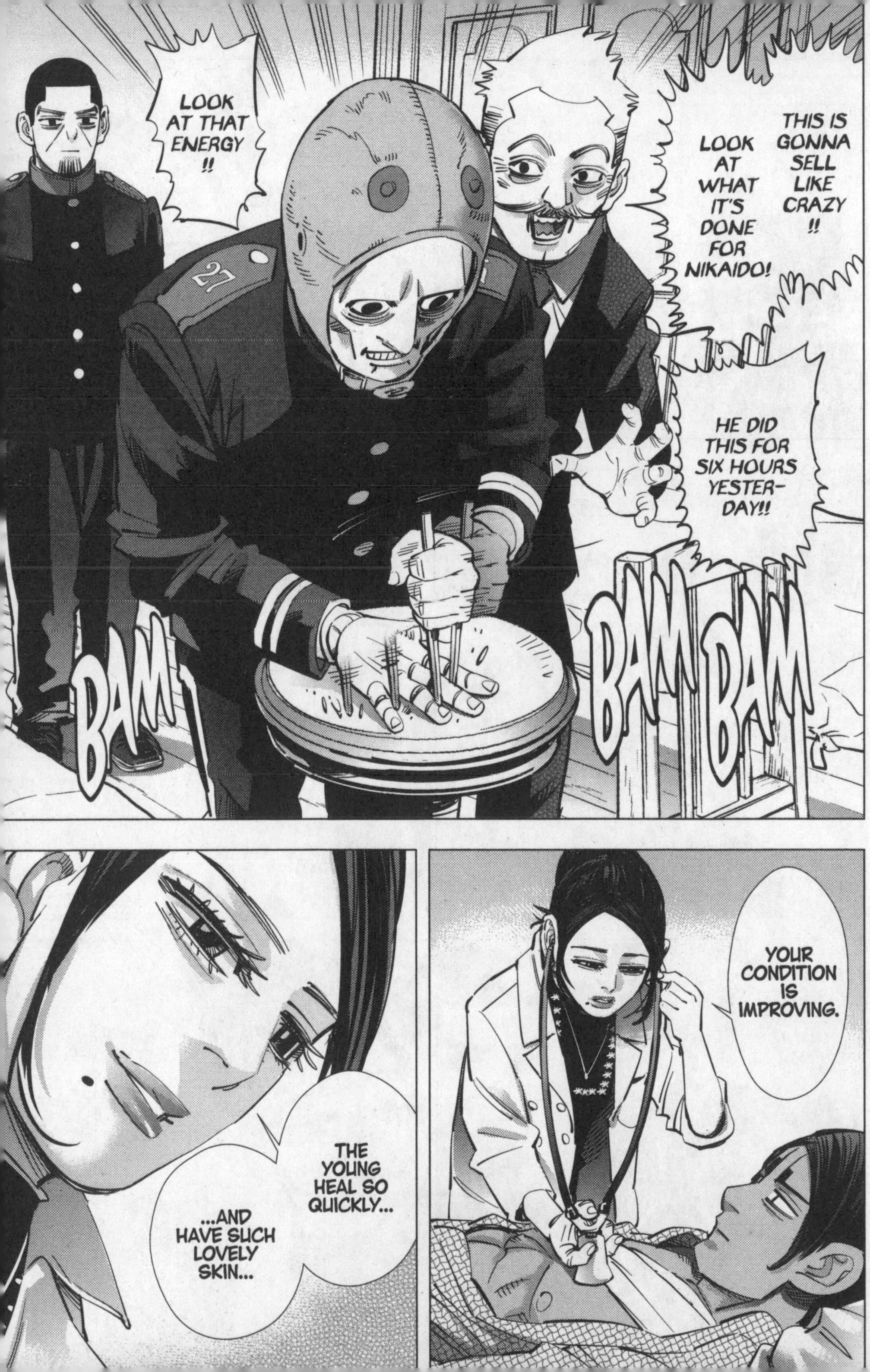
THIS IS GONNA SELL LIKE CRAZY!!
LOOK AT WHAT IT'S DONE FOR NIKAIDO!
HE DID THIS FOR SIX HOURS YESTER-DAY!!
BAM BAM
LOOK AT THAT ENERGY!!
BAM
YOUR CONDITION IS IMPROVING.
THE YOUNG HEAL SO QUICKLY...
...AND HAVE SUCH LOVELY SKIN...

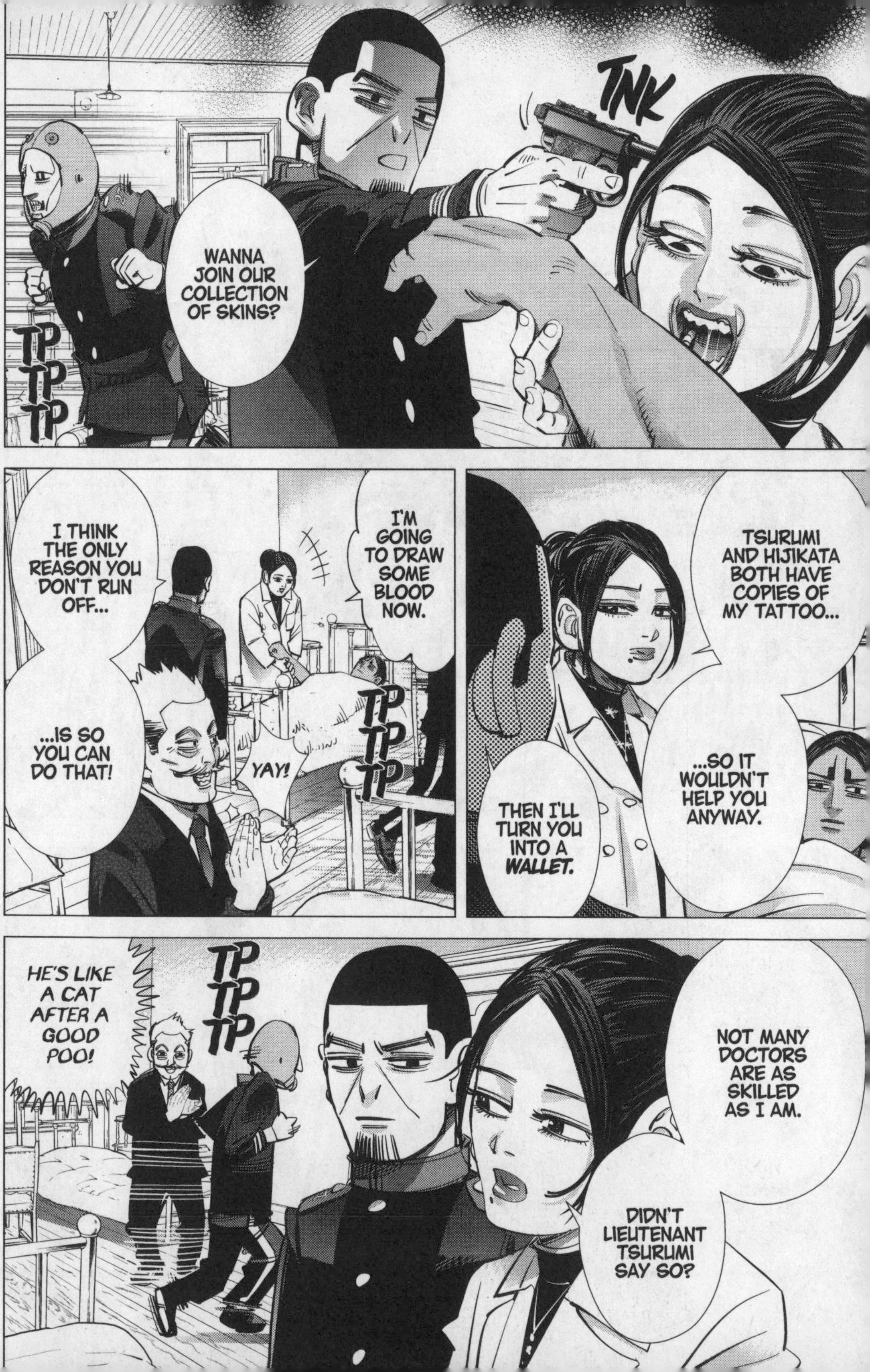
TNK
WANNA JOIN OUR COLLECTION OF SKINS?
TP TP TP
TSURUMI AND HIJIKATA BOTH HAVE COPIES OF MY TATTOO...
...SO IT WOULDN'T HELP YOU ANYWAY.
THEN I'LL TURN YOU INTO A WALLET.
I'M GOING TO DRAW SOME BLOOD NOW.
TP TP TP
I THINK THE ONLY REASON YOU DON'T RUN OFF...
...IS SO YOU CAN DO THAT!
YAY!
NOT MANY DOCTORS ARE AS SKILLED AS I AM.
DIDN'T LIEUTENANT TSURUMI SAY SO?
TP TP TP
HE'S LIKE A CAT AFTER A GOOD POO!

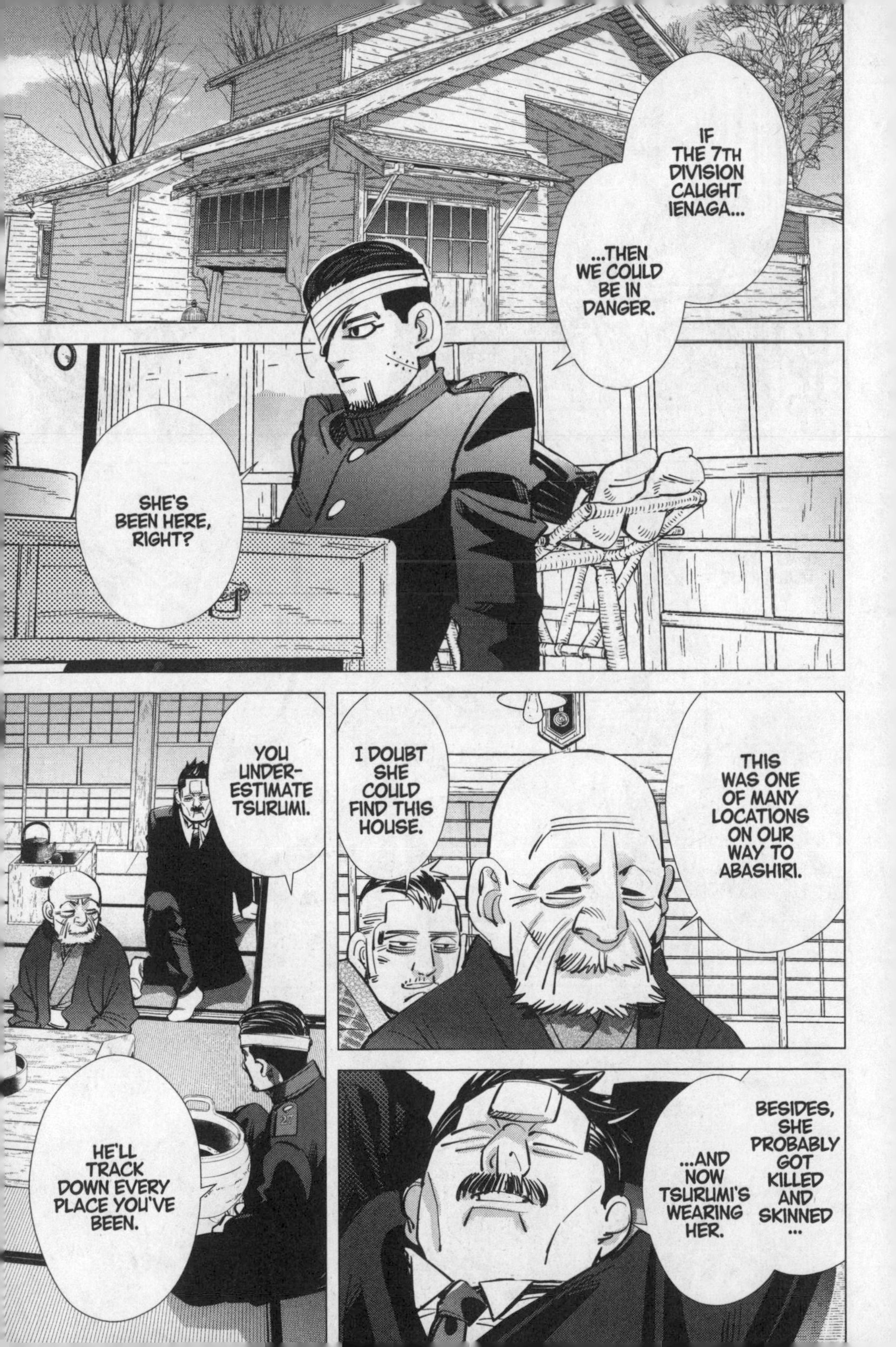
IF THE 7TH DIVISION CAUGHT IENAGA...
...THEN WE COULD BE IN DANGER.
SHE'S BEEN HERE, RIGHT?
THIS WAS ONE OF MANY LOCATIONS ON OUR WAY TO ABASHIRI.
I DOUBT SHE COULD FIND THIS HOUSE.
BESIDES, SHE PROBABLY GOT KILLED AND SKINNED...
...AND NOW TSURUMI'S WEARING HER.
YOU UNDER-ESTIMATE TSURUMI.
HE'LL TRACK DOWN EVERY PLACE YOU'VE BEEN.

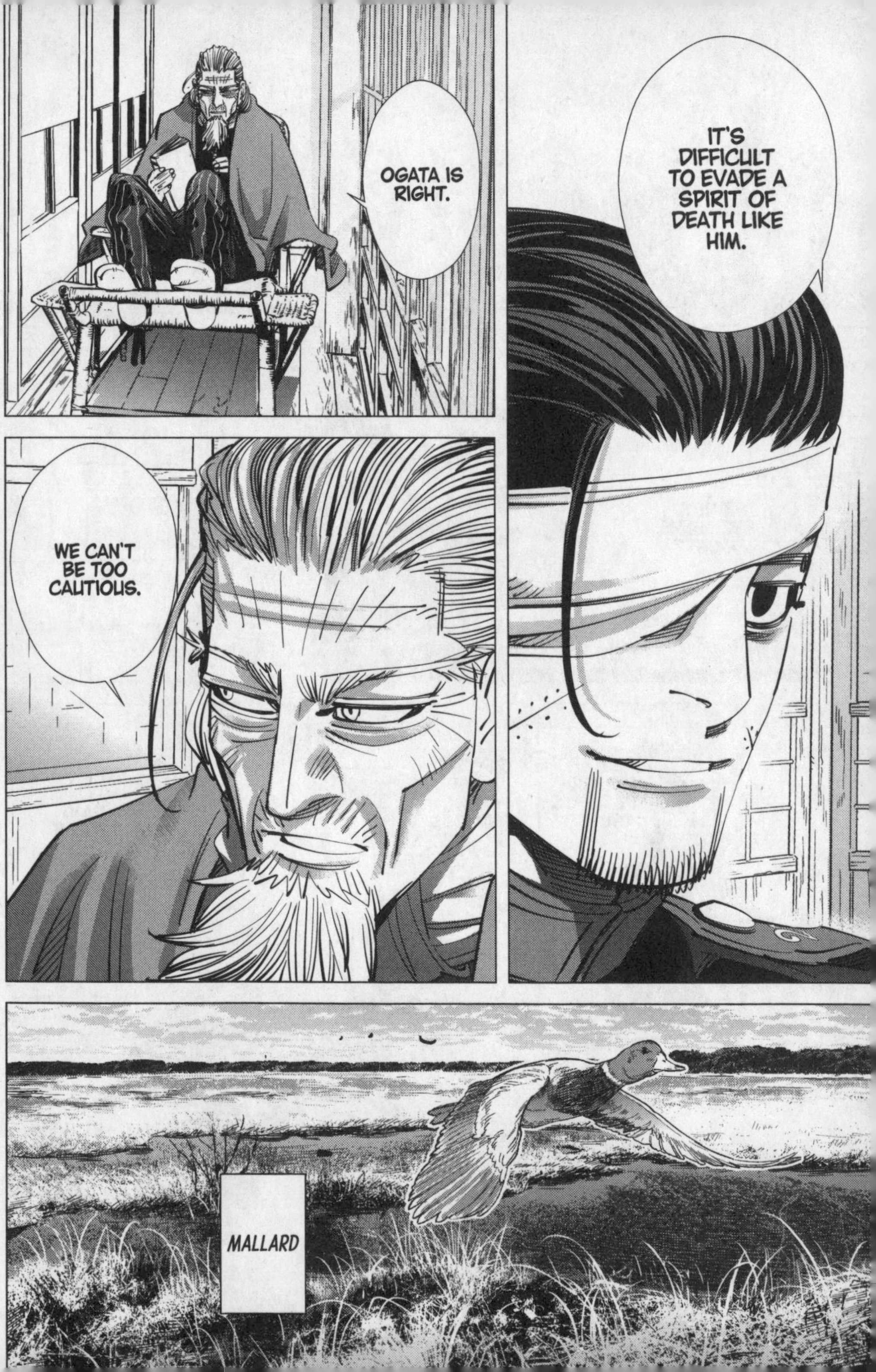
It's difficult to evade a spirit of death like him.
Ogata is right.
We can't be too cautious.
Mallard

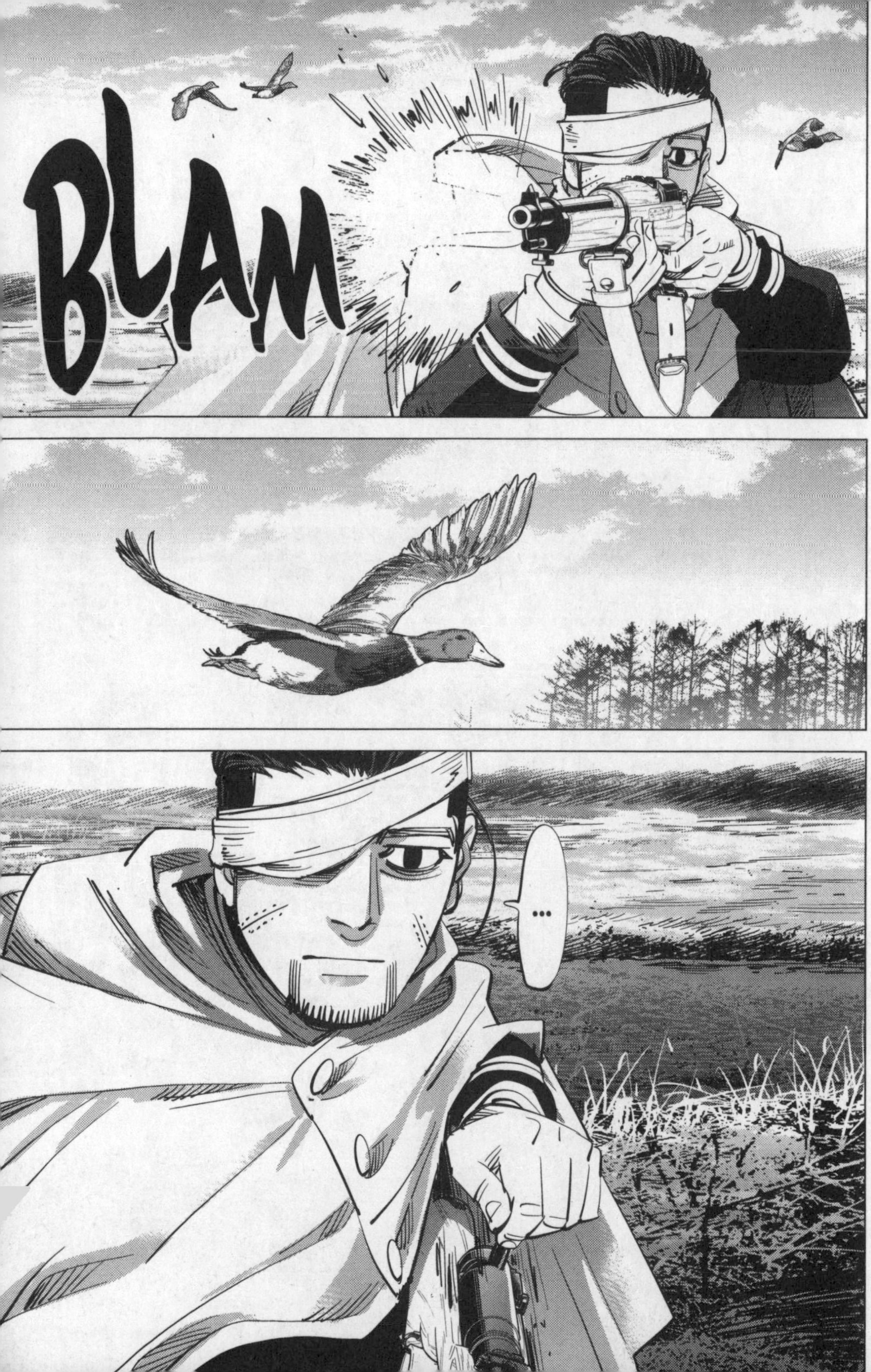
BLAM
...

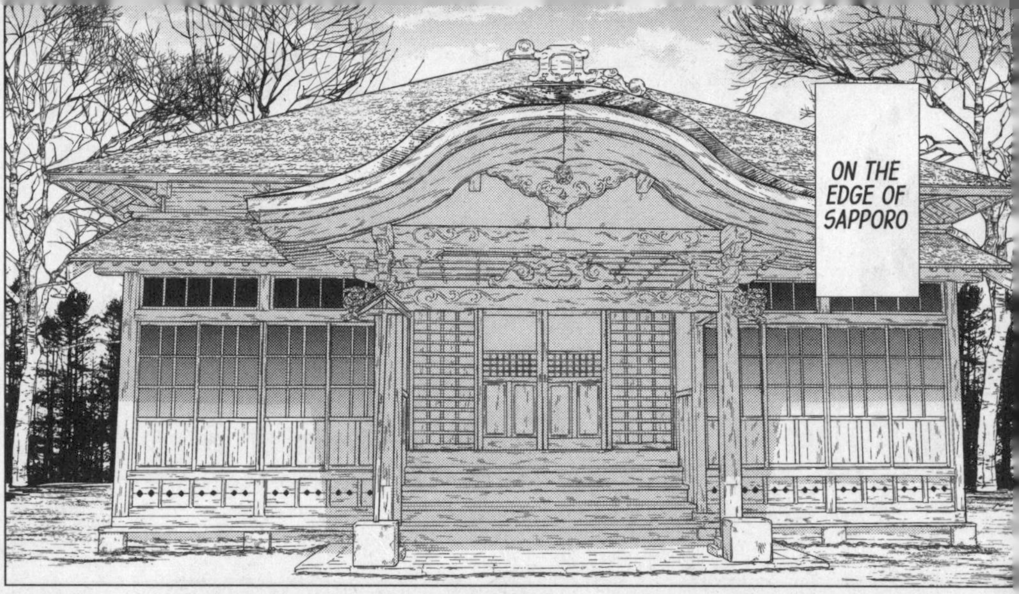
ON THE EDGE OF SAPPORO

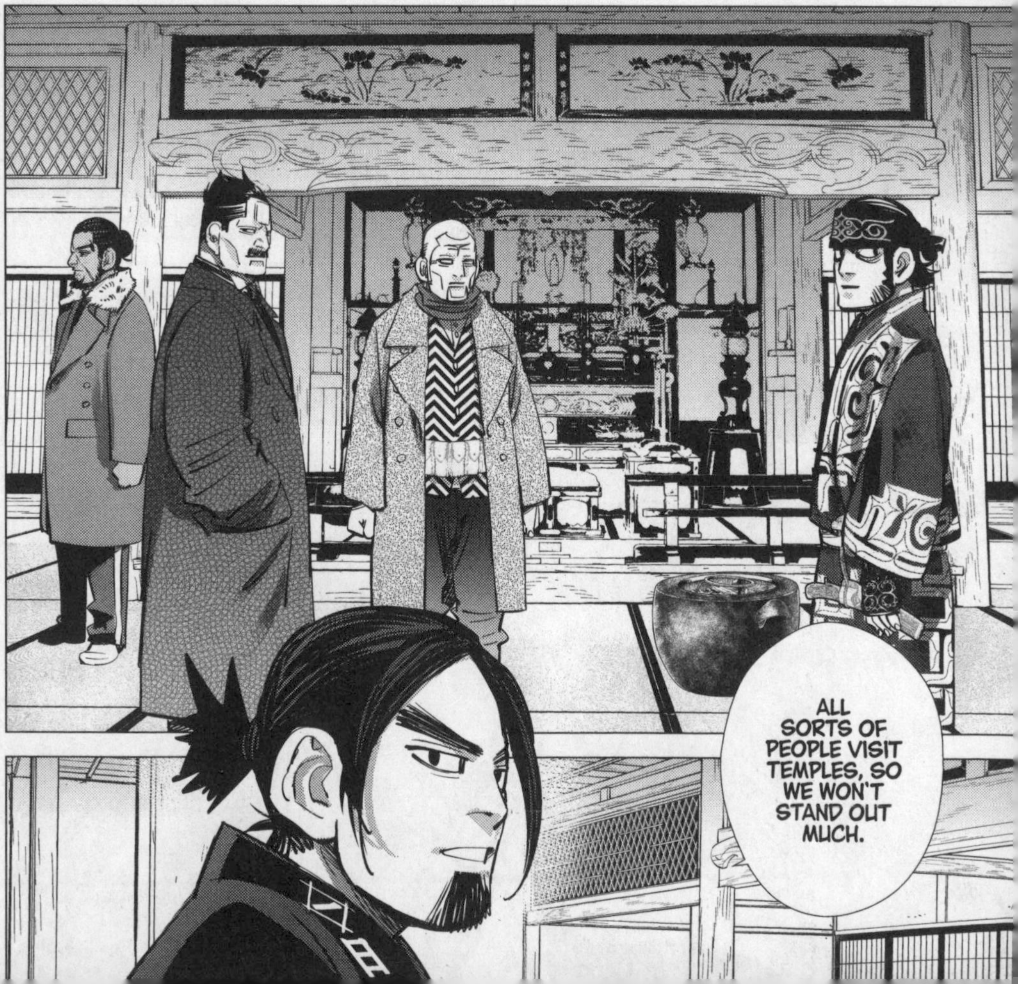
ALL SORTS OF PEOPLE VISIT TEMPLES, SO WE WON'T STAND OUT MUCH.

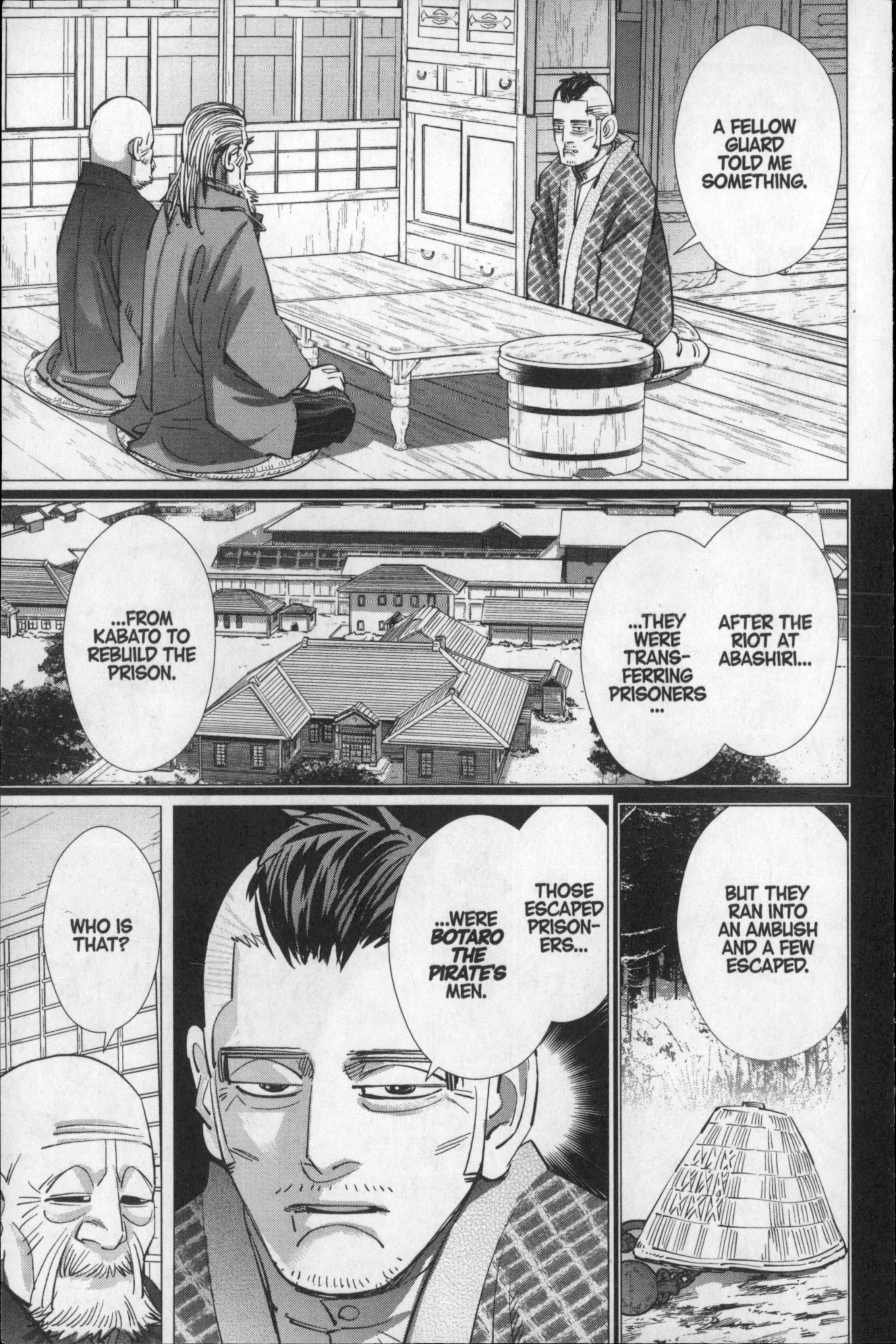
A FELLOW GUARD TOLD ME SOMETHING.
AFTER THE RIOT AT ABASHIRI...
...THEY WERE TRANS-FERRING PRISONERS...
...FROM KABATO TO REBUILD THE PRISON.
BUT THEY RAN INTO AN AMBUSH AND A FEW ESCAPED.
THOSE ESCAPED PRISON-ERS...
...WERE BOTARO THE PIRATE'S MEN.
WHO IS THAT?

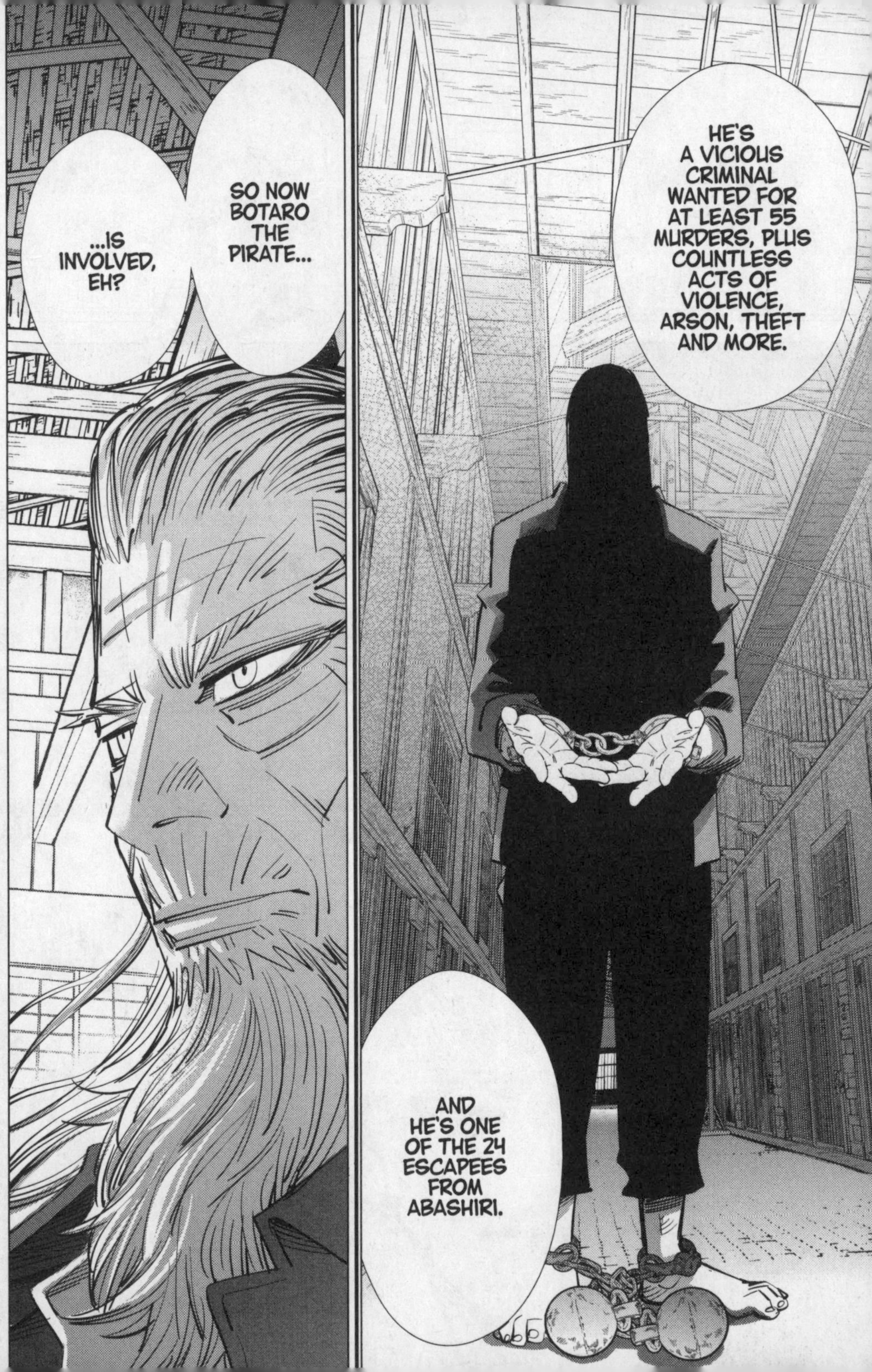
HE'S A VICIOUS CRIMINAL WANTED FOR AT LEAST 55 MURDERS, PLUS COUNTLESS ACTS OF VIOLENCE, ARSON, THEFT AND MORE.
AND HE'S ONE OF THE 24 ESCAPEES FROM ABASHIRI.
SO NOW BOTARO THE PIRATE...
...IS INVOLVED, EH?

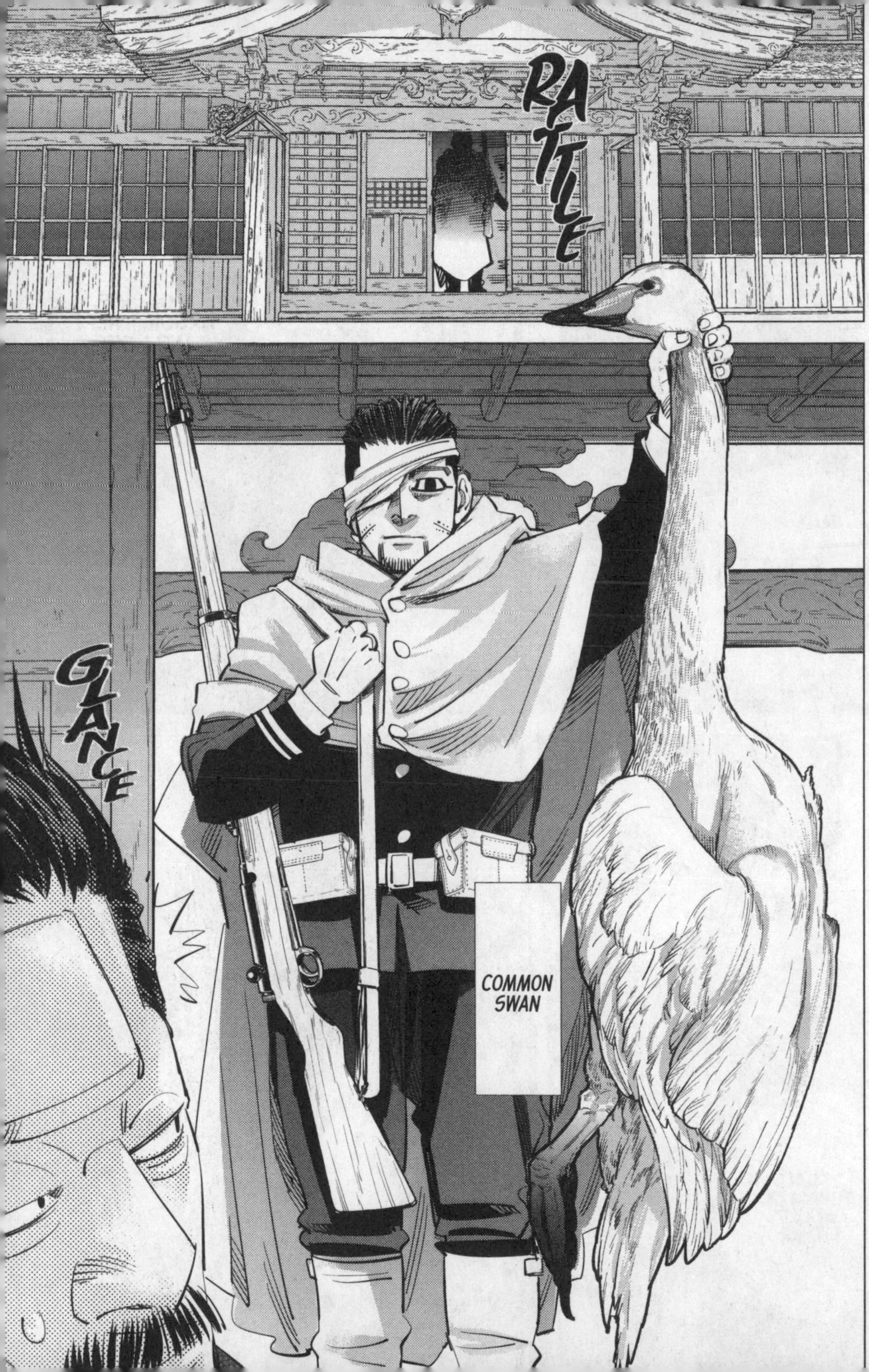
RATTLE
GLANCE
COMMON SWAN

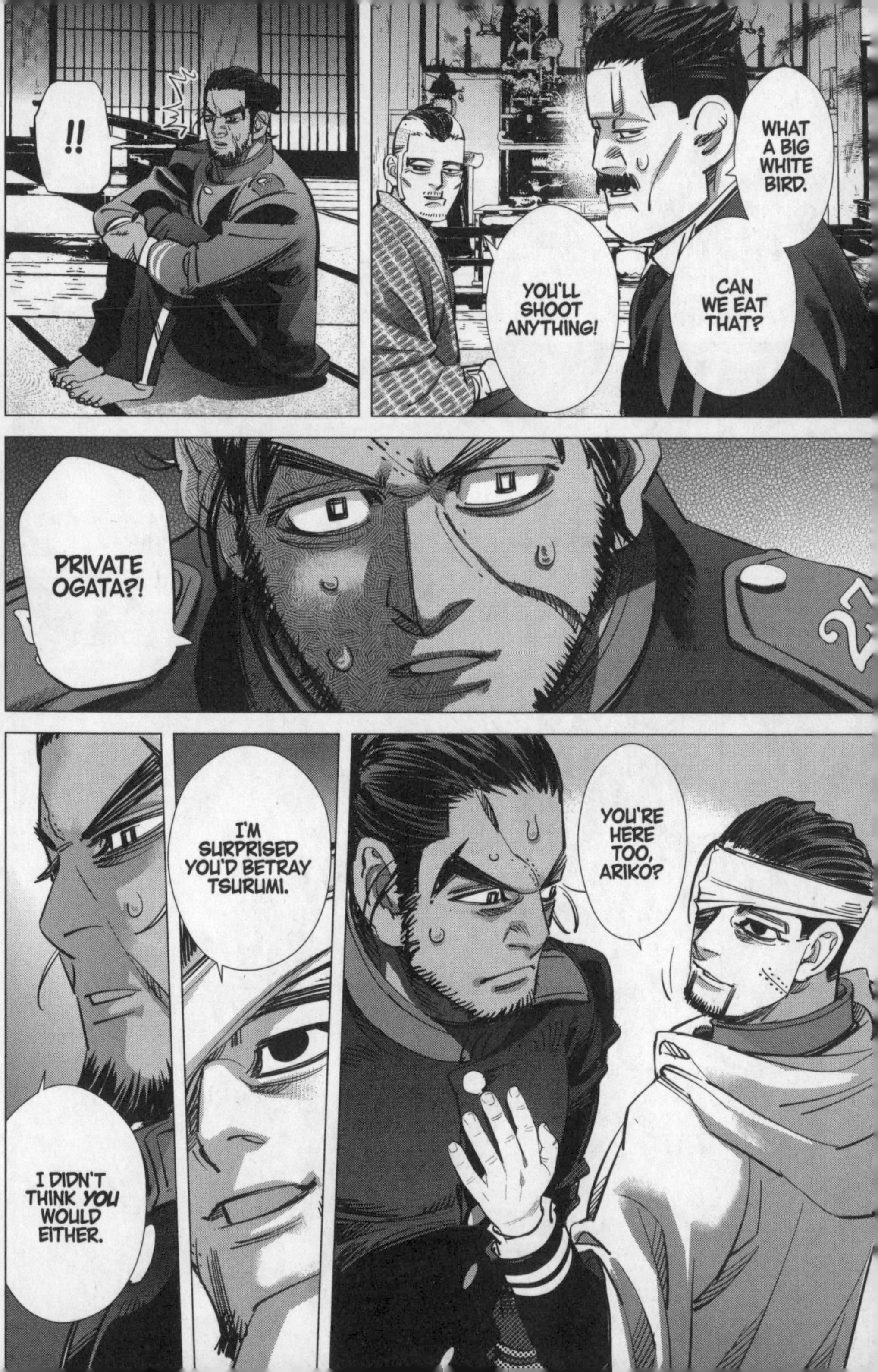
WHAT A BIG WHITE BIRD.
CAN WE EAT THAT?
YOU'LL SHOOT ANYTHING!
!!
PRIVATE OGATA?!
YOU'RE HERE TOO, ARIKO?
I'M SURPRISED YOU'D BETRAY TSURUMI.
I DIDN'T THINK *YOU* WOULD EITHER.

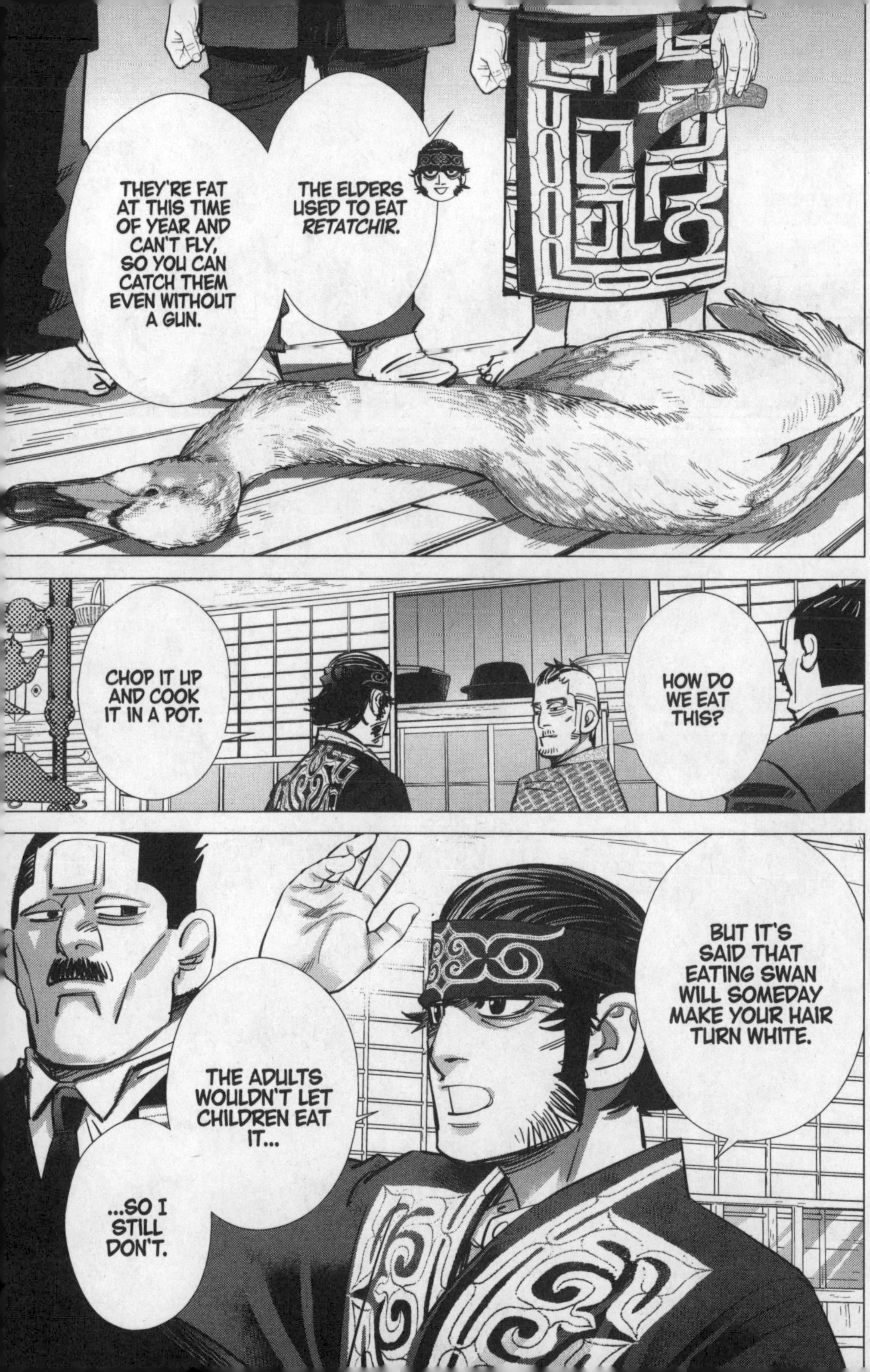
THE ELDERS USED TO EAT *RETATCHIR*.
THEY'RE FAT AT THIS TIME OF YEAR AND CAN'T FLY, SO YOU CAN CATCH THEM EVEN WITHOUT A GUN.
HOW DO WE EAT THIS?
CHOP IT UP AND COOK IT IN A POT.
BUT IT'S SAID THAT EATING SWAN WILL SOMEDAY MAKE YOUR HAIR TURN WHITE.
THE ADULTS WOULDN'T LET CHILDREN EAT IT...
...SO I STILL DON'T.

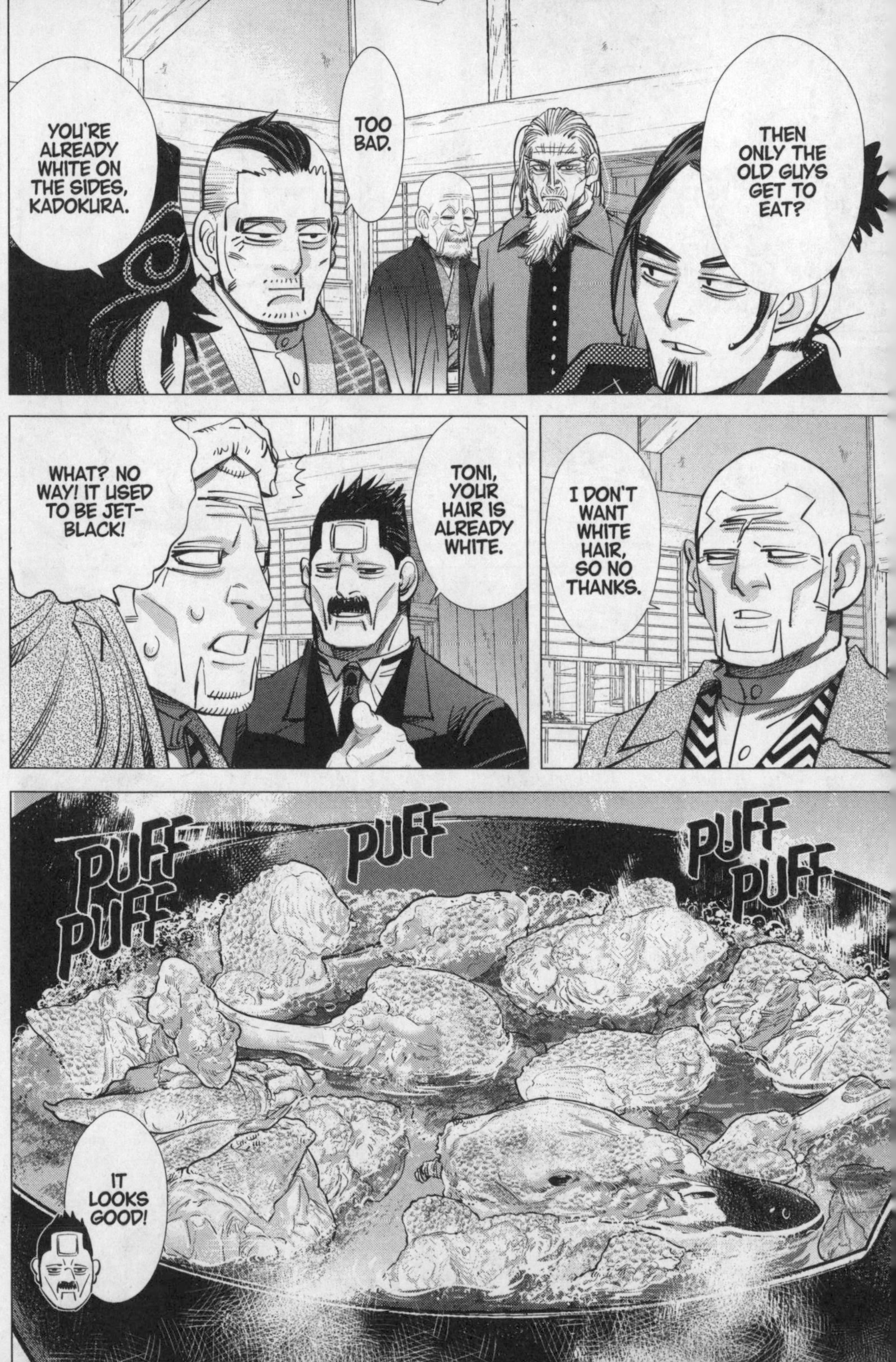
THEN ONLY THE OLD GUYS GET TO EAT?
TOO BAD.
YOU'RE ALREADY WHITE ON THE SIDES, KADOKURA.
I DON'T WANT WHITE HAIR, SO NO THANKS.
TONI, YOUR HAIR IS ALREADY WHITE.
WHAT? NO WAY! IT USED TO BE JET-BLACK!
PUFF PUFF
PUFF
PUFF PUFF
IT LOOKS GOOD!

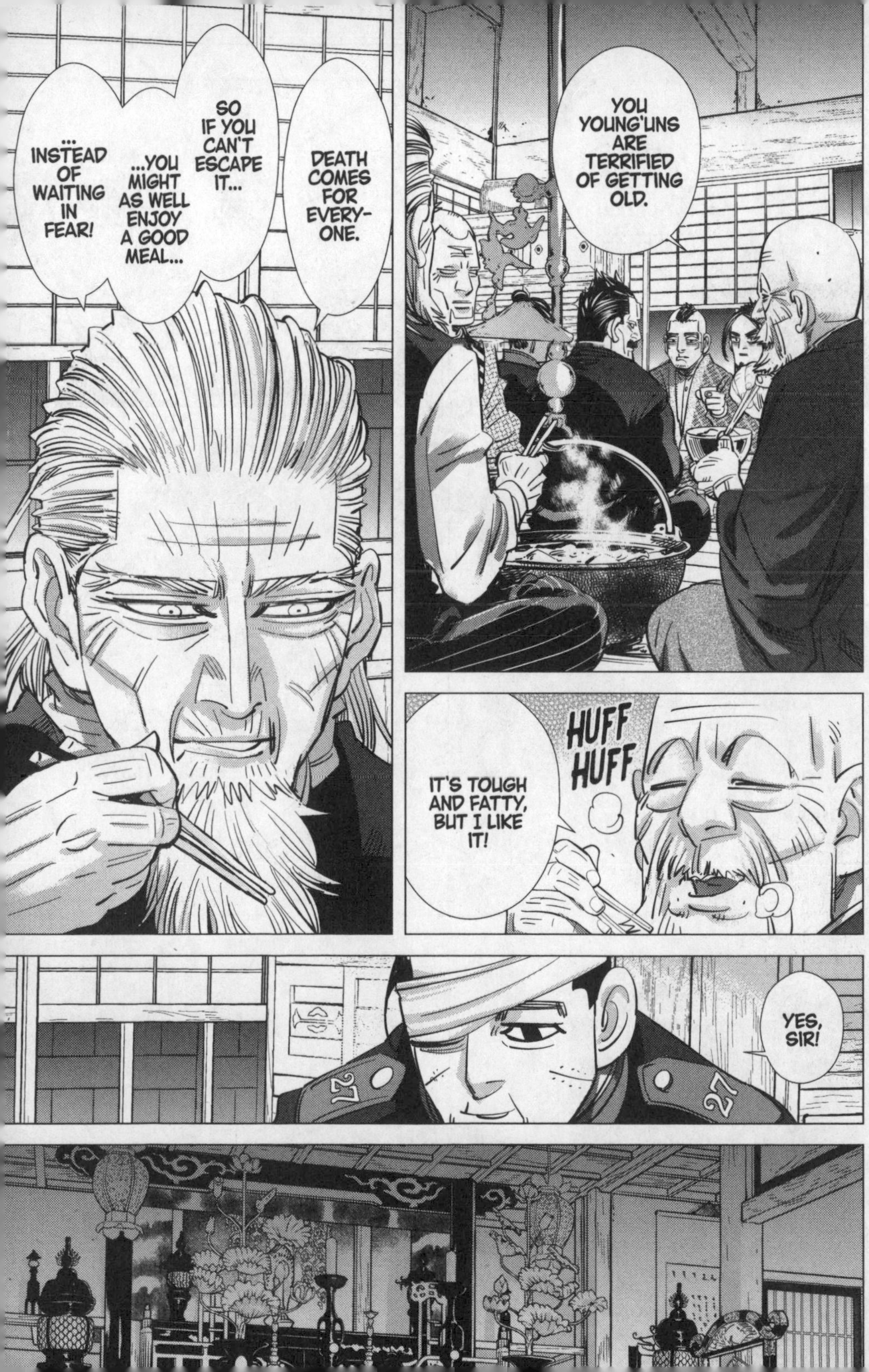
YOU YOUNG'UNS ARE TERRIFIED OF GETTING OLD.
DEATH COMES FOR EVERY-ONE.
SO IF YOU CAN'T ESCAPE IT...
...YOU MIGHT AS WELL ENJOY A GOOD MEAL...
...INSTEAD OF WAITING IN FEAR!
HUFF HUFF
IT'S TOUGH AND FATTY, BUT I LIKE IT!
YES, SIR!

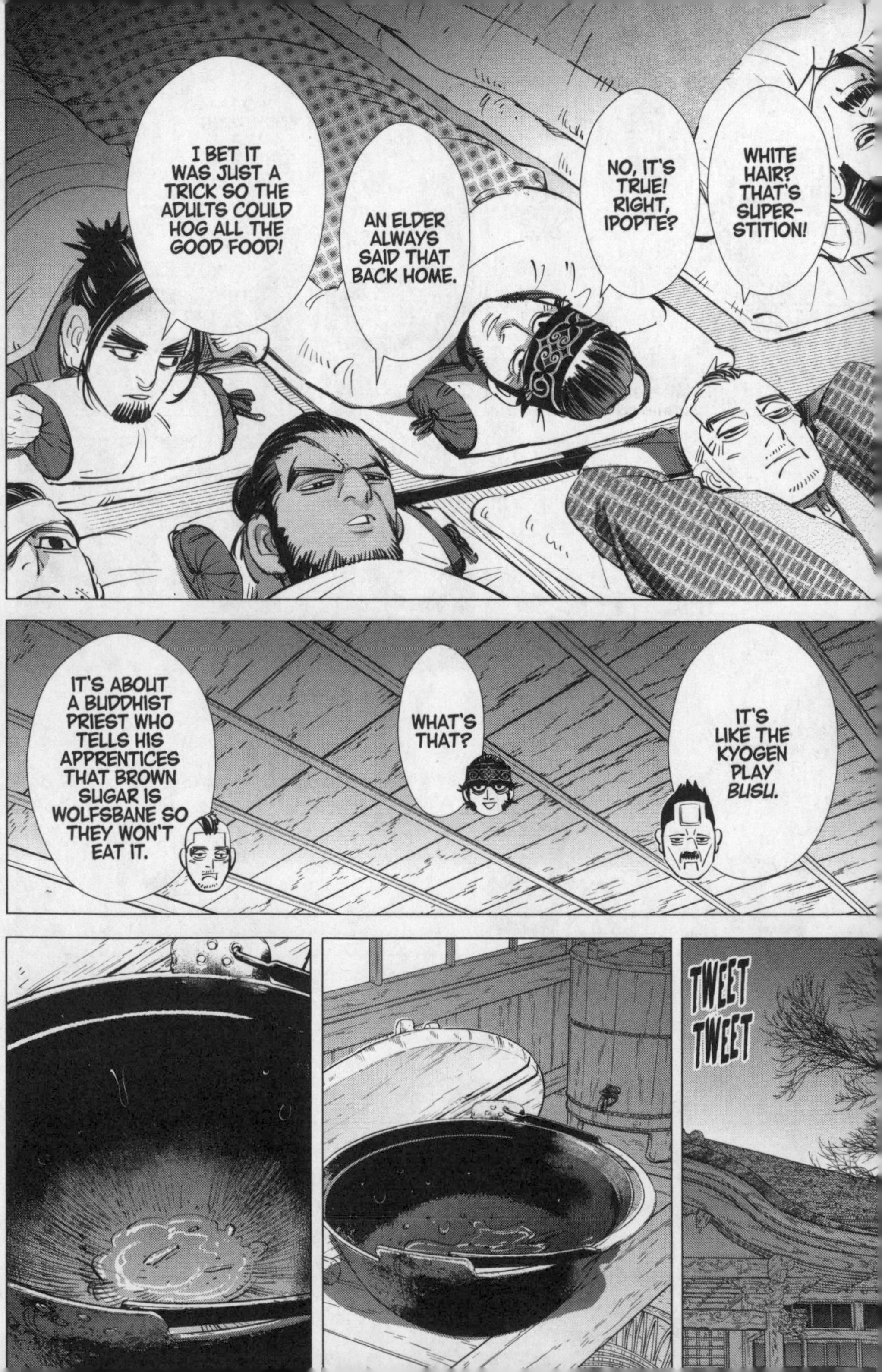
WHITE HAIR? THAT'S SUPER-STITION!
NO, IT'S TRUE! RIGHT, IPOPTE?
AN ELDER ALWAYS SAID THAT BACK HOME.
I BET IT WAS JUST A TRICK SO THE ADULTS COULD HOG ALL THE GOOD FOOD!
IT'S LIKE THE KYOGEN PLAY BUSU.
WHAT'S THAT?
IT'S ABOUT A BUDDHIST PRIEST WHO TELLS HIS APPRENTICES THAT BROWN SUGAR IS WOLFSBANE SO THEY WON'T EAT IT.
TWEET TWEET

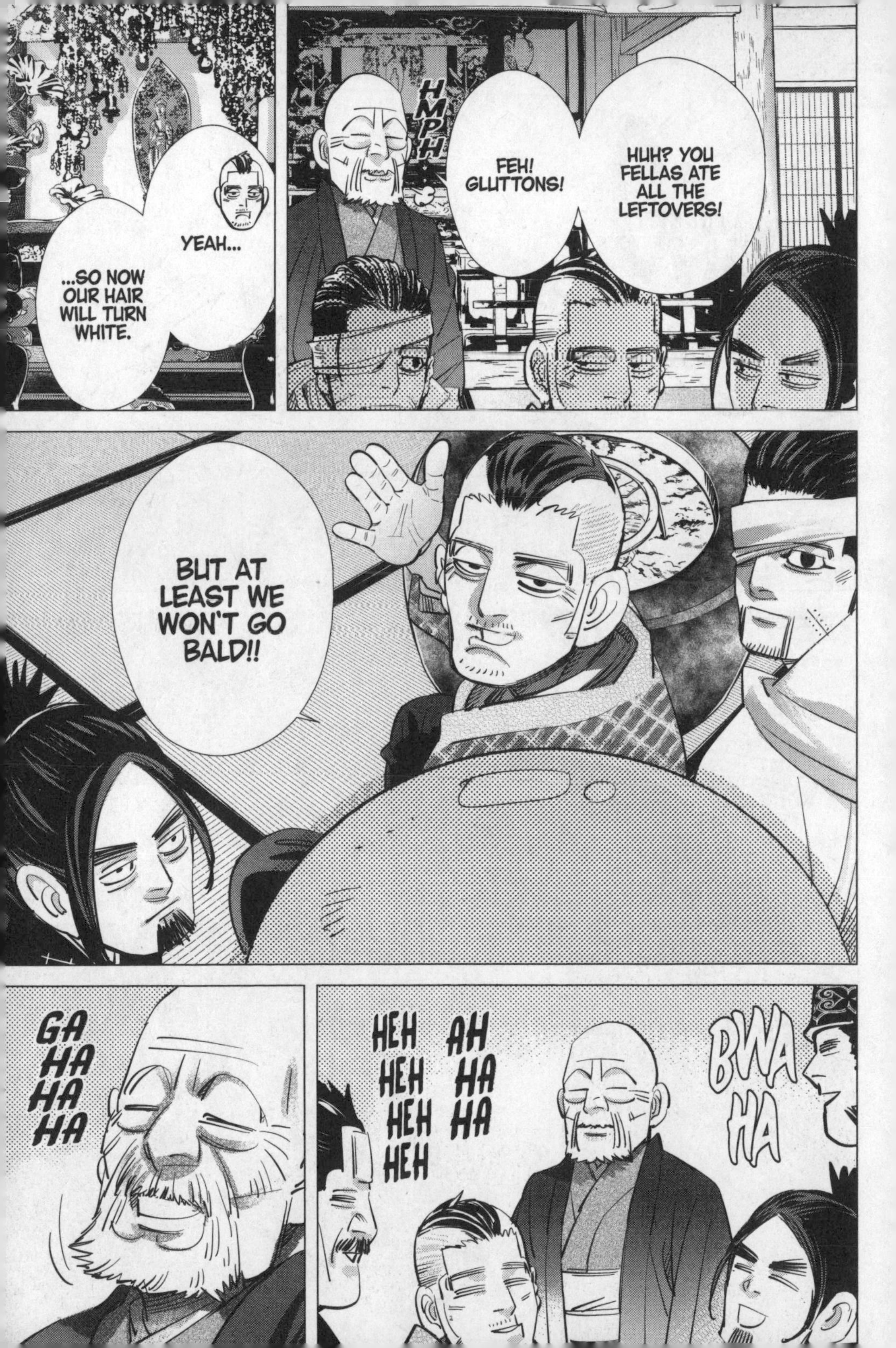
HUH? YOU FELLAS ATE ALL THE LEFTOVERS!
FEH! GLUTTONS!
HMPH
YEAH...
...SO NOW OUR HAIR WILL TURN WHITE.
BUT AT LEAST WE WON'T GO BALD!!
BWA HA
AH HA HA HA
HEH HEH HEH HEH
GA HA HA HA

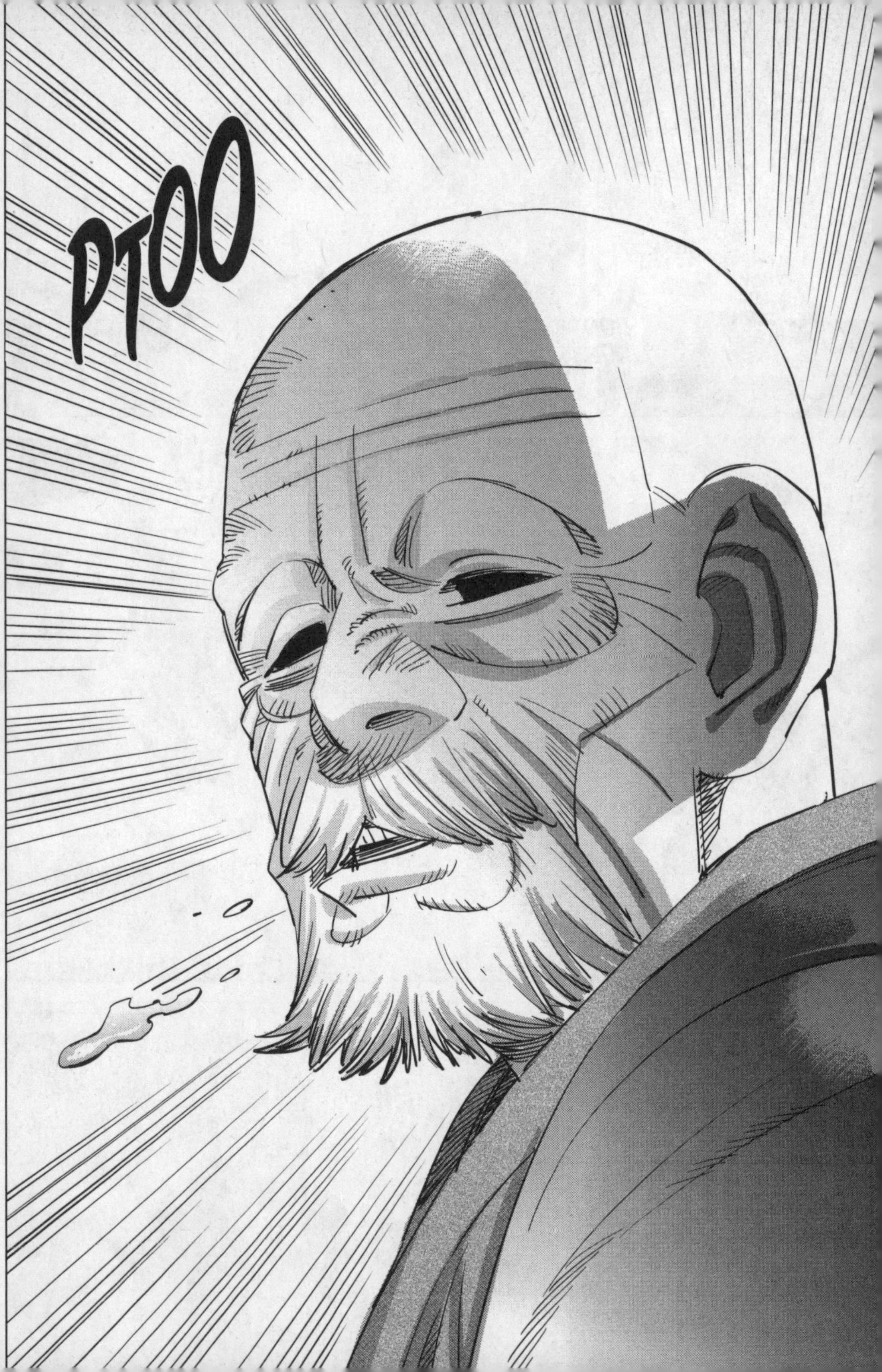
PTOO

Chapter 224: Near Lake Shikotsu

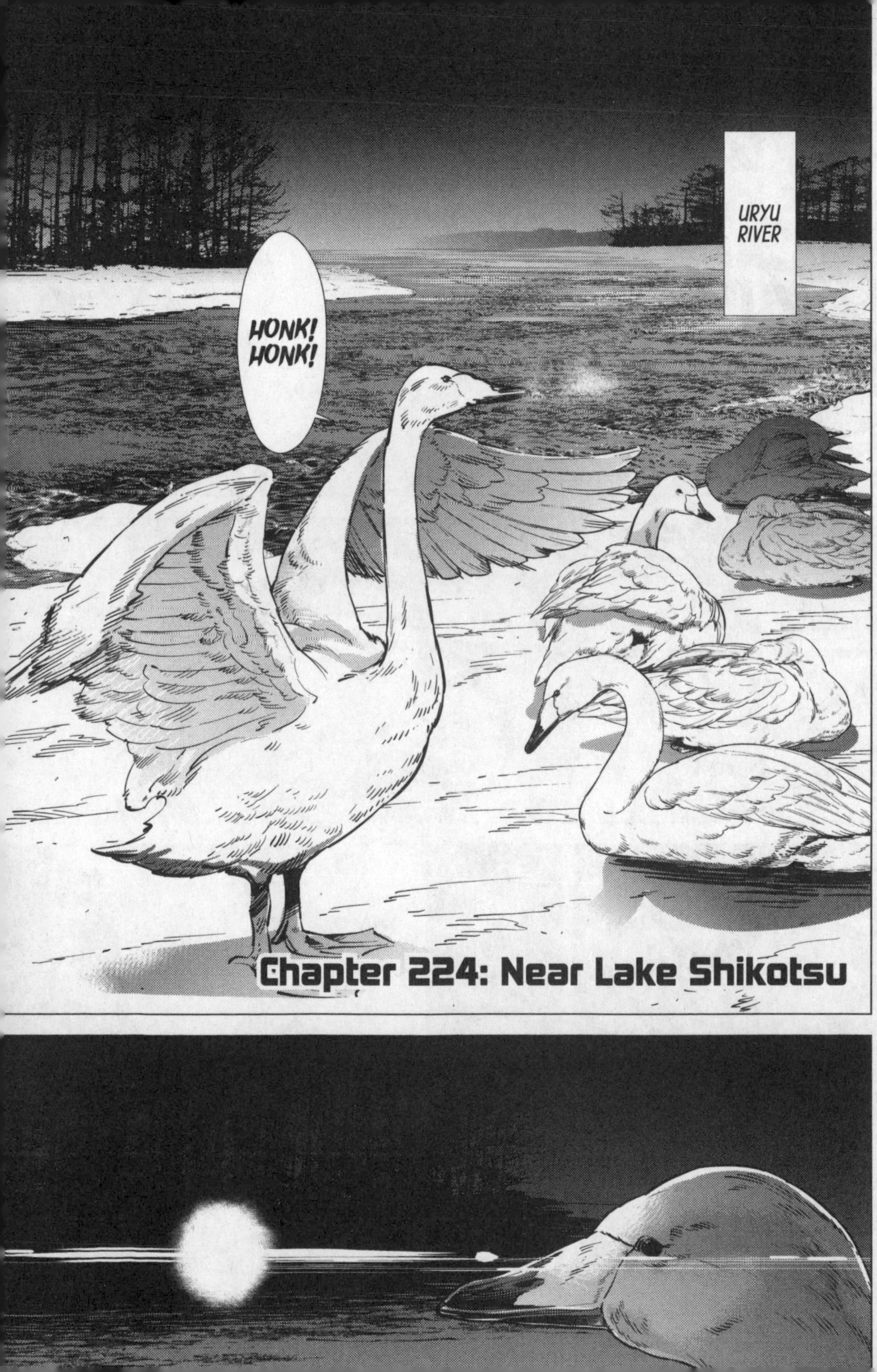
URYU RIVER
HONK! HONK!

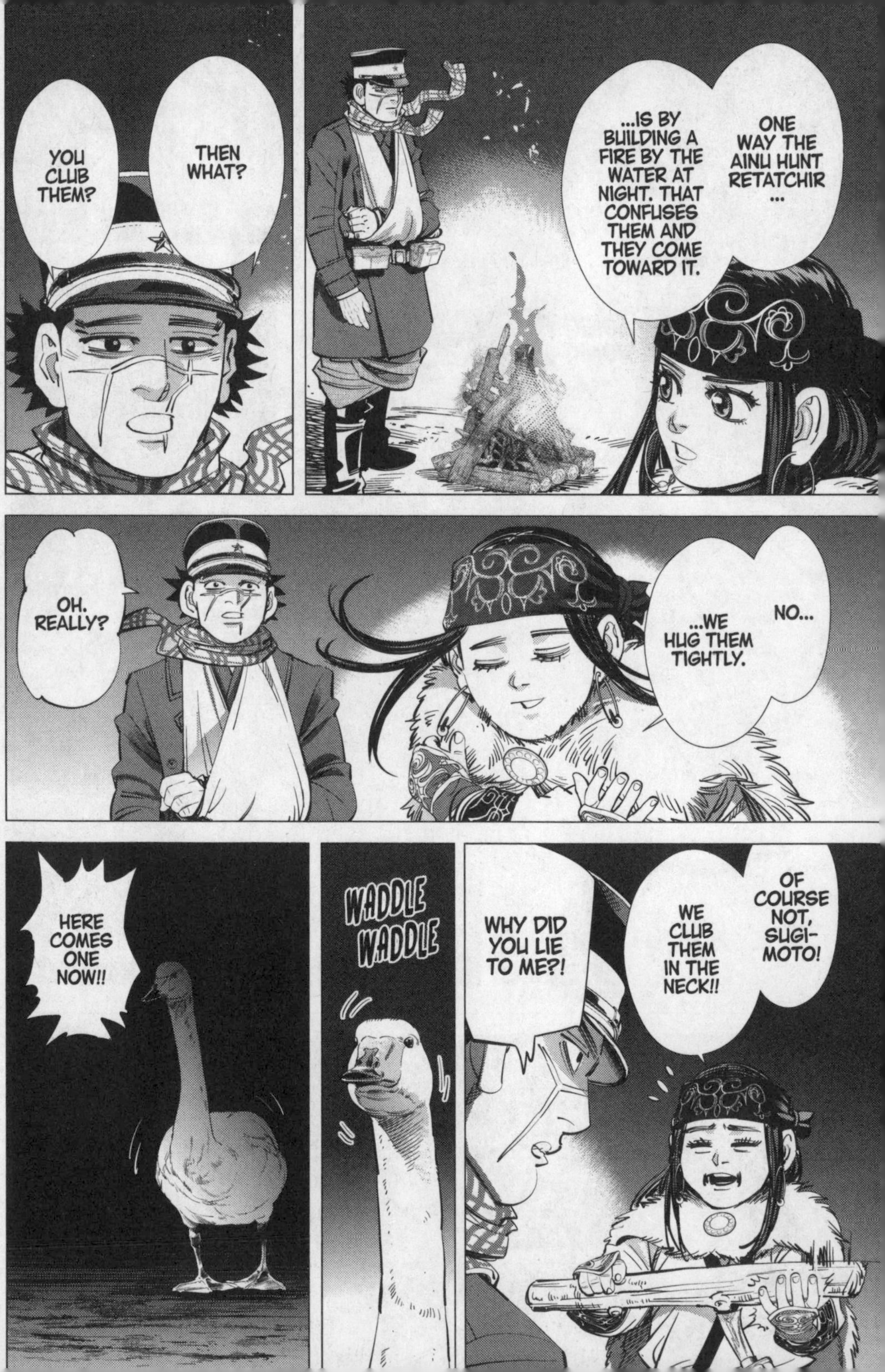
ONE WAY THE AINU HUNT RETATCHIR ...
...IS BY BUILDING A FIRE BY THE WATER AT NIGHT. THAT CONFUSES THEM AND THEY COME TOWARD IT.
THEN WHAT?
YOU CLUB THEM?
NO...
...WE HUG THEM TIGHTLY.
OH. REALLY?
OF COURSE NOT, SUGI-MOTO!
WE CLUB THEM IN THE NECK!!
WHY DID YOU LIE TO ME?!
WADDLE WADDLE
HERE COMES ONE NOW!!

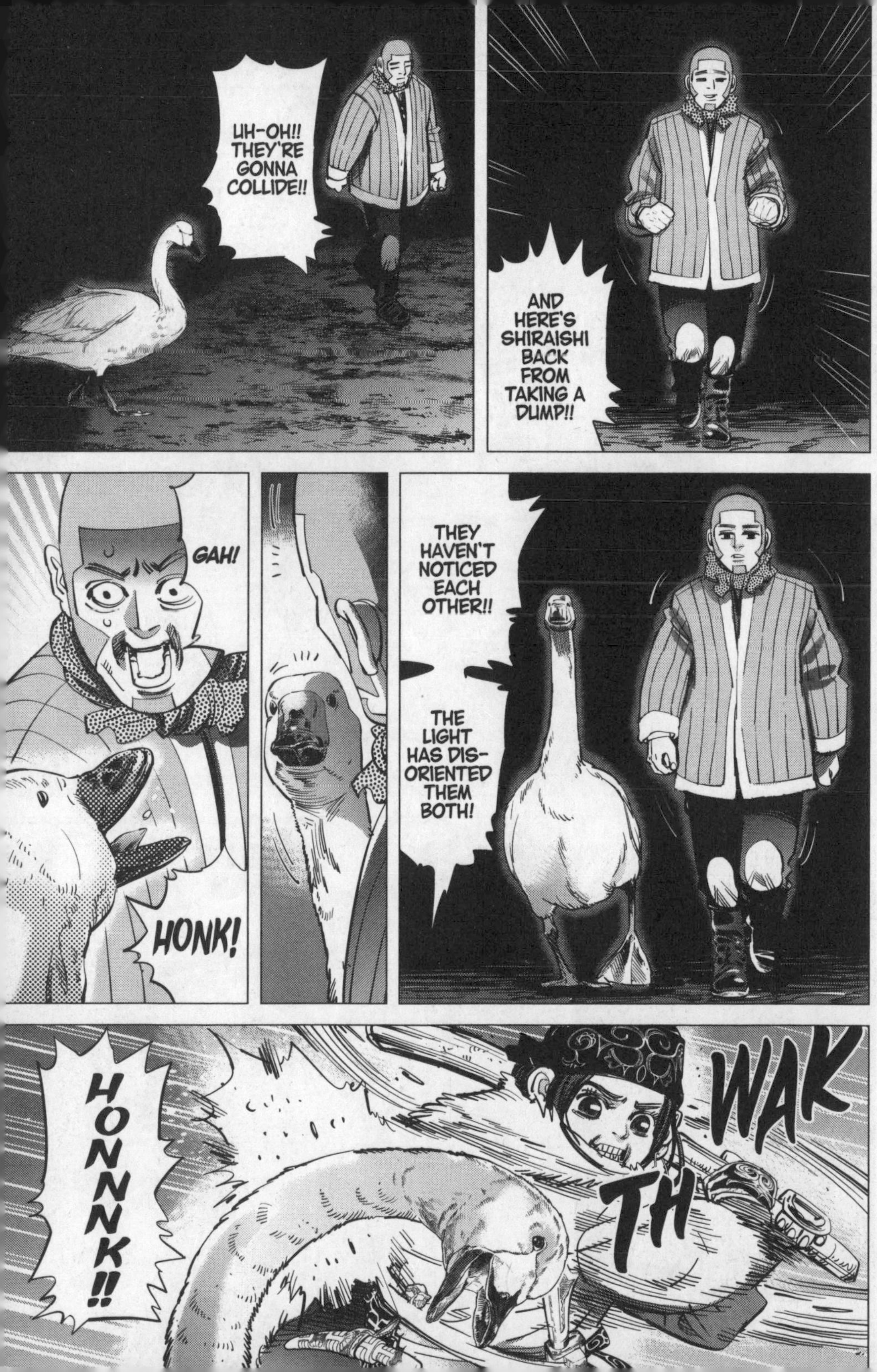
AND HERE'S SHIRAISHI BACK FROM TAKING A DUMP!!
UH-OH!! THEY'RE GONNA COLLIDE!!
THEY HAVEN'T NOTICED EACH OTHER!!
THE LIGHT HAS DIS-ORIENTED THEM BOTH!
GAH!
HONK!
WAK
TH
HONNNK!!

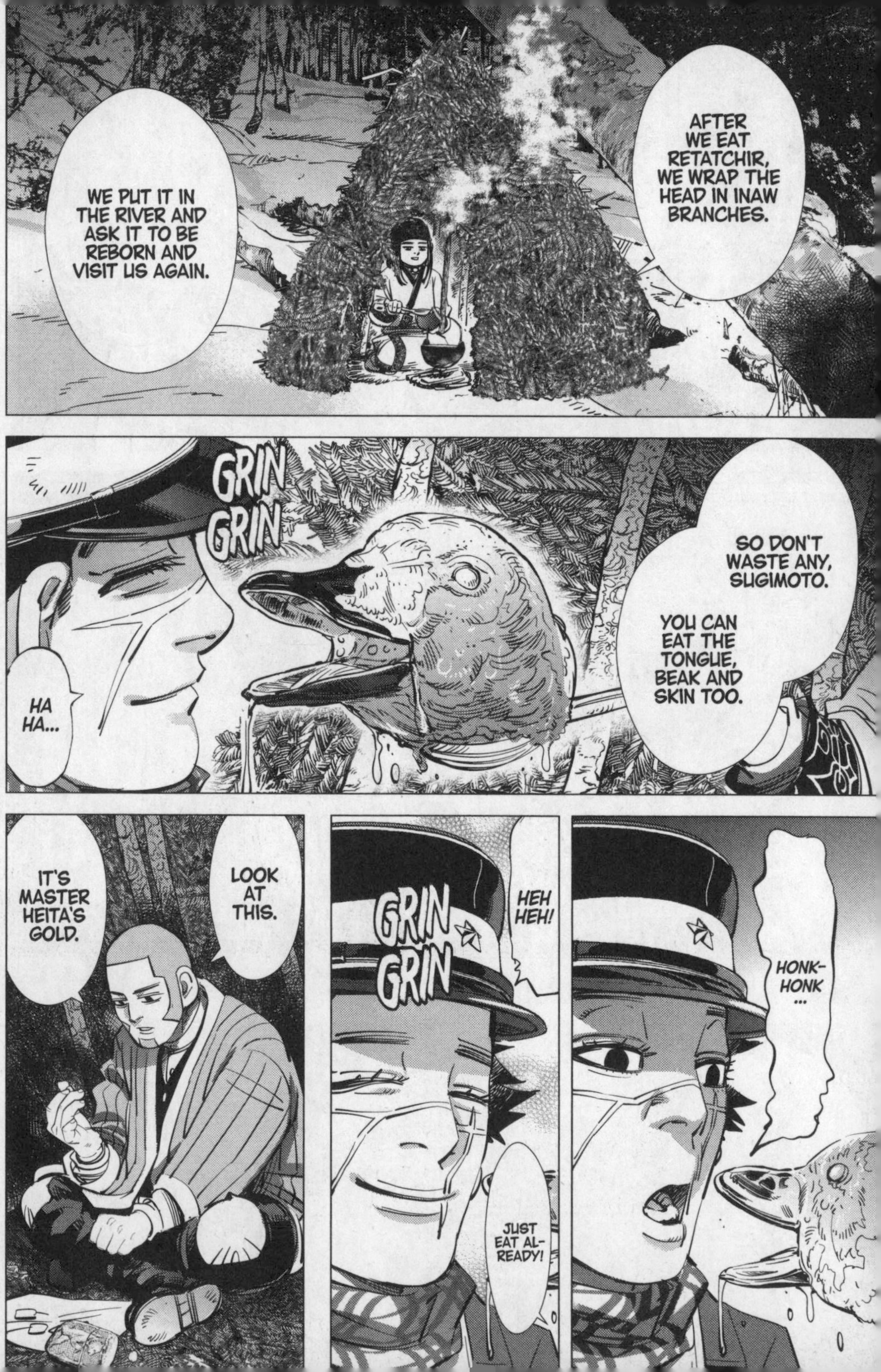
AFTER WE EAT RETATCHIR, WE WRAP THE HEAD IN INAW BRANCHES.
WE PUT IT IN THE RIVER AND ASK IT TO BE REBORN AND VISIT US AGAIN.
SO DON'T WASTE ANY, SUGIMOTO.
YOU CAN EAT THE TONGUE, BEAK AND SKIN TOO.
GRIN GRIN
HA HA...
HONK-HONK ...
HEH HEH!
GRIN GRIN
JUST EAT AL-READY!
LOOK AT THIS.
IT'S MASTER HEITA'S GOLD.

HE KEPT SAMPLES HE COLLECTED FROM EACH RIVER.
*YUBARI RIVER
*REKIFUNE RIVER
*MOSHOSANBETSU RIVER
EACH KIND OF GOLD HAS ITS OWN "FACE."
IT CAN BE GRANULAR, SCALY OR TABULAR.
THE GOLD IN EACH PLACE IS DIFFERENT.
Yubari River
Shiribeshi-Toshibetsu River
SOME IS ROUND AND SOME IS ANGULAR.
Tonbetsu River
Shiriuchi River
A VETERAN PANNER CAN TELL WHERE GOLD CAME FROM JUST BY LOOKING AT ITS FACE.

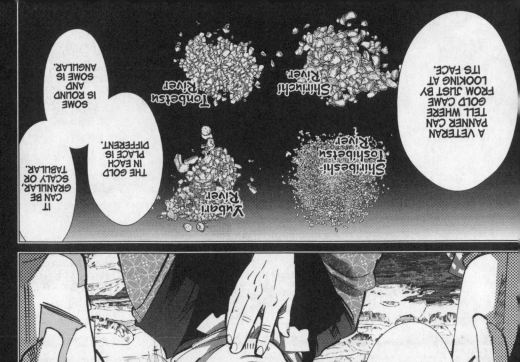

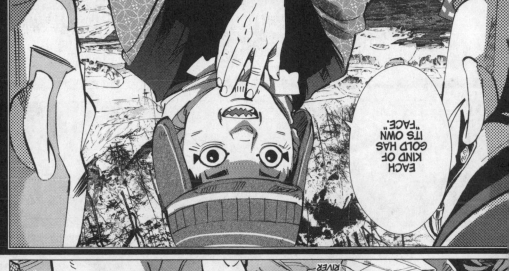

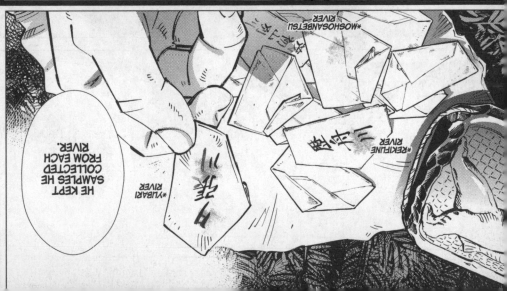

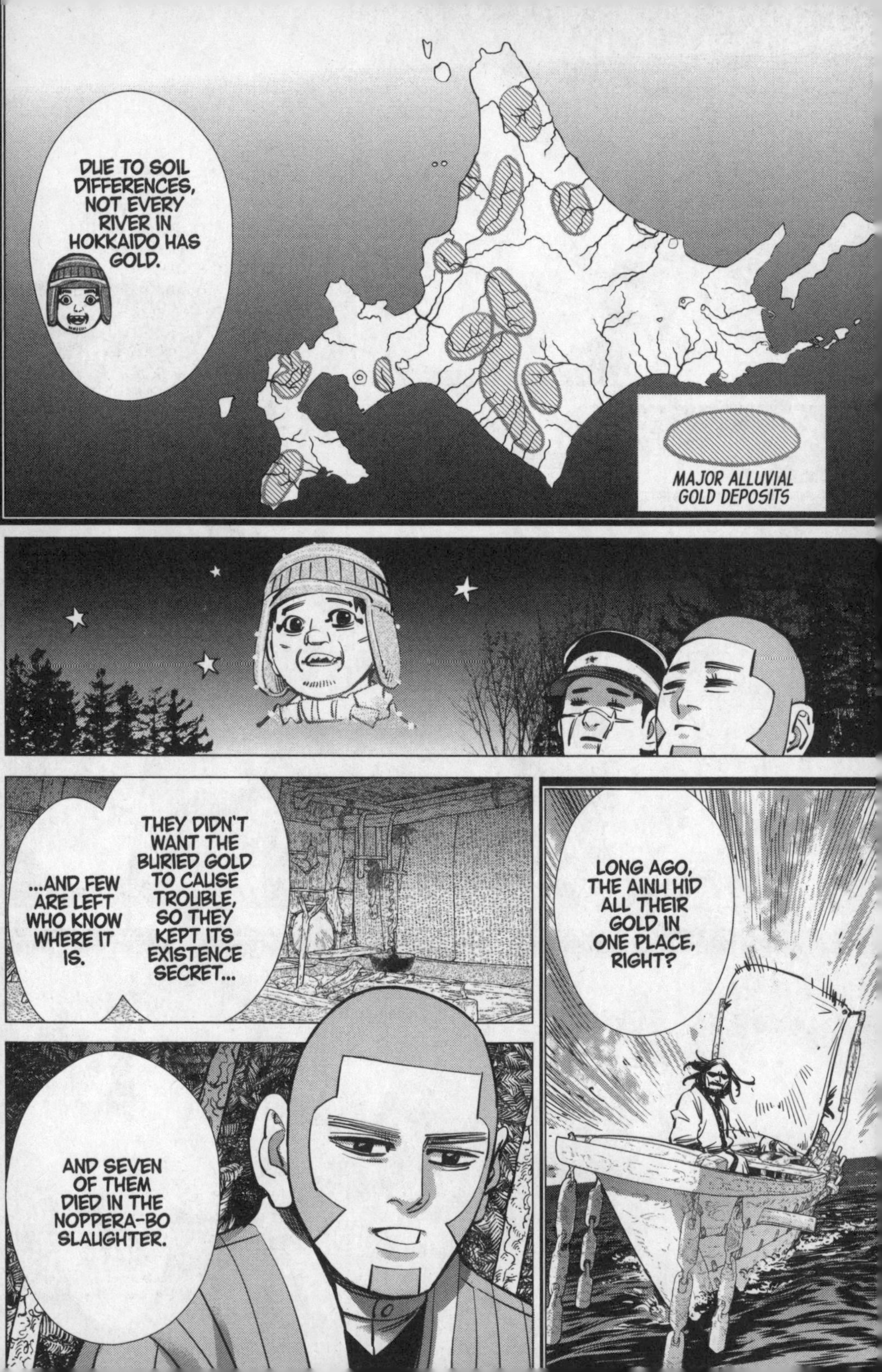
DUE TO SOIL DIFFERENCES, NOT EVERY RIVER IN HOKKAIDO HAS GOLD.
MAJOR ALLUVIAL GOLD DEPOSITS
LONG AGO, THE AINU HID ALL THEIR GOLD IN ONE PLACE, RIGHT?
THEY DIDN'T WANT THE BURIED GOLD TO CAUSE TROUBLE, SO THEY KEPT ITS EXISTENCE SECRET...
...AND FEW ARE LEFT WHO KNOW WHERE IT IS.
AND SEVEN OF THEM DIED IN THE NOPPERA-BO SLAUGHTER.

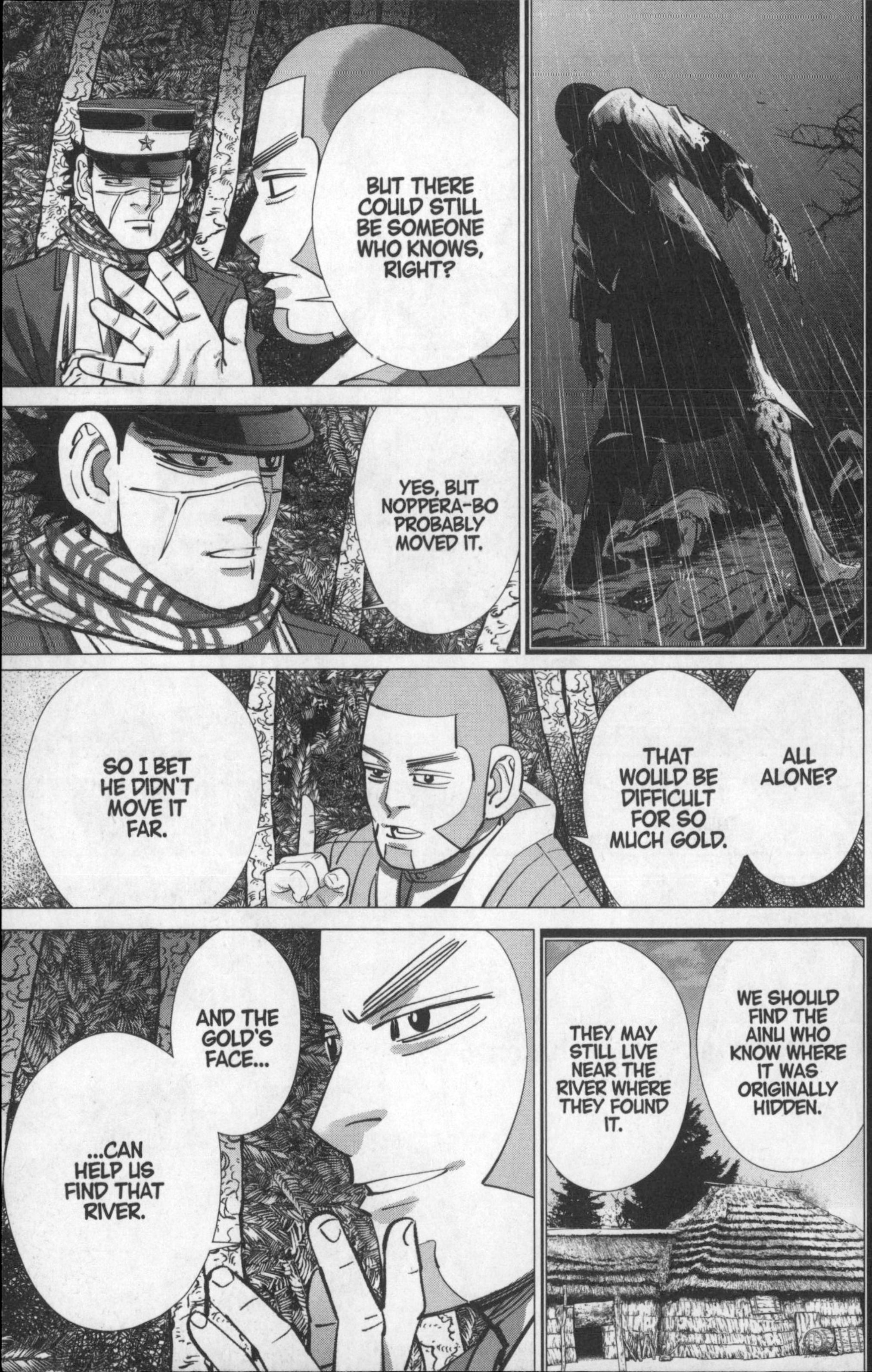
BUT THERE COULD STILL BE SOMEONE WHO KNOWS, RIGHT?
YES, BUT NOPPERA-BO PROBABLY MOVED IT.
ALL ALONE?
THAT WOULD BE DIFFICULT FOR SO MUCH GOLD.
SO I BET HE DIDN'T MOVE IT FAR.
WE SHOULD FIND THE AINU WHO KNOW WHERE IT WAS ORIGINALLY HIDDEN.
THEY MAY STILL LIVE NEAR THE RIVER WHERE THEY FOUND IT.
AND THE GOLD'S FACE...
...CAN HELP US FIND THAT RIVER.

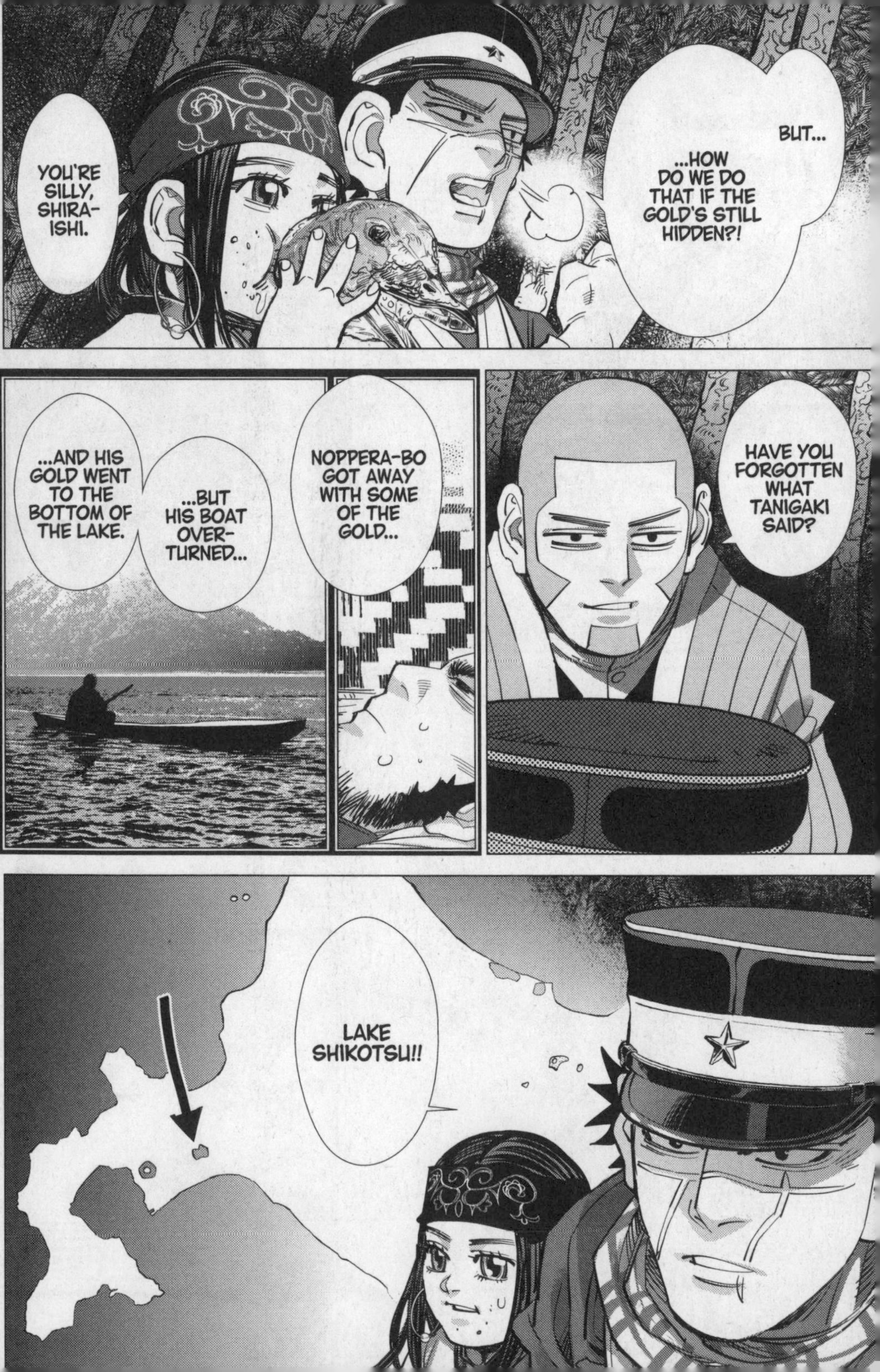
BUT...
...HOW DO WE DO THAT IF THE GOLD'S STILL HIDDEN?!
YOU'RE SILLY, SHIRA-ISHI.
HAVE YOU FORGOTTEN WHAT TANIGAKI SAID?
NOPPERA-BO GOT AWAY WITH SOME OF THE GOLD...
...BUT HIS BOAT OVER-TURNED...
...AND HIS GOLD WENT TO THE BOTTOM OF THE LAKE.
LAKE SHIKOTSU!!

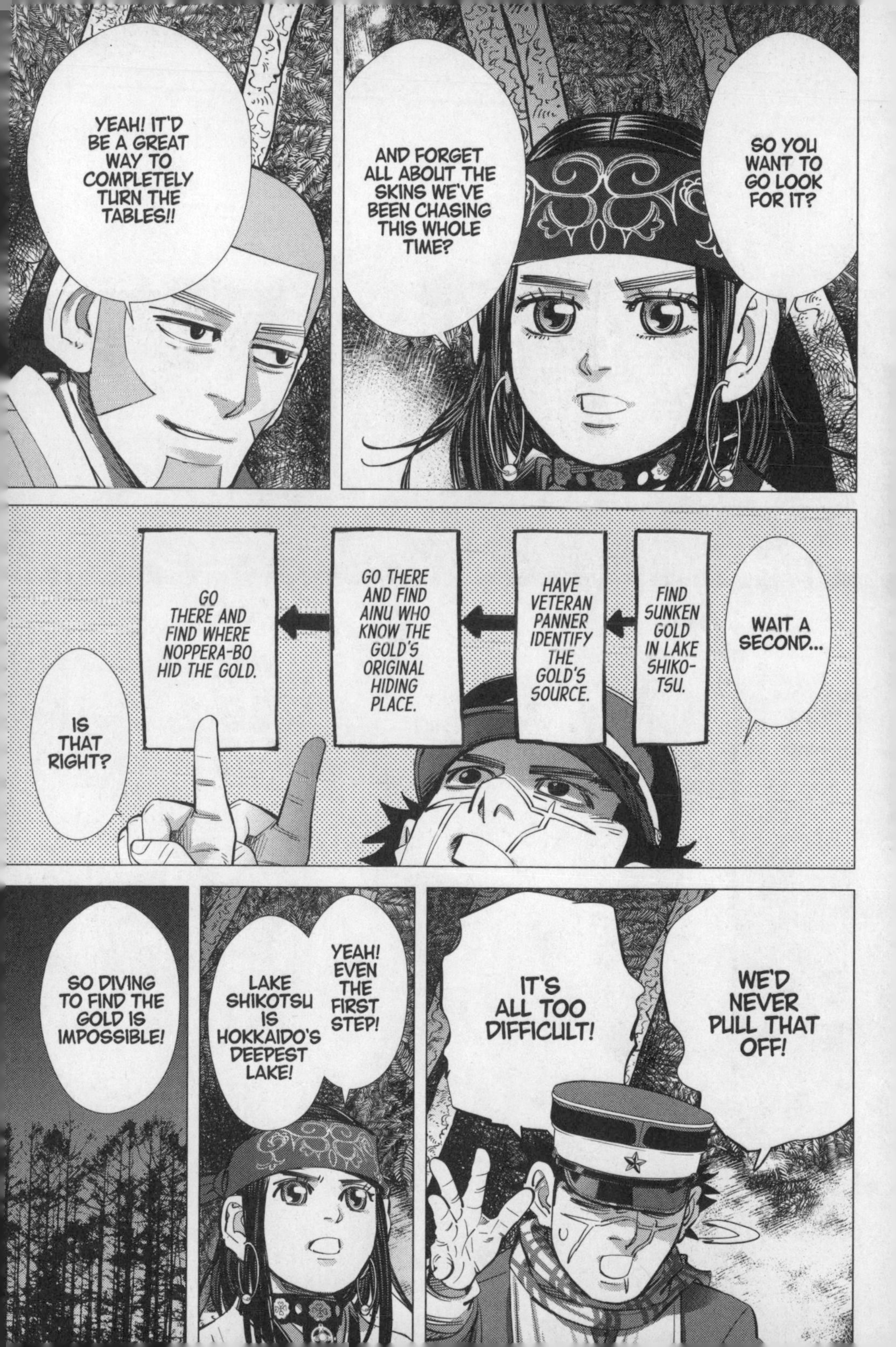
SO YOU WANT TO GO LOOK FOR IT?
AND FORGET ALL ABOUT THE SKINS WE'VE BEEN CHASING THIS WHOLE TIME?
YEAH! IT'D BE A GREAT WAY TO COMPLETELY TURN THE TABLES!!
WAIT A SECOND...
FIND SUNKEN GOLD IN LAKE SHIKO-TSU.
HAVE VETERAN PANNER IDENTIFY THE GOLD'S SOURCE.
GO THERE AND FIND AINU WHO KNOW THE GOLD'S ORIGINAL HIDING PLACE.
GO THERE AND FIND WHERE NOPPERA-BO HID THE GOLD.
IS THAT RIGHT?
WE'D NEVER PULL THAT OFF!
IT'S ALL TOO DIFFICULT!
YEAH! EVEN THE FIRST STEP!
LAKE SHIKOTSU IS HOKKAIDO'S DEEPEST LAKE!
SO DIVING TO FIND THE GOLD IS IMPOSSIBLE!

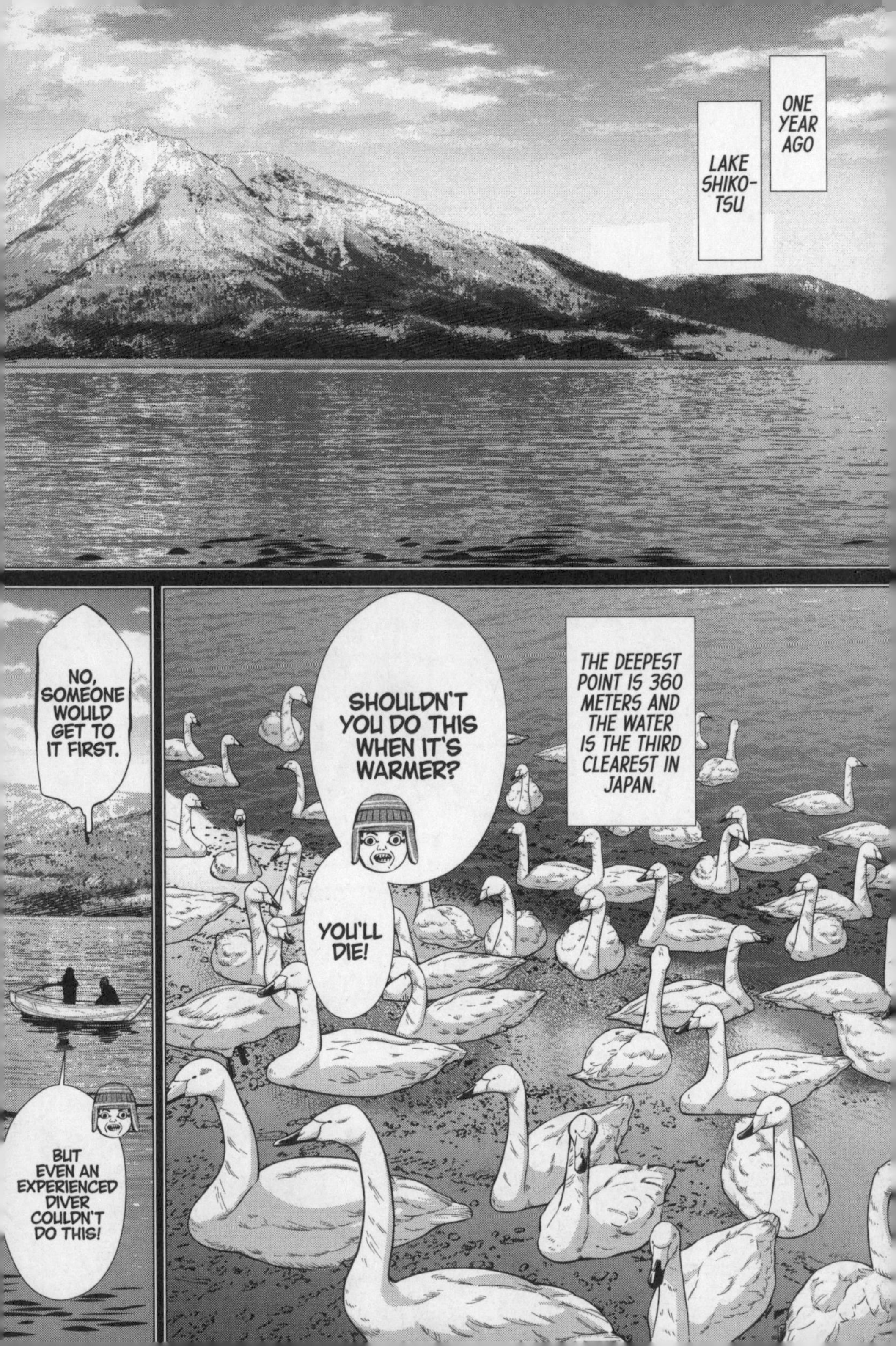
ONE YEAR AGO
LAKE SHIKO-TSU
THE DEEPEST POINT IS 360 METERS AND THE WATER IS THE THIRD CLEAREST IN JAPAN.
SHOULDN'T YOU DO THIS WHEN IT'S WARMER?
YOU'LL DIE!
NO, SOMEONE WOULD GET TO IT FIRST.
BUT EVEN AN EXPERIENCED DIVER COULDN'T DO THIS!

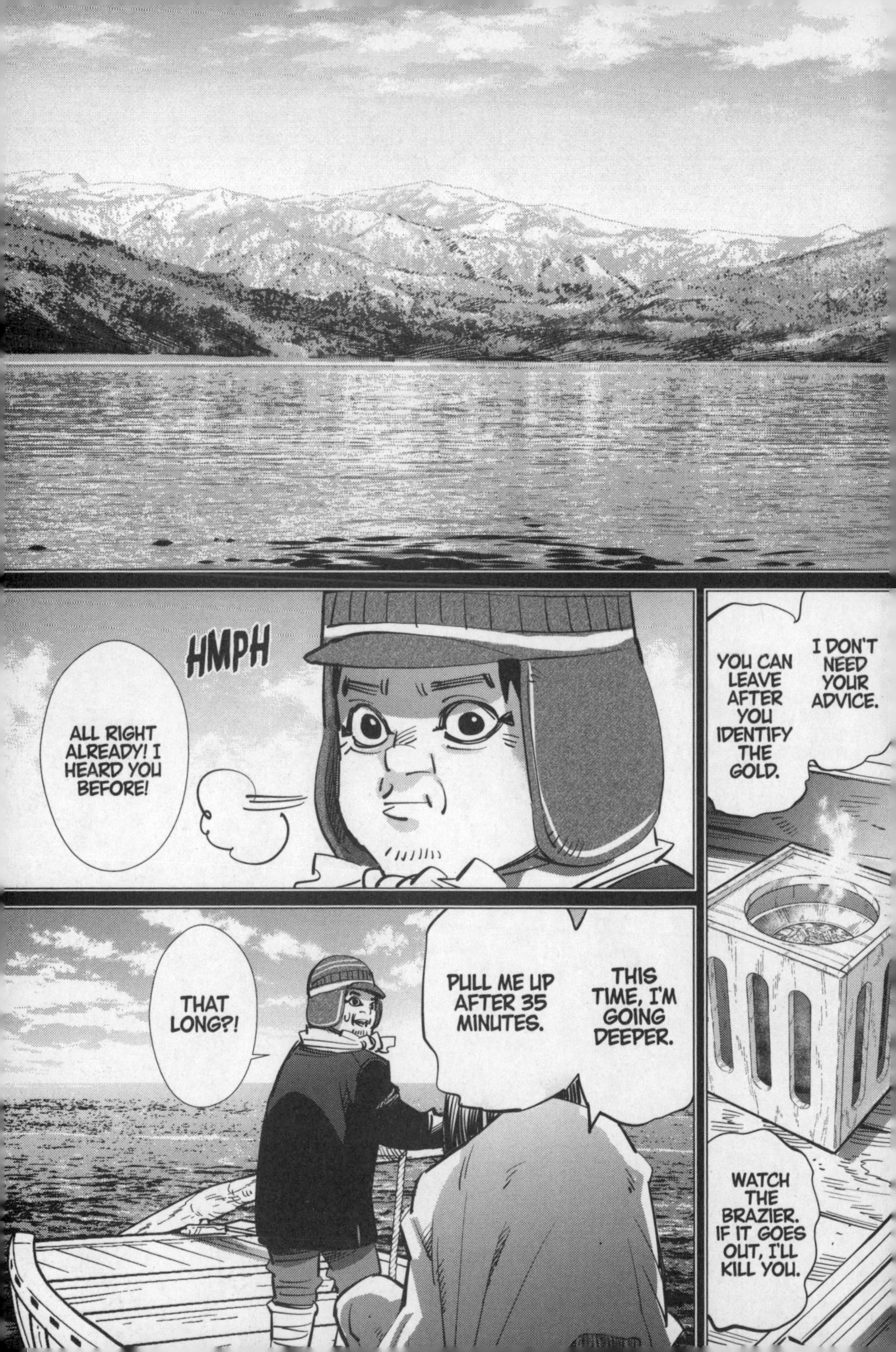
I DON'T NEED YOUR ADVICE.
YOU CAN LEAVE AFTER YOU IDENTIFY THE GOLD.
WATCH THE BRAZIER. IF IT GOES OUT, I'LL KILL YOU.
HMPH
ALL RIGHT ALREADY! I HEARD YOU BEFORE!
THIS TIME, I'M GOING DEEPER.
PULL ME UP AFTER 35 MINUTES.
THAT LONG?!

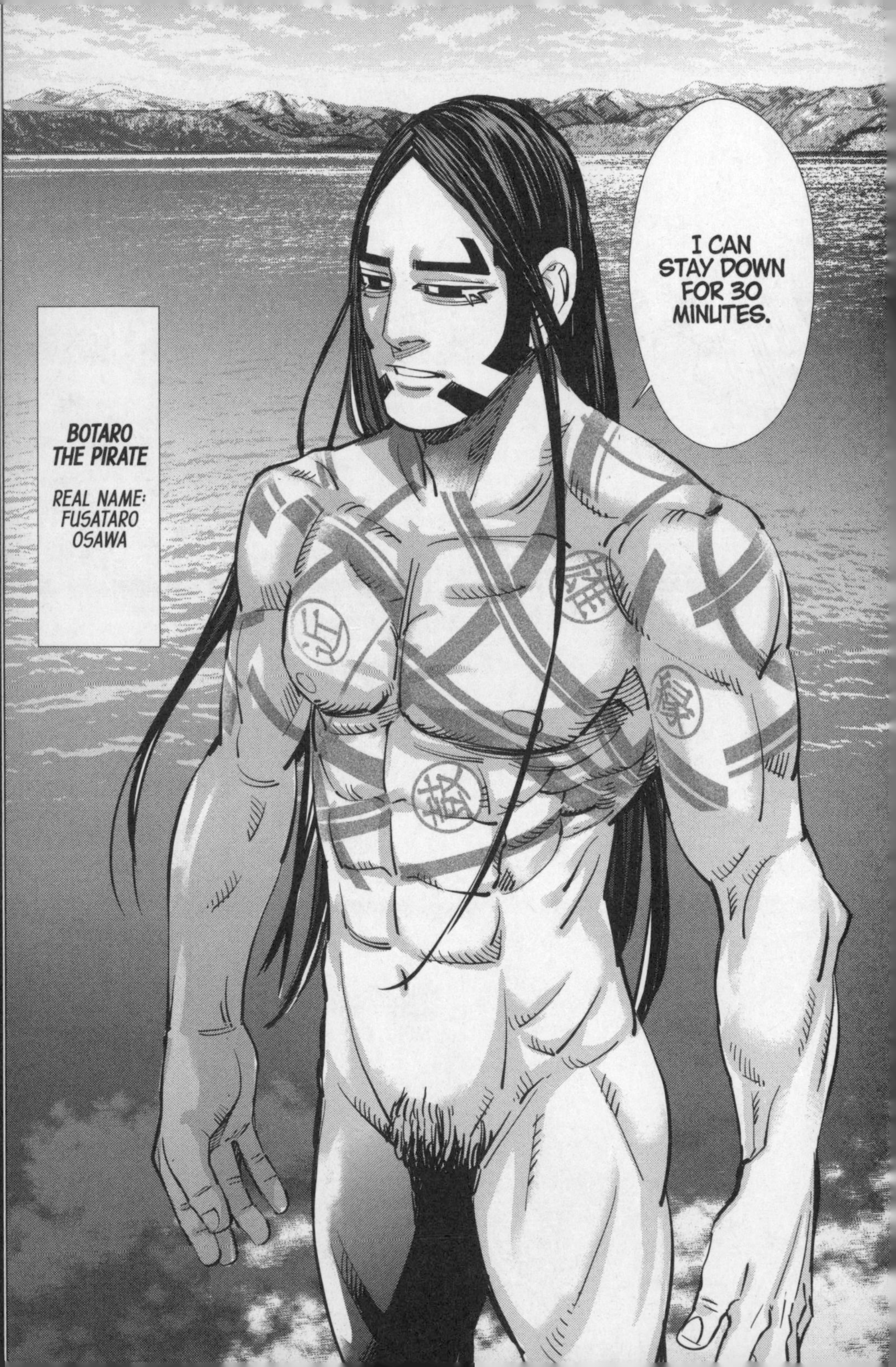
I CAN STAY DOWN FOR 30 MINUTES.
BOTARO THE PIRATE
REAL NAME: FUSATARO OSAWA

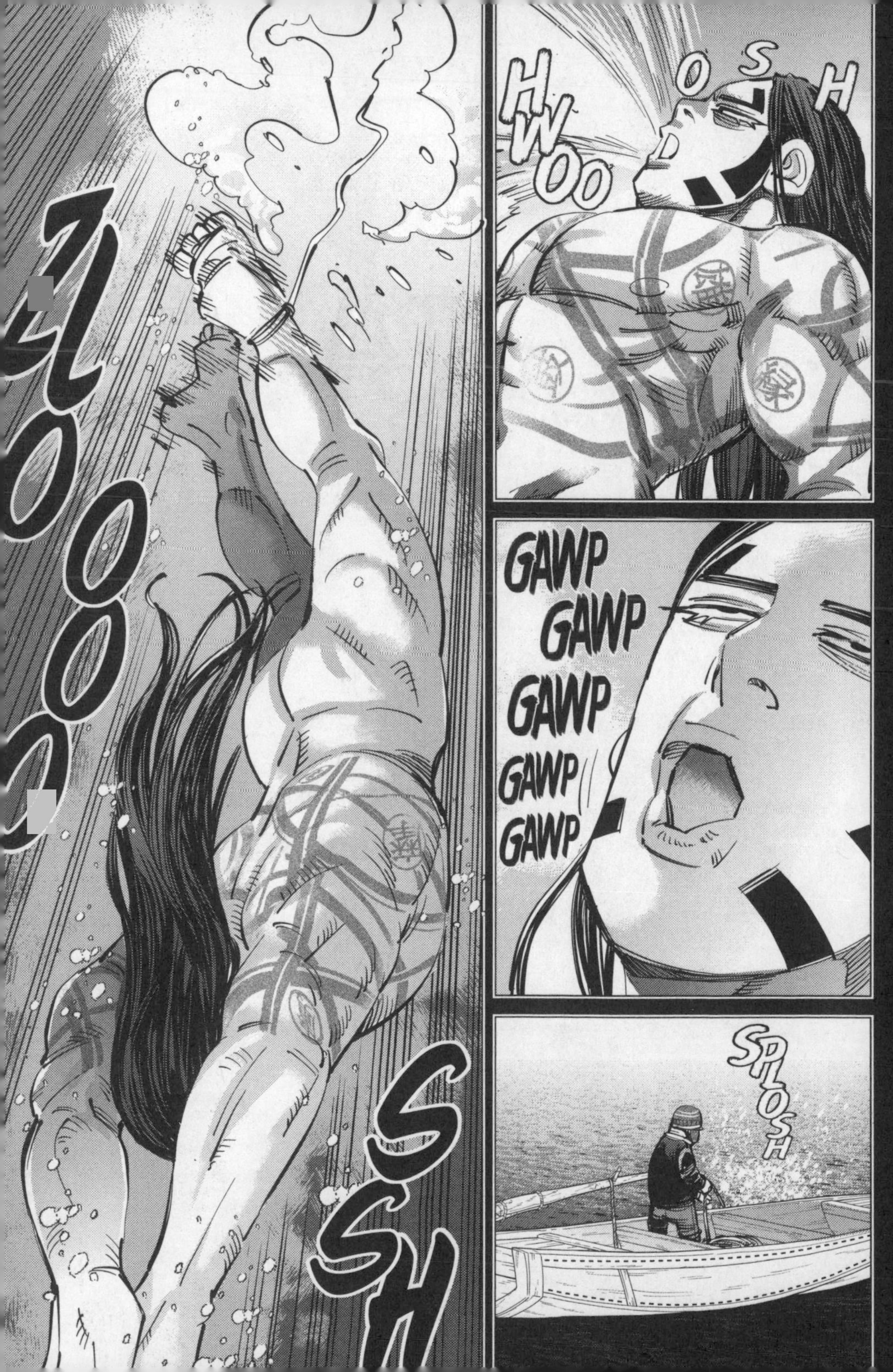
HWOOOSH
GAWP GAWP GAWP GAWP GAWP
SPLOSH
ZOOOO
SSH

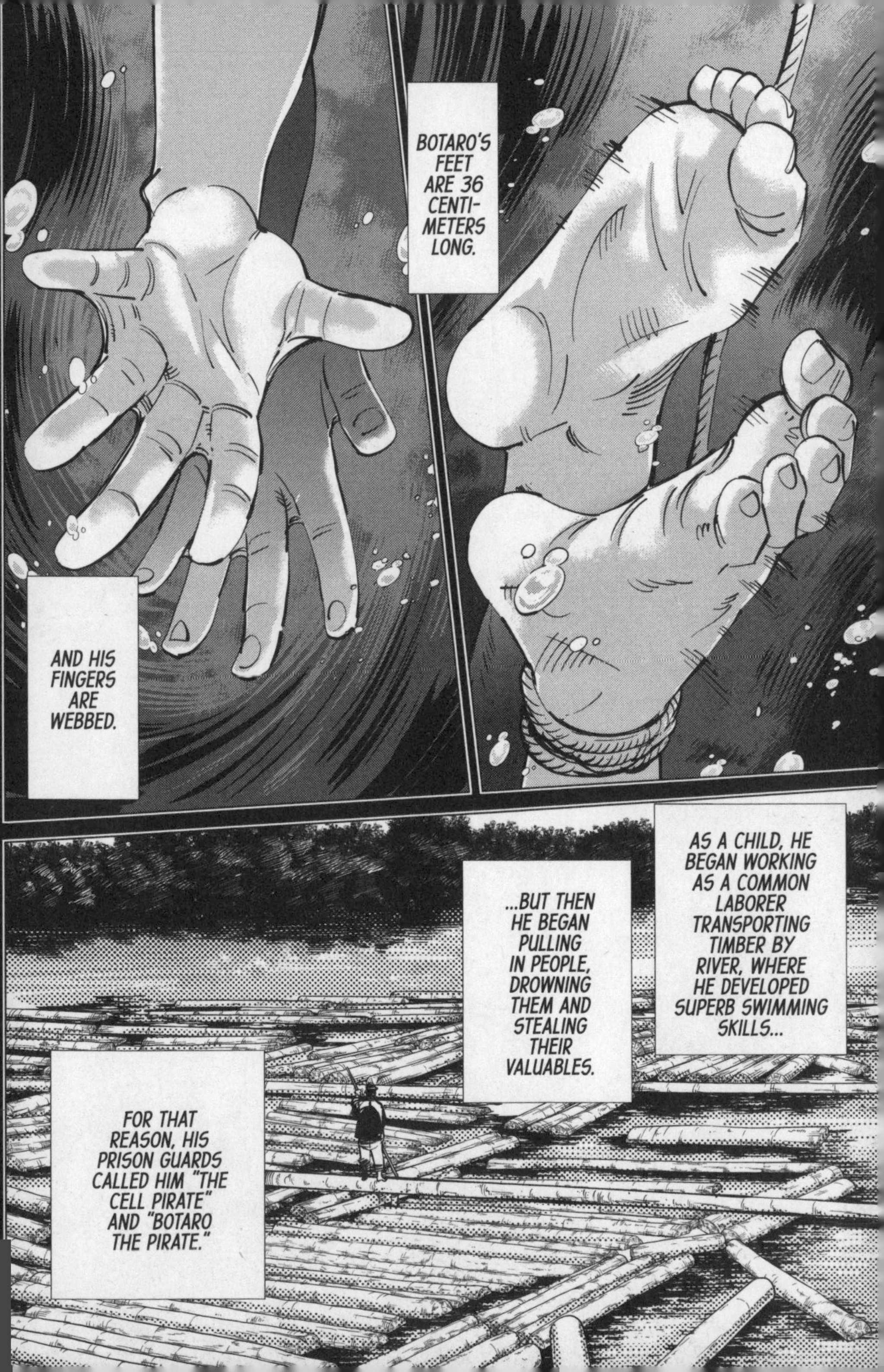
BOTARO'S FEET ARE 36 CENTI-METERS LONG.
AND HIS FINGERS ARE WEBBED.
AS A CHILD, HE BEGAN WORKING AS A COMMON LABORER TRANSPORTING TIMBER BY RIVER, WHERE HE DEVELOPED SUPERB SWIMMING SKILLS...
...BUT THEN HE BEGAN PULLING IN PEOPLE, DROWNING THEM AND STEALING THEIR VALUABLES.
FOR THAT REASON, HIS PRISON GUARDS CALLED HIM "THE CELL PIRATE" AND "BOTARO THE PIRATE."

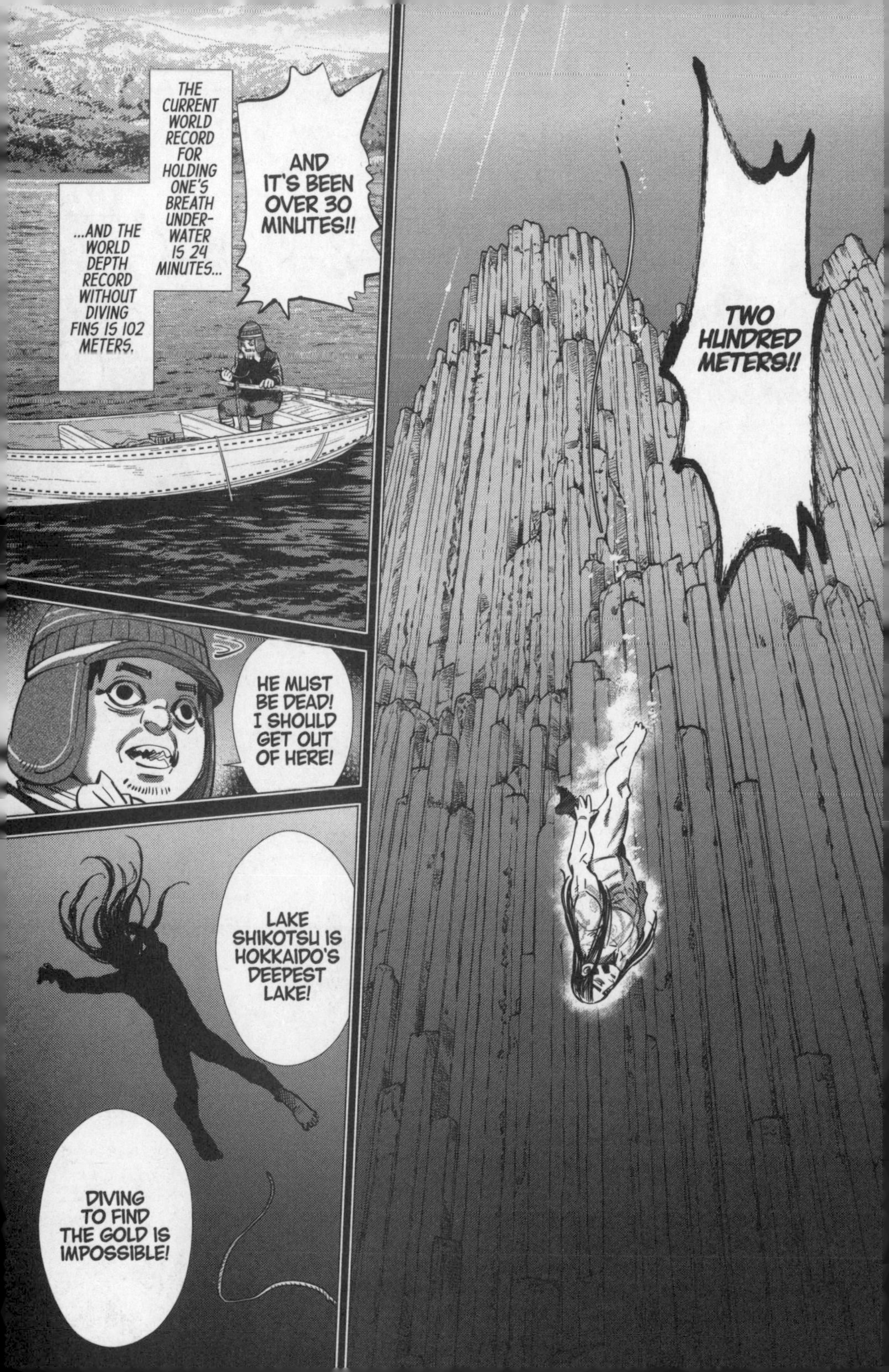
TWO HUNDRED METERS!!
THE CURRENT WORLD RECORD FOR HOLDING ONE'S BREATH UNDER-WATER IS 24 MINUTES...
...AND THE WORLD DEPTH RECORD WITHOUT DIVING FINS IS 102 METERS.
AND IT'S BEEN OVER 30 MINUTES!!
HE MUST BE DEAD! I SHOULD GET OUT OF HERE!
LAKE SHIKOTSU IS HOKKAIDO'S DEEPEST LAKE!
DIVING TO FIND THE GOLD IS IMPOSSIBLE!

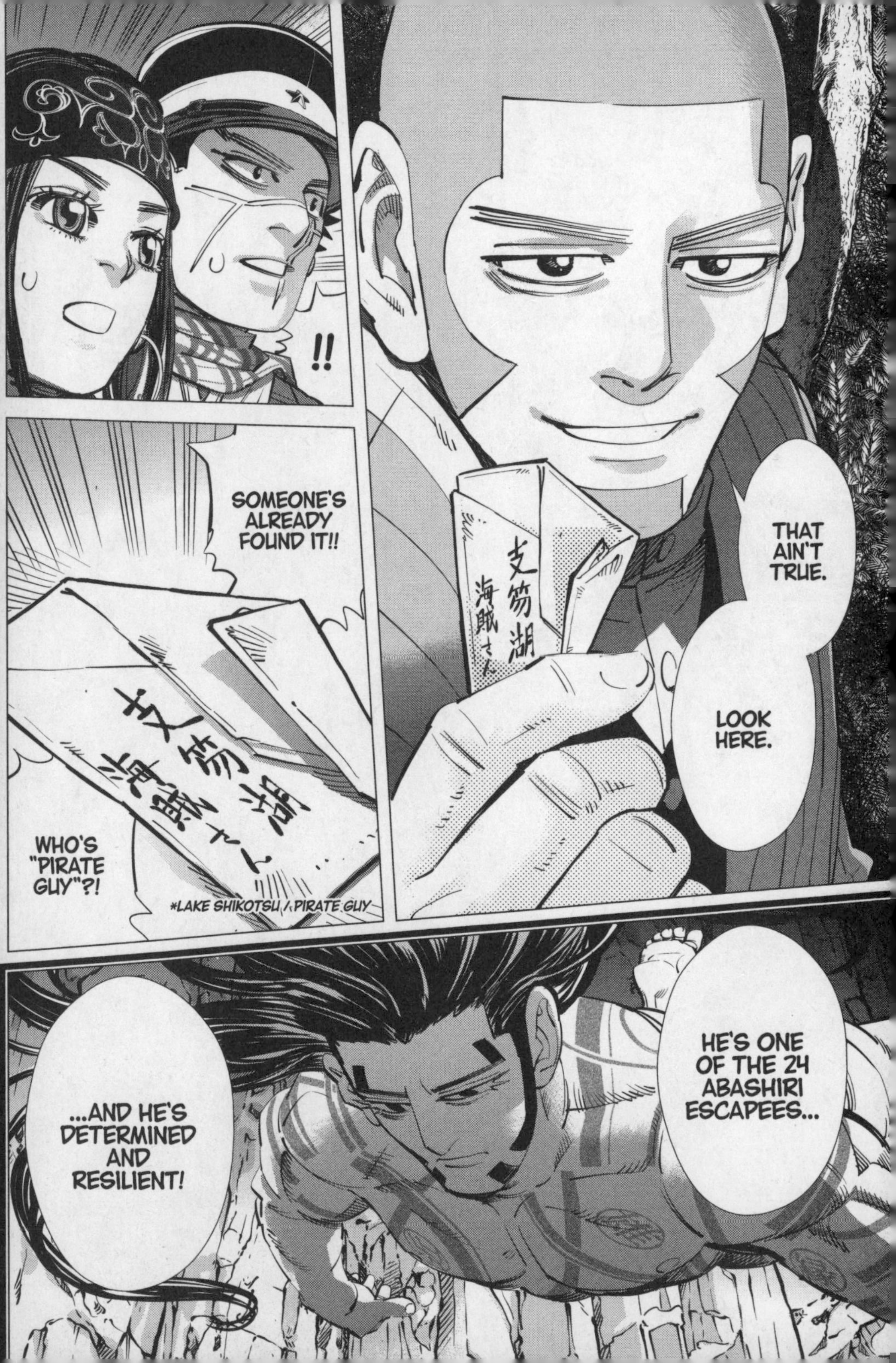
THAT AIN'T TRUE.
LOOK HERE.
支笏湖
海賊さん
!!
SOMEONE'S ALREADY FOUND IT!!
支笏湖
海賊さん
WHO'S "PIRATE GUY"?!
*LAKE SHIKOTSU / PIRATE GUY
HE'S ONE OF THE 24 ABASHIRI ESCAPEES...
...AND HE'S DETERMINED AND RESILIENT!

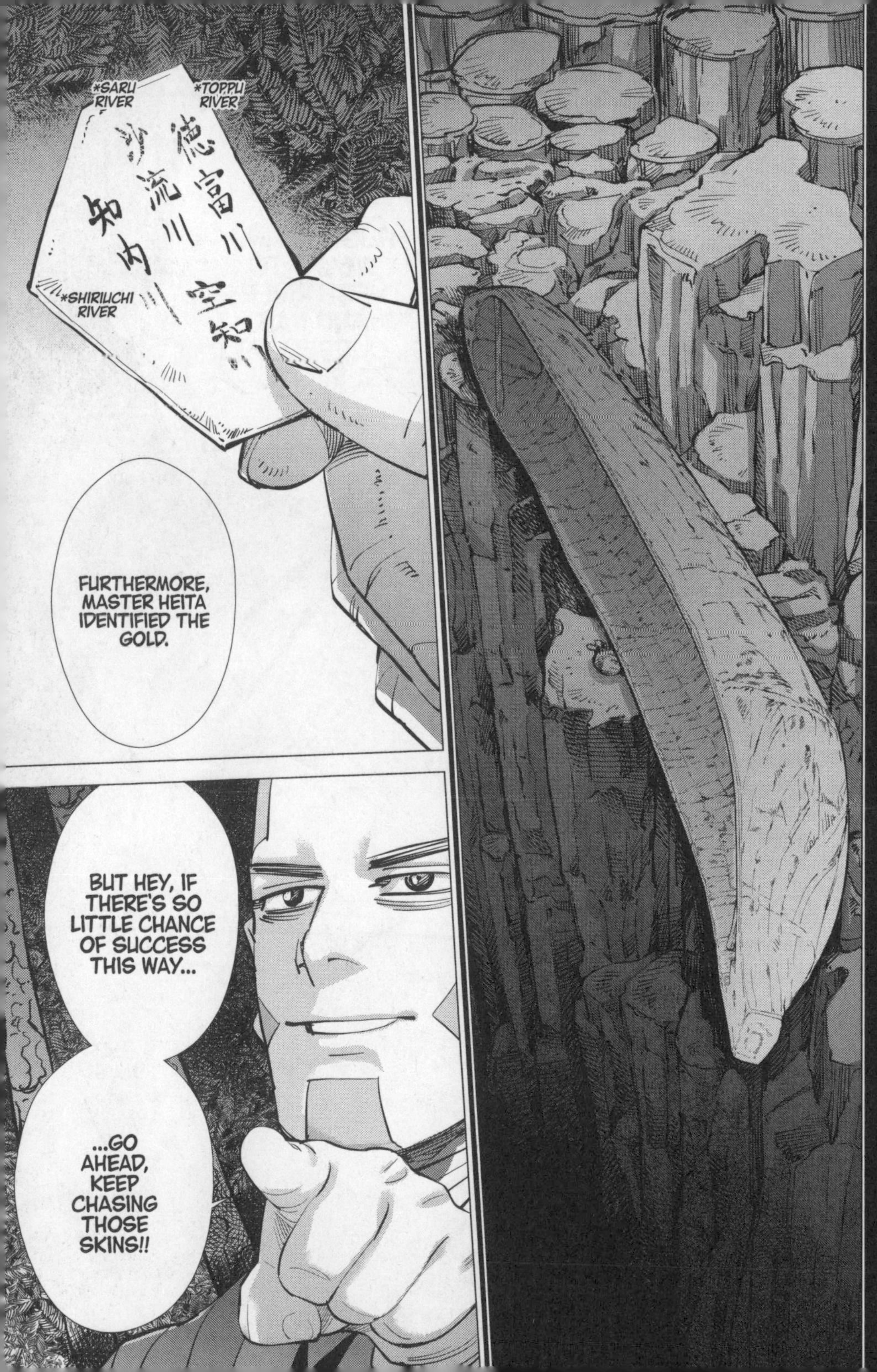

徳富川 空知川
沙流川
知内川
*TOPPU RIVER
*SARU RIVER
*SHIRIUCHI RIVER
FURTHERMORE, MASTER HEITA IDENTIFIED THE GOLD.
BUT HEY, IF THERE'S SO LITTLE CHANCE OF SUCCESS THIS WAY...
...GO AHEAD, KEEP CHASING THOSE SKINS!!

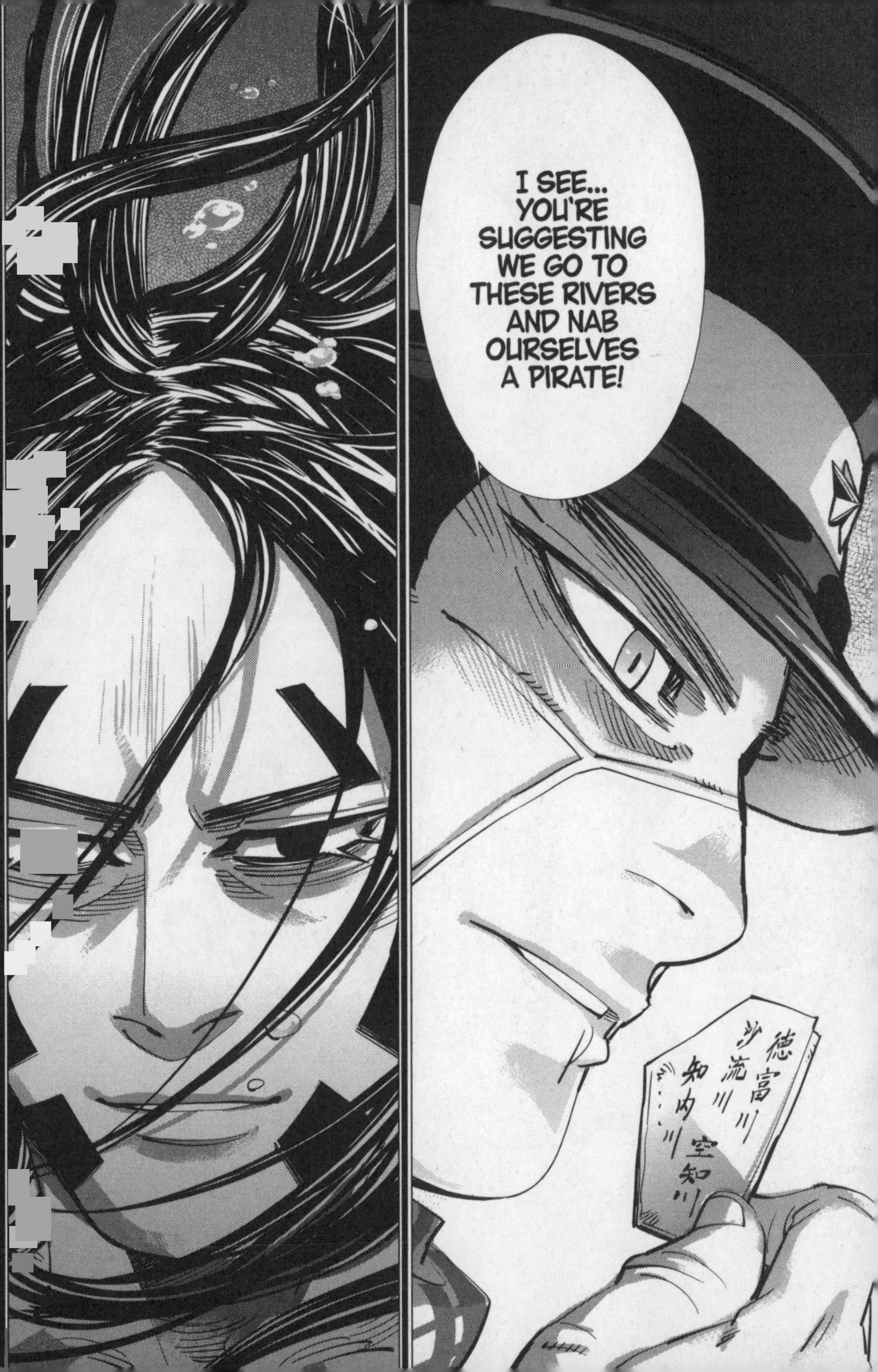
I SEE... YOU'RE SUGGESTING WE GO TO THESE RIVERS AND NAB OURSELVES A PIRATE!
徳富川 空知川
沙流川 知内川

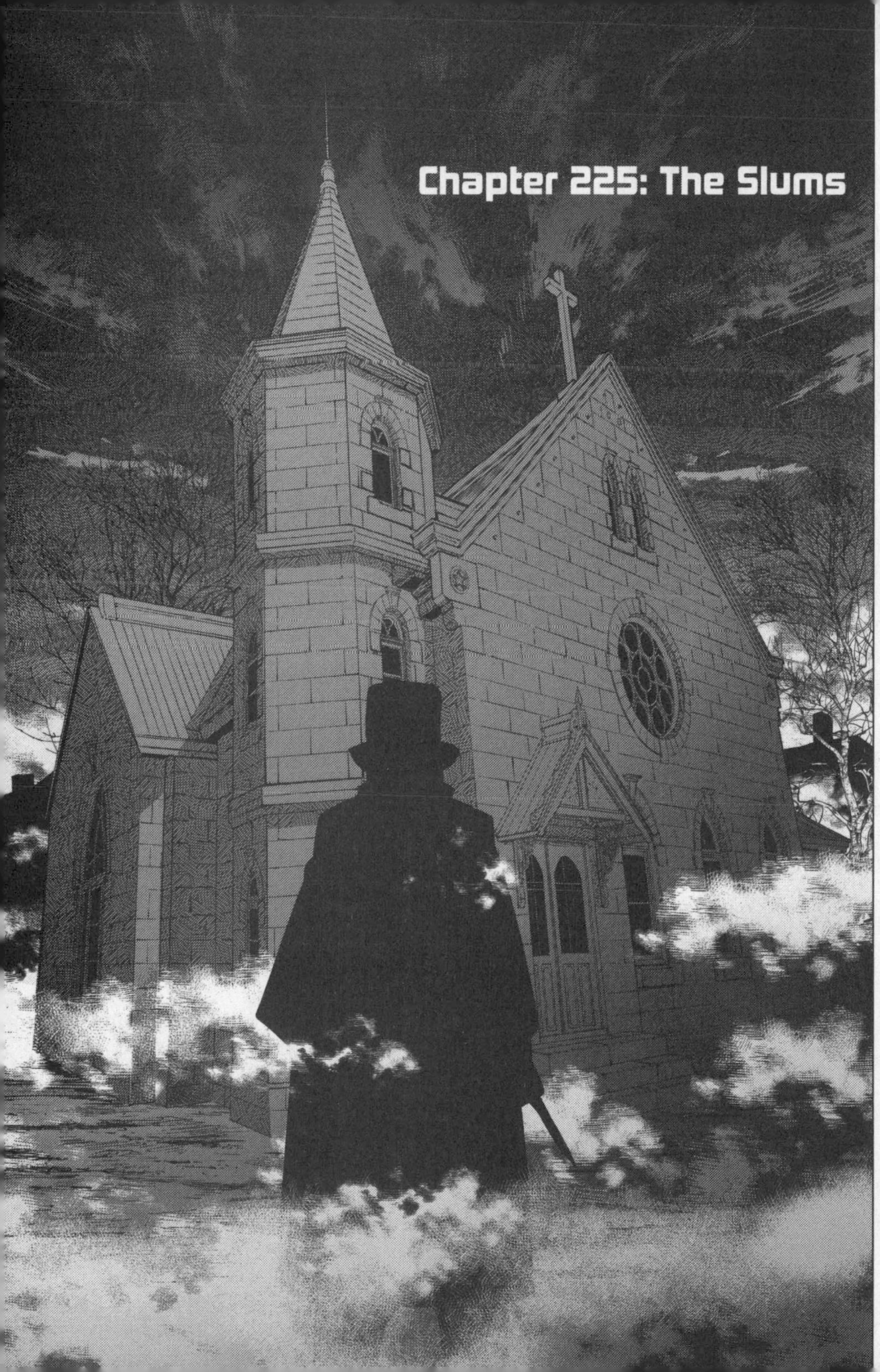
Chapter 225: The Slums

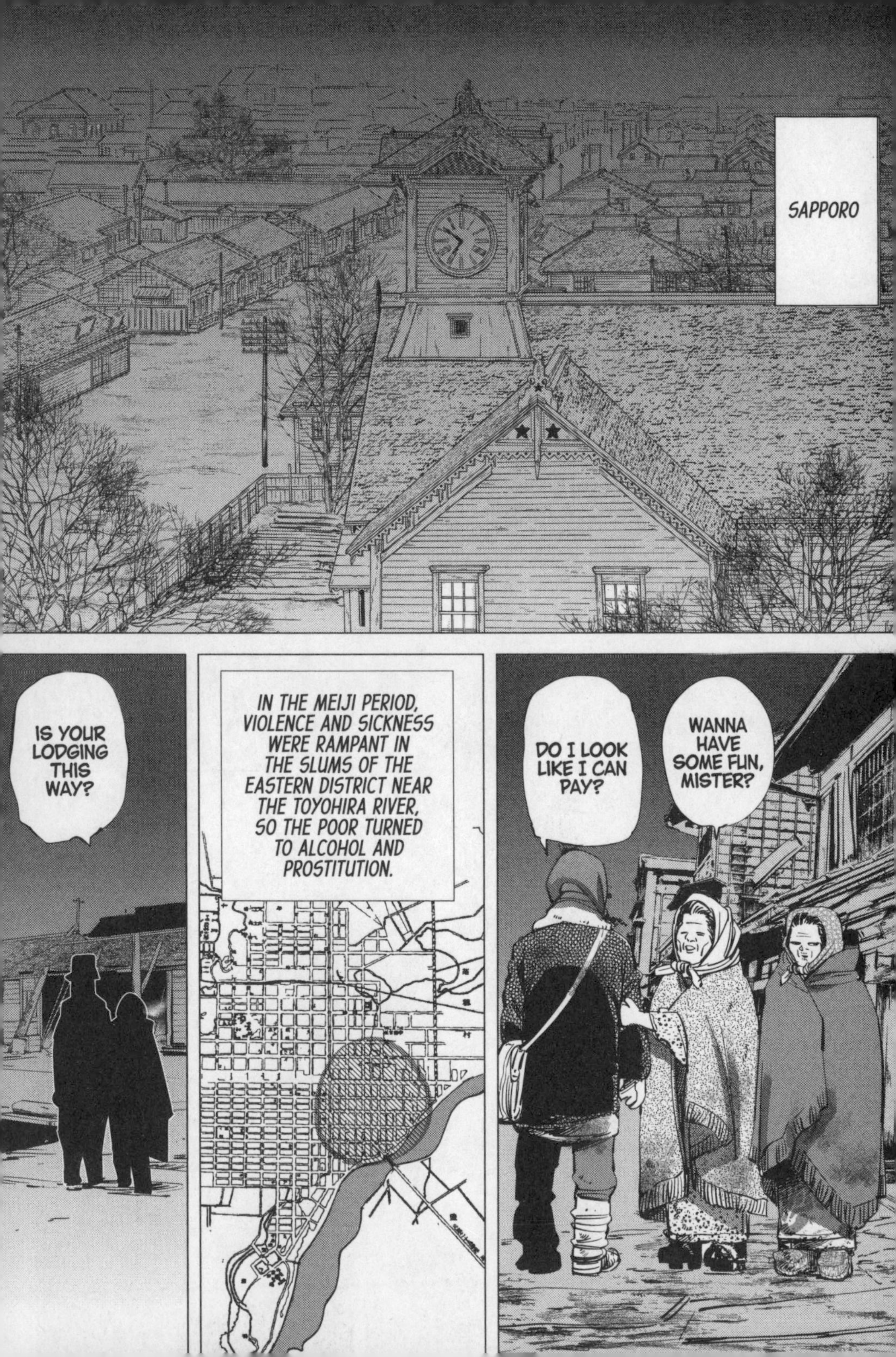
SAPPORO
WANNA HAVE SOME FUN, MISTER?
DO I LOOK LIKE I CAN PAY?
IN THE MEIJI PERIOD, VIOLENCE AND SICKNESS WERE RAMPANT IN THE SLUMS OF THE EASTERN DISTRICT NEAR THE TOYOHIRA RIVER, SO THE POOR TURNED TO ALCOHOL AND PROSTITUTION.
IS YOUR LODGING THIS WAY?

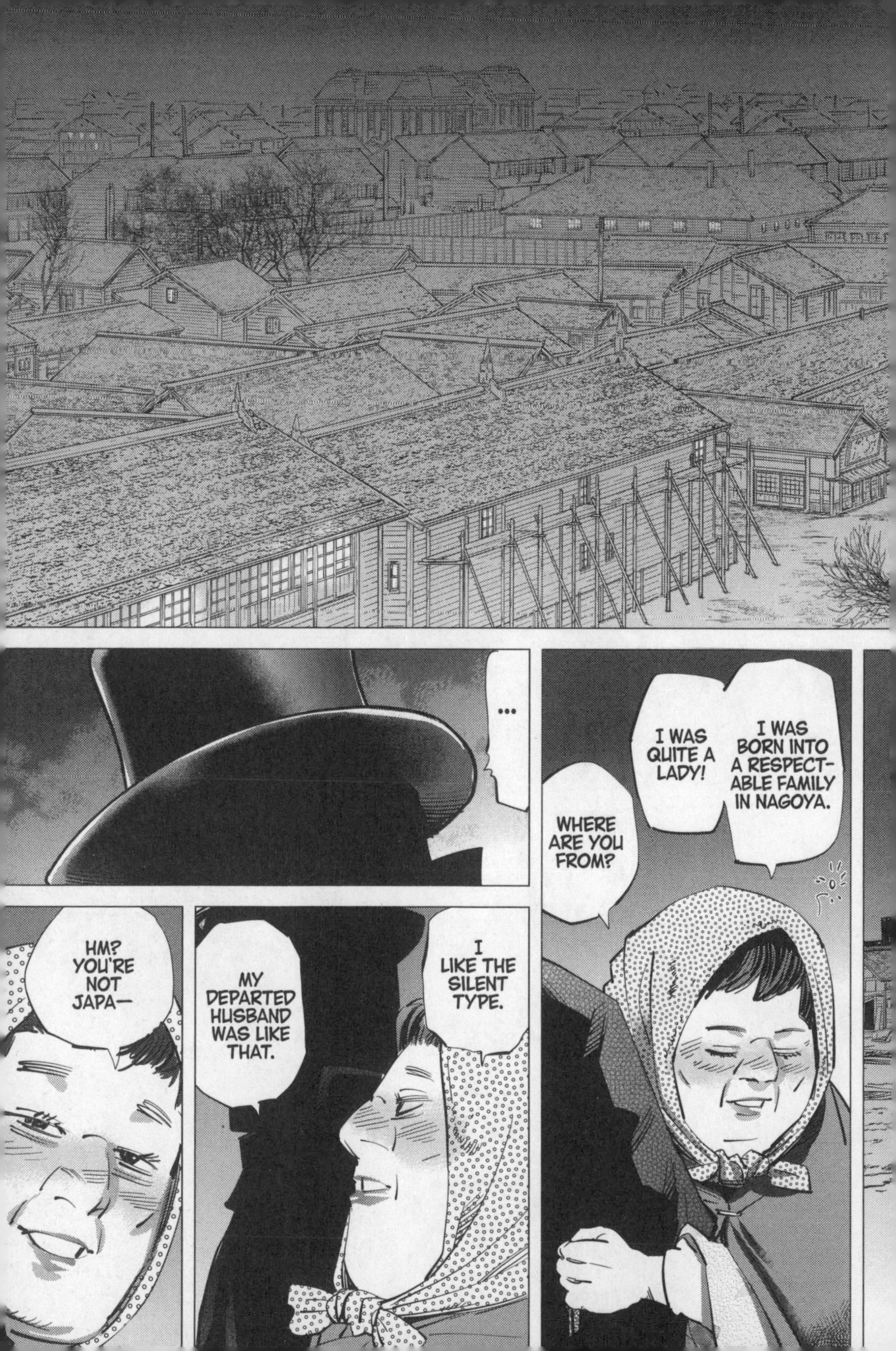
I WAS BORN INTO A RESPECTABLE FAMILY IN NAGOYA.
I WAS QUITE A LADY!
WHERE ARE YOU FROM?
...
I LIKE THE SILENT TYPE.
MY DEPARTED HUSBAND WAS LIKE THAT.
HM? YOU'RE NOT JAPA—

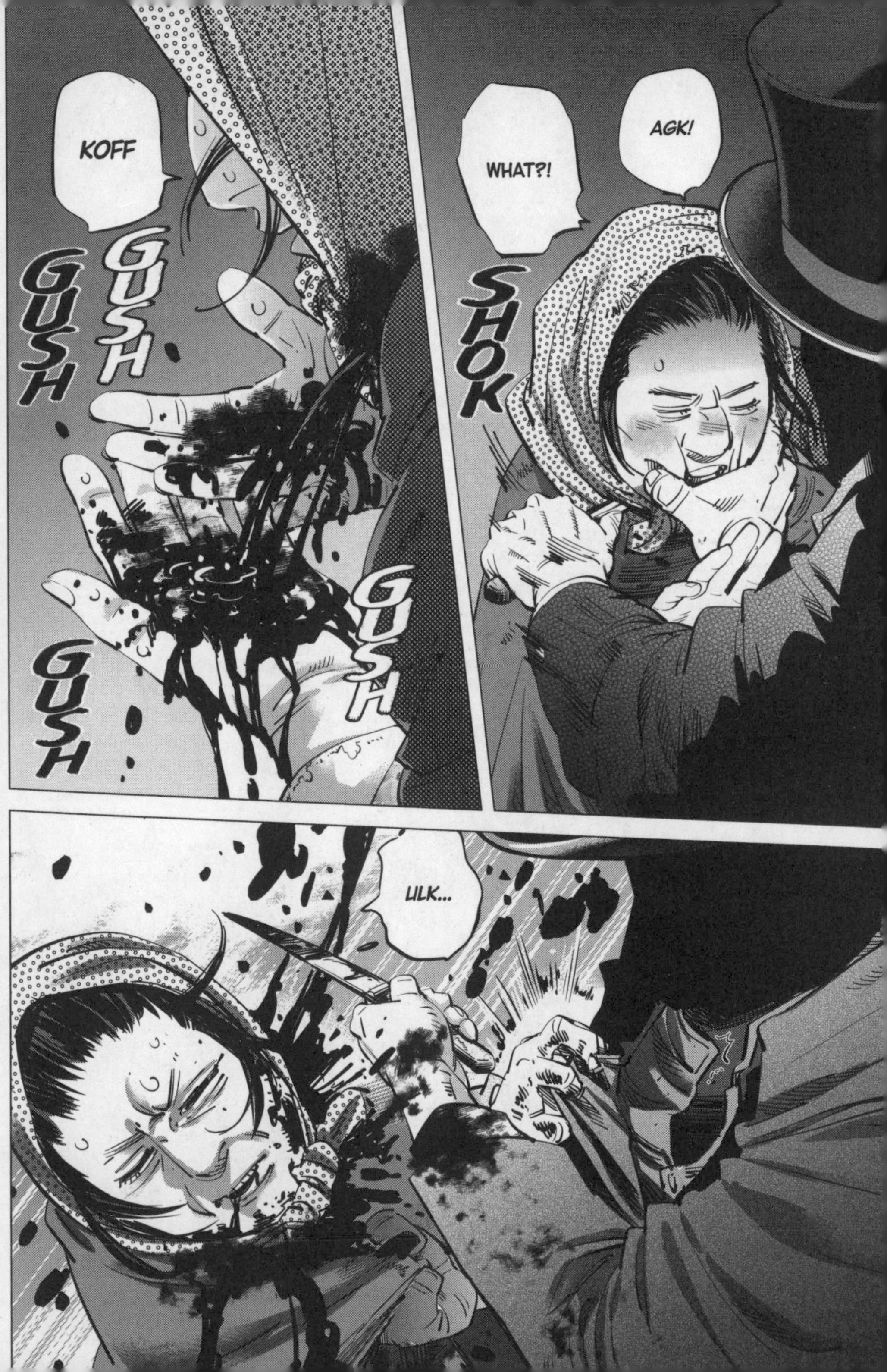
AGK!
WHAT?!
SHOK
KOFF
GUSH
GUSH
GUSH
GUSH
ULK...

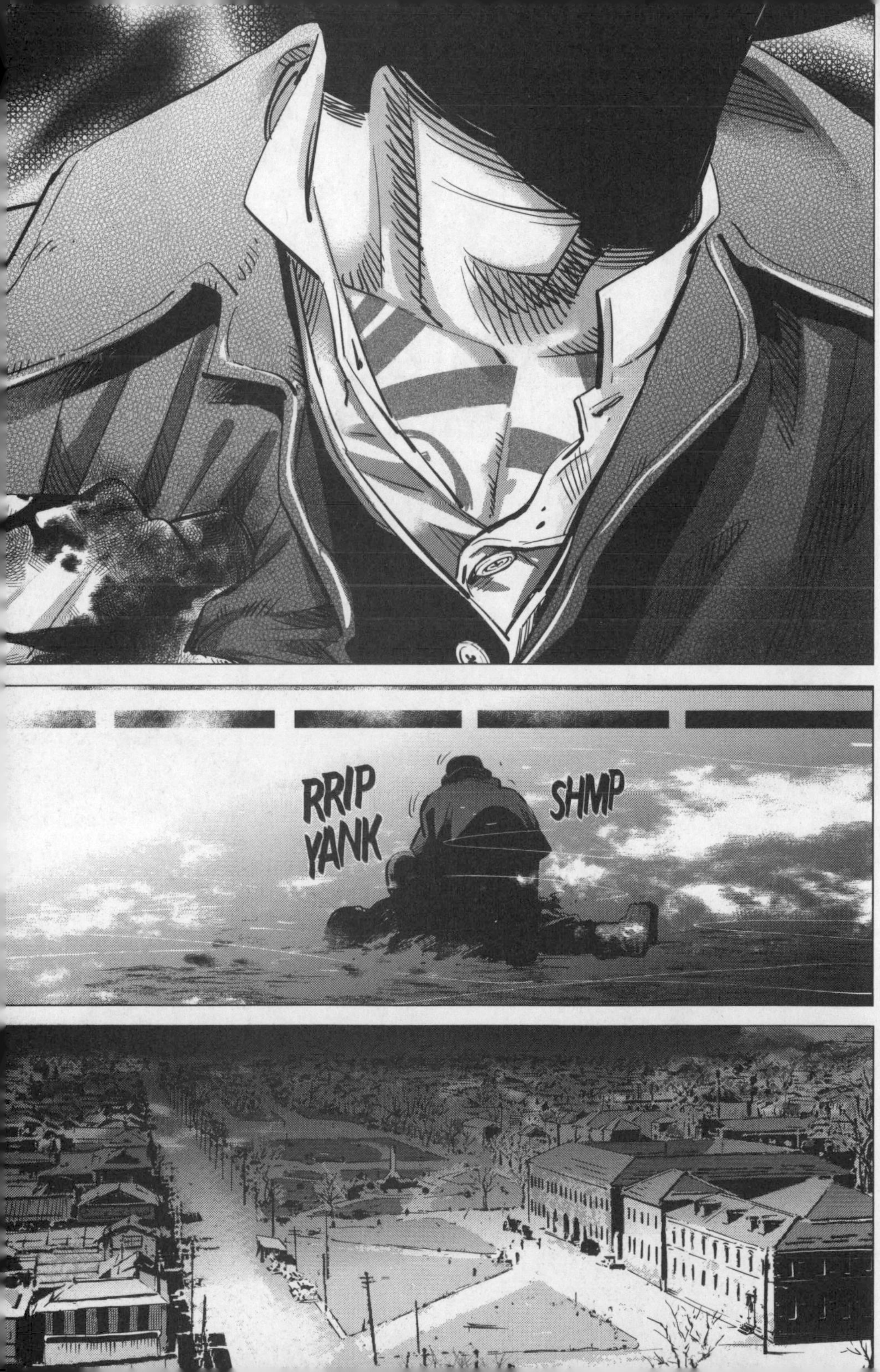
SHMP
RRIP
YANK

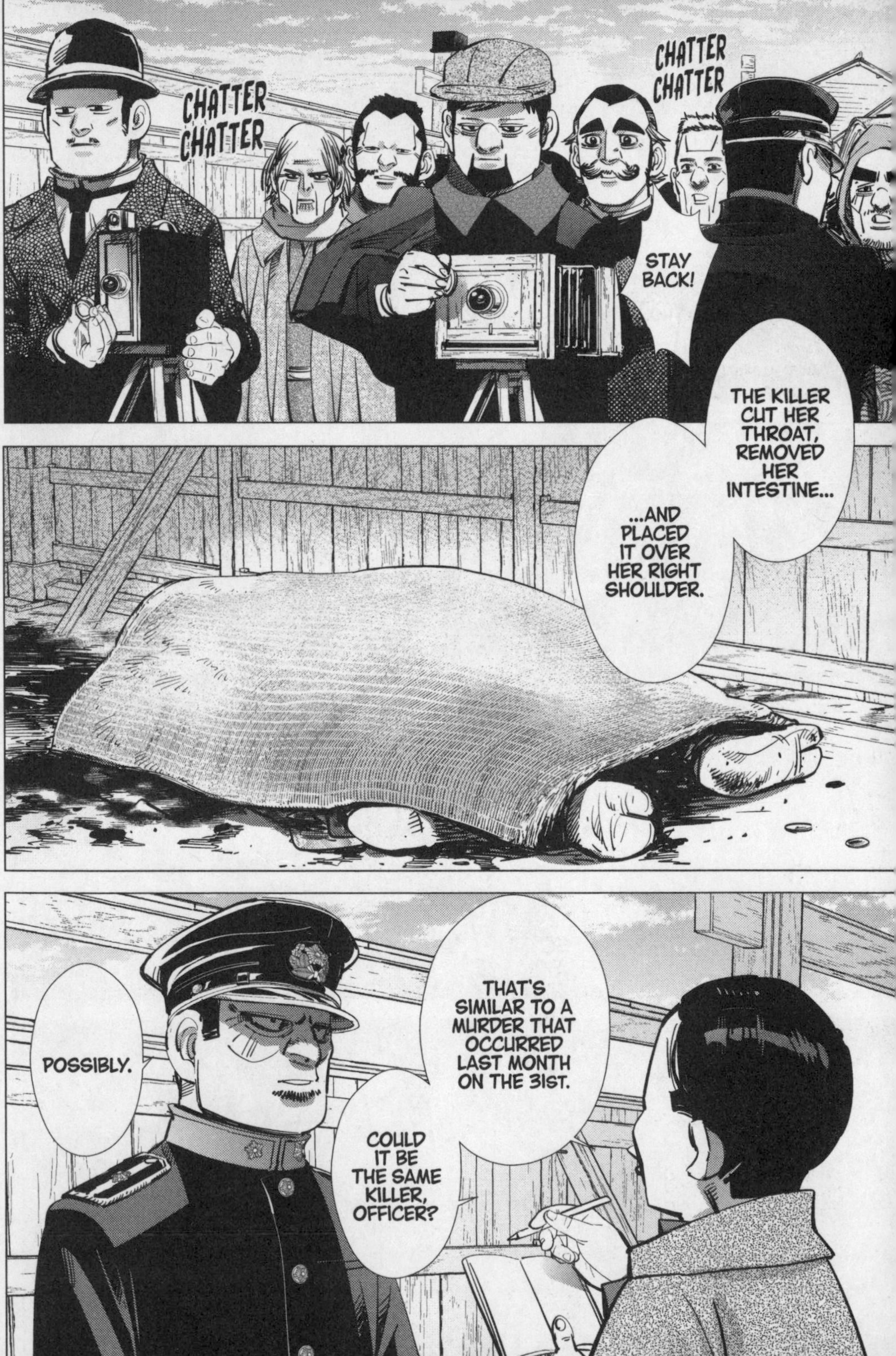
CHATTER CHATTER
CHATTER CHATTER
STAY BACK!
THE KILLER CUT HER THROAT, REMOVED HER INTESTINE...
...AND PLACED IT OVER HER RIGHT SHOULDER.
THAT'S SIMILAR TO A MURDER THAT OCCURRED LAST MONTH ON THE 31ST.
COULD IT BE THE SAME KILLER, OFFICER?
POSSIBLY.

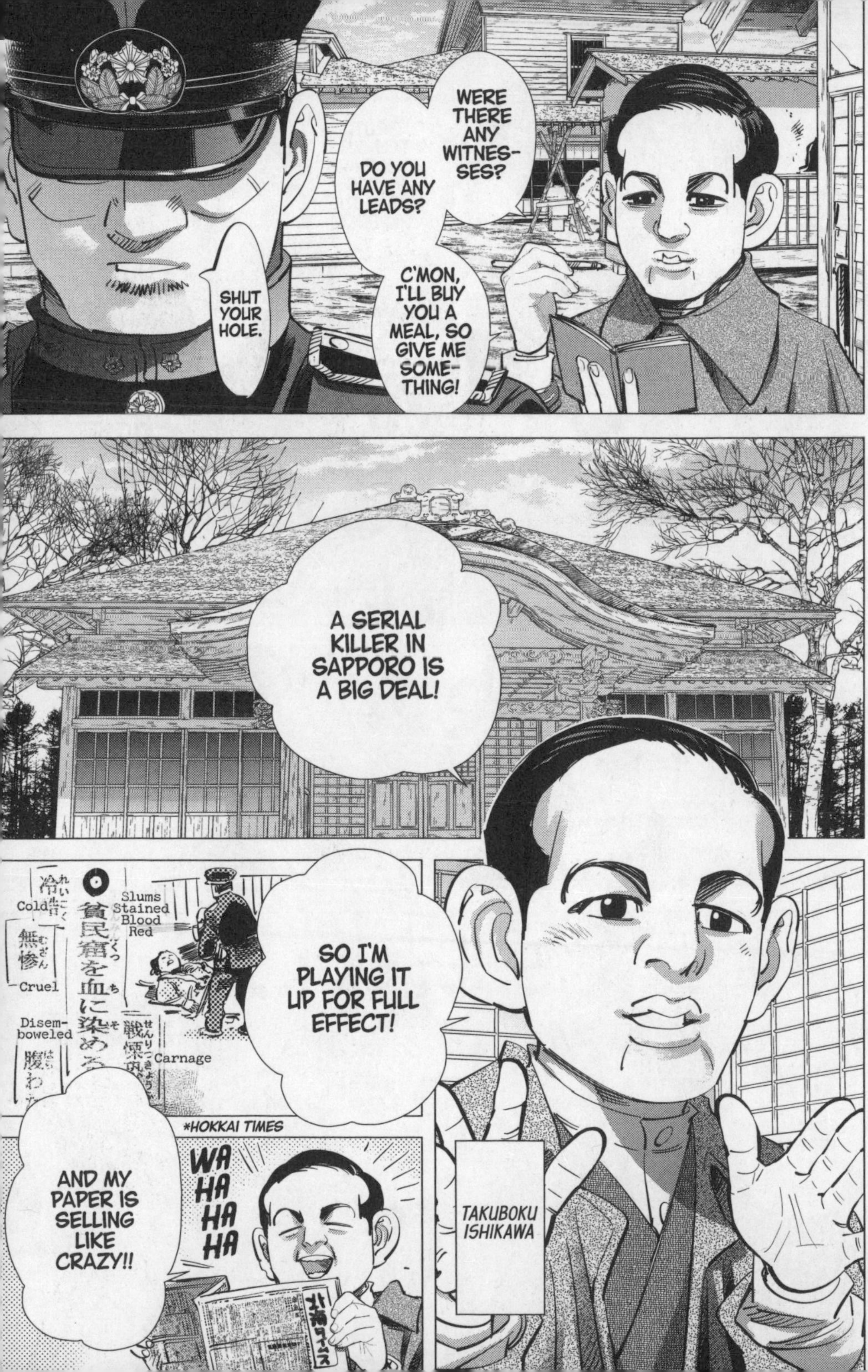
WERE THERE ANY WITNES-SES?
DO YOU HAVE ANY LEADS?
C'MON, I'LL BUY YOU A MEAL, SO GIVE ME SOME-THING!
SHUT YOUR HOLE.
A SERIAL KILLER IN SAPPORO IS A BIG DEAL!
SO I'M PLAYING IT UP FOR FULL EFFECT!
TAKUBOKU ISHIKAWA
Cold
Slums Stained Blood Red
Cruel
Disem-boweled
Carnage
*HOKKAI TIMES
WA HA HA HA
AND MY PAPER IS SELLING LIKE CRAZY!!

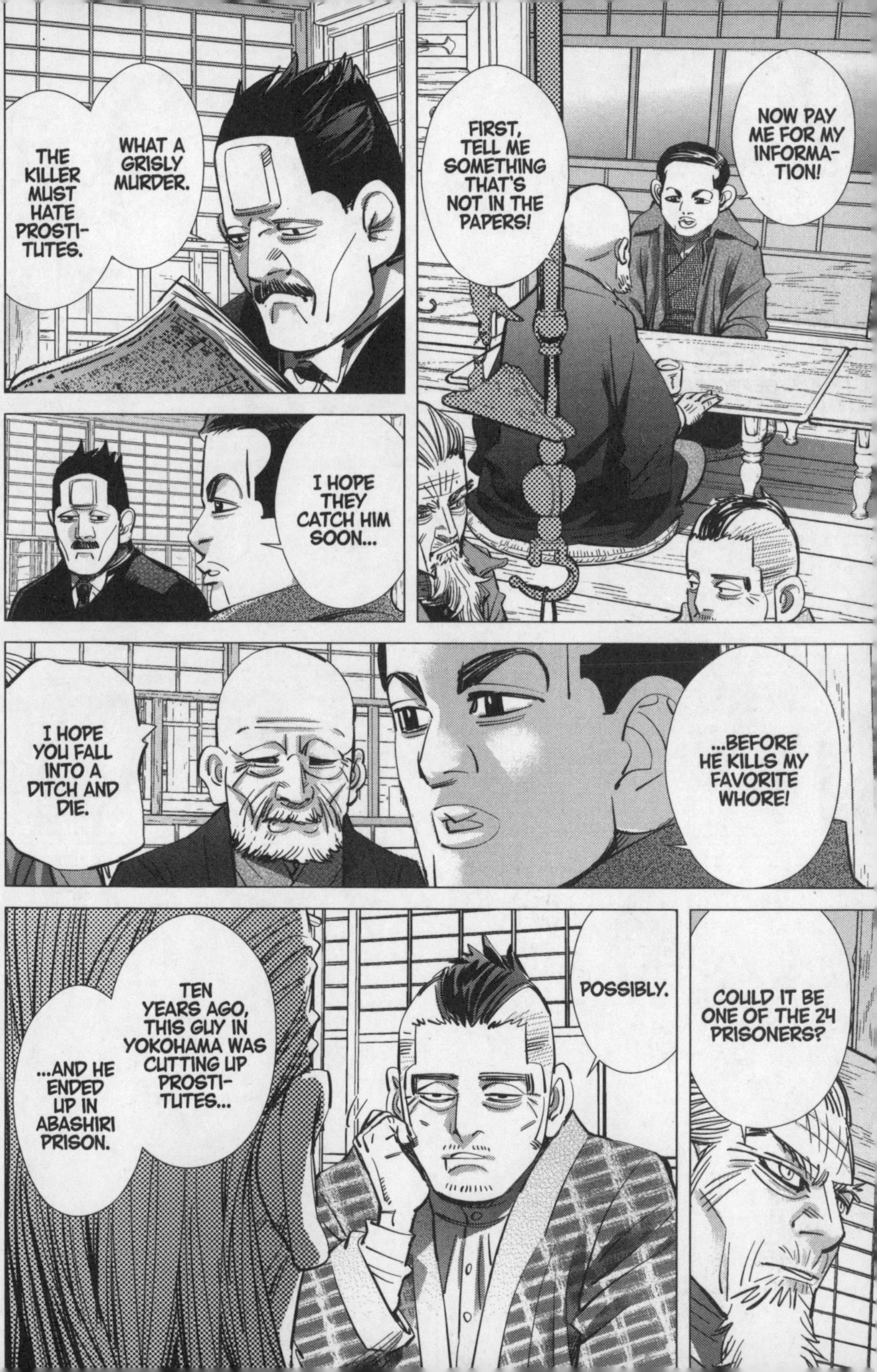
NOW PAY ME FOR MY INFORMA-TION!
FIRST, TELL ME SOMETHING THAT'S NOT IN THE PAPERS!
WHAT A GRISLY MURDER.
THE KILLER MUST HATE PROSTI-TUTES.
I HOPE THEY CATCH HIM SOON...
...BEFORE HE KILLS MY FAVORITE WHORE!
I HOPE YOU FALL INTO A DITCH AND DIE.
COULD IT BE ONE OF THE 24 PRISONERS?
POSSIBLY.
TEN YEARS AGO, THIS GUY IN YOKOHAMA WAS CUTTING UP PROSTI-TUTES...
...AND HE ENDED UP IN ABASHIRI PRISON.

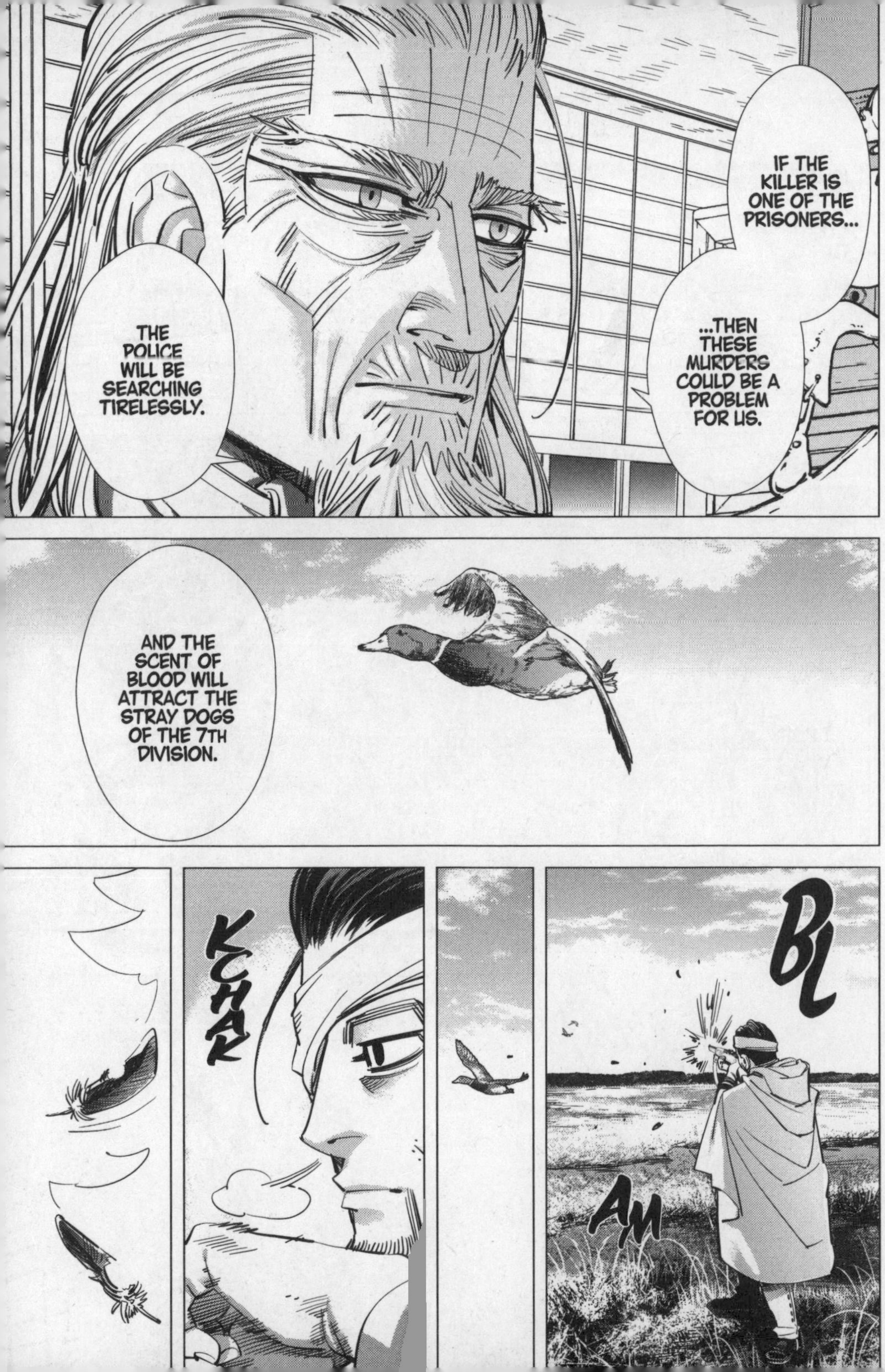
IF THE KILLER IS ONE OF THE PRISONERS...
...THEN THESE MURDERS COULD BE A PROBLEM FOR US.
THE POLICE WILL BE SEARCHING TIRELESSLY.
AND THE SCENT OF BLOOD WILL ATTRACT THE STRAY DOGS OF THE 7TH DIVISION.
BLAM
KCHAK

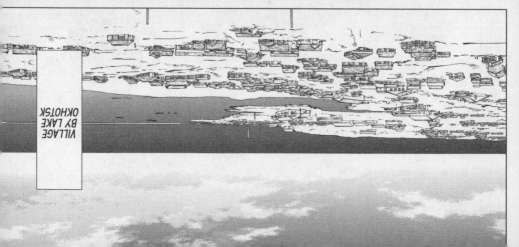

VILLAGE BY LAKE OKHOTSK

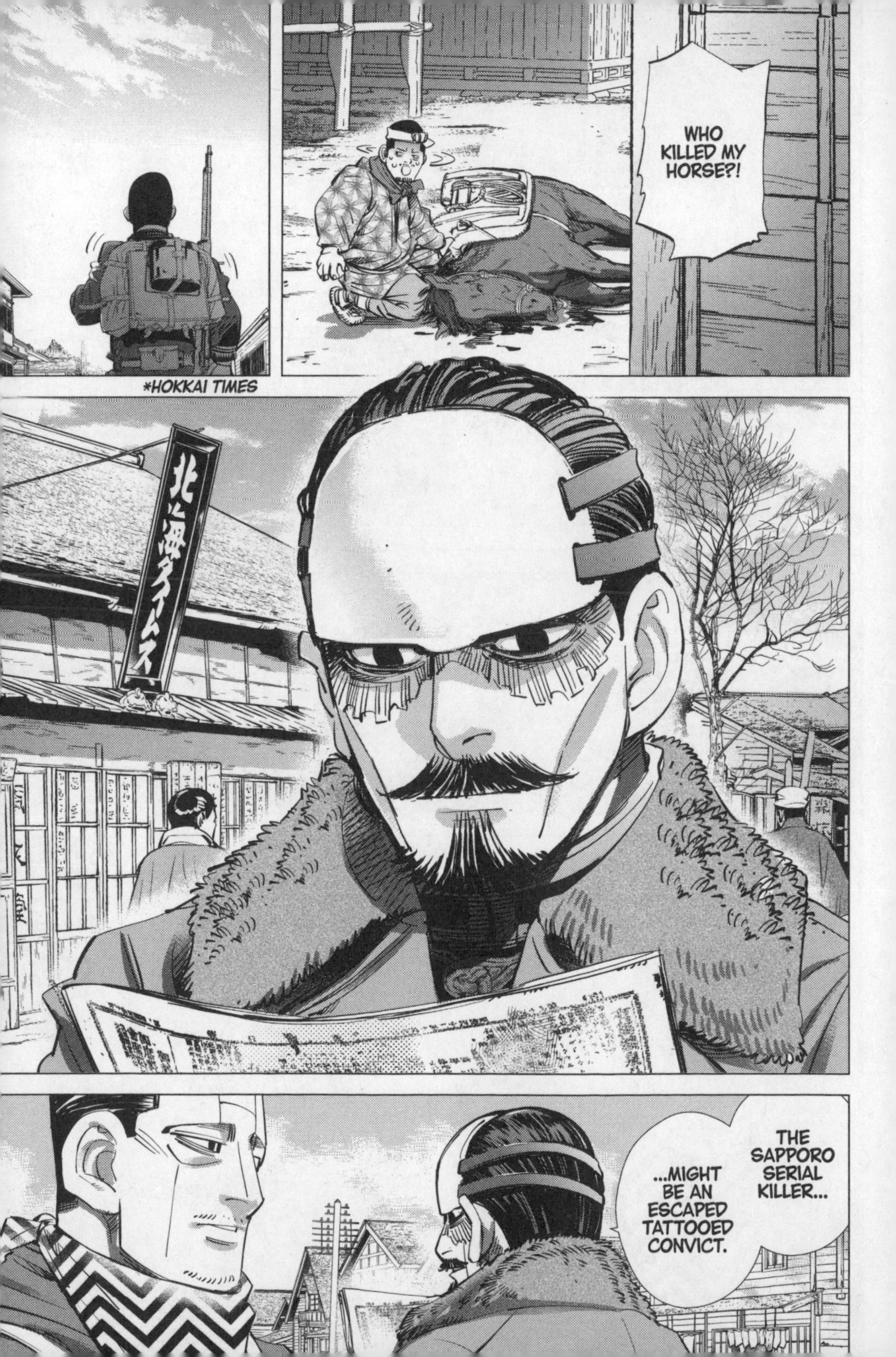
WHO KILLED MY HORSE?!
*HOKKAI TIMES
北海タイムス
THE SAPPORO SERIAL KILLER...
...MIGHT BE AN ESCAPED TATTOOED CONVICT.

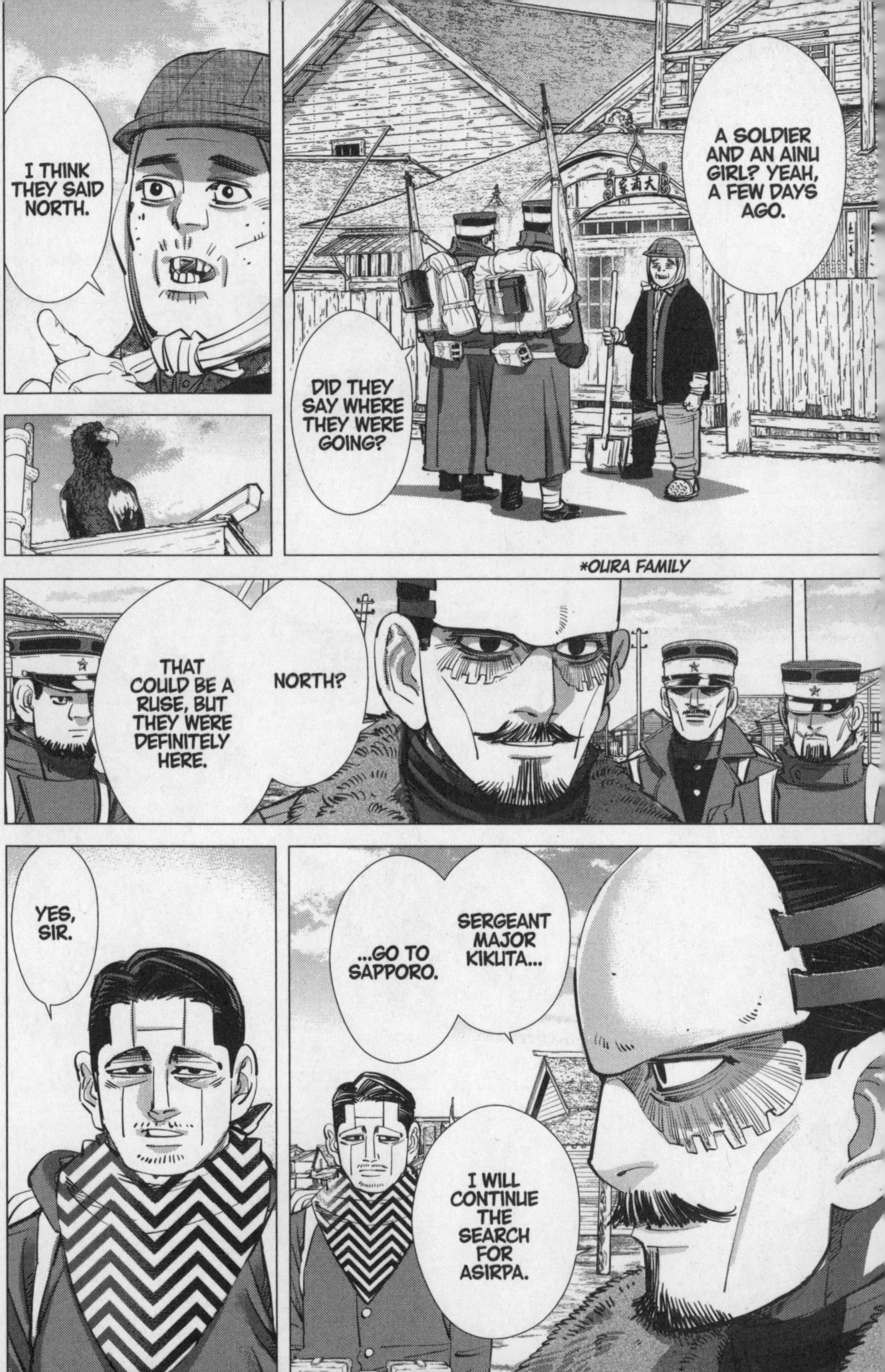
A SOLDIER AND AN AINU GIRL? YEAH, A FEW DAYS AGO.
DID THEY SAY WHERE THEY WERE GOING?
I THINK THEY SAID NORTH.
*OURA FAMILY
NORTH?
THAT COULD BE A RUSE, BUT THEY WERE DEFINITELY HERE.
SERGEANT MAJOR KIKUTA...
...GO TO SAPPORO.
I WILL CONTINUE THE SEARCH FOR ASIRPA.
YES, SIR.

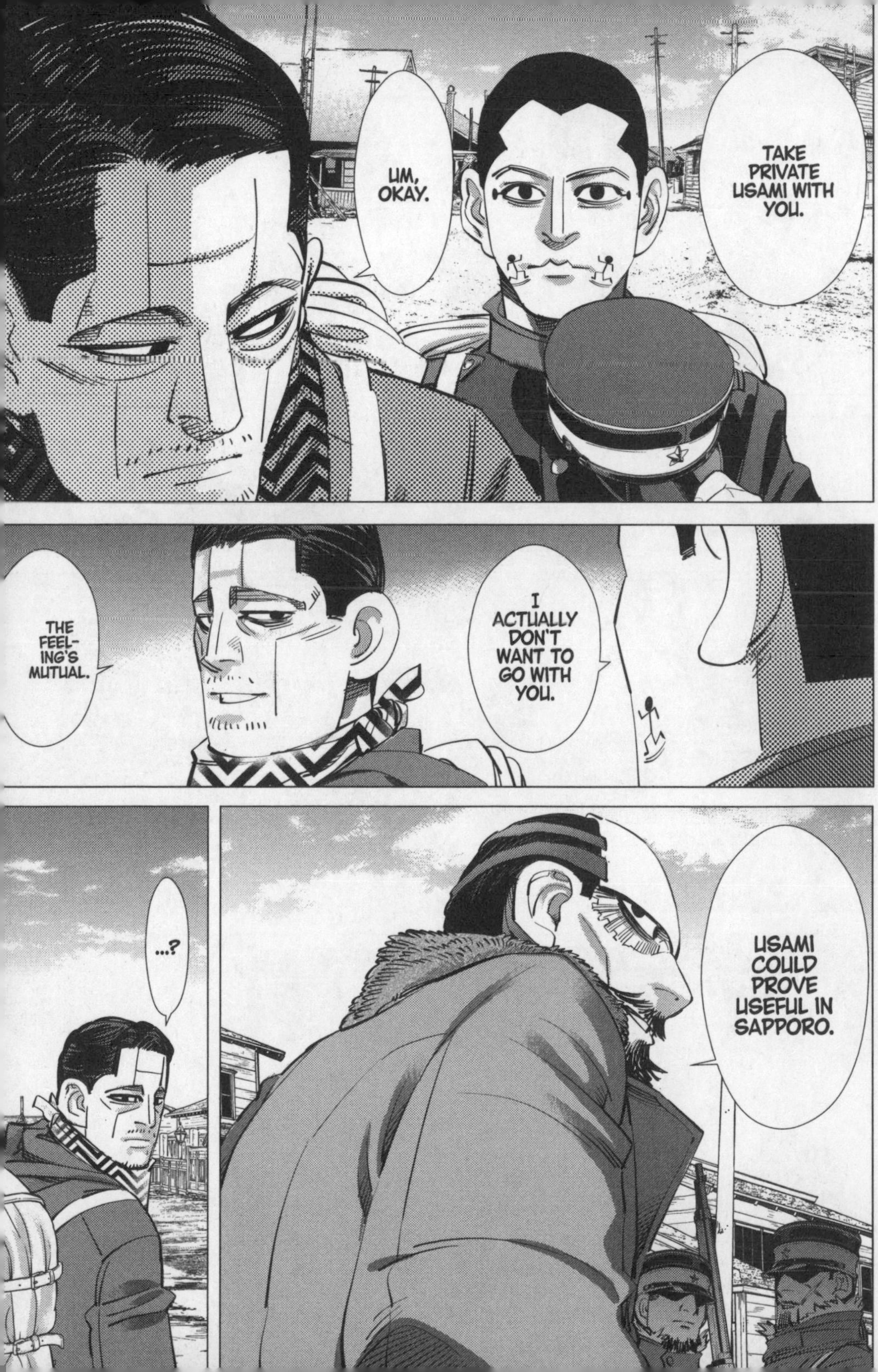
TAKE PRIVATE USAMI WITH YOU.
UM, OKAY.
I ACTUALLY DON'T WANT TO GO WITH YOU.
THE FEEL-ING'S MUTUAL.
USAMI COULD PROVE USEFUL IN SAPPORO.
...?

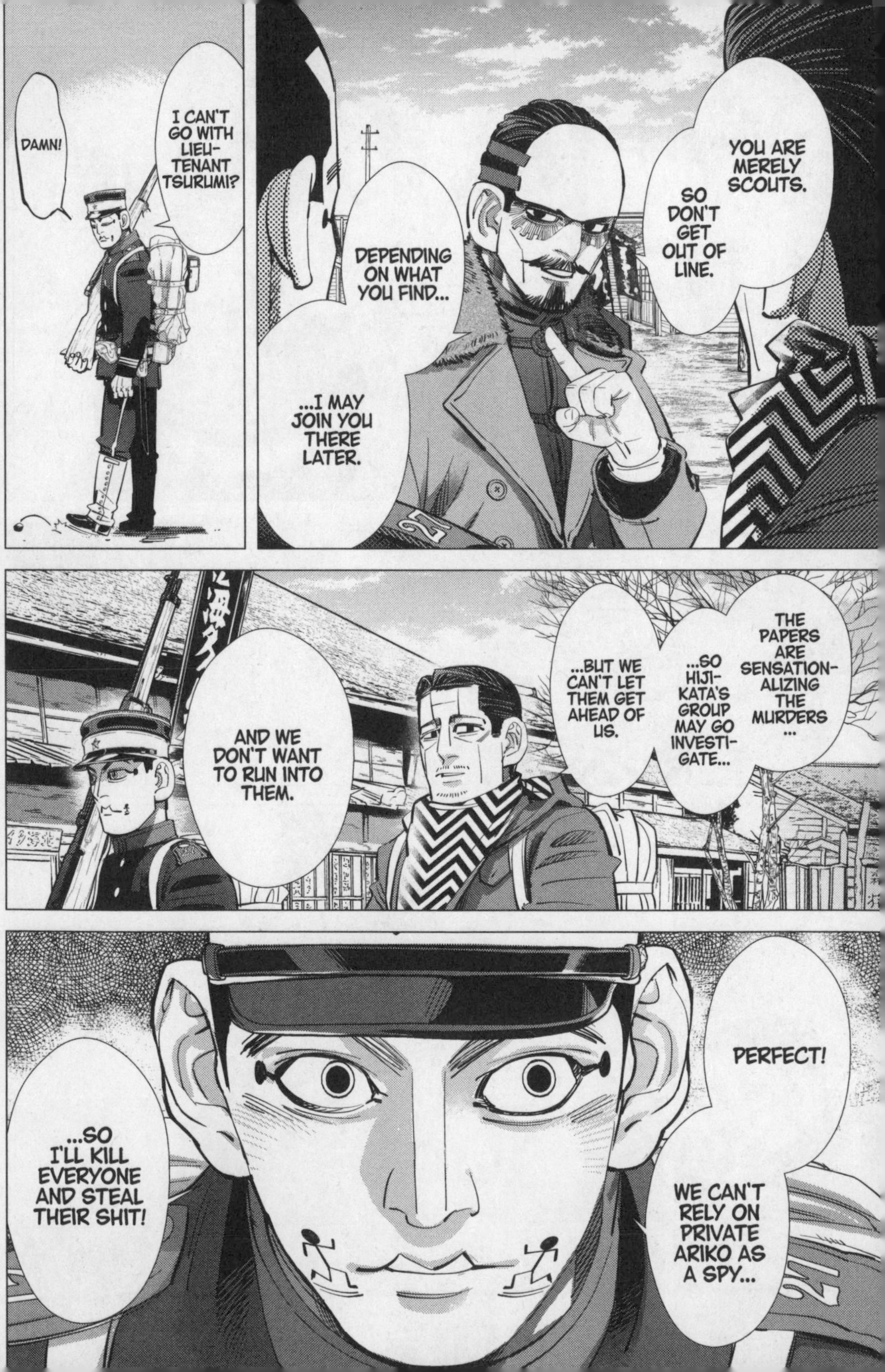
YOU ARE MERELY SCOUTS.
SO DON'T GET OUT OF LINE.
DEPENDING ON WHAT YOU FIND...
...I MAY JOIN YOU THERE LATER.
I CAN'T GO WITH LIEU-TENANT TSURUMI?
DAMN!
THE PAPERS ARE SENSATION-ALIZING THE MURDERS ...
...SO HIJI-KATA'S GROUP MAY GO INVESTI-GATE...
...BUT WE CAN'T LET THEM GET AHEAD OF US.
AND WE DON'T WANT TO RUN INTO THEM.
PERFECT!
WE CAN'T RELY ON PRIVATE ARIKO AS A SPY...
...SO I'LL KILL EVERYONE AND STEAL THEIR SHIT!

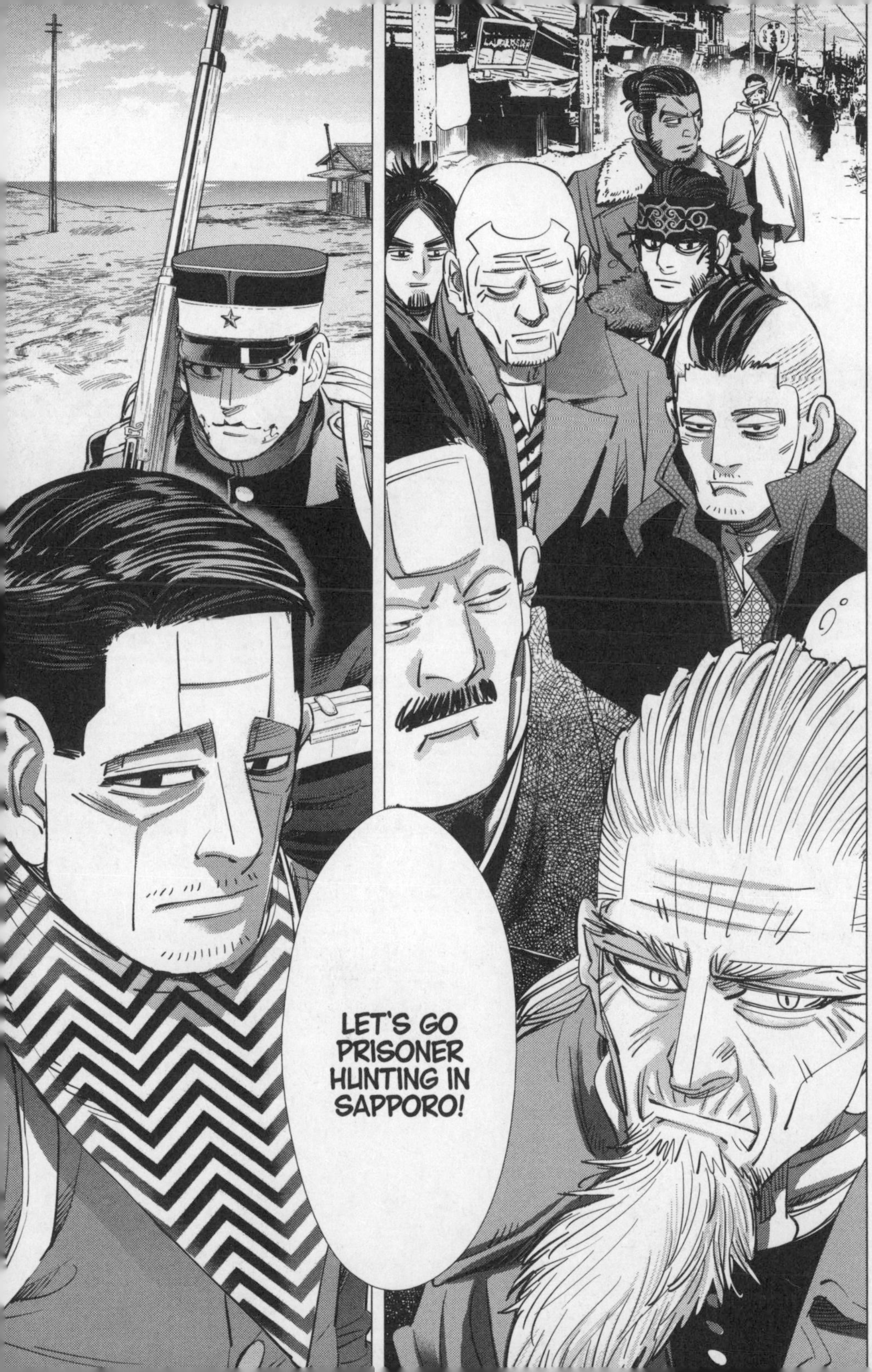
LET'S GO PRISONER HUNTING IN SAPPORO!

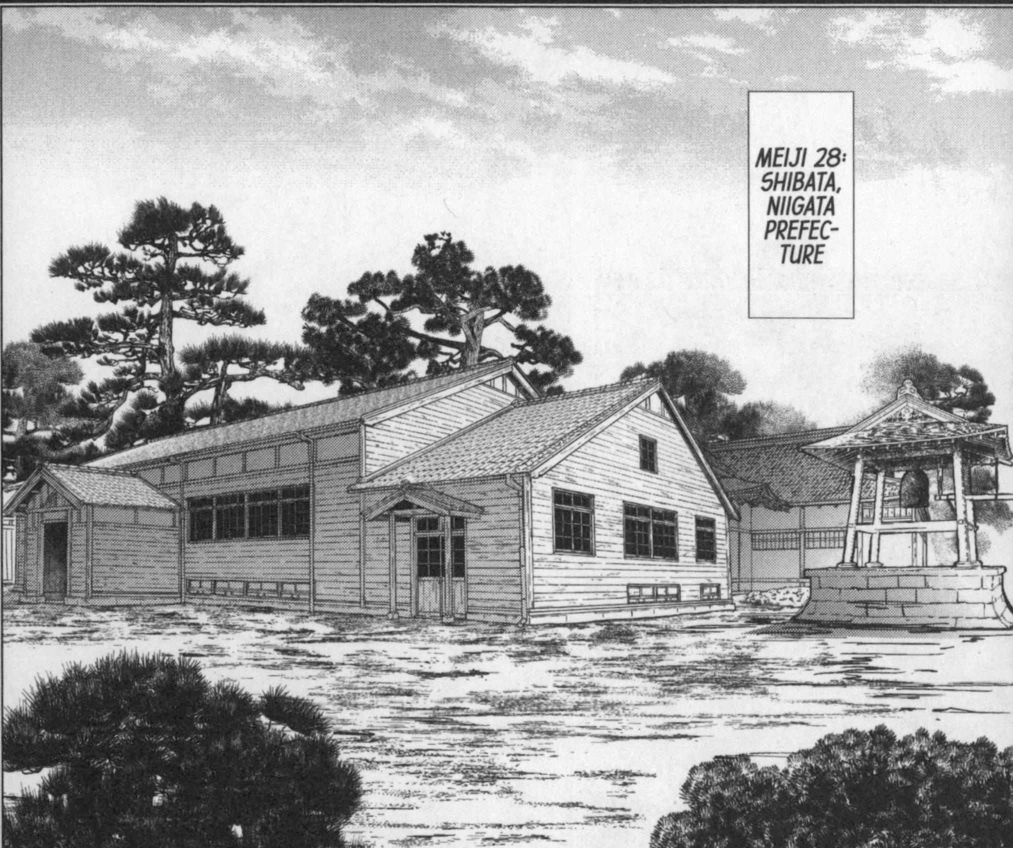
MEIJI 28: SHIBATA, NIIGATA PREFEC-TURE
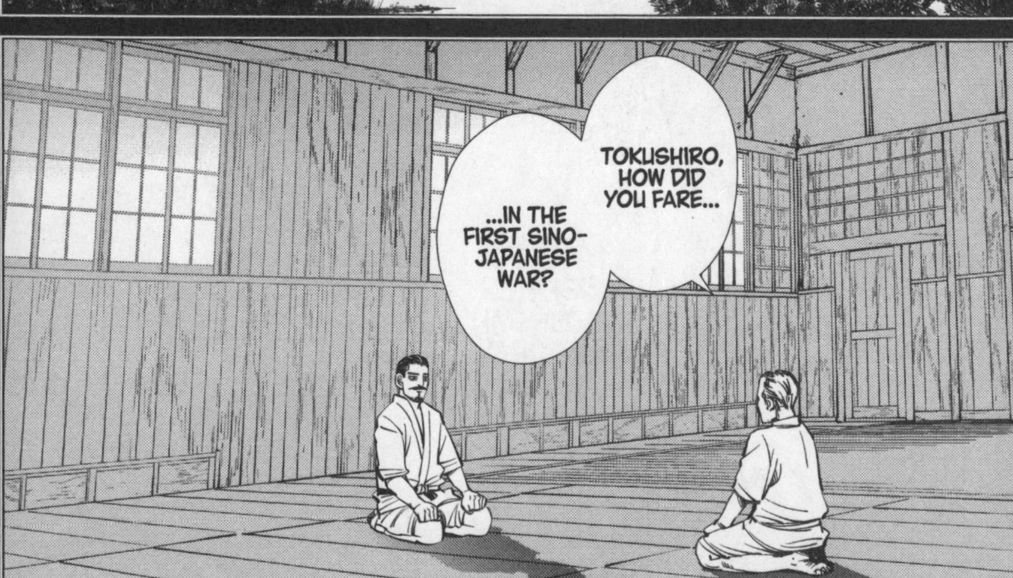
TOKUSHIRO, HOW DID YOU FARE...
...IN THE FIRST SINO-JAPANESE WAR?

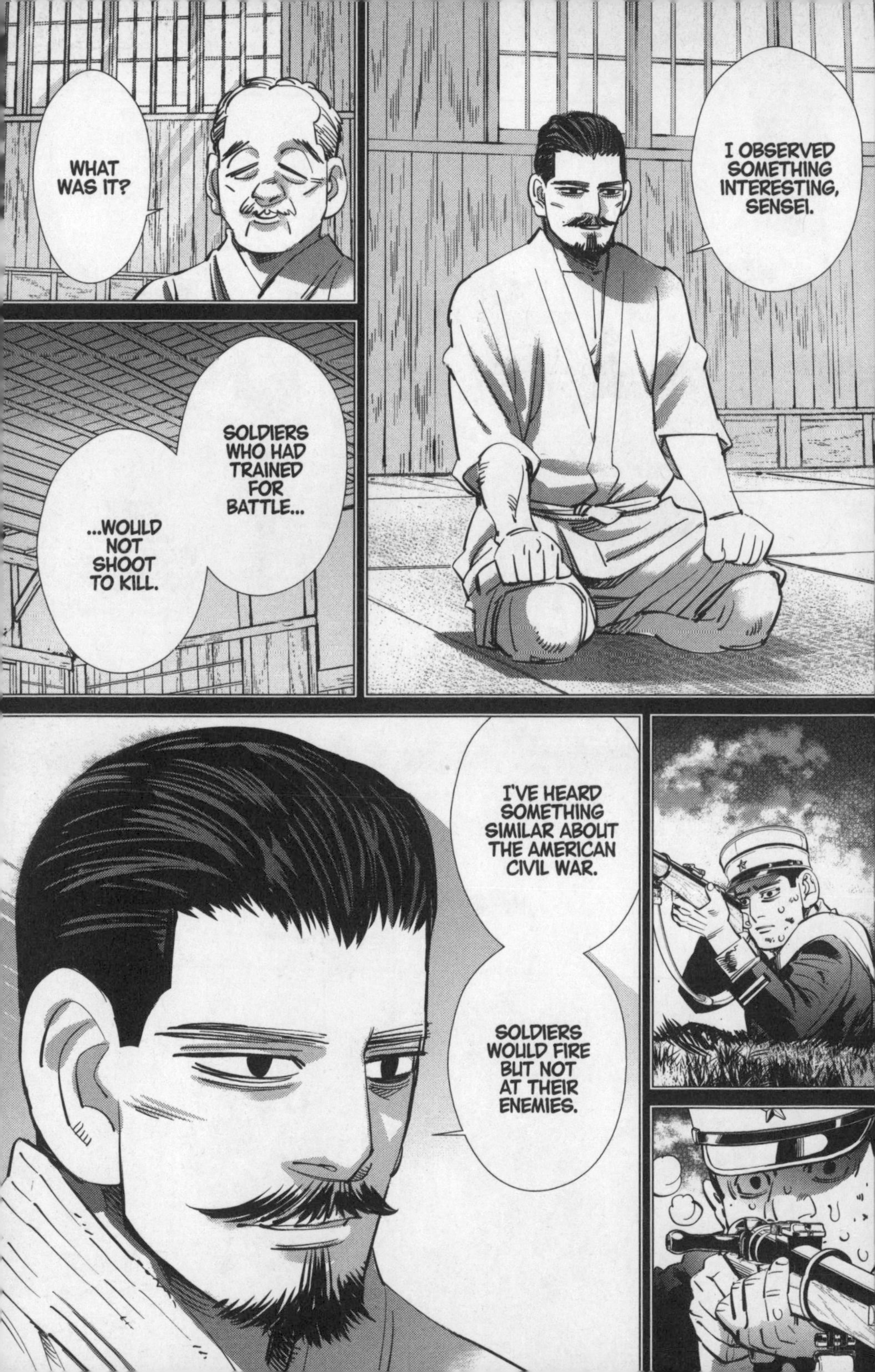
I OBSERVED SOMETHING INTERESTING, SENSEI.
WHAT WAS IT?
SOLDIERS WHO HAD TRAINED FOR BATTLE...
...WOULD NOT SHOOT TO KILL.
I'VE HEARD SOMETHING SIMILAR ABOUT THE AMERICAN CIVIL WAR.
SOLDIERS WOULD FIRE BUT NOT AT THEIR ENEMIES.

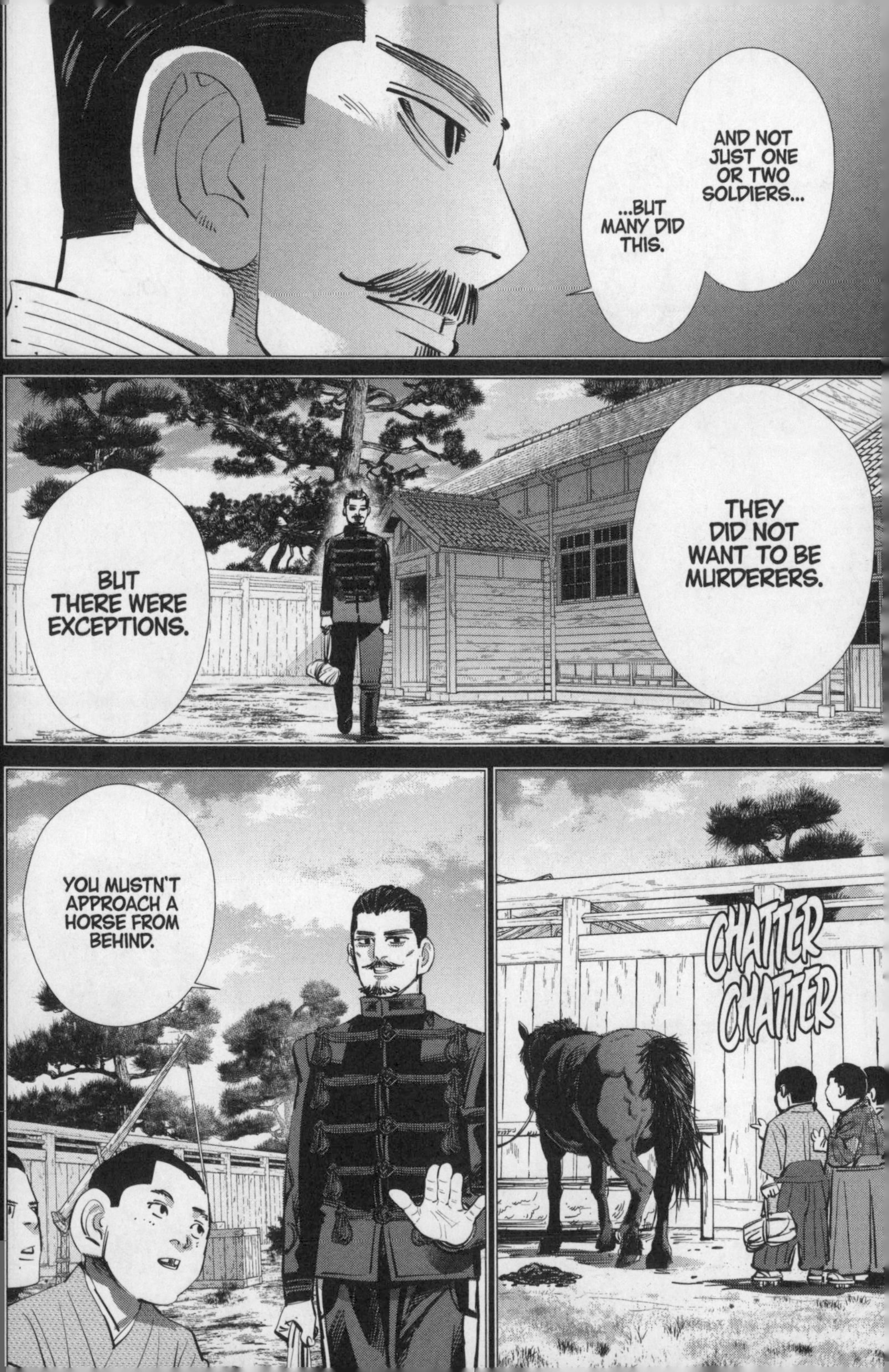
AND NOT JUST ONE OR TWO SOLDIERS...
...BUT MANY DID THIS.
THEY DID NOT WANT TO BE MURDERERS.
BUT THERE WERE EXCEPTIONS.
CHATTER CHATTER
YOU MUSTN'T APPROACH A HORSE FROM BEHIND.

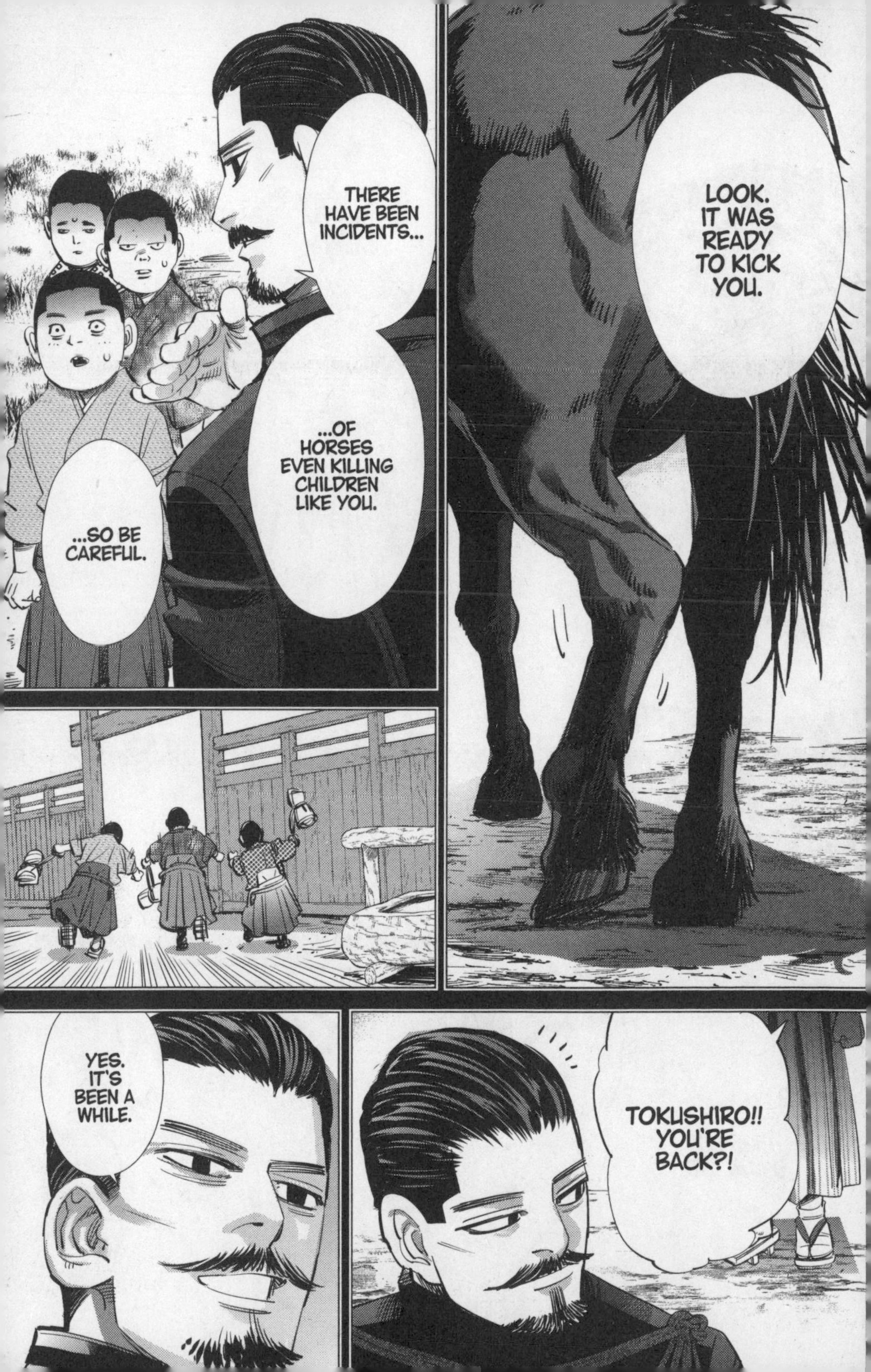
LOOK. IT WAS READY TO KICK YOU.
THERE HAVE BEEN INCIDENTS...
...OF HORSES EVEN KILLING CHILDREN LIKE YOU.
...SO BE CAREFUL.
TOKUSHIRO!! YOU'RE BACK?!
YES. IT'S BEEN A WHILE.

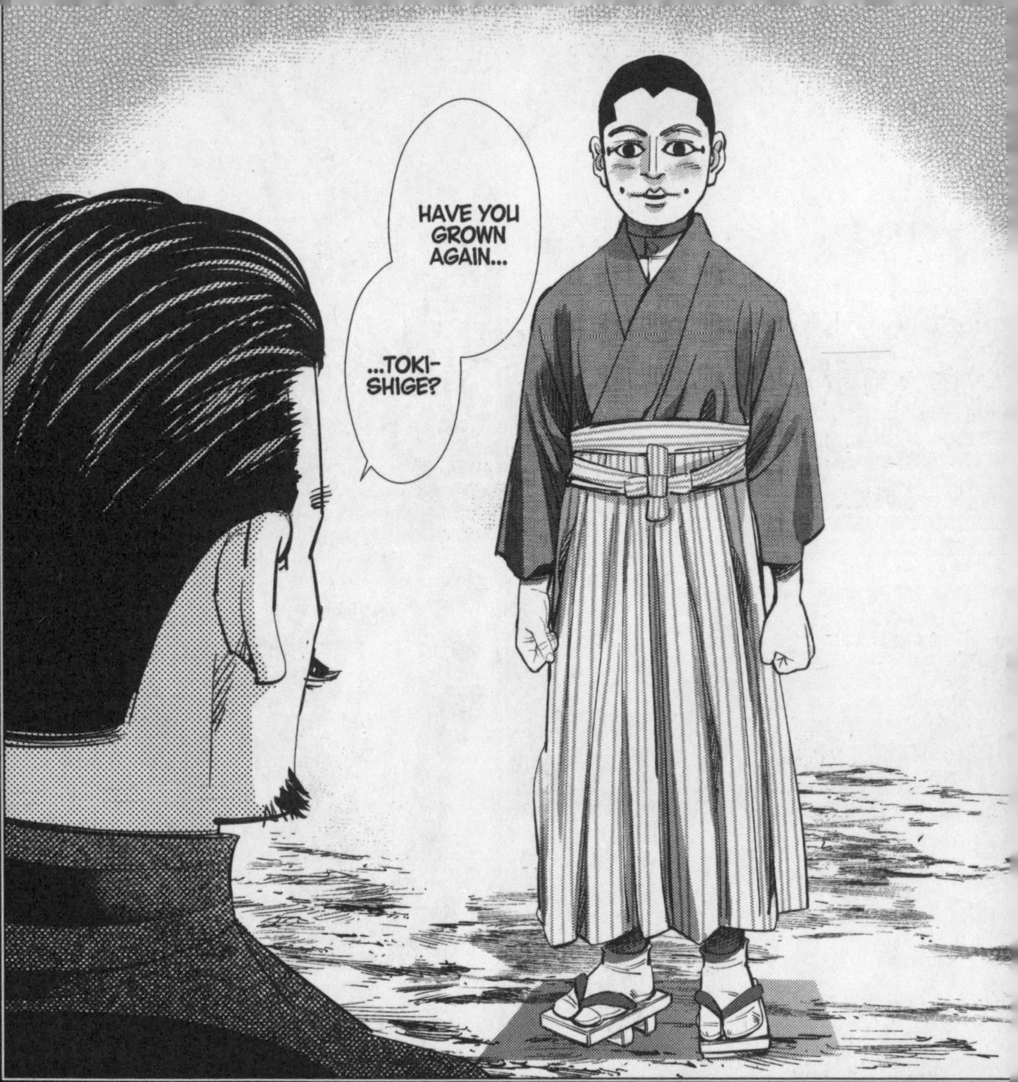
HAVE YOU GROWN AGAIN...
...TOKI-SHIGE?
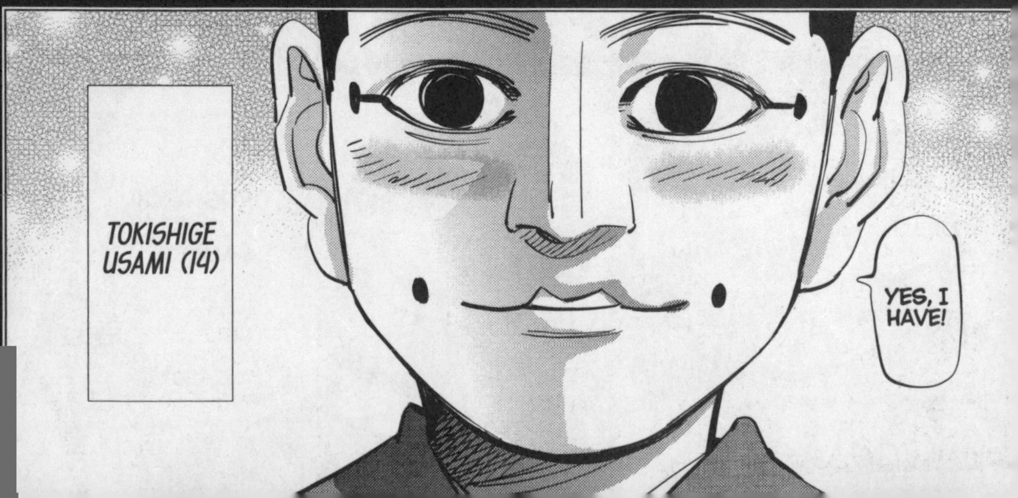
YES, I HAVE!
TOKISHIGE USAMI (14)

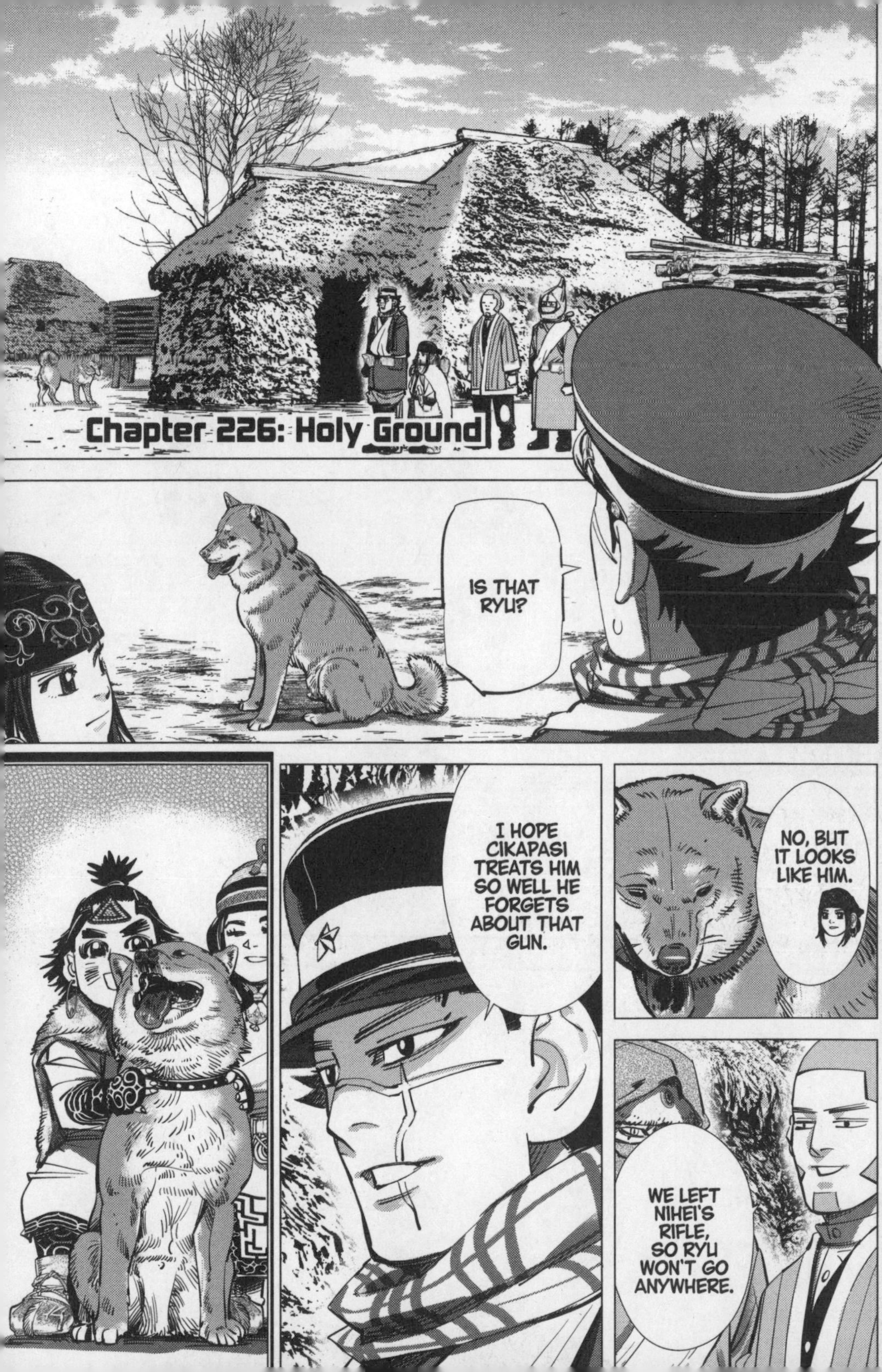
Chapter 226: Holy Ground
IS THAT RYU?
NO, BUT IT LOOKS LIKE HIM.
WE LEFT NIHEI'S RIFLE, SO RYU WON'T GO ANYWHERE.
I HOPE CIKAPASI TREATS HIM SO WELL HE FORGETS ABOUT THAT GUN.

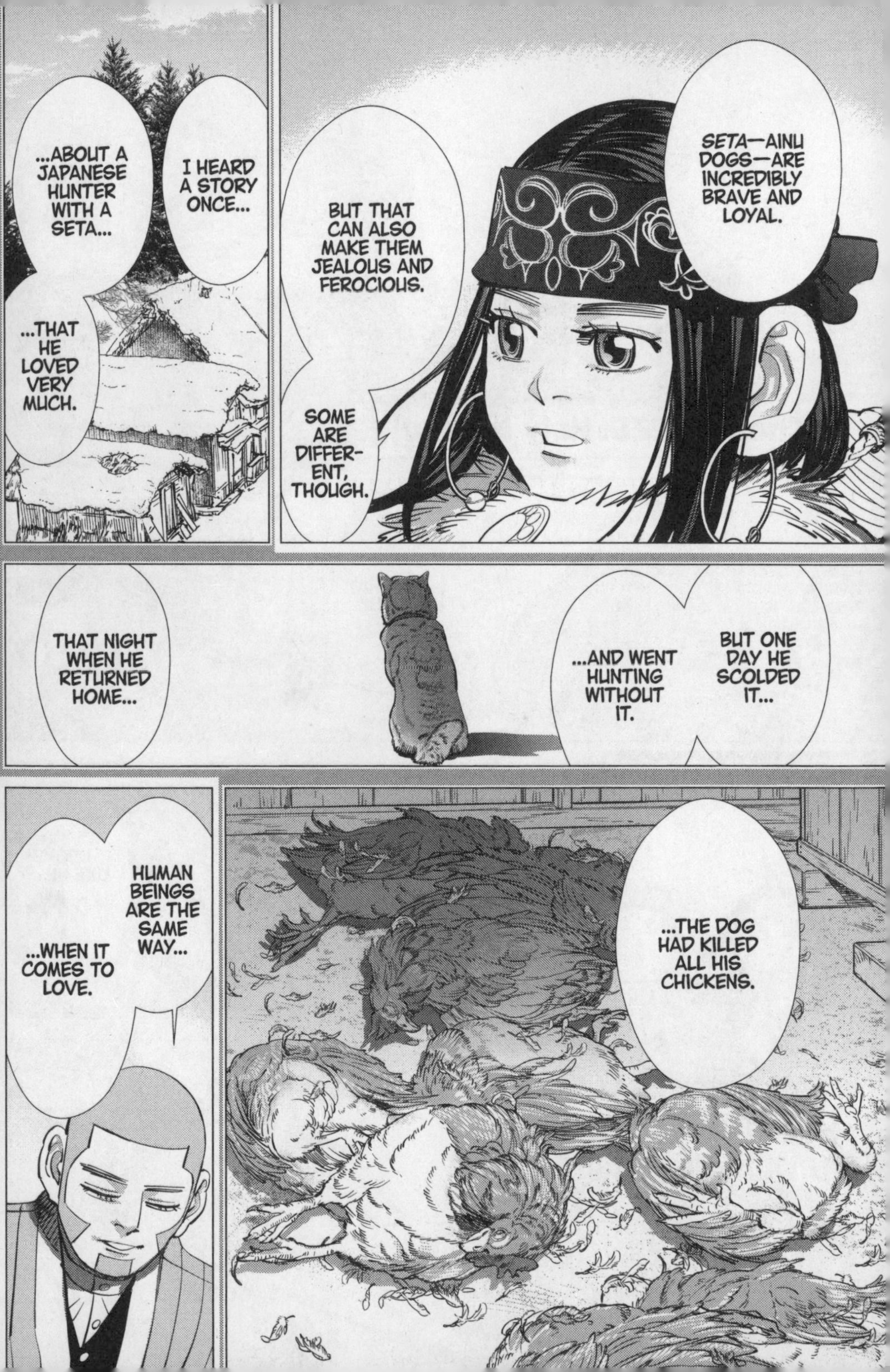
SETA—AINU DOGS—ARE INCREDIBLY BRAVE AND LOYAL.
BUT THAT CAN ALSO MAKE THEM JEALOUS AND FEROCIOUS.
SOME ARE DIFFERENT, THOUGH.
I HEARD A STORY ONCE...
...ABOUT A JAPANESE HUNTER WITH A SETA...
...THAT HE LOVED VERY MUCH.
BUT ONE DAY HE SCOLDED IT...
...AND WENT HUNTING WITHOUT IT.
THAT NIGHT WHEN HE RETURNED HOME...
...THE DOG HAD KILLED ALL HIS CHICKENS.
HUMAN BEINGS ARE THE SAME WAY...
...WHEN IT COMES TO LOVE.

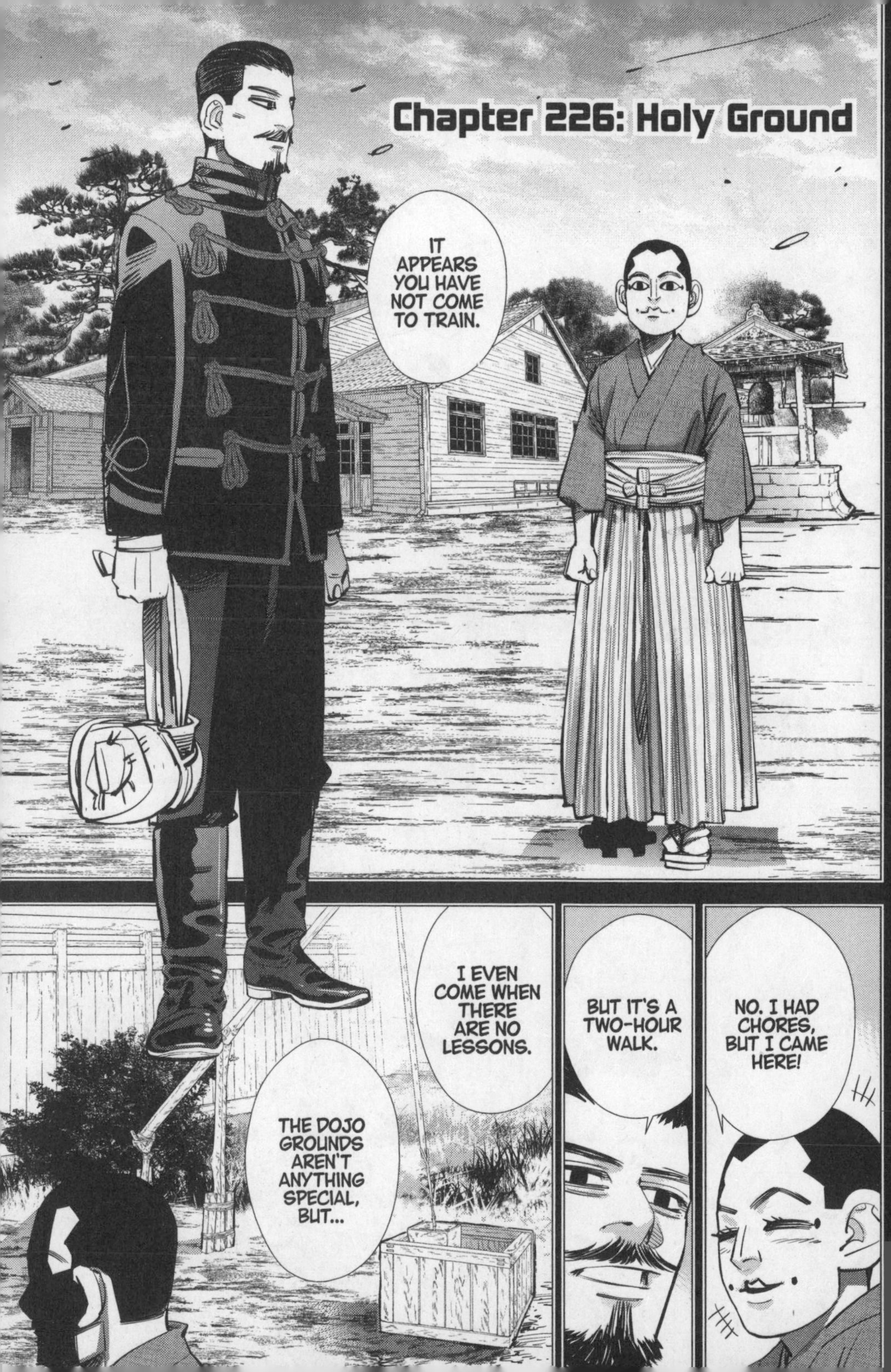
Chapter 226: Holy Ground
IT APPEARS YOU HAVE NOT COME TO TRAIN.
NO. I HAD CHORES, BUT I CAME HERE!
BUT IT'S A TWO-HOUR WALK.
I EVEN COME WHEN THERE ARE NO LESSONS.
THE DOJO GROUNDS AREN'T ANYTHING SPECIAL, BUT...

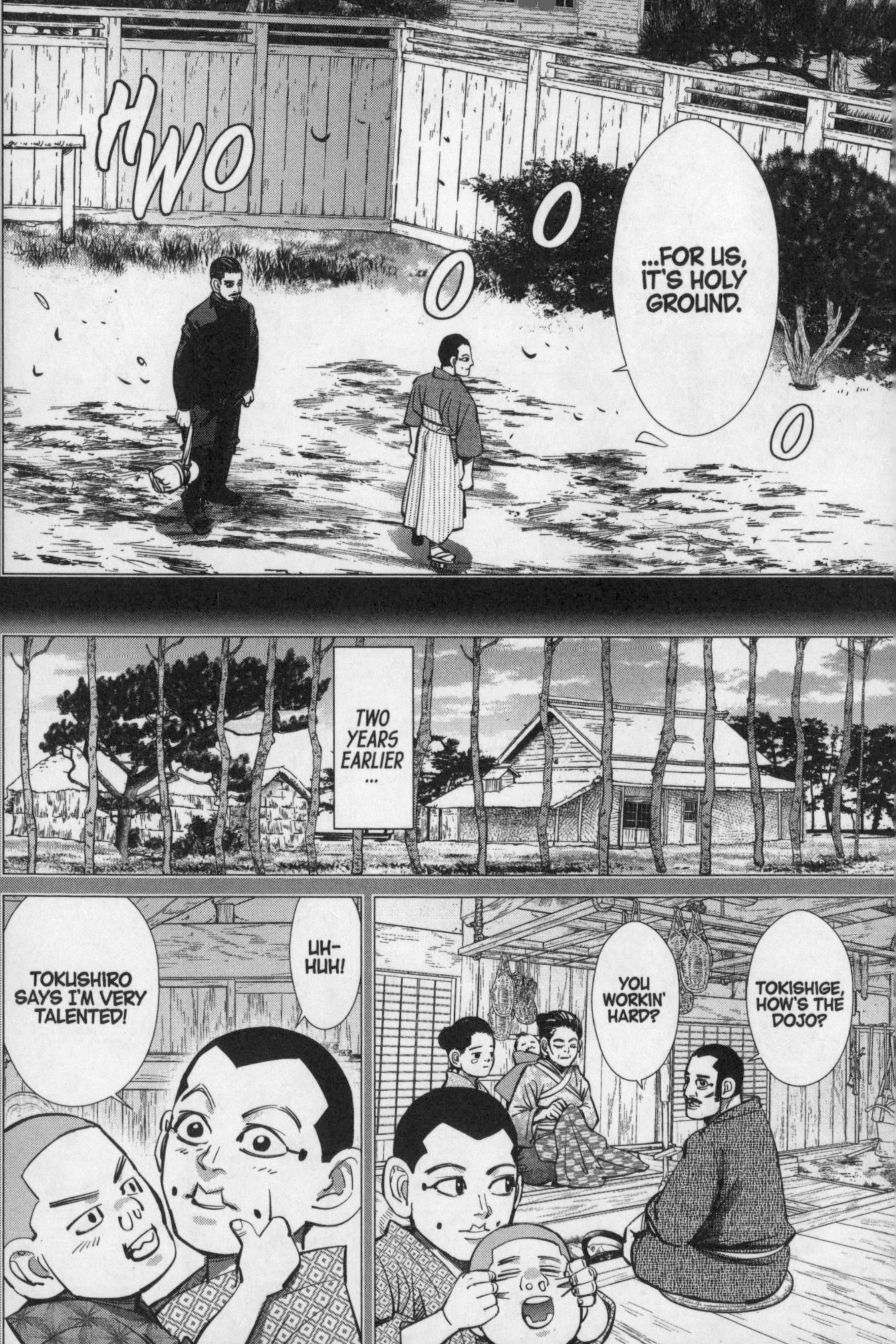
...FOR US, IT'S HOLY GROUND.
HWOOOO
TWO YEARS EARLIER ...
TOKISHIGE, HOW'S THE DOJO?
YOU WORKIN' HARD?
UH-HUH!
TOKUSHIRO SAYS I'M VERY TALENTED!

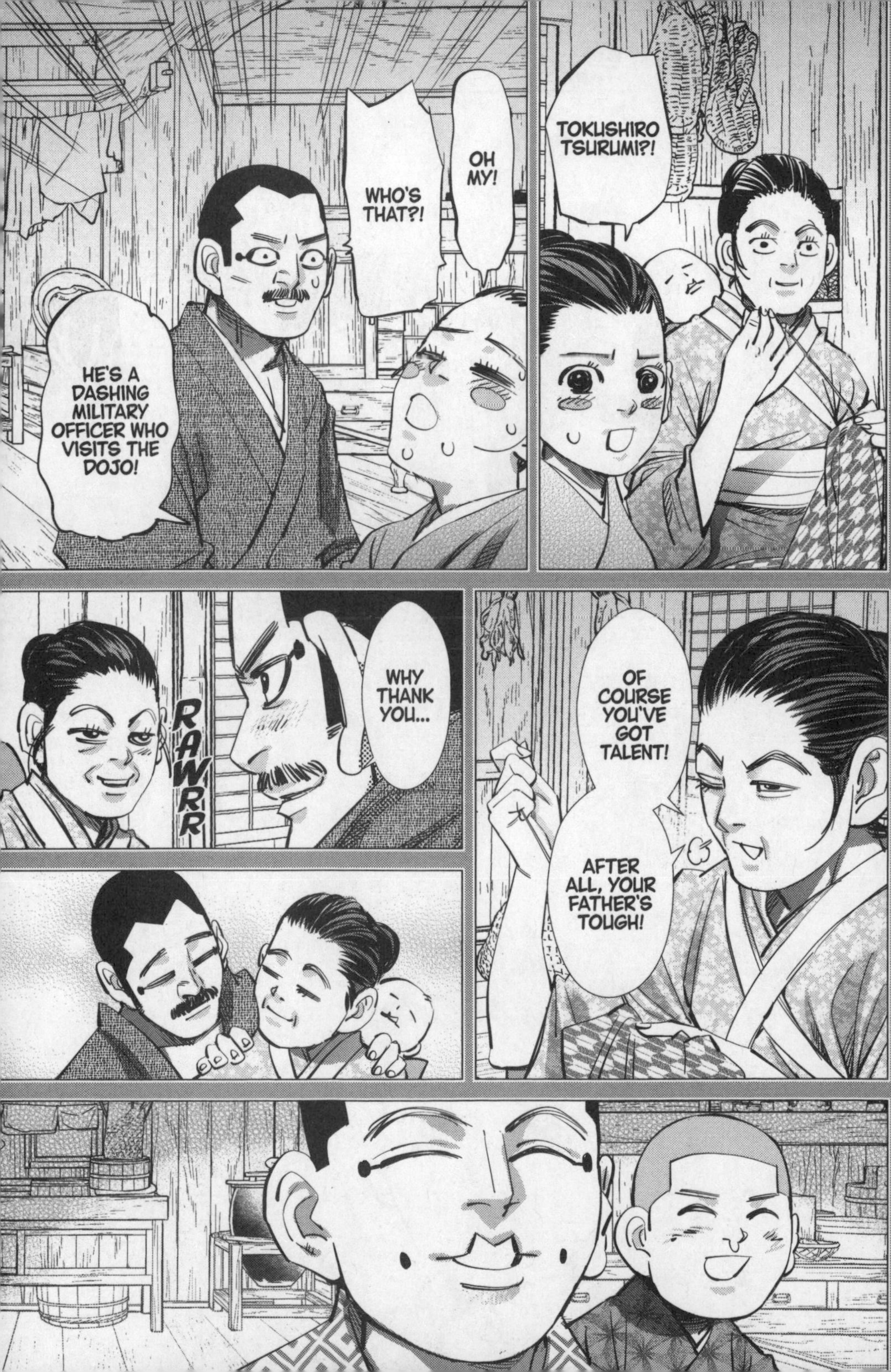
TOKUSHIRO TSURUMI?!
OH MY!
WHO'S THAT?!
HE'S A DASHING MILITARY OFFICER WHO VISITS THE DOJO!
OF COURSE YOU'VE GOT TALENT!
AFTER ALL, YOUR FATHER'S TOUGH!
WHY THANK YOU...
RAWRR

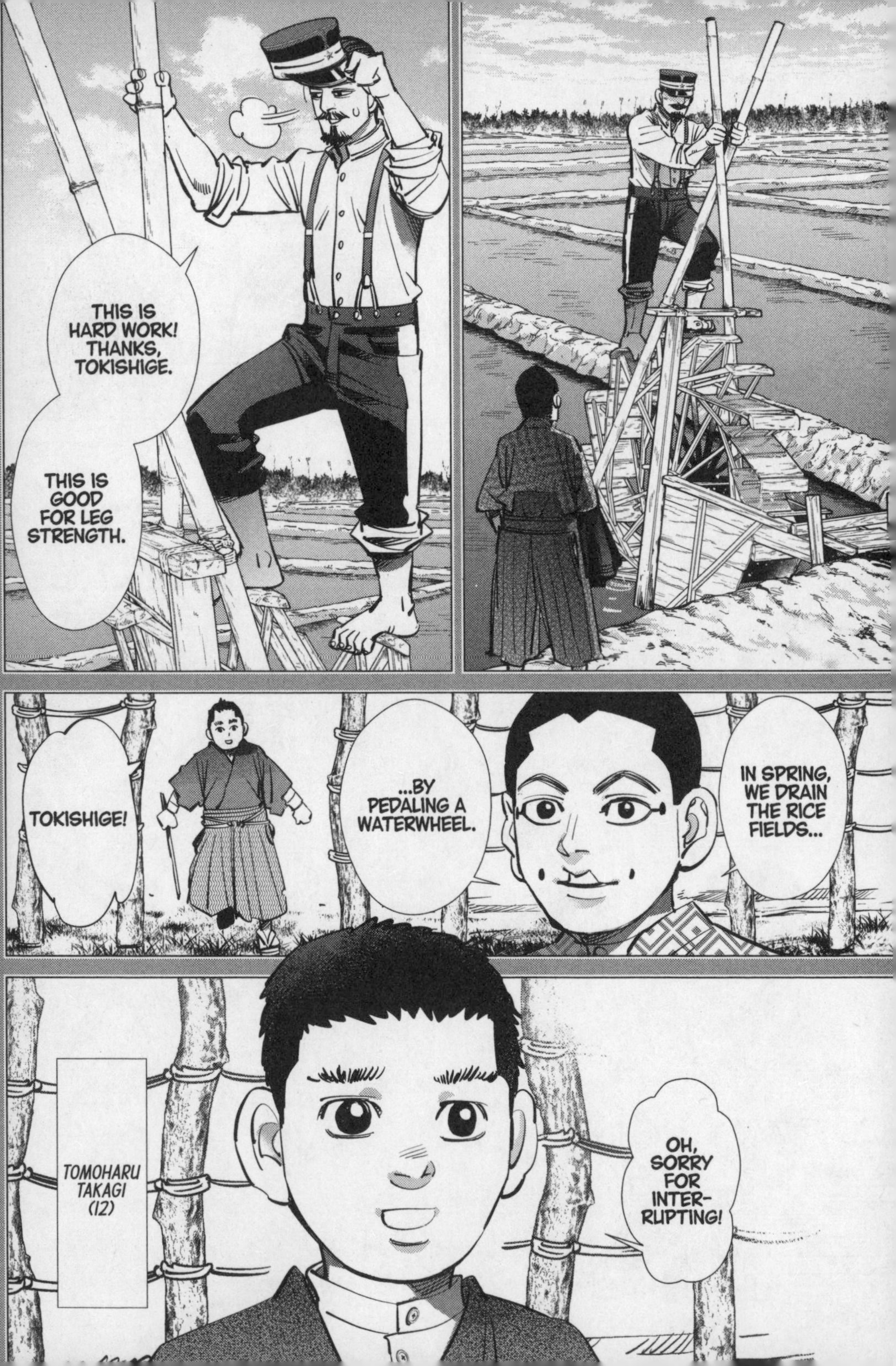
THIS IS HARD WORK! THANKS, TOKISHIGE.
THIS IS GOOD FOR LEG STRENGTH.
IN SPRING, WE DRAIN THE RICE FIELDS...
...BY PEDALING A WATERWHEEL.
TOKISHIGE!
TOMOHARU TAKAGI (12)
OH, SORRY FOR INTER-RUPTING!

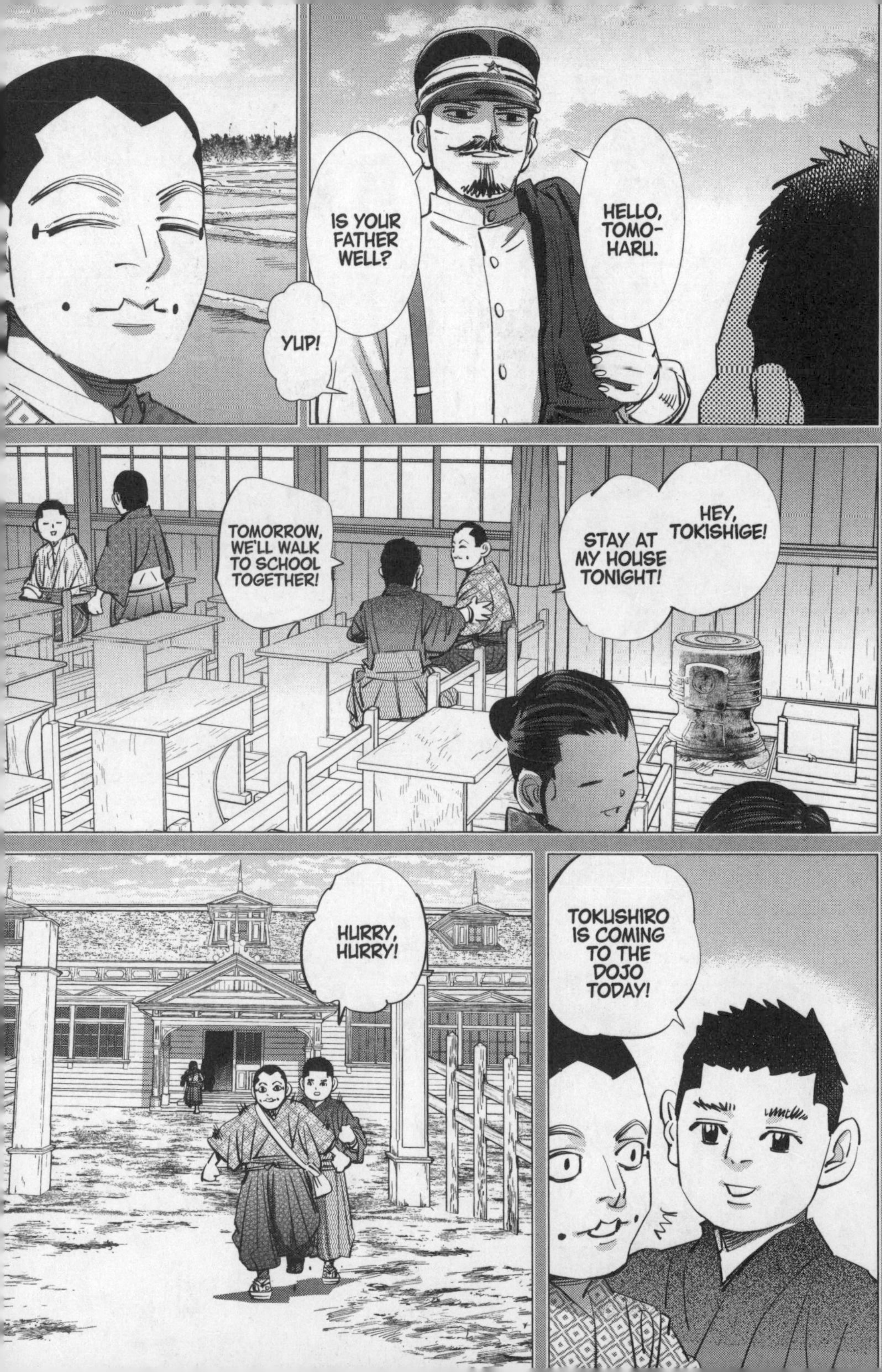
HELLO, TOMO-HARU.
IS YOUR FATHER WELL?
YUP!
HEY, TOKISHIGE!
STAY AT MY HOUSE TONIGHT!
TOMORROW, WE'LL WALK TO SCHOOL TOGETHER!
TOKUSHIRO IS COMING TO THE DOJO TODAY!
HURRY, HURRY!

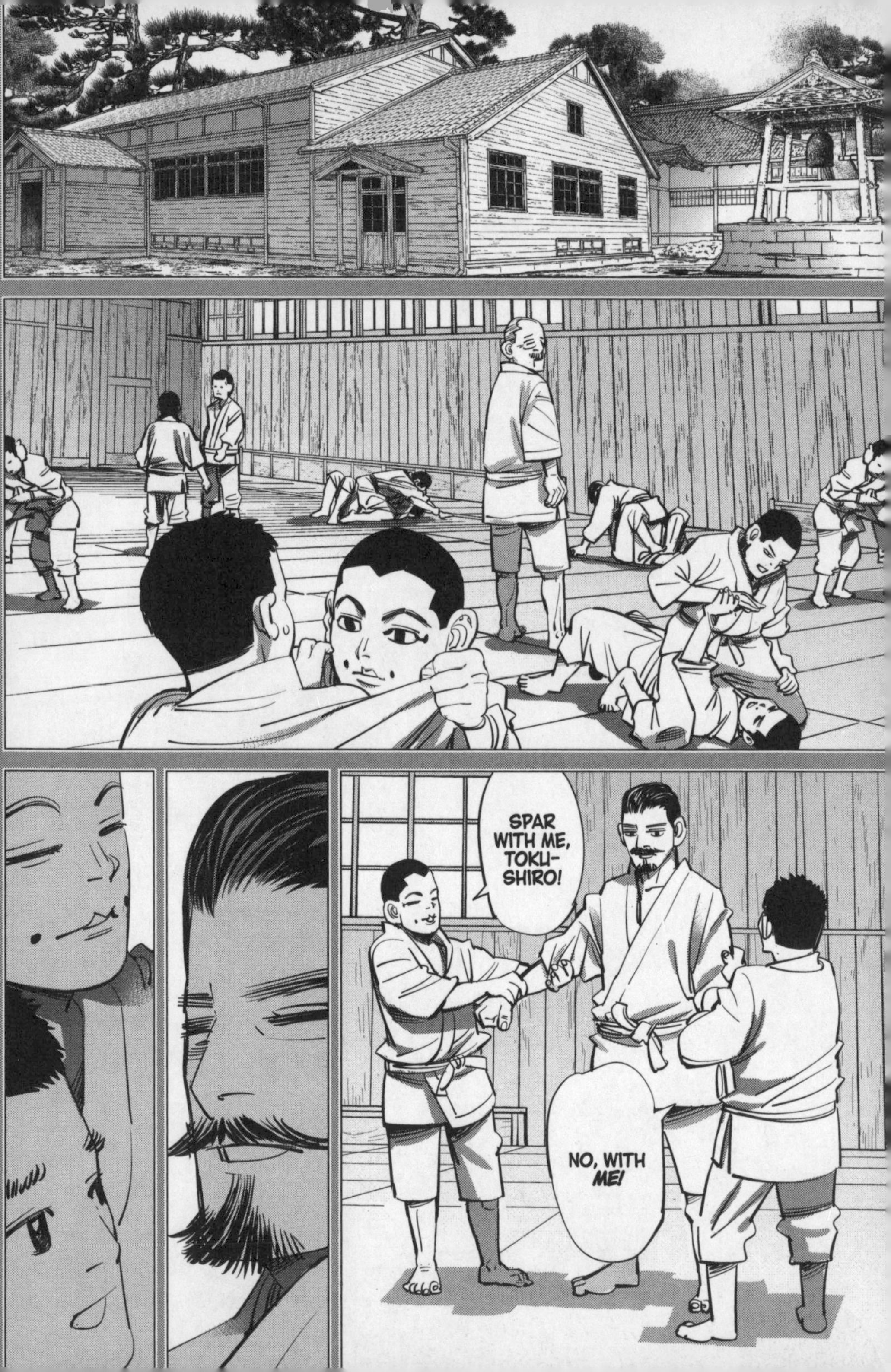
SPAR WITH ME, TOKU-SHIRO!
NO, WITH ME!

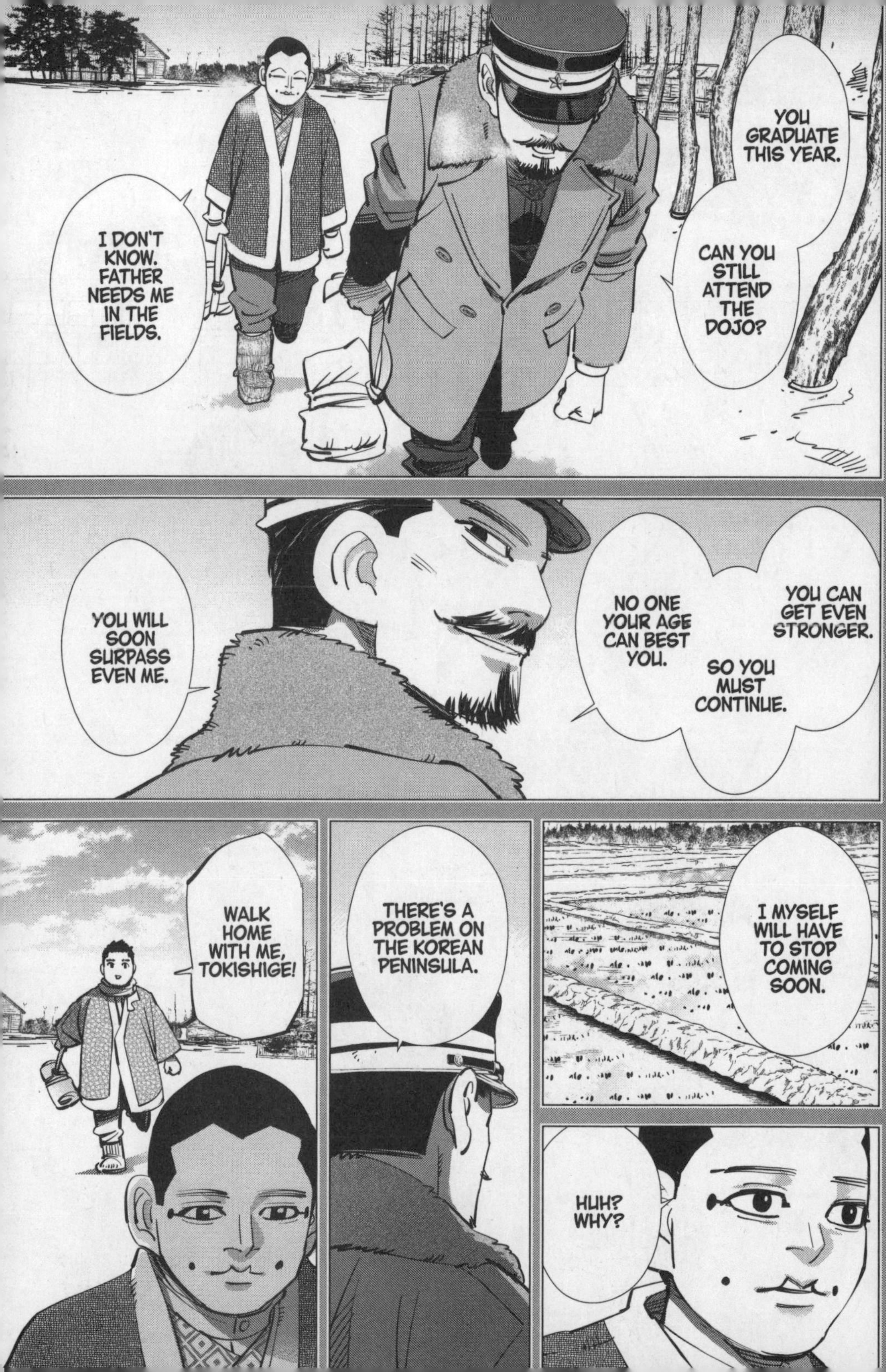
YOU GRADUATE THIS YEAR.
CAN YOU STILL ATTEND THE DOJO?
I DON'T KNOW. FATHER NEEDS ME IN THE FIELDS.
YOU CAN GET EVEN STRONGER.
NO ONE YOUR AGE CAN BEST YOU.
SO YOU MUST CONTINUE.
YOU WILL SOON SURPASS EVEN ME.
I MYSELF WILL HAVE TO STOP COMING SOON.
HUH? WHY?
THERE'S A PROBLEM ON THE KOREAN PENINSULA.
WALK HOME WITH ME, TOKISHIGE!

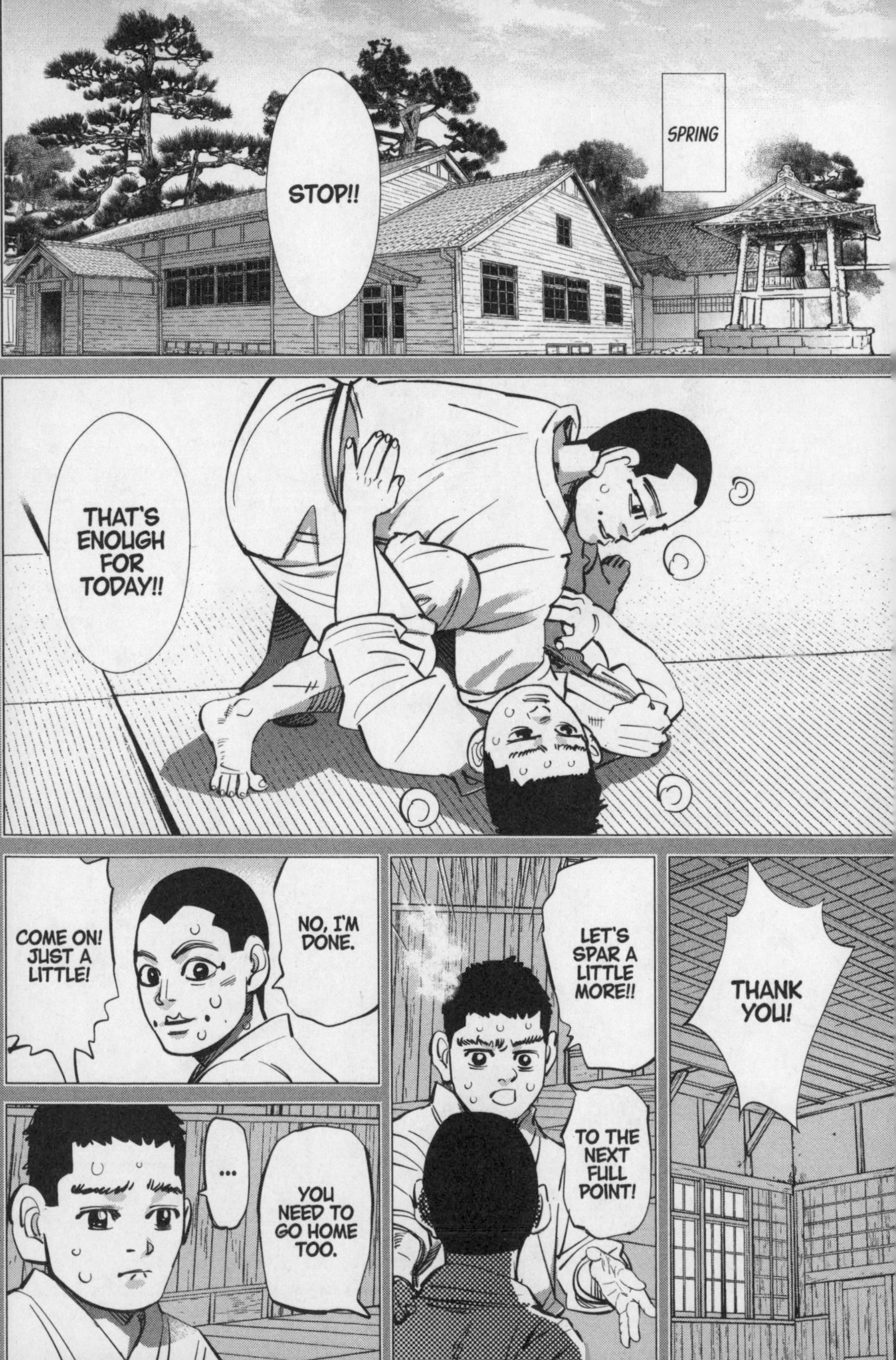
SPRING
STOP!!
THAT'S ENOUGH FOR TODAY!!
THANK YOU!
LET'S SPAR A LITTLE MORE!!
TO THE NEXT FULL POINT!
NO, I'M DONE.
COME ON! JUST A LITTLE!
...
YOU NEED TO GO HOME TOO.

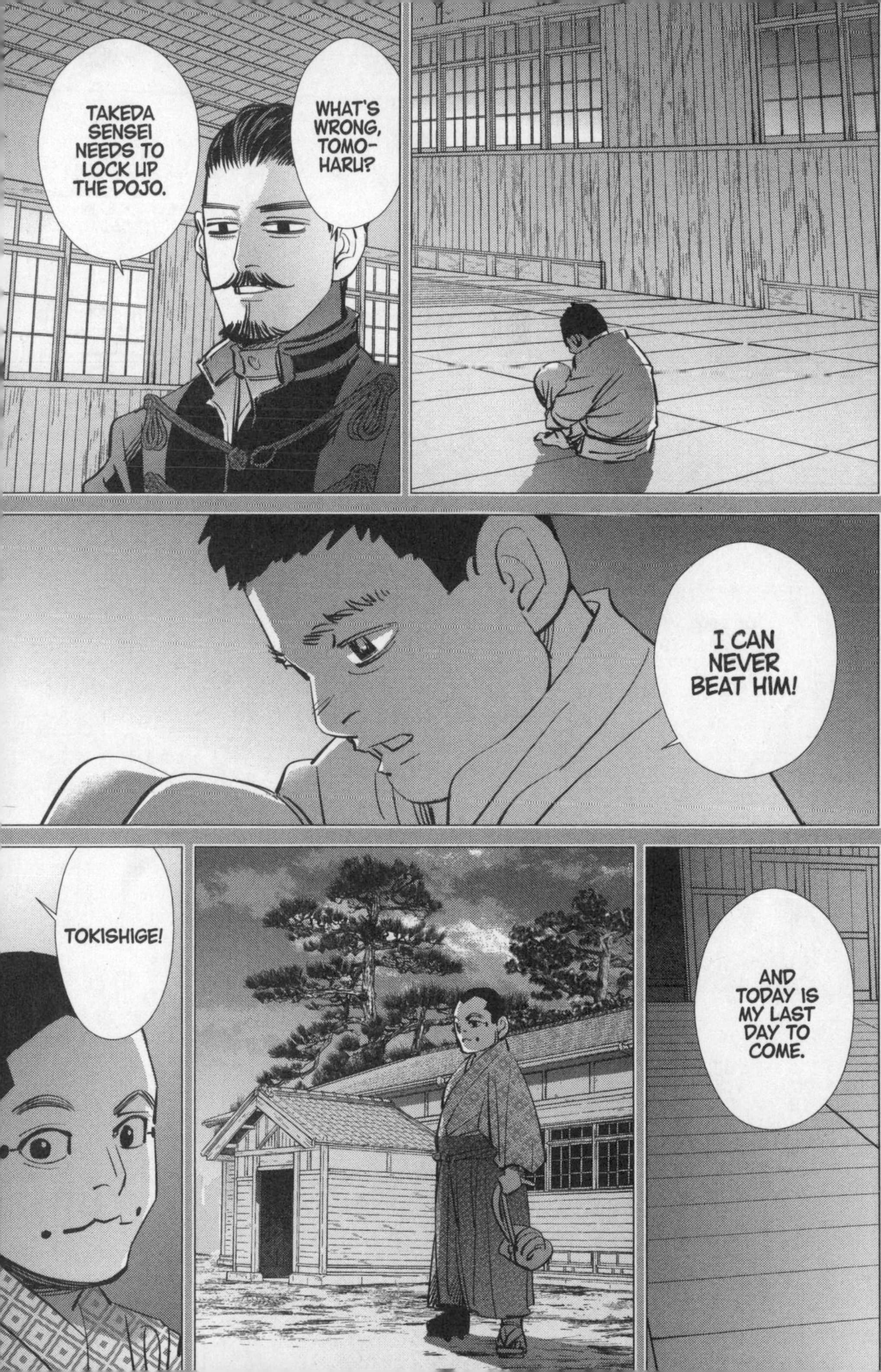
WHAT'S WRONG, TOMO-HARU?
TAKEDA SENSEI NEEDS TO LOCK UP THE DOJO.
I CAN NEVER BEAT HIM!
AND TODAY IS MY LAST DAY TO COME.
TOKISHIGE!

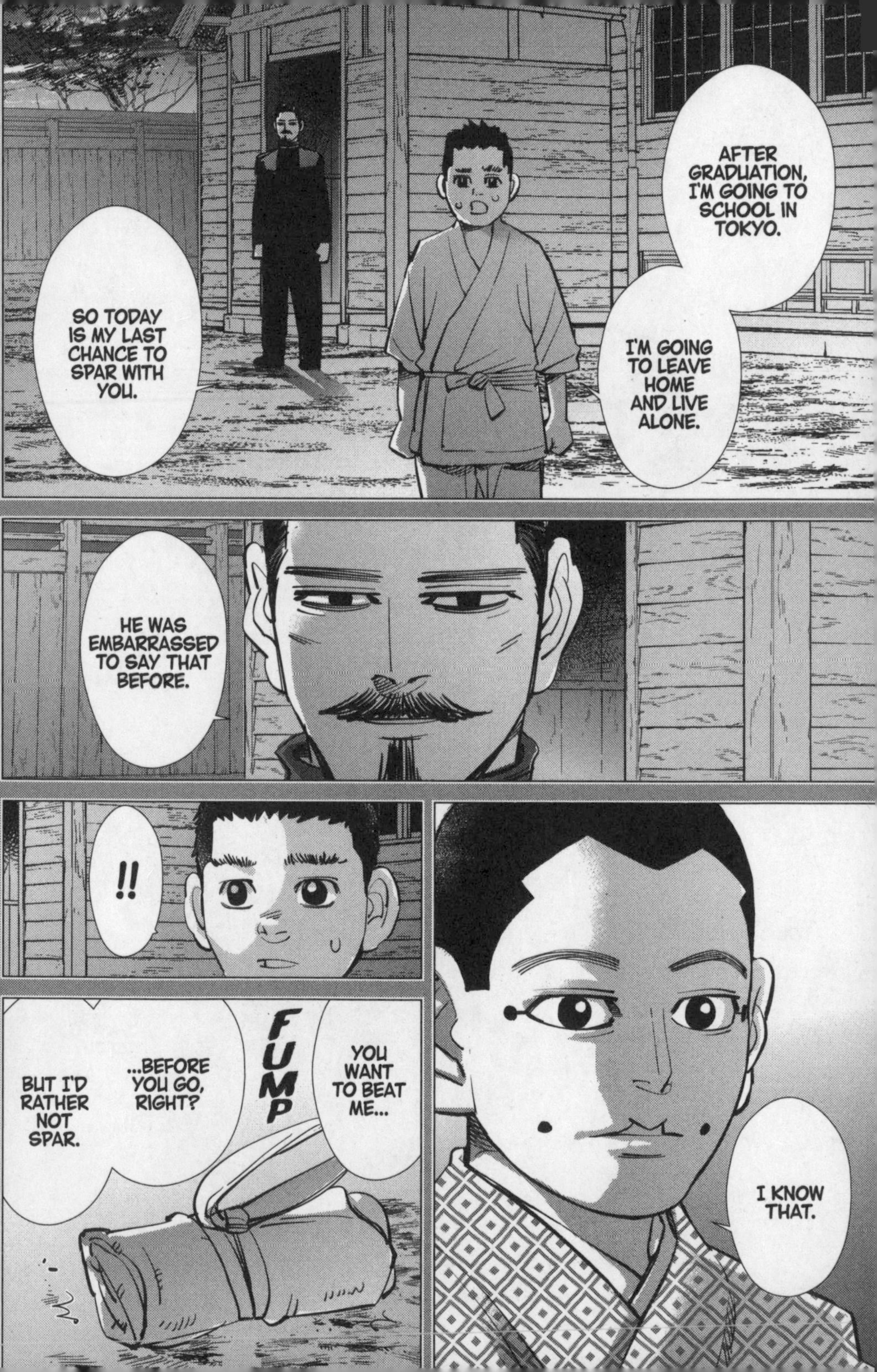
AFTER GRADUATION, I'M GOING TO SCHOOL IN TOKYO.
I'M GOING TO LEAVE HOME AND LIVE ALONE.
SO TODAY IS MY LAST CHANCE TO SPAR WITH YOU.
HE WAS EMBARRASSED TO SAY THAT BEFORE.
I KNOW THAT.
!!
YOU WANT TO BEAT ME...
FUMP
...BEFORE YOU GO, RIGHT?
BUT I'D RATHER NOT SPAR.

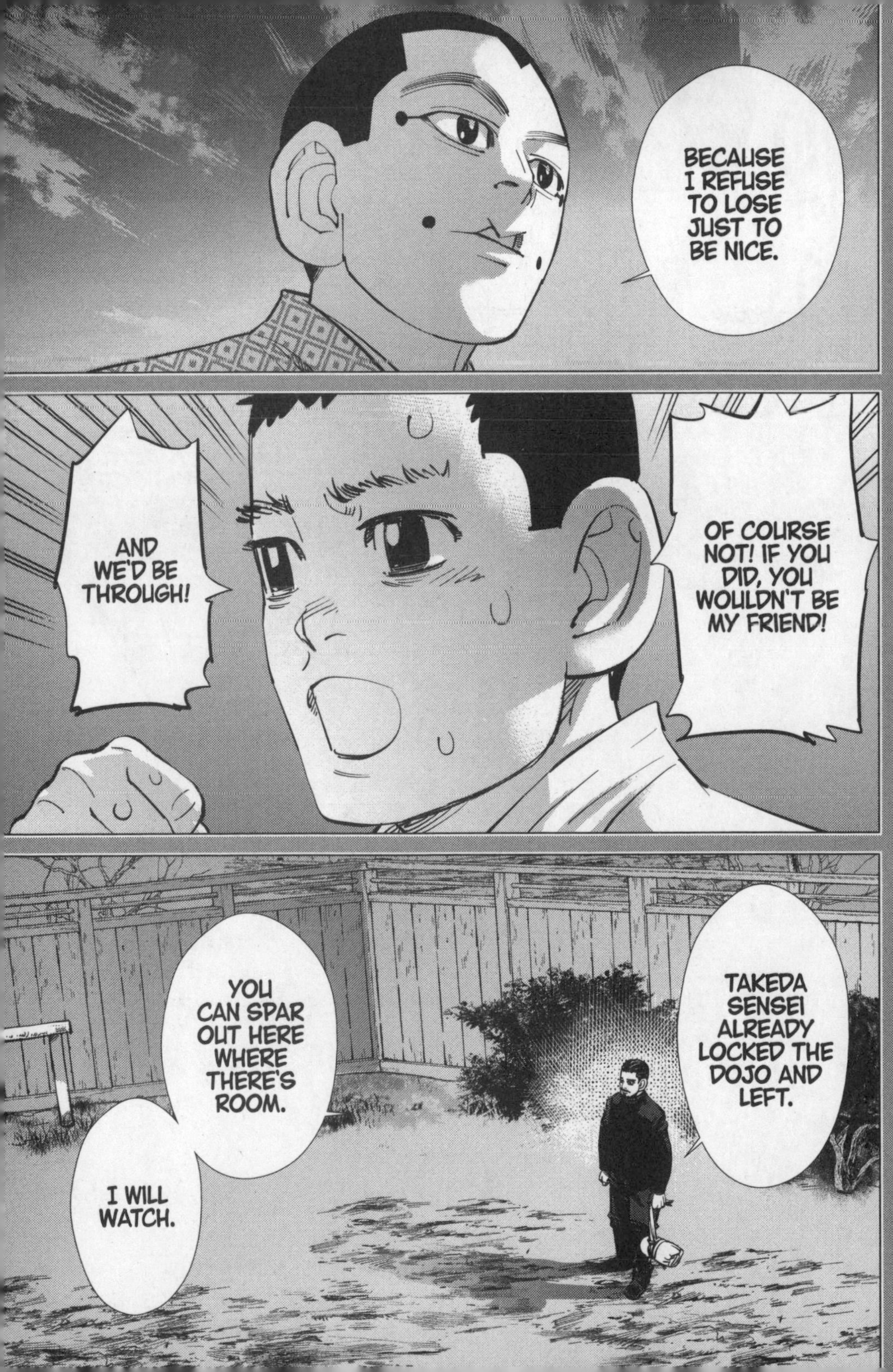
BECAUSE I REFUSE TO LOSE JUST TO BE NICE.
OF COURSE NOT! IF YOU DID, YOU WOULDN'T BE MY FRIEND!
AND WE'D BE THROUGH!
TAKEDA SENSEI ALREADY LOCKED THE DOJO AND LEFT.
YOU CAN SPAR OUT HERE WHERE THERE'S ROOM.
I WILL WATCH.

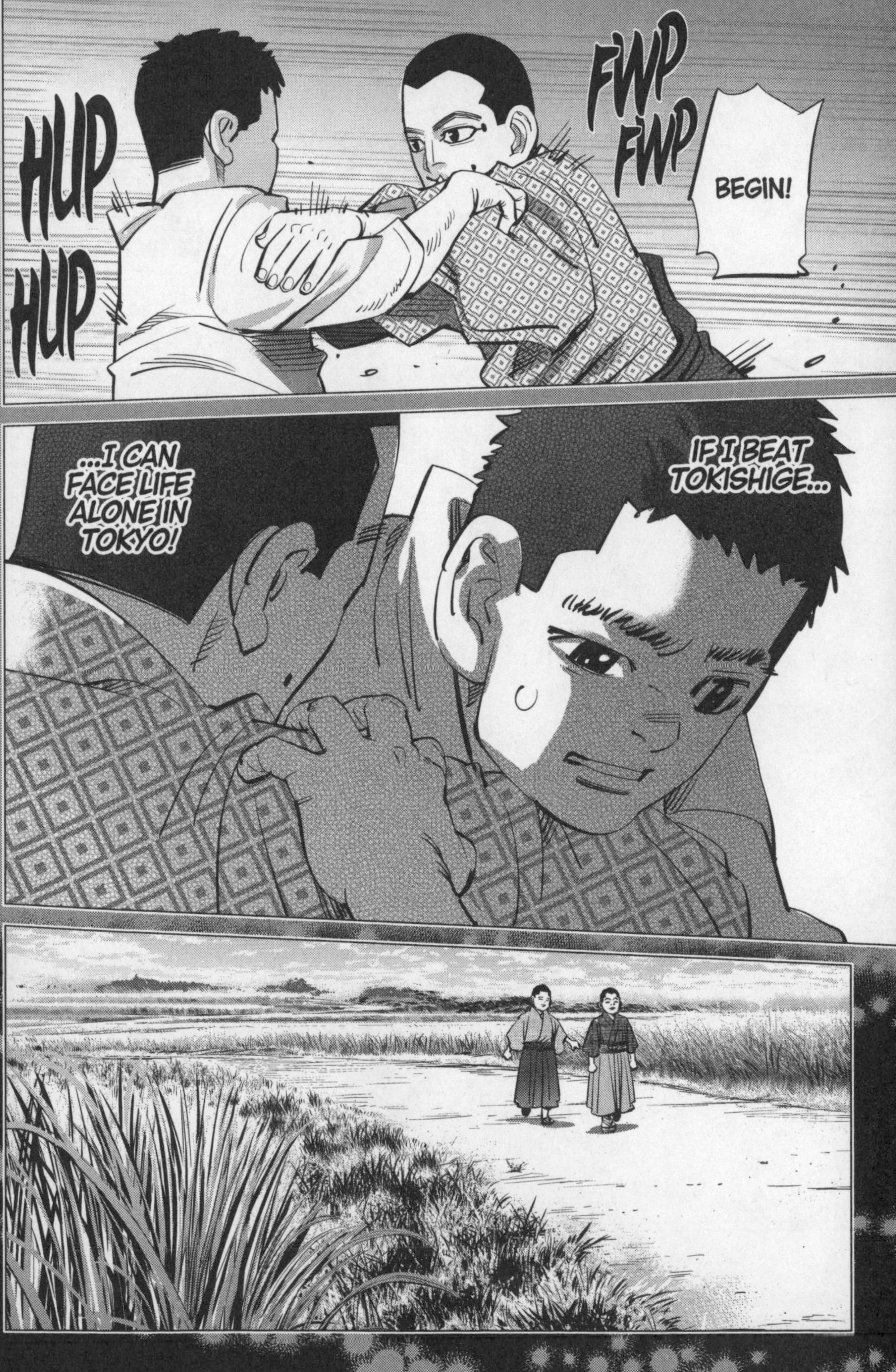
BEGIN!
FWP FWP
HUP HUP
IF I BEAT TOKISHIGE...
...I CAN FACE LIFE ALONE IN TOKYO!

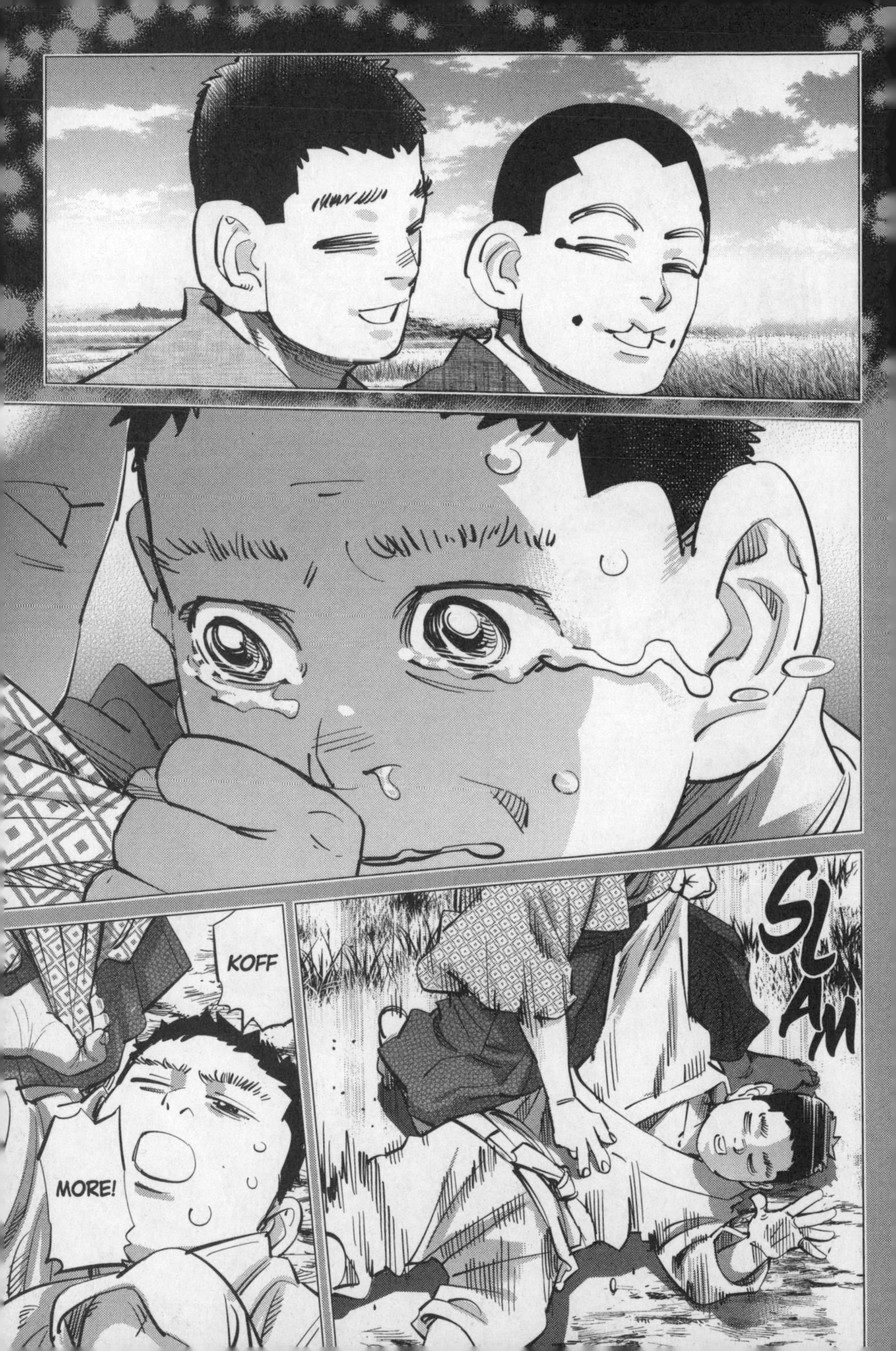
SLAM
KOFF
MORE!

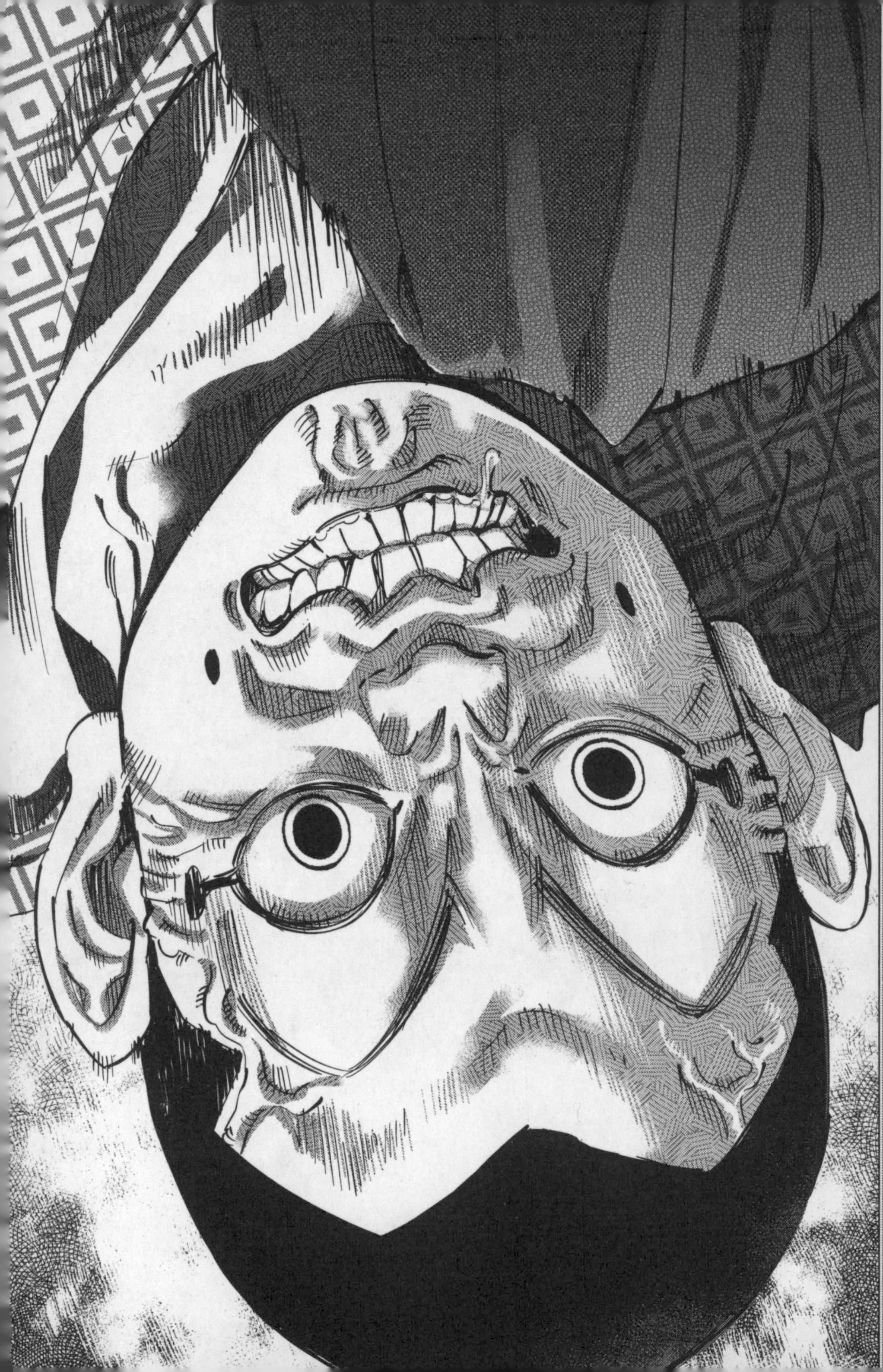

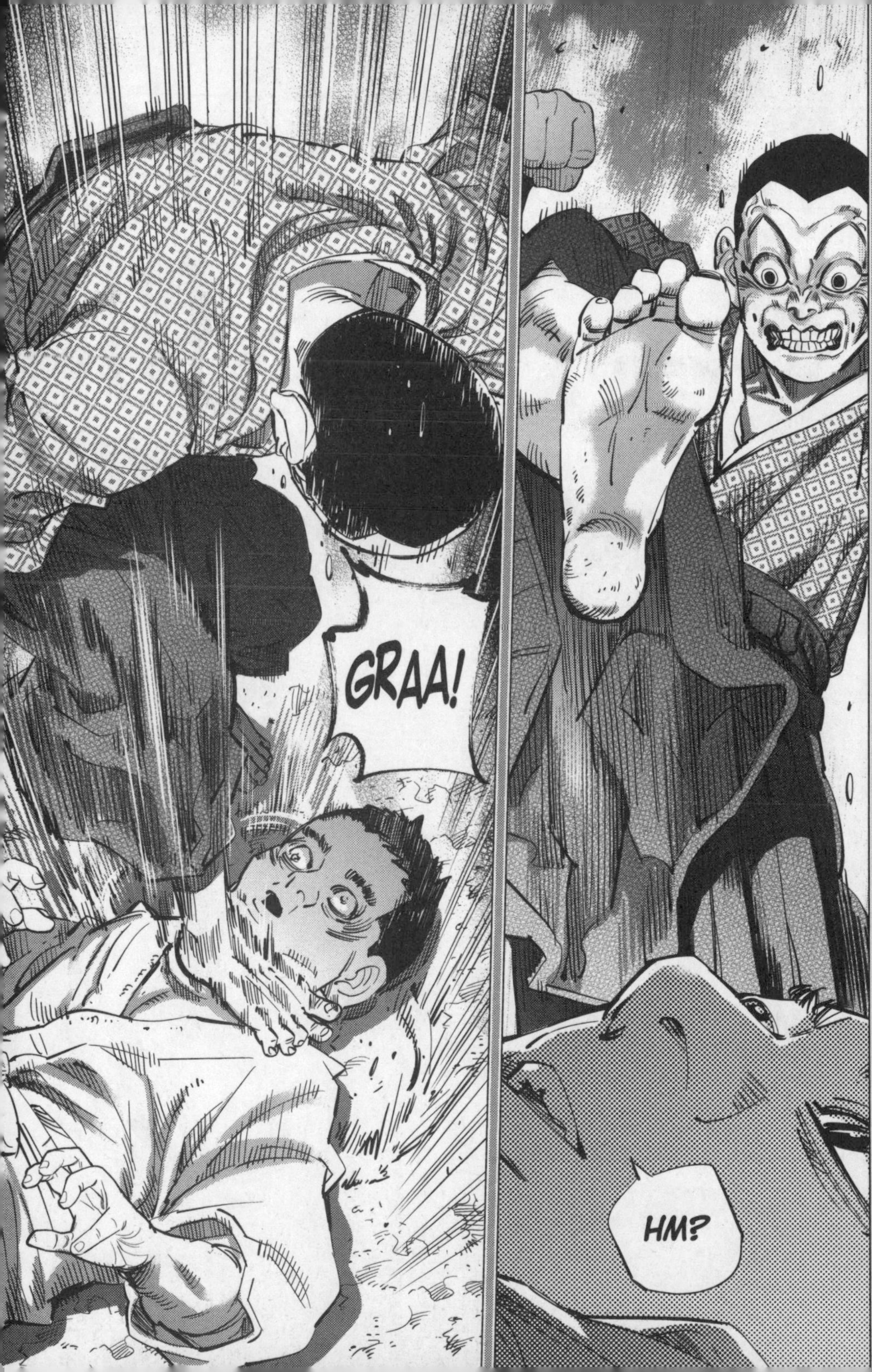
HM?
GRAA!

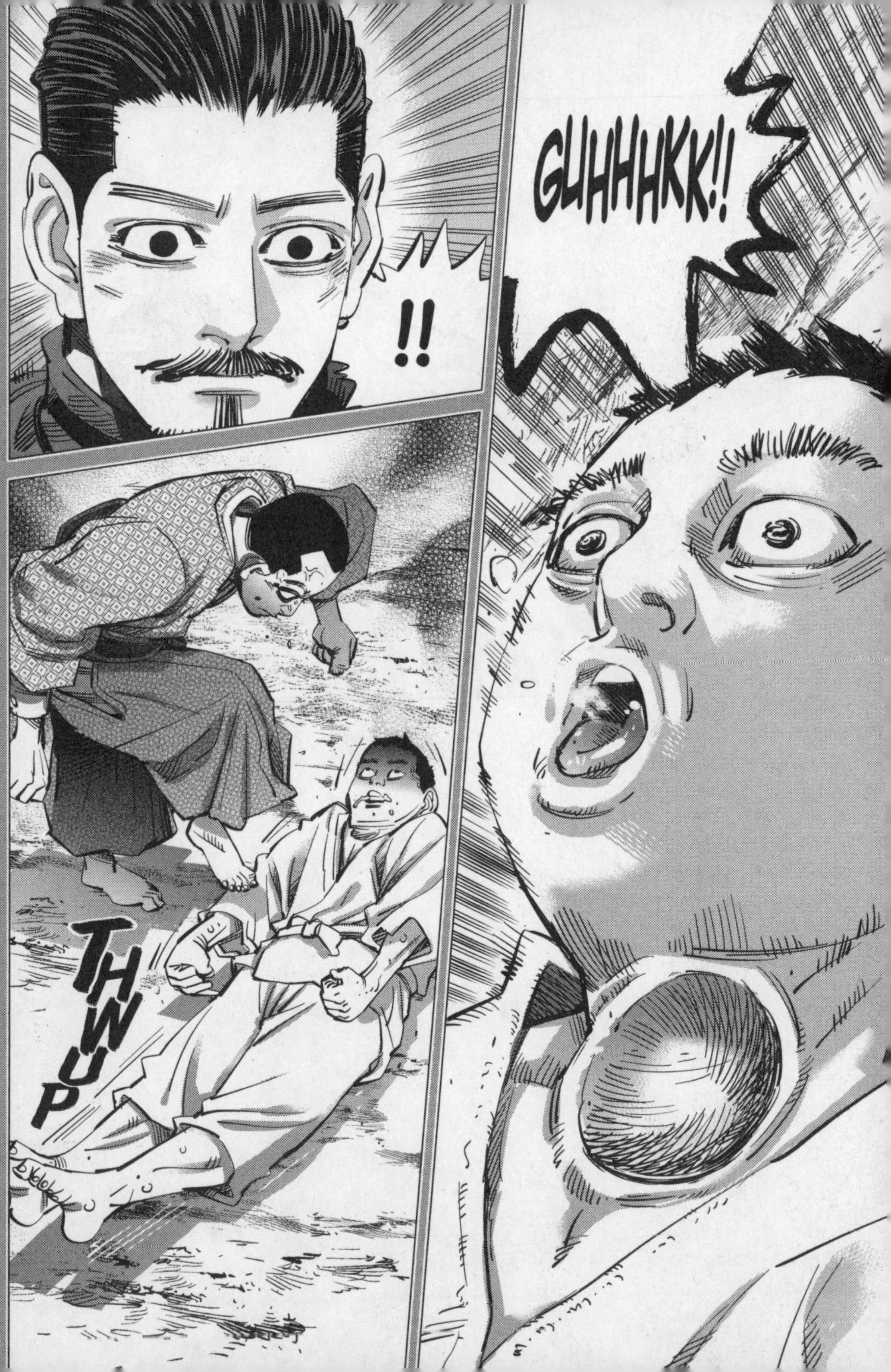
GUHHHKK!!
!!
THWUP

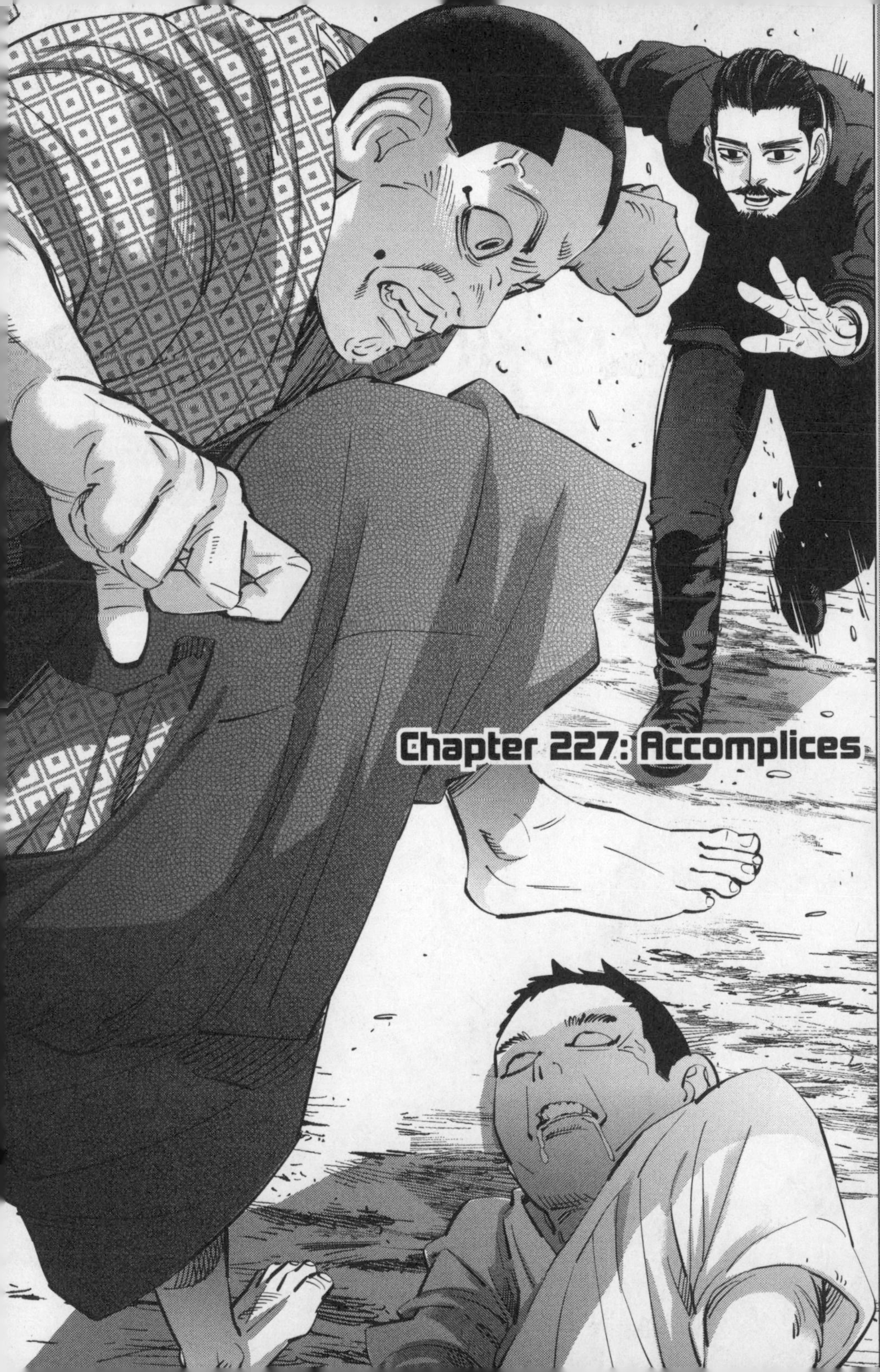
Chapter 227: Accomplices

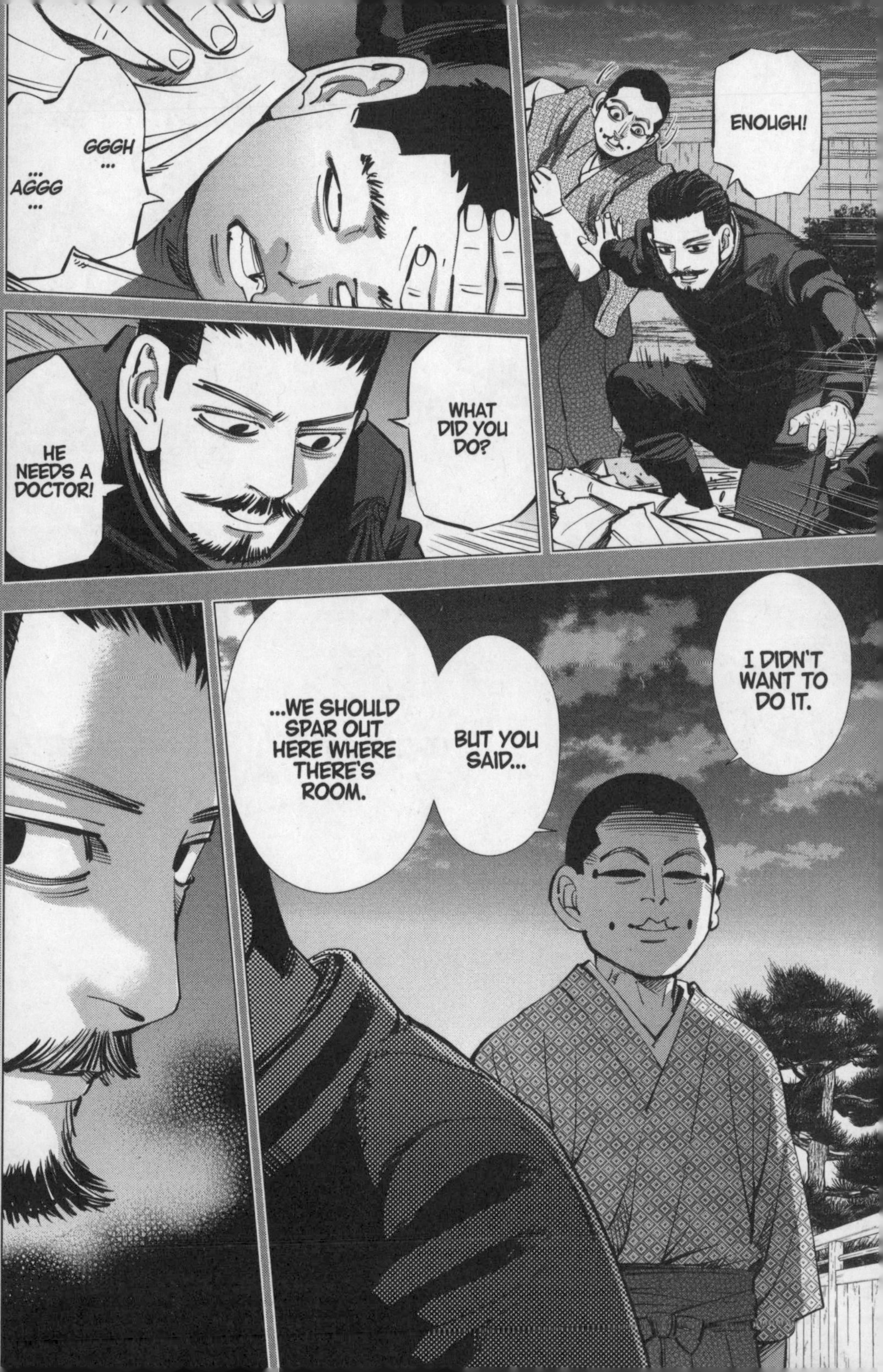
ENOUGH!
GGGH ...
... AGGG ...
WHAT DID YOU DO?
HE NEEDS A DOCTOR!
I DIDN'T WANT TO DO IT.
BUT YOU SAID...
...WE SHOULD SPAR OUT HERE WHERE THERE'S ROOM.

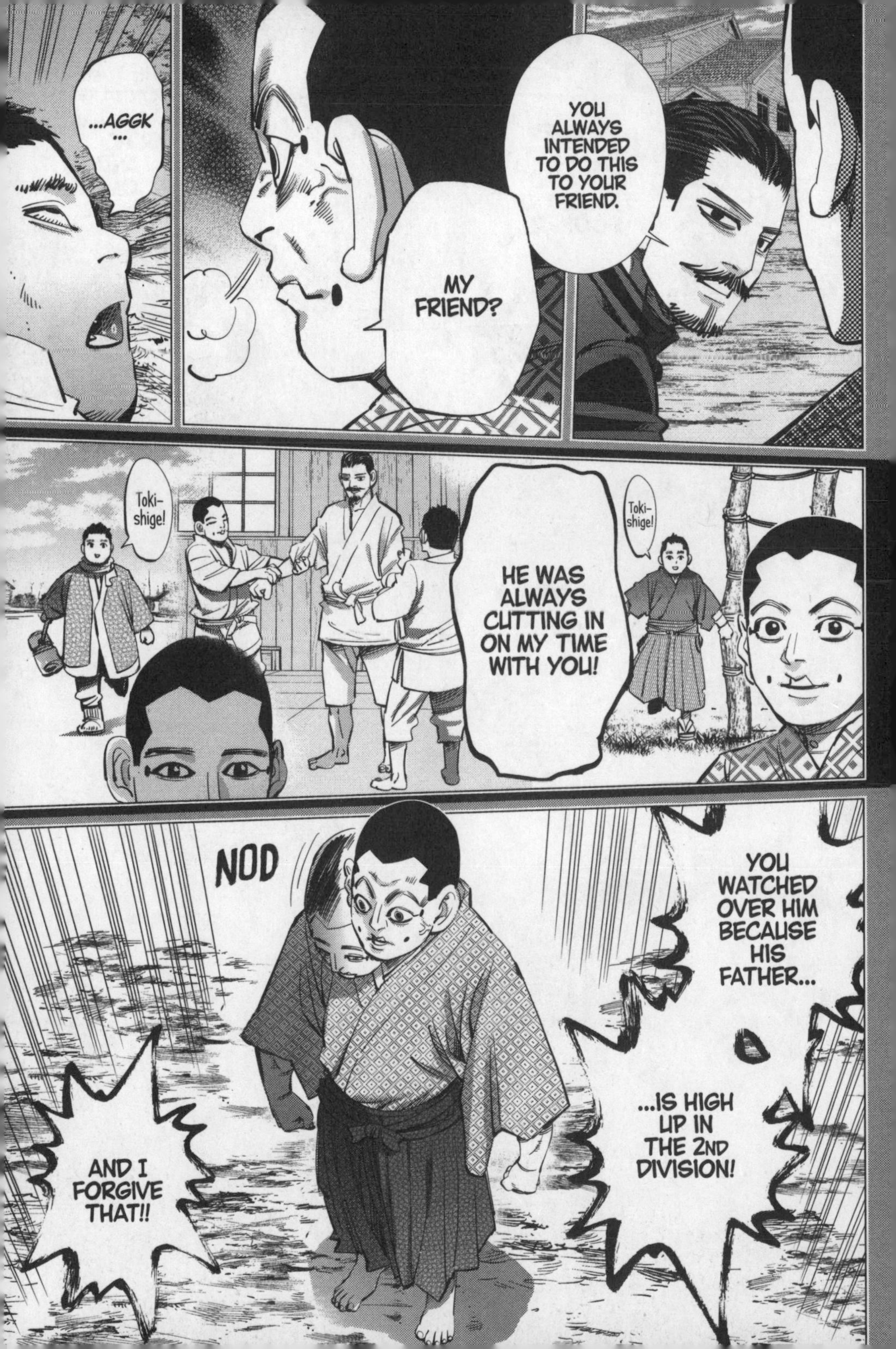
YOU ALWAYS INTENDED TO DO THIS TO YOUR FRIEND.
MY FRIEND?
...AGGK ...
Toki-shige!
HE WAS ALWAYS CUTTING IN ON MY TIME WITH YOU!
Toki-shige!
YOU WATCHED OVER HIM BECAUSE HIS FATHER...
...IS HIGH UP IN THE 2ND DIVISION!
NOD
AND I FORGIVE THAT!!

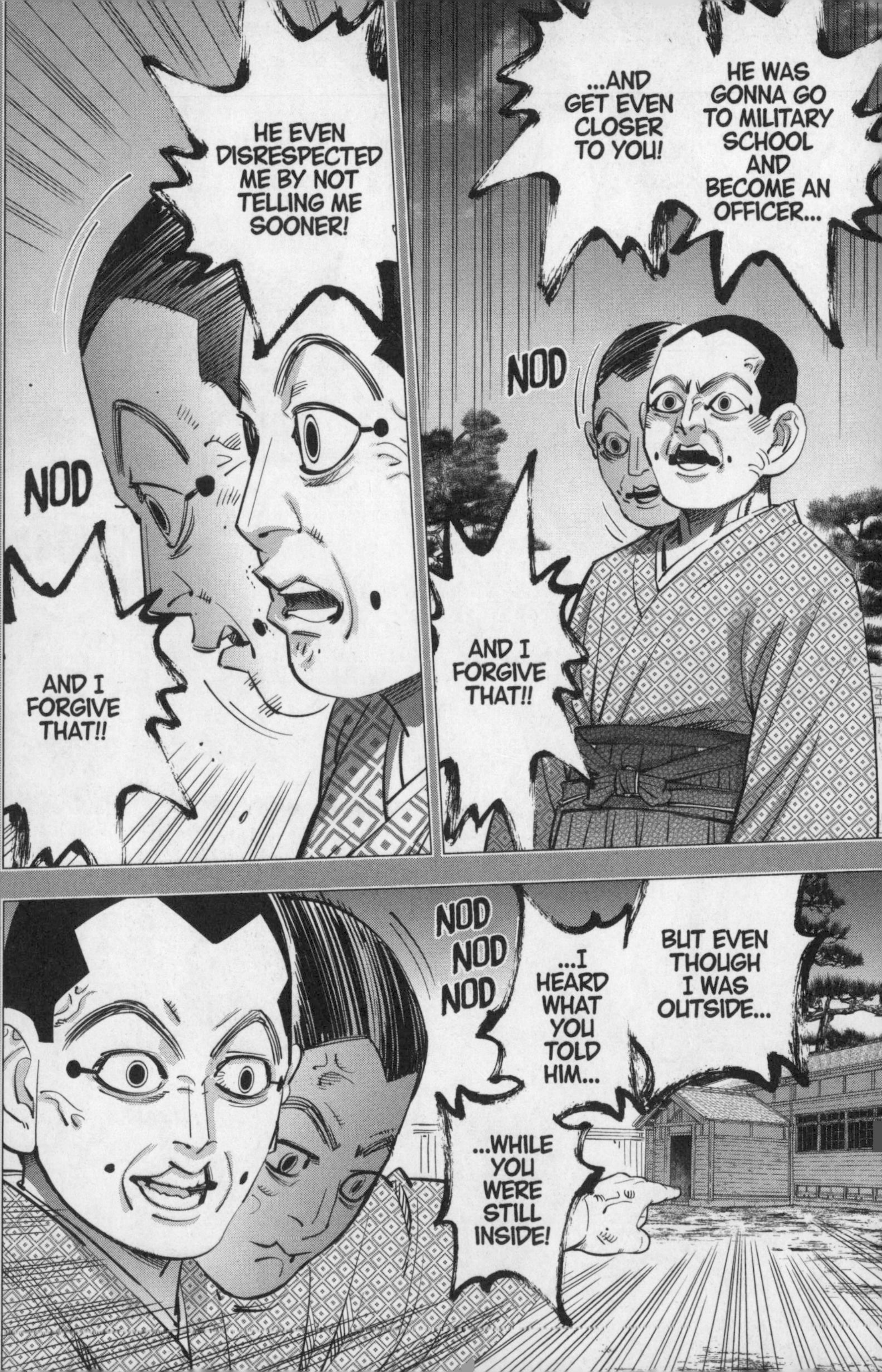
HE WAS GONNA GO TO MILITARY SCHOOL AND BECOME AN OFFICER...
...AND GET EVEN CLOSER TO YOU!
NOD
AND I FORGIVE THAT!!
HE EVEN DISRESPECTED ME BY NOT TELLING ME SOONER!
NOD
AND I FORGIVE THAT!!
BUT EVEN THOUGH I WAS OUTSIDE...
...I HEARD WHAT YOU TOLD HIM...
...WHILE YOU WERE STILL INSIDE!
NOD NOD NOD

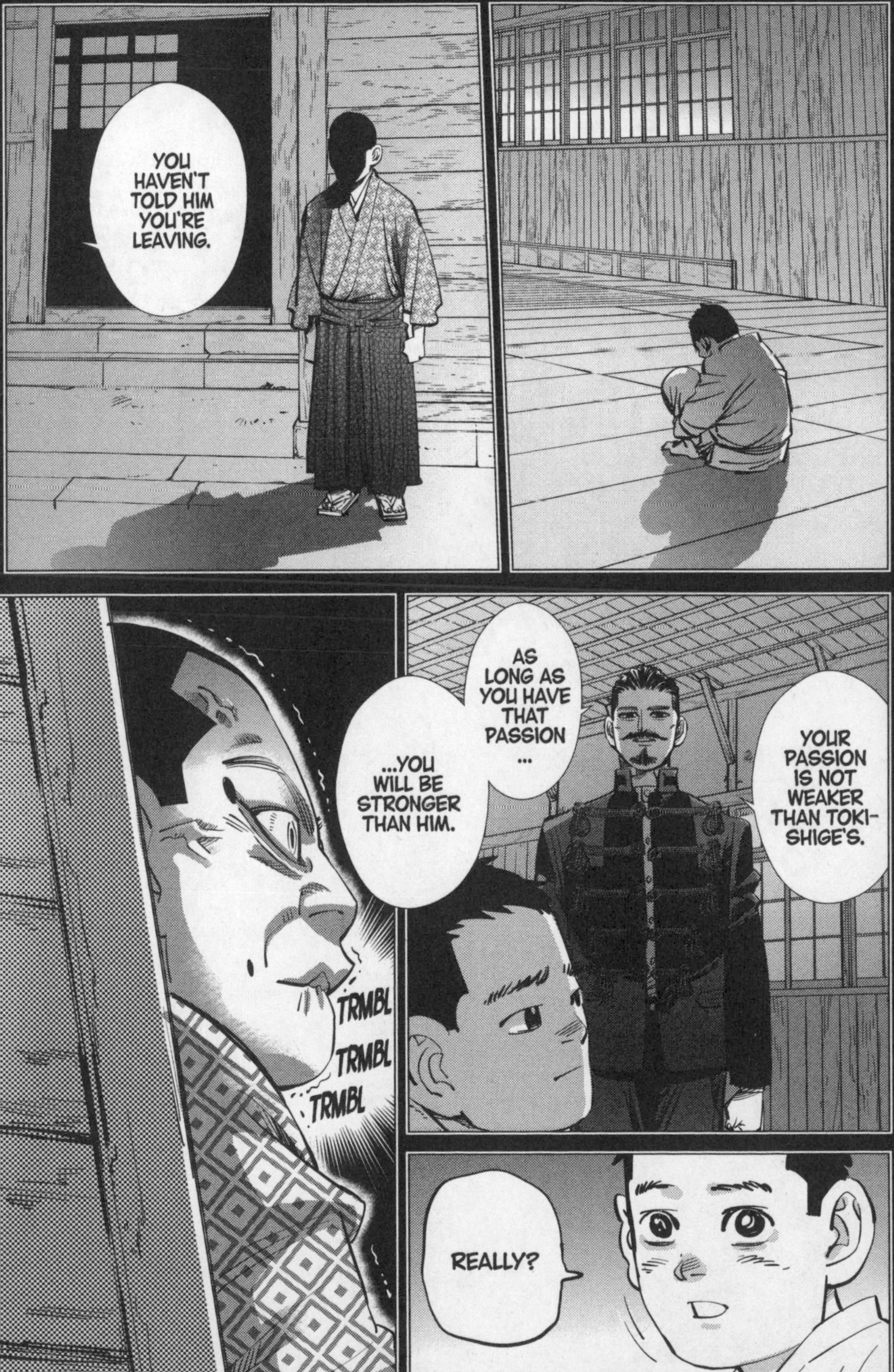
YOU HAVEN'T TOLD HIM YOU'RE LEAVING.
YOUR PASSION IS NOT WEAKER THAN TOKI-SHIGE'S.
AS LONG AS YOU HAVE THAT PASSION ...
...YOU WILL BE STRONGER THAN HIM.
REALLY?
TRMBL
TRMBL
TRMBL

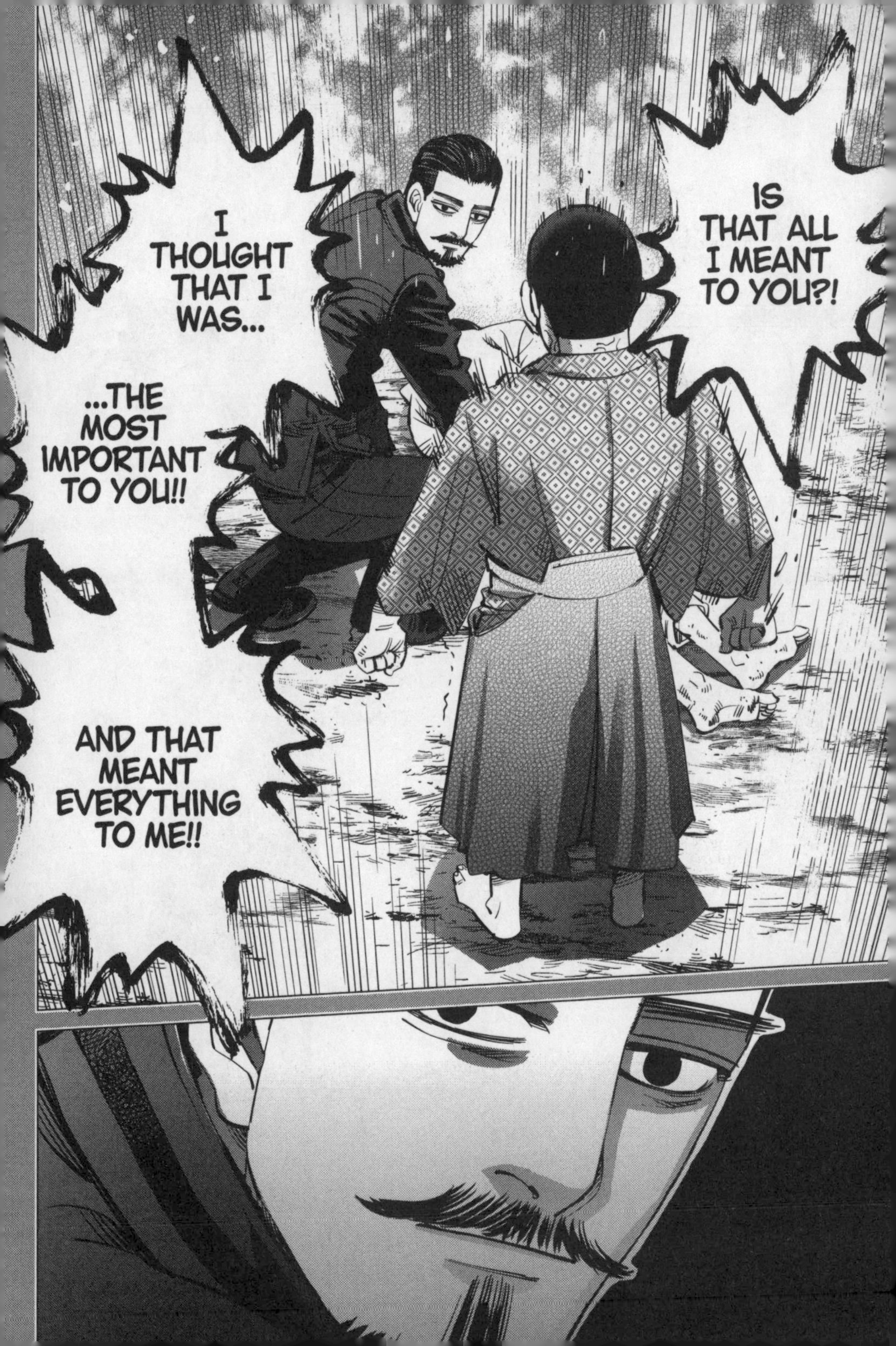
IS THAT ALL I MEANT TO YOU?!
I THOUGHT THAT I WAS...
...THE MOST IMPORTANT TO YOU!!
AND THAT MEANT EVERYTHING TO ME!!

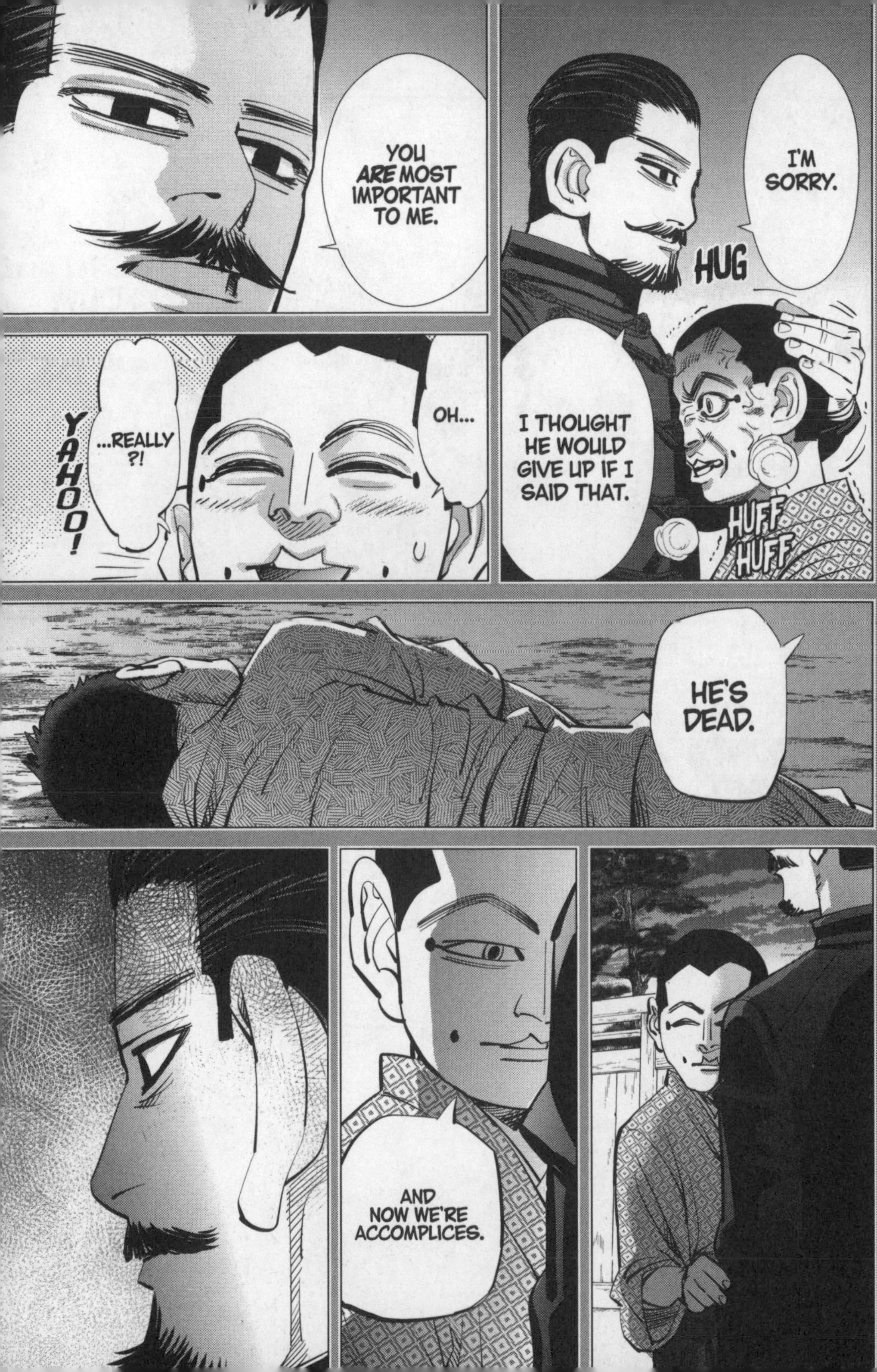
I'M SORRY.
HUG
I THOUGHT HE WOULD GIVE UP IF I SAID THAT.
HUFF HUFF
YOU ARE MOST IMPORTANT TO ME.
OH...
...REALLY ?!
YAHOO!
HE'S DEAD.
AND NOW WE'RE ACCOMPLICES.

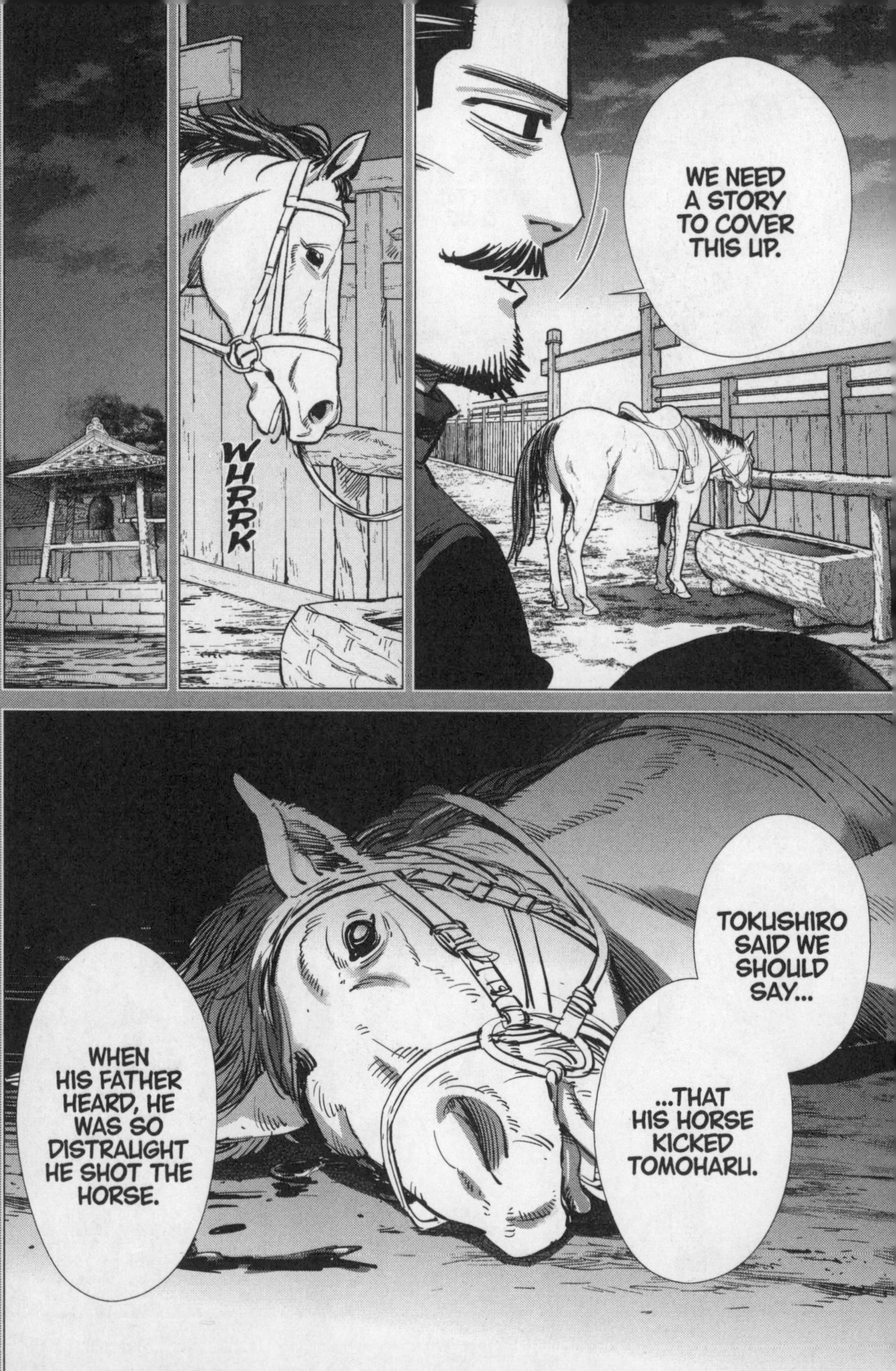
WE NEED A STORY TO COVER THIS UP.
WHRRK
TOKUSHIRO SAID WE SHOULD SAY...
...THAT HIS HORSE KICKED TOMOHARU.
WHEN HIS FATHER HEARD, HE WAS SO DISTRAUGHT HE SHOT THE HORSE.

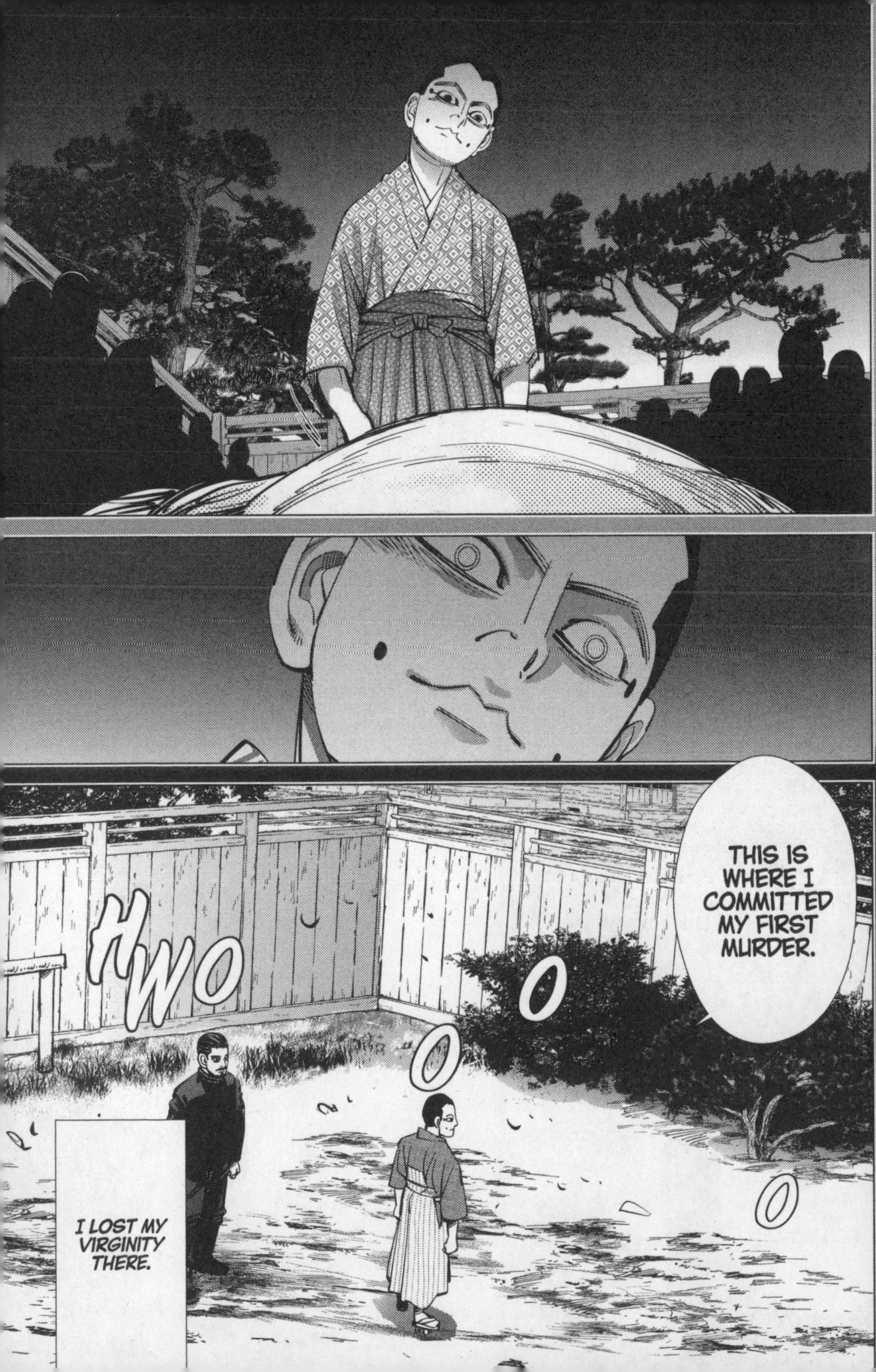
THIS IS WHERE I COMMITTED MY FIRST MURDER.
HWOOOO
I LOST MY VIRGINITY THERE.

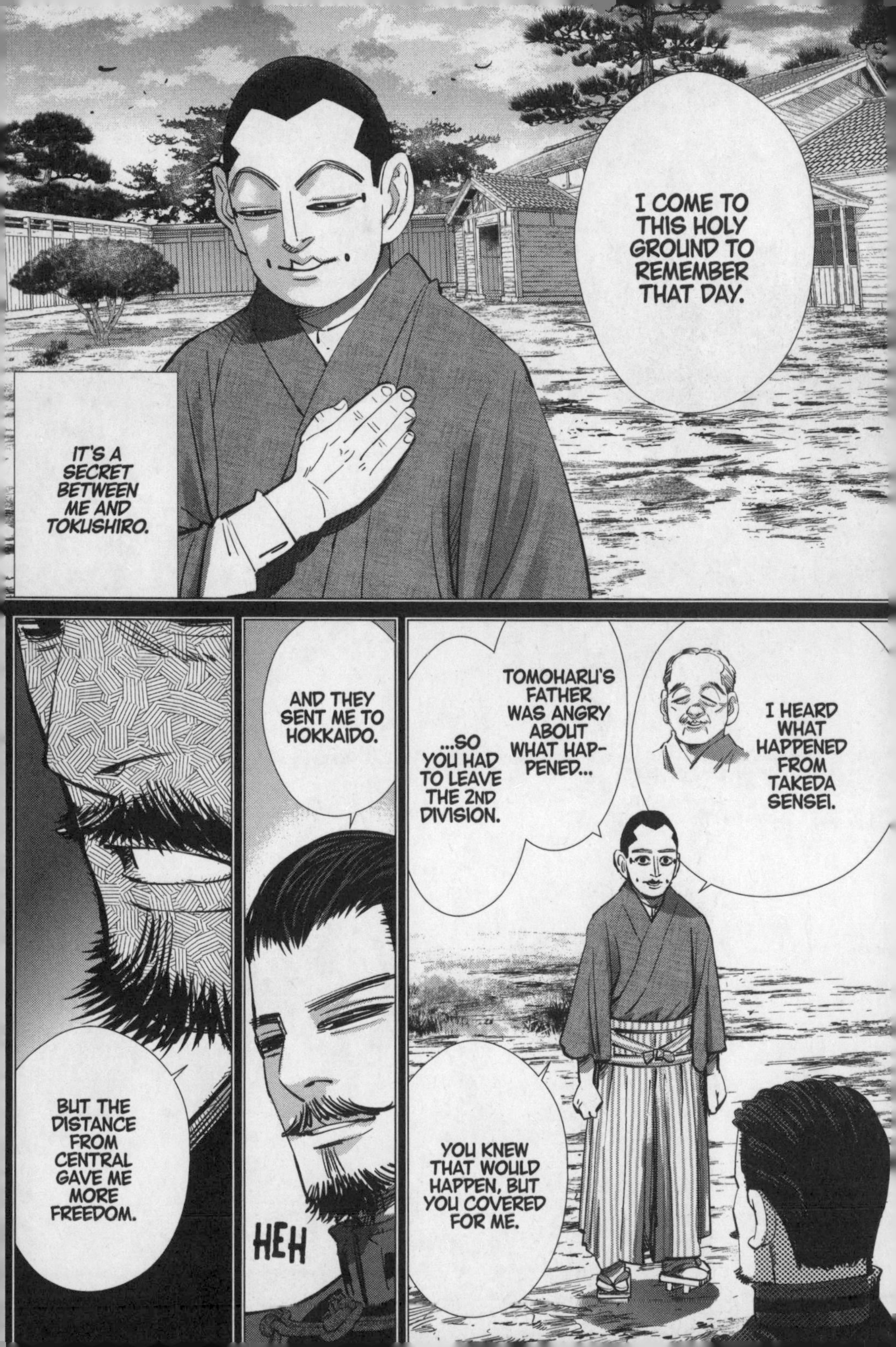
I COME TO THIS HOLY GROUND TO REMEMBER THAT DAY.
IT'S A SECRET BETWEEN ME AND TOKUSHIRO.
I HEARD WHAT HAPPENED FROM TAKEDA SENSEI.
TOMOHARU'S FATHER WAS ANGRY ABOUT WHAT HAP-PENED...
...SO YOU HAD TO LEAVE THE 2ND DIVISION.
YOU KNEW THAT WOULD HAPPEN, BUT YOU COVERED FOR ME.
AND THEY SENT ME TO HOKKAIDO.
HEH
BUT THE DISTANCE FROM CENTRAL GAVE ME MORE FREEDOM.

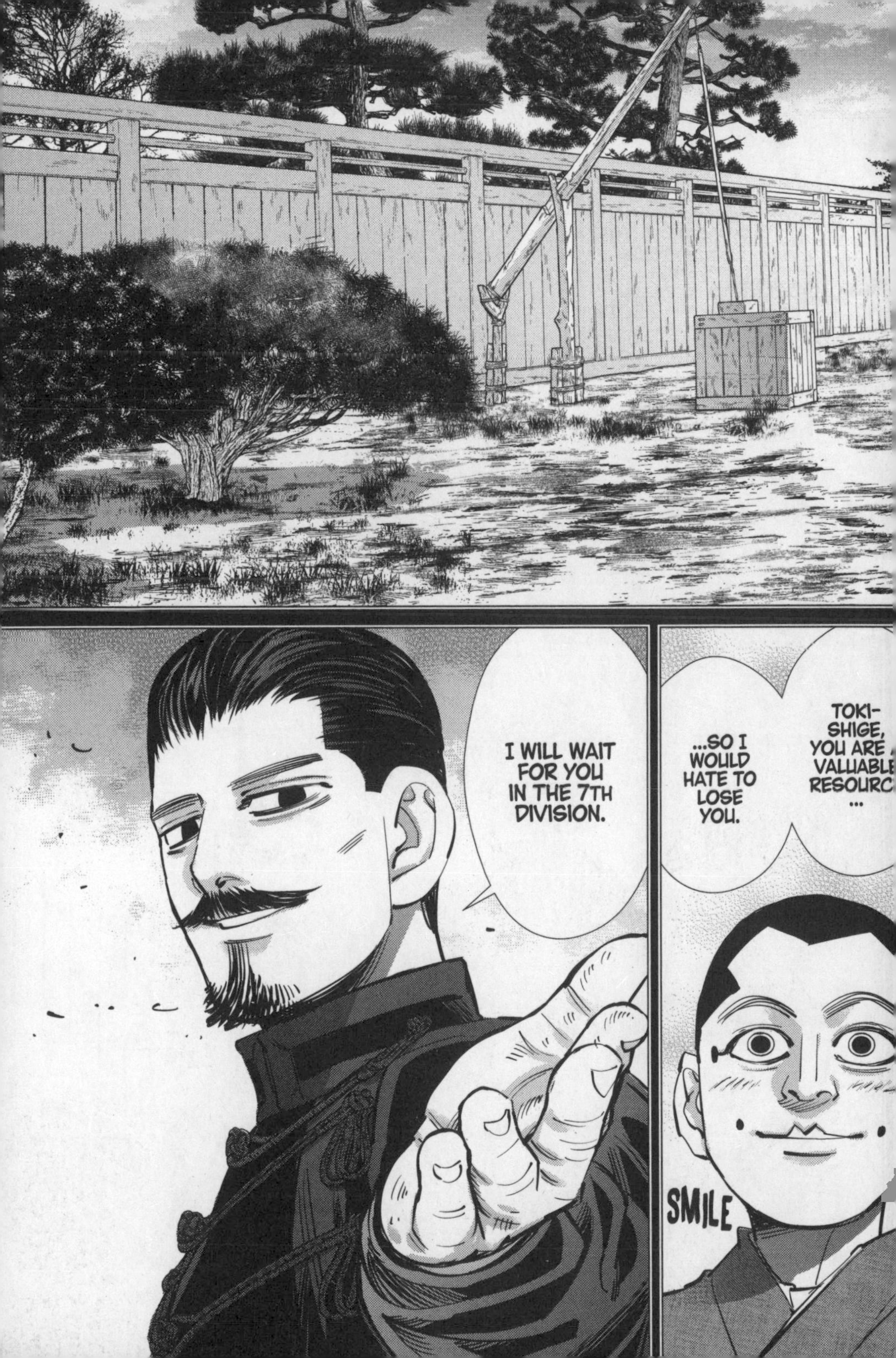
TOKI-SHIGE, YOU ARE VALUABL RESOURC ...
...SO I WOULD HATE TO LOSE YOU.
SMILE
I WILL WAIT FOR YOU IN THE 7TH DIVISION.

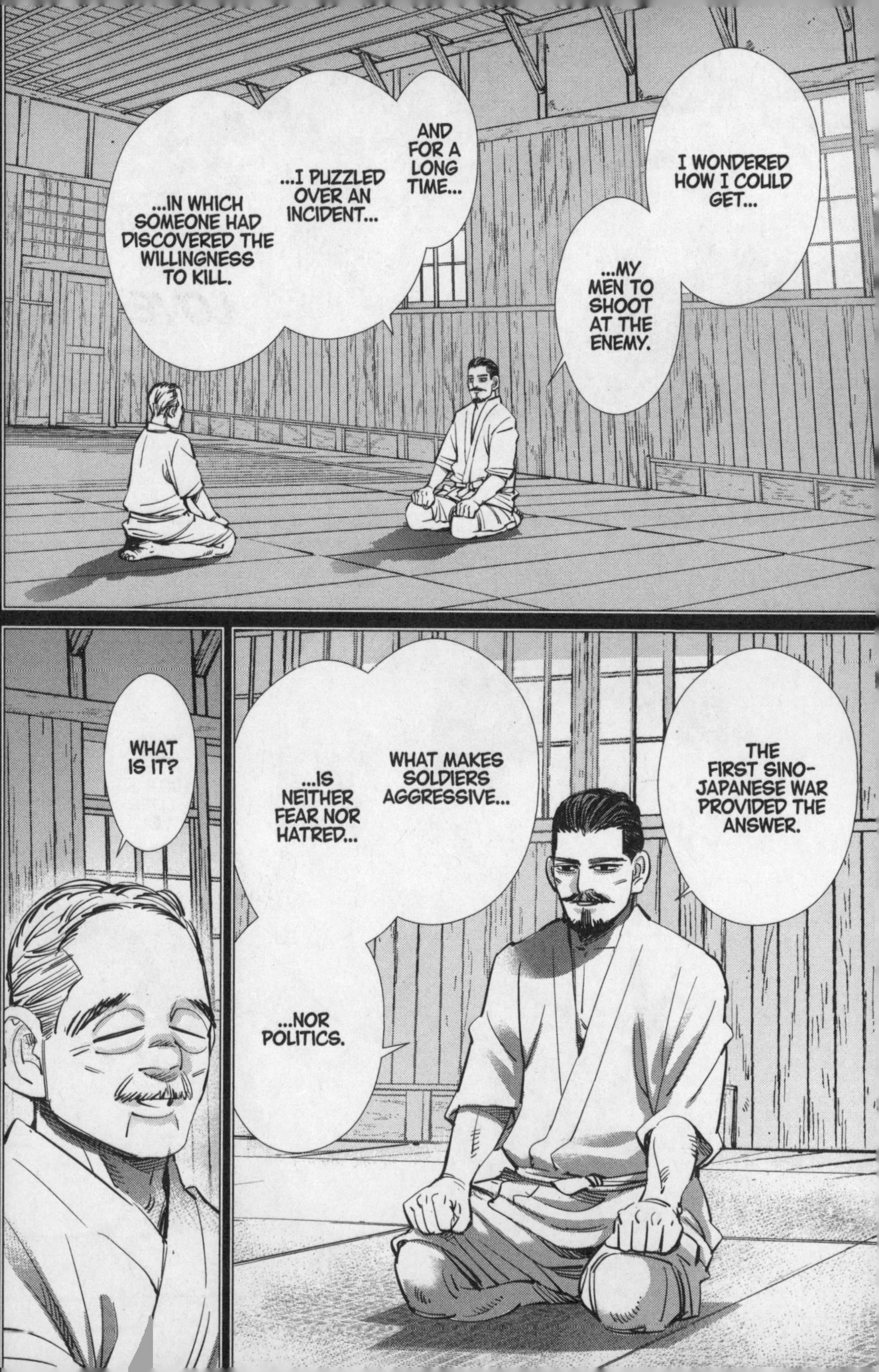
I WONDERED HOW I COULD GET...
...MY MEN TO SHOOT AT THE ENEMY.
AND FOR A LONG TIME...
...I PUZZLED OVER AN INCIDENT...
...IN WHICH SOMEONE HAD DISCOVERED THE WILLINGNESS TO KILL.
THE FIRST SINO-JAPANESE WAR PROVIDED THE ANSWER.
WHAT MAKES SOLDIERS AGGRESSIVE...
...IS NEITHER FEAR NOR HATRED...
...NOR POLITICS.
WHAT IS IT?

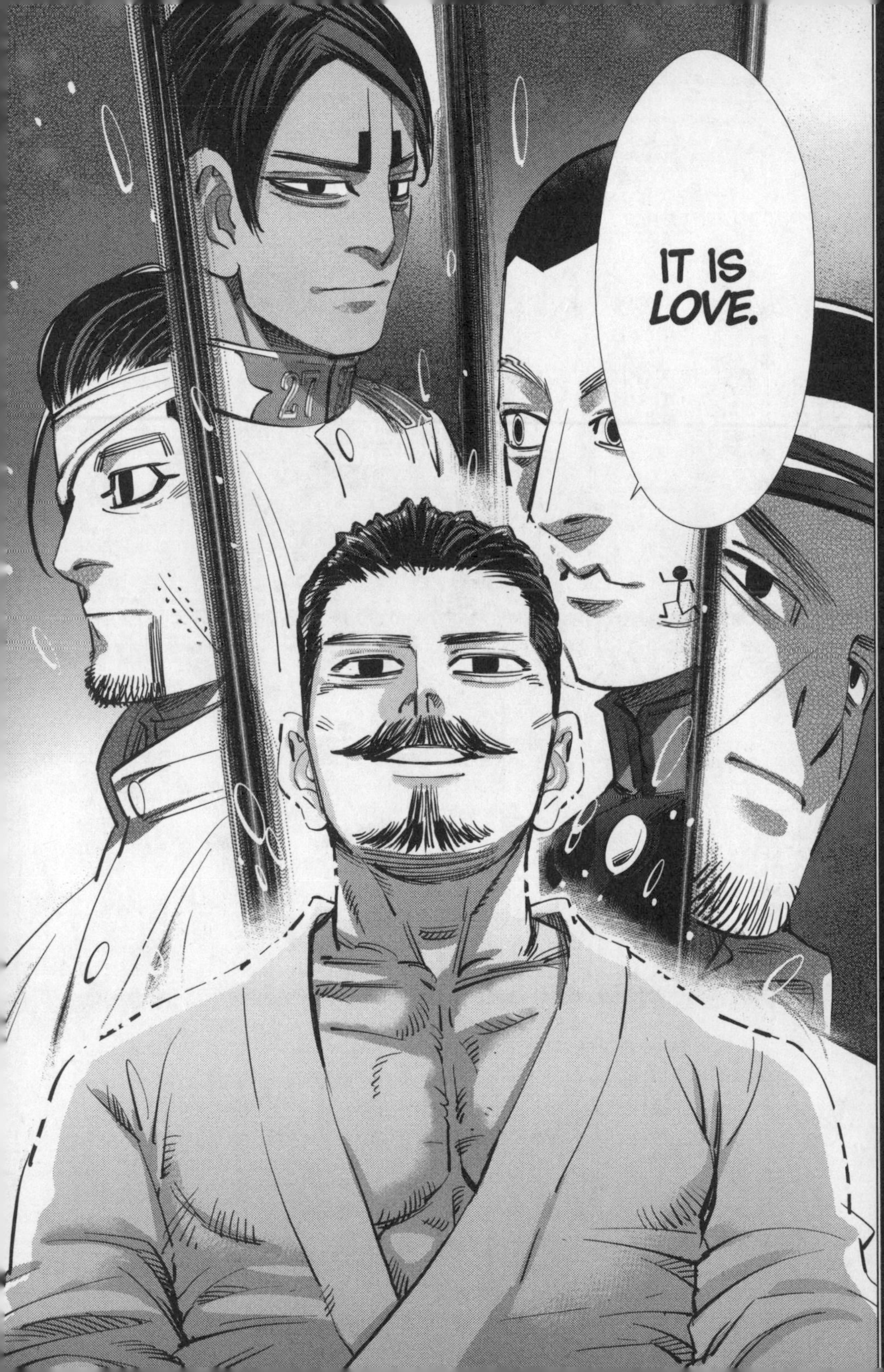
IT IS LOVE.

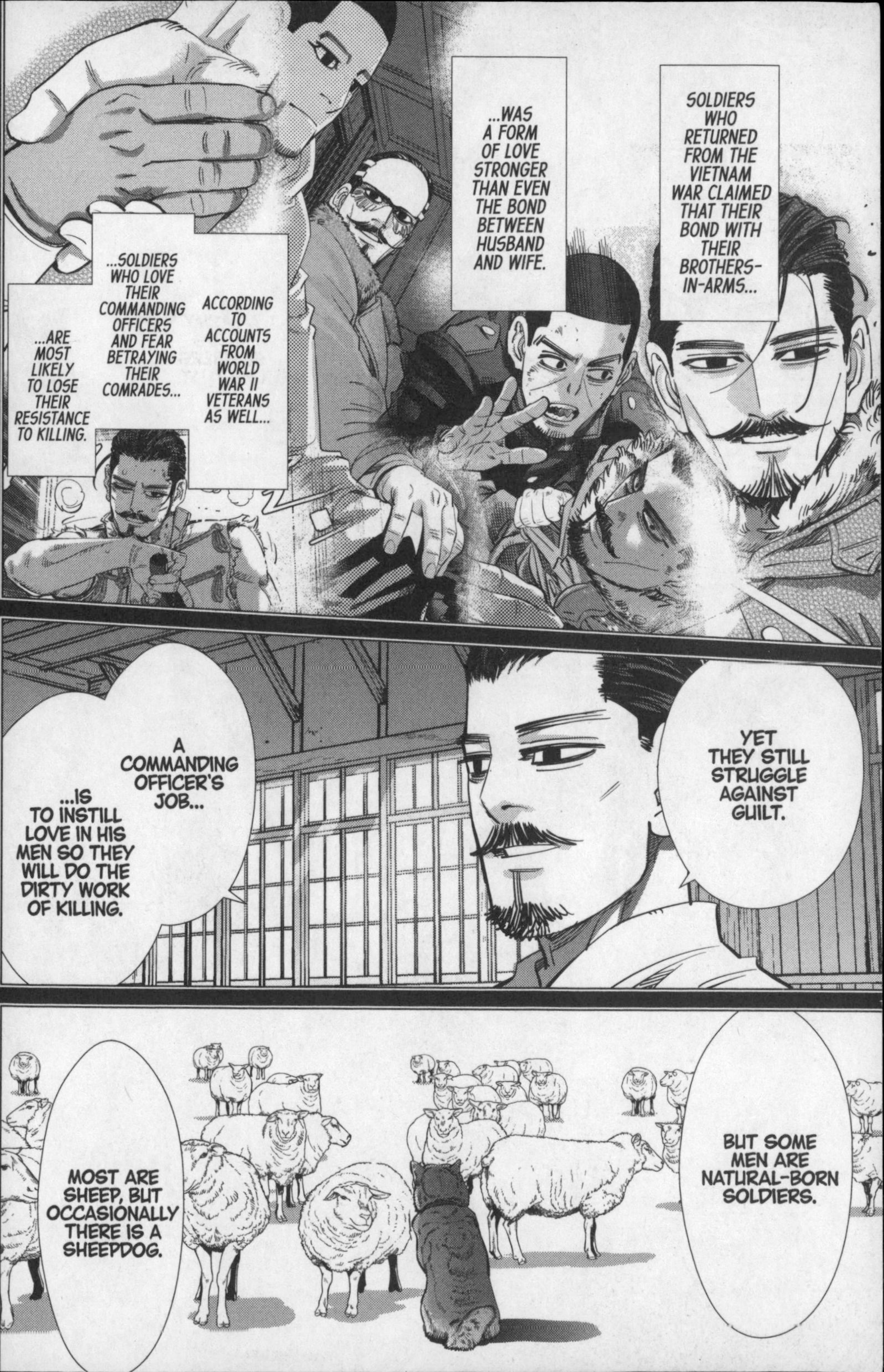
SOLDIERS WHO RETURNED FROM THE VIETNAM WAR CLAIMED THAT THEIR BOND WITH THEIR BROTHERS-IN-ARMS...
...WAS A FORM OF LOVE STRONGER THAN EVEN THE BOND BETWEEN HUSBAND AND WIFE.
ACCORDING TO ACCOUNTS FROM WORLD WAR II VETERANS AS WELL...
...SOLDIERS WHO LOVE THEIR COMMANDING OFFICERS AND FEAR BETRAYING THEIR COMRADES...
...ARE MOST LIKELY TO LOSE THEIR RESISTANCE TO KILLING.
YET THEY STILL STRUGGLE AGAINST GUILT.
A COMMANDING OFFICER'S JOB...
...IS TO INSTILL LOVE IN HIS MEN SO THEY WILL DO THE DIRTY WORK OF KILLING.
BUT SOME MEN ARE NATURAL-BORN SOLDIERS.
MOST ARE SHEEP, BUT OCCASIONALLY THERE IS A SHEEPDOG.

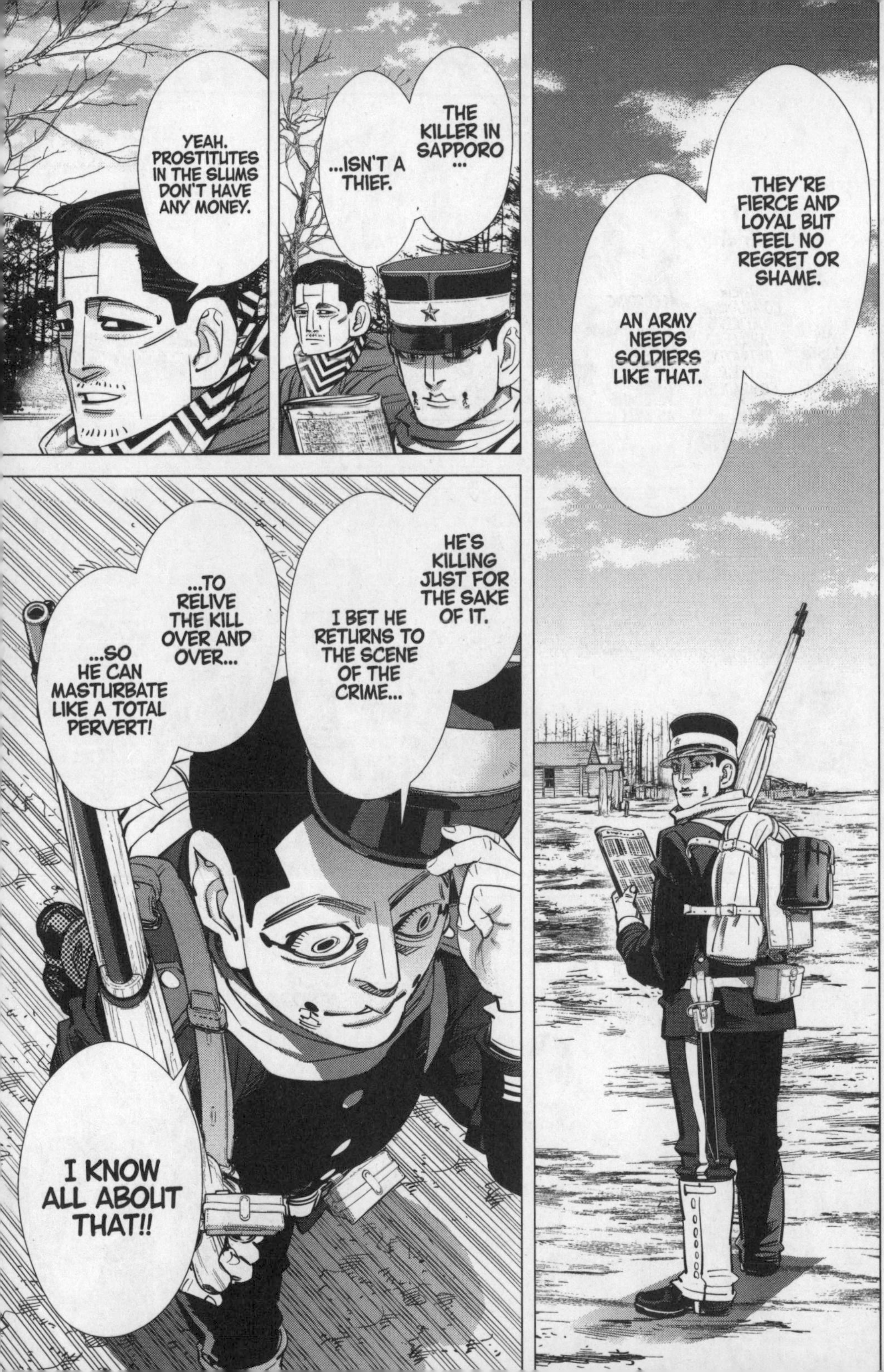
THEY'RE FIERCE AND LOYAL BUT FEEL NO REGRET OR SHAME.
AN ARMY NEEDS SOLDIERS LIKE THAT.
THE KILLER IN SAPPORO ...
...ISN'T A THIEF.
YEAH. PROSTITUTES IN THE SLUMS DON'T HAVE ANY MONEY.
HE'S KILLING JUST FOR THE SAKE OF IT.
I BET HE RETURNS TO THE SCENE OF THE CRIME...
...TO RELIVE THE KILL OVER AND OVER...
...SO HE CAN MASTURBATE LIKE A TOTAL PERVERT!
I KNOW ALL ABOUT THAT!!

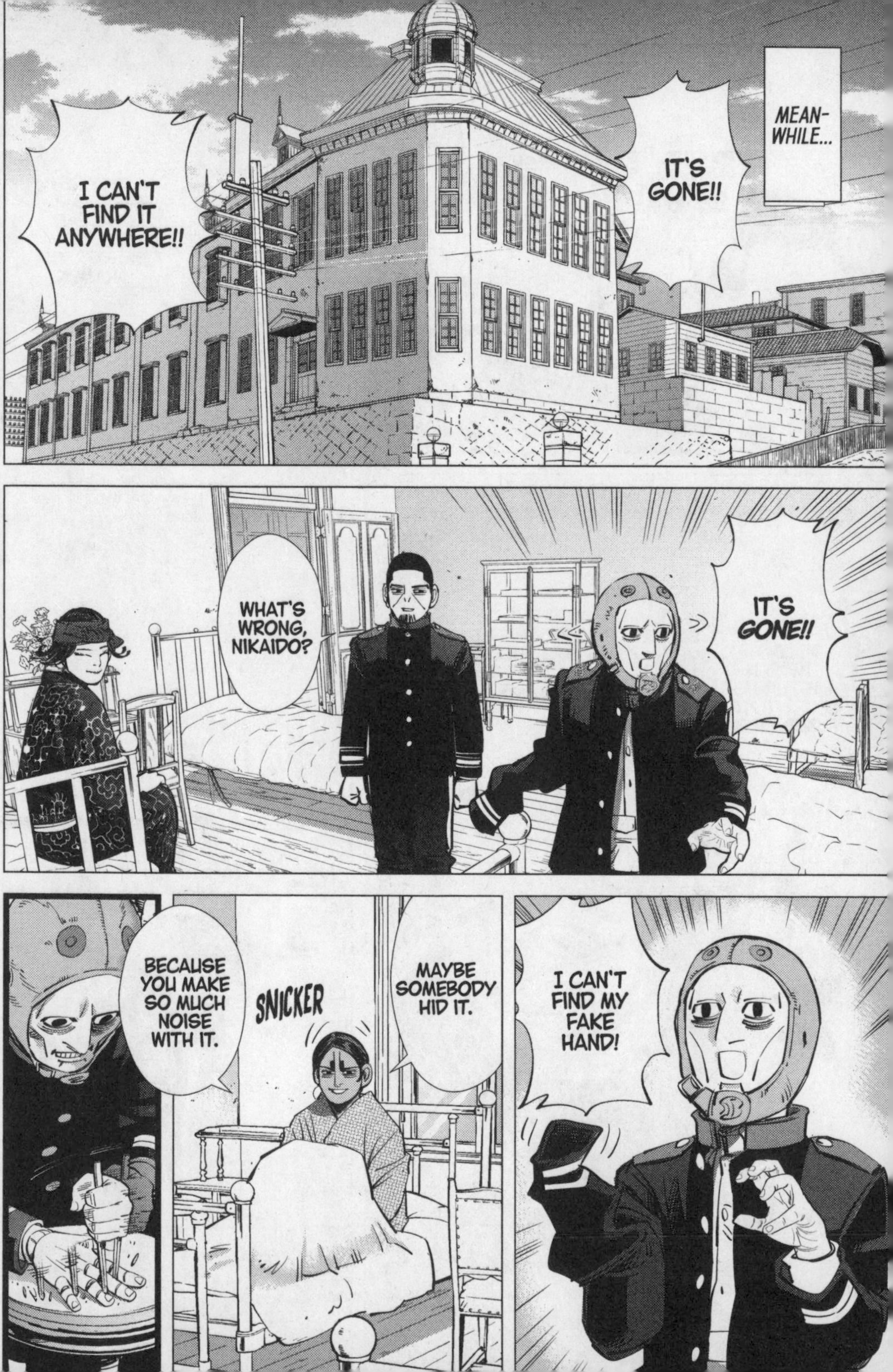
MEAN-WHILE...
IT'S GONE!!
I CAN'T FIND IT ANYWHERE!!
IT'S GONE!!
WHAT'S WRONG, NIKAIDO?
I CAN'T FIND MY FAKE HAND!
MAYBE SOMEBODY HID IT.
SNICKER
BECAUSE YOU MAKE SO MUCH NOISE WITH IT.

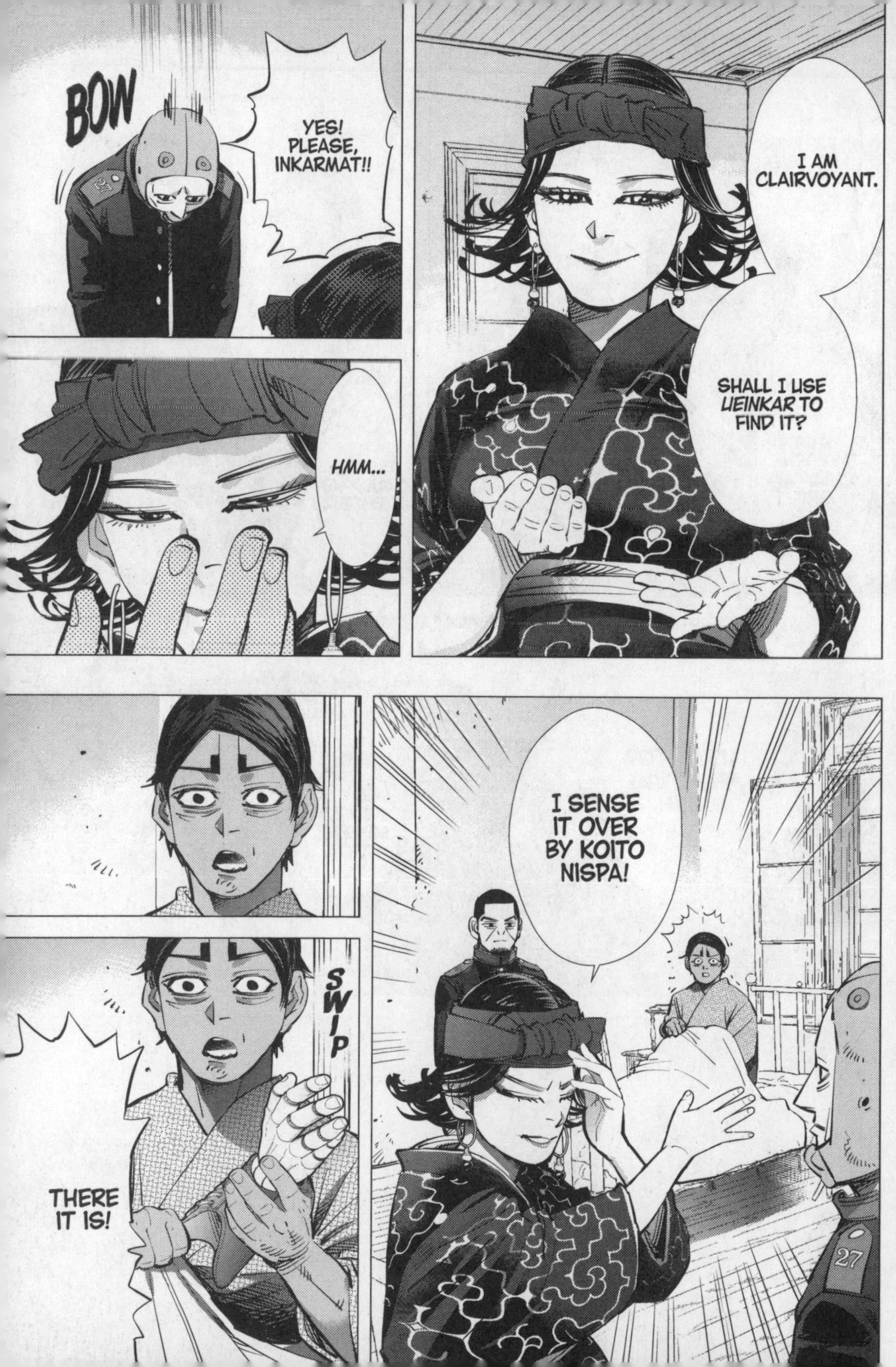
I AM CLAIRVOYANT.
SHALL I USE UEINKAR TO FIND IT?
BOW
YES! PLEASE, INKARMAT!!
HMM...
I SENSE IT OVER BY KOITO NISPA!
SWIP
THERE IT IS!

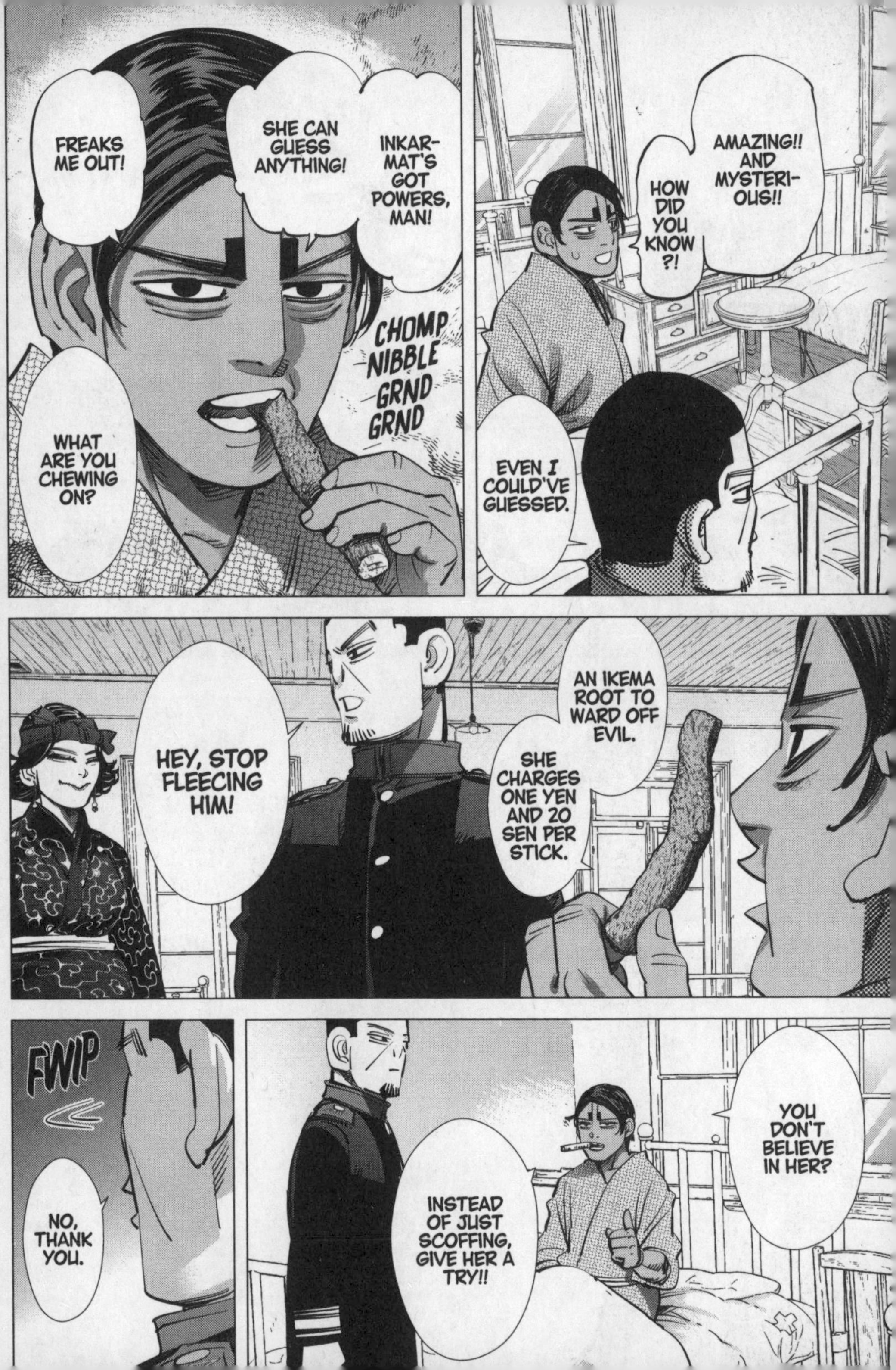
AMAZING!! AND MYSTERIOUS!!
HOW DID YOU KNOW?!
EVEN I COULD'VE GUESSED.
SHE CAN GUESS ANYTHING! INKARMAT'S GOT POWERS, MAN!
FREAKS ME OUT!
CHOMP NIBBLE GRND GRND
WHAT ARE YOU CHEWING ON?
AN IKEMA ROOT TO WARD OFF EVIL.
SHE CHARGES ONE YEN AND 20 SEN PER STICK.
HEY, STOP FLEECING HIM!
YOU DON'T BELIEVE IN HER?
INSTEAD OF JUST SCOFFING, GIVE HER A TRY!!
FWIP
NO, THANK YOU.

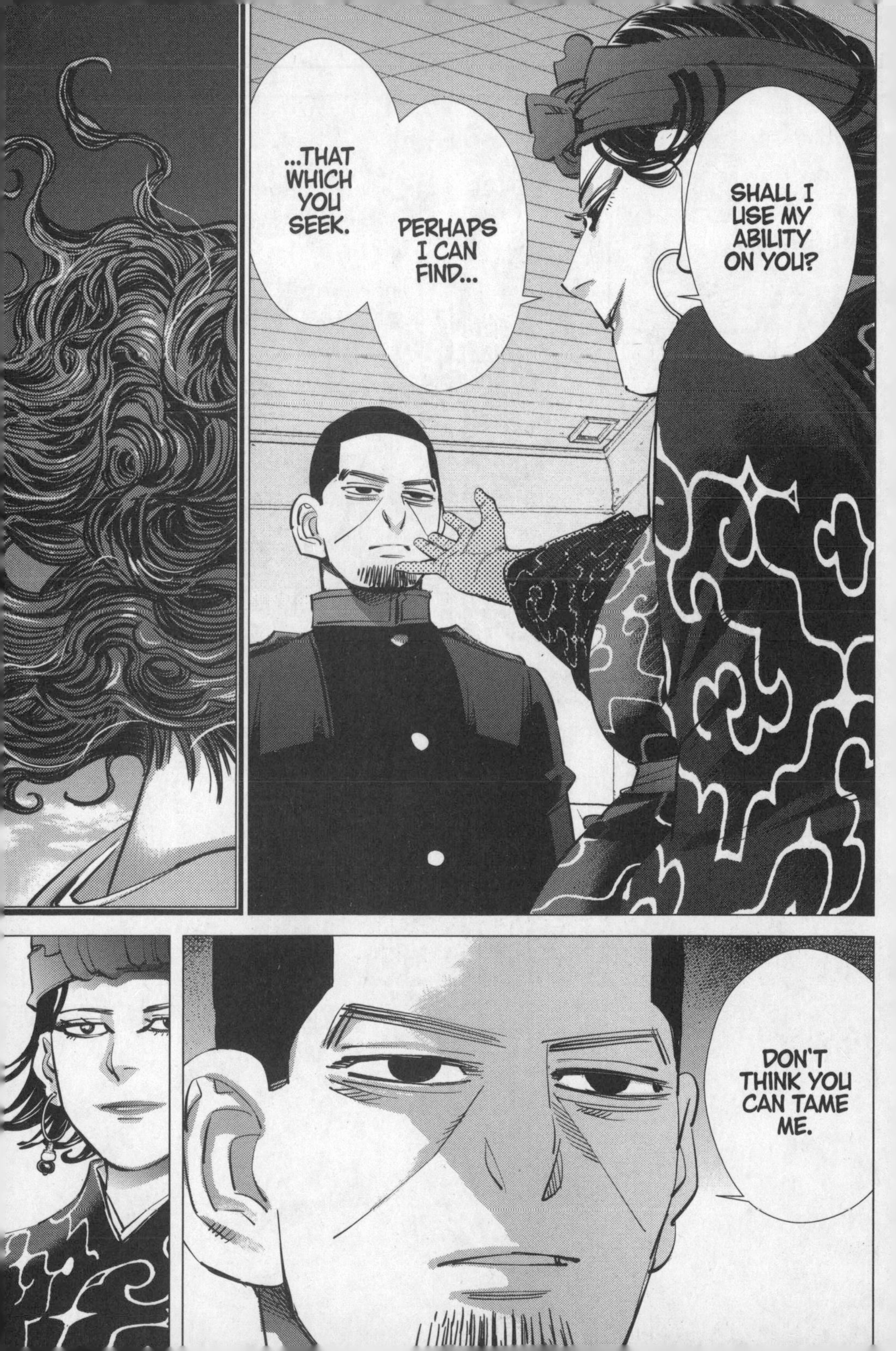
SHALL I USE MY ABILITY ON YOU?
PERHAPS I CAN FIND...
...THAT WHICH YOU SEEK.
DON'T THINK YOU CAN TAME ME.

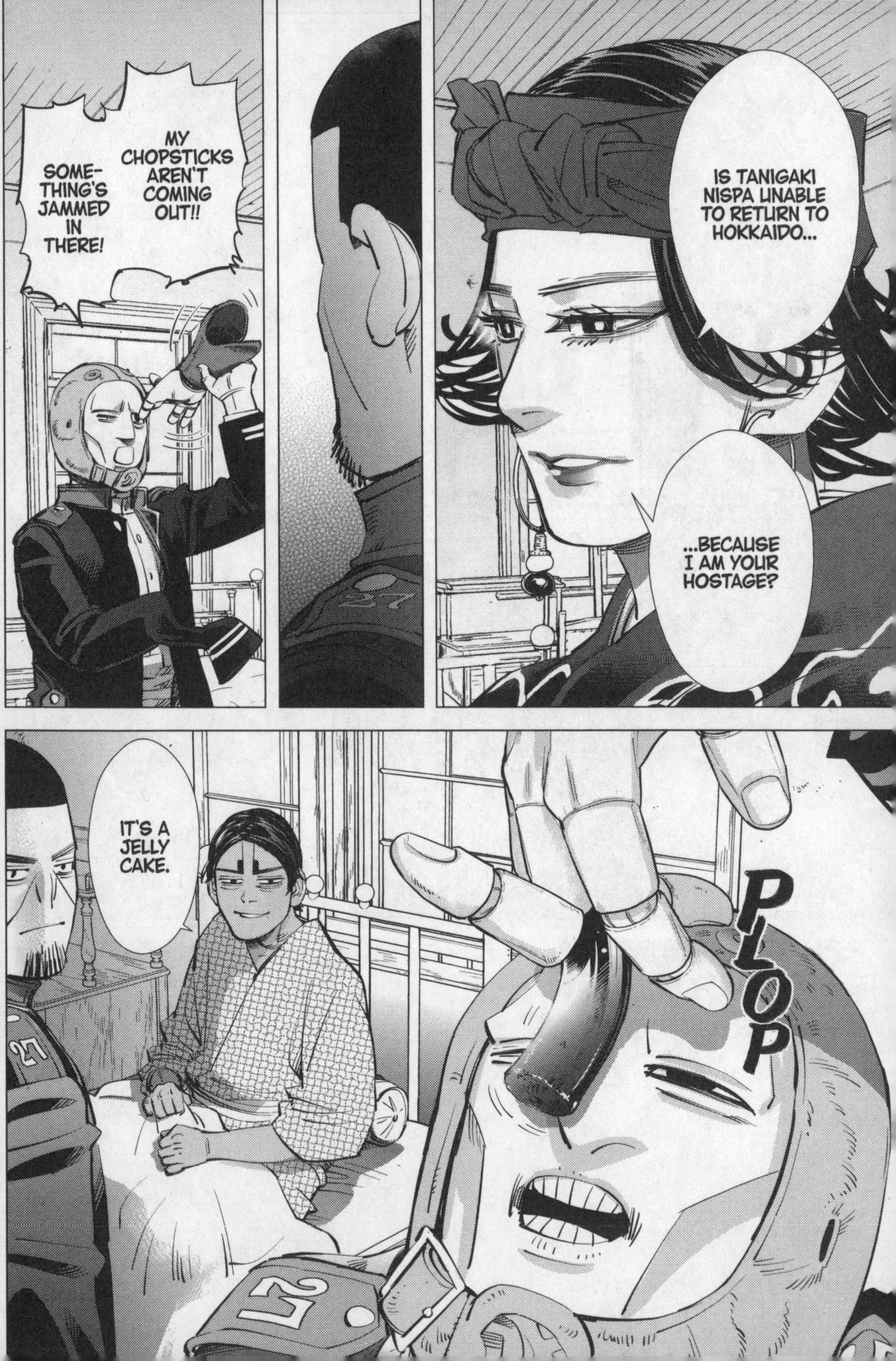
IS TANIGAKI NISPA UNABLE TO RETURN TO HOKKAIDO...
...BECAUSE I AM YOUR HOSTAGE?
MY CHOPSTICKS AREN'T COMING OUT!!
SOME-THING'S JAMMED IN THERE!
PLOP
IT'S A JELLY CAKE.

Chapter 228: Long-Tailed Tit

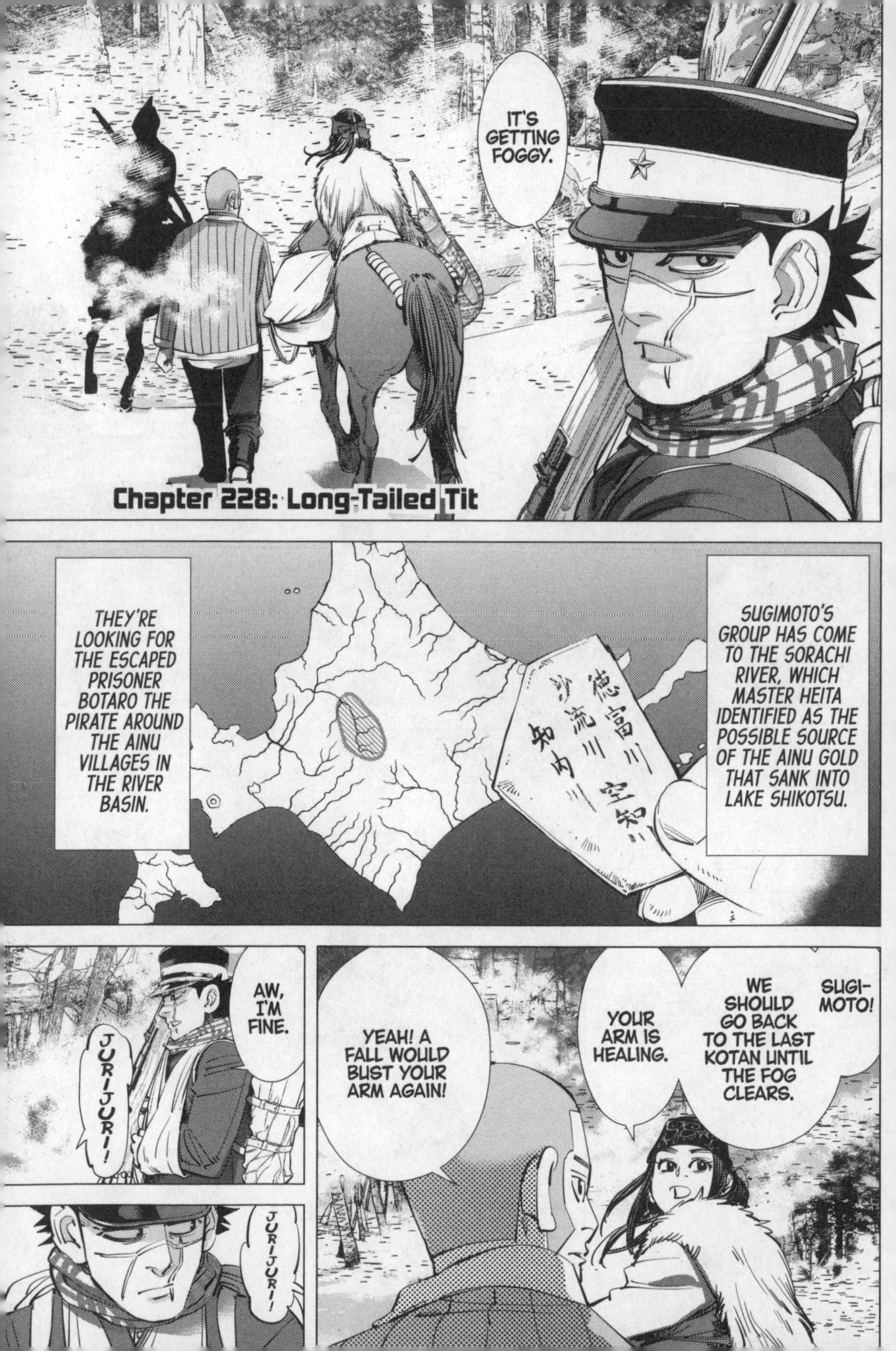
IT'S GETTING FOGGY.
Chapter 228: Long-Tailed Tit
SUGIMOTO'S GROUP HAS COME TO THE SORACHI RIVER, WHICH MASTER HEITA IDENTIFIED AS THE POSSIBLE SOURCE OF THE AINU GOLD THAT SANK INTO LAKE SHIKOTSU.
THEY'RE LOOKING FOR THE ESCAPED PRISONER BOTARO THE PIRATE AROUND THE AINU VILLAGES IN THE RIVER BASIN.
SUGI-MOTO!
WE SHOULD GO BACK TO THE LAST KOTAN UNTIL THE FOG CLEARS.
YOUR ARM IS HEALING.
YEAH! A FALL WOULD BUST YOUR ARM AGAIN!
AW, I'M FINE.
JURIJURI!
JURIJURI!

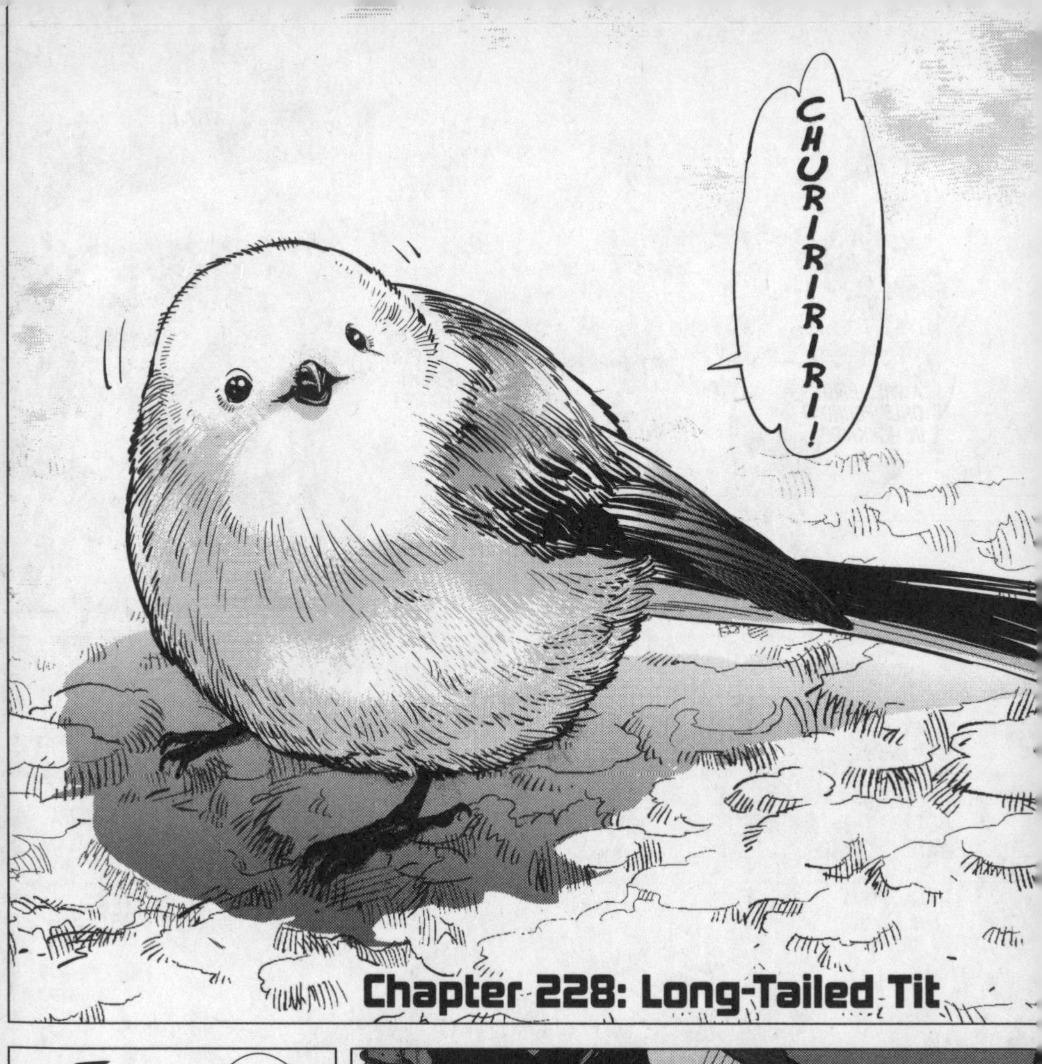
CHURIRIRIRI!

Chapter 228: Long-Tailed Tit

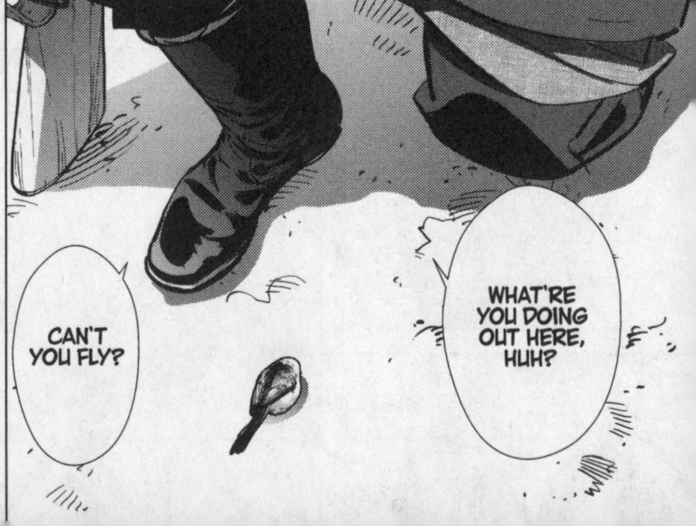
WHAT'RE YOU DOING OUT HERE, HUH?
CAN'T YOU FLY?

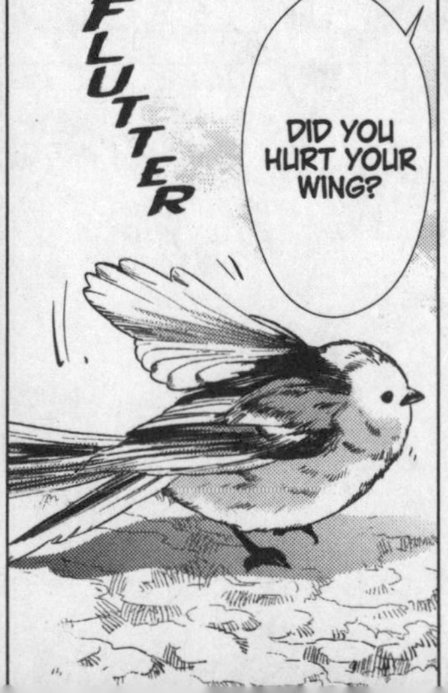
DID YOU HURT YOUR WING?
FLUTTER

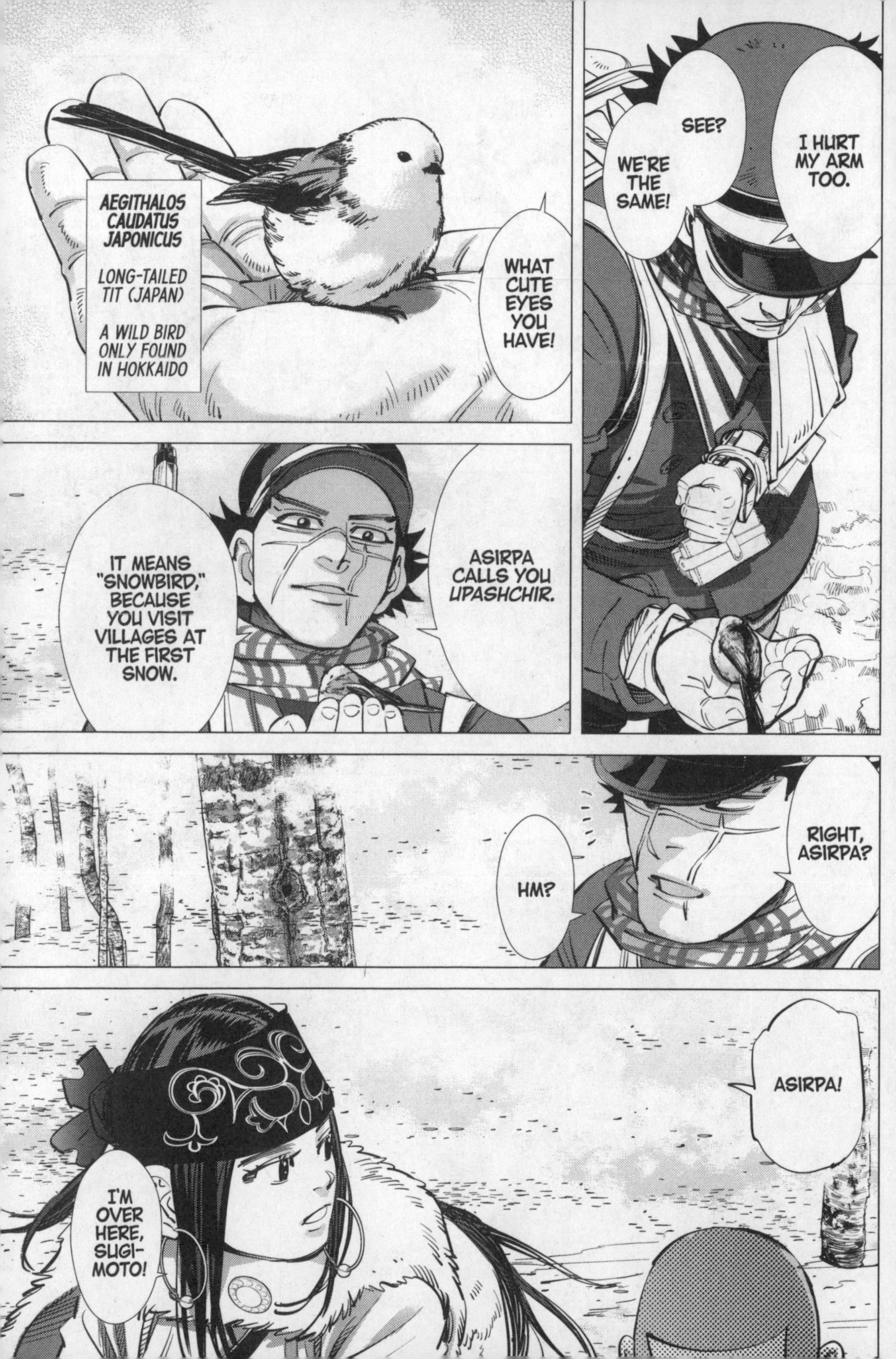
I HURT MY ARM TOO.
SEE?
WE'RE THE SAME!
WHAT CUTE EYES YOU HAVE!
AEGITHALOS CAUDATUS JAPONICUS
LONG-TAILED TIT (JAPAN)
A WILD BIRD ONLY FOUND IN HOKKAIDO
ASIRPA CALLS YOU UPASHCHIR.
IT MEANS "SNOWBIRD," BECAUSE YOU VISIT VILLAGES AT THE FIRST SNOW.
RIGHT, ASIRPA?
HM?
ASIRPA!
I'M OVER HERE, SUGI-MOTO!

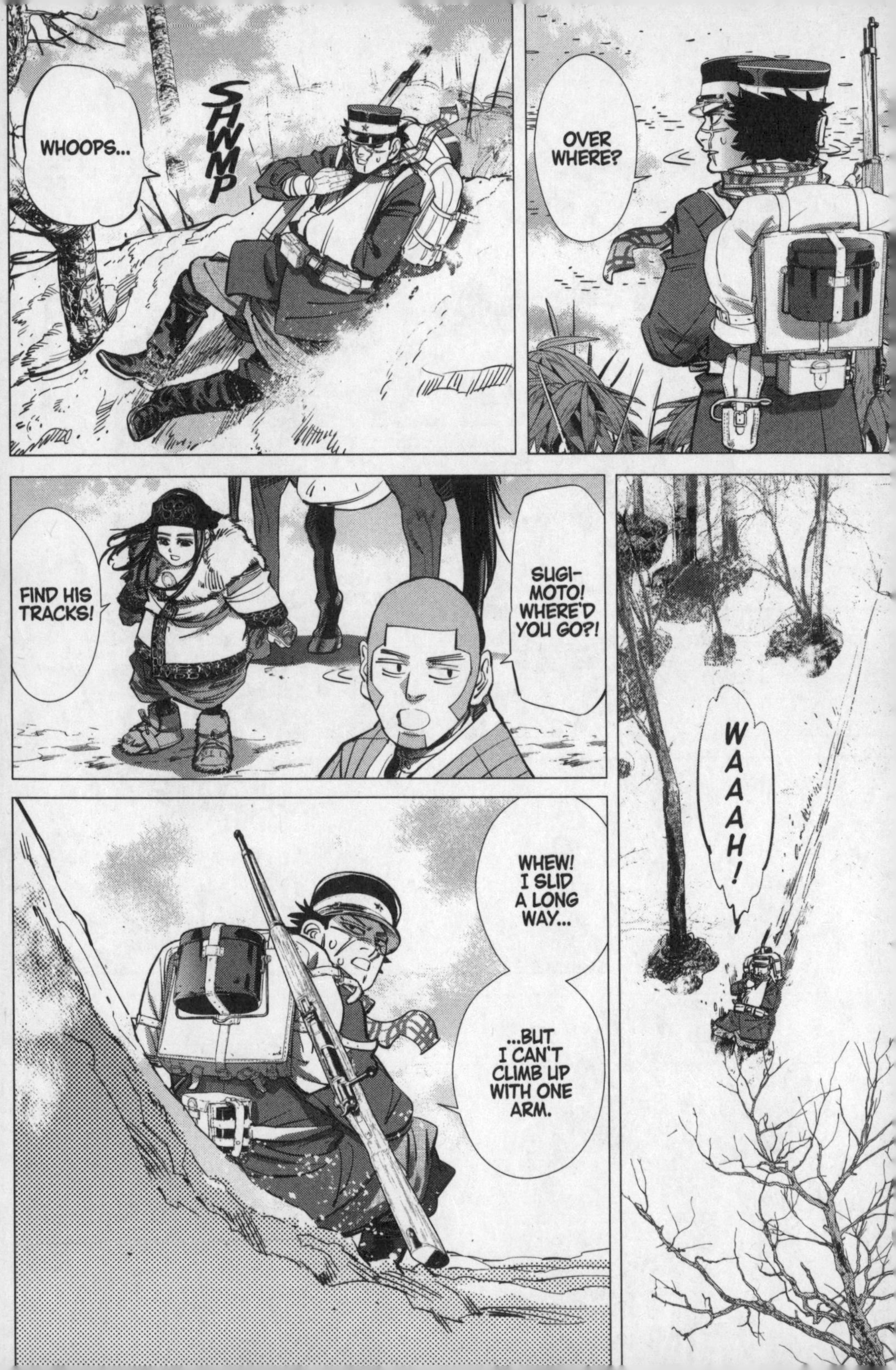
OVER WHERE?
WHOOPS...
SHWMP
WAAAAH!
SUGI-MOTO! WHERE'D YOU GO?!
FIND HIS TRACKS!
WHEW! I SLID A LONG WAY...
...BUT I CAN'T CLIMB UP WITH ONE ARM.

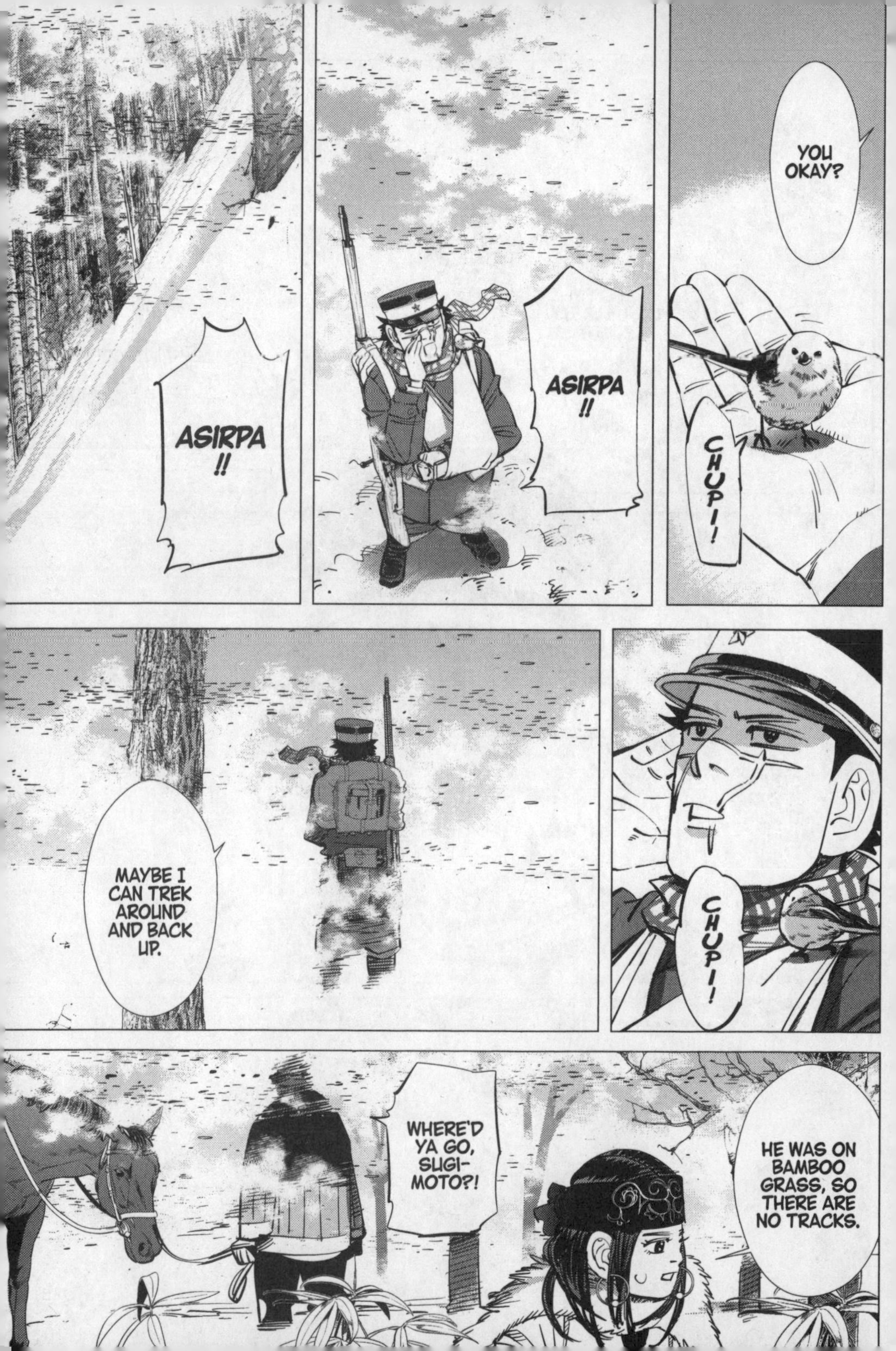
YOU OKAY?
CHUPI!
ASIRPA !!
ASIRPA !!
CHUPI!
MAYBE I CAN TREK AROUND AND BACK UP.
HE WAS ON BAMBOO GRASS, SO THERE ARE NO TRACKS.
WHERE'D YA GO, SUGI-MOTO?!

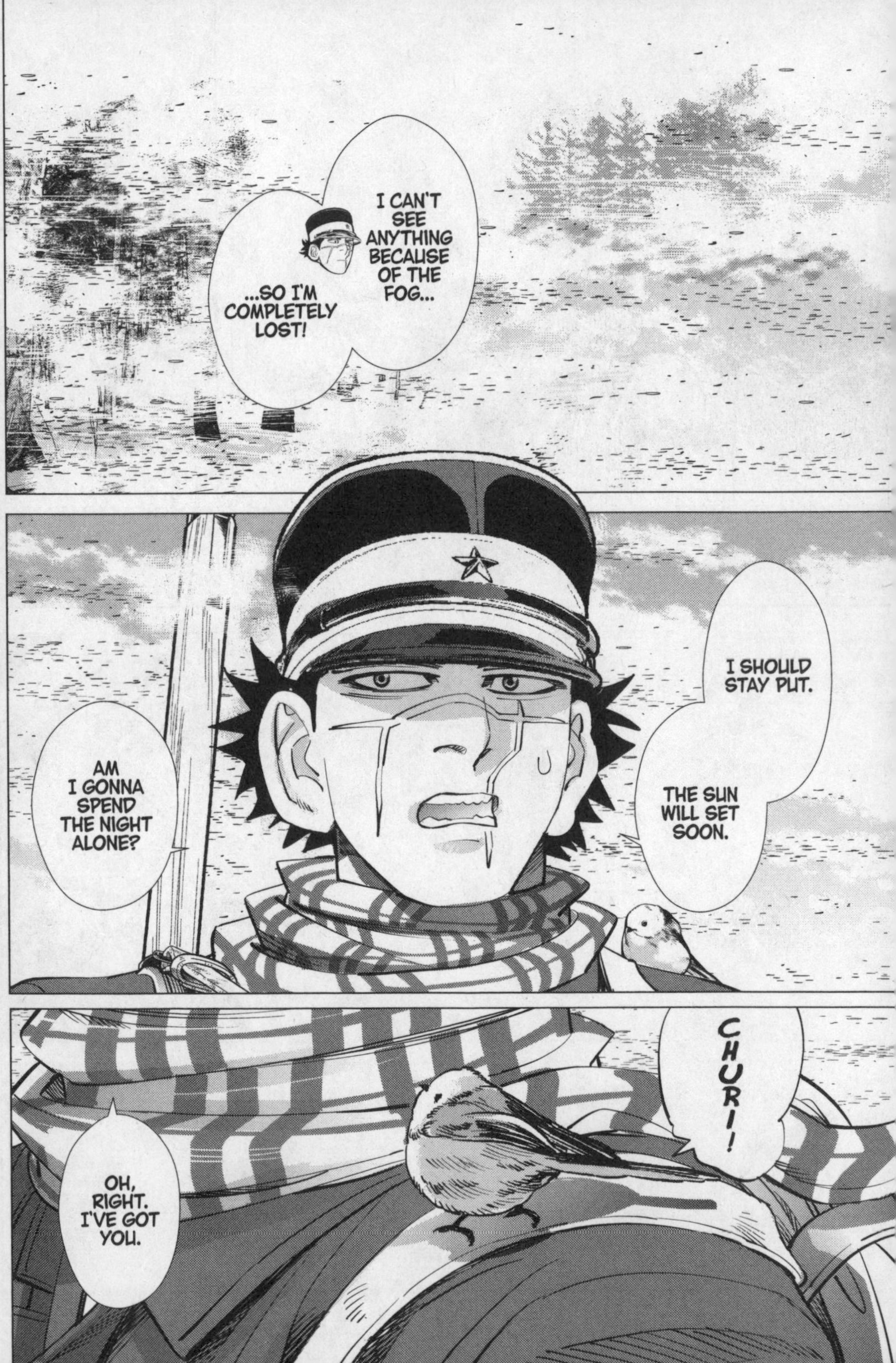
I CAN'T SEE ANYTHING BECAUSE OF THE FOG...
...SO I'M COMPLETELY LOST!
I SHOULD STAY PUT.
THE SUN WILL SET SOON.
AM I GONNA SPEND THE NIGHT ALONE?
CHURI!
OH, RIGHT. I'VE GOT YOU.

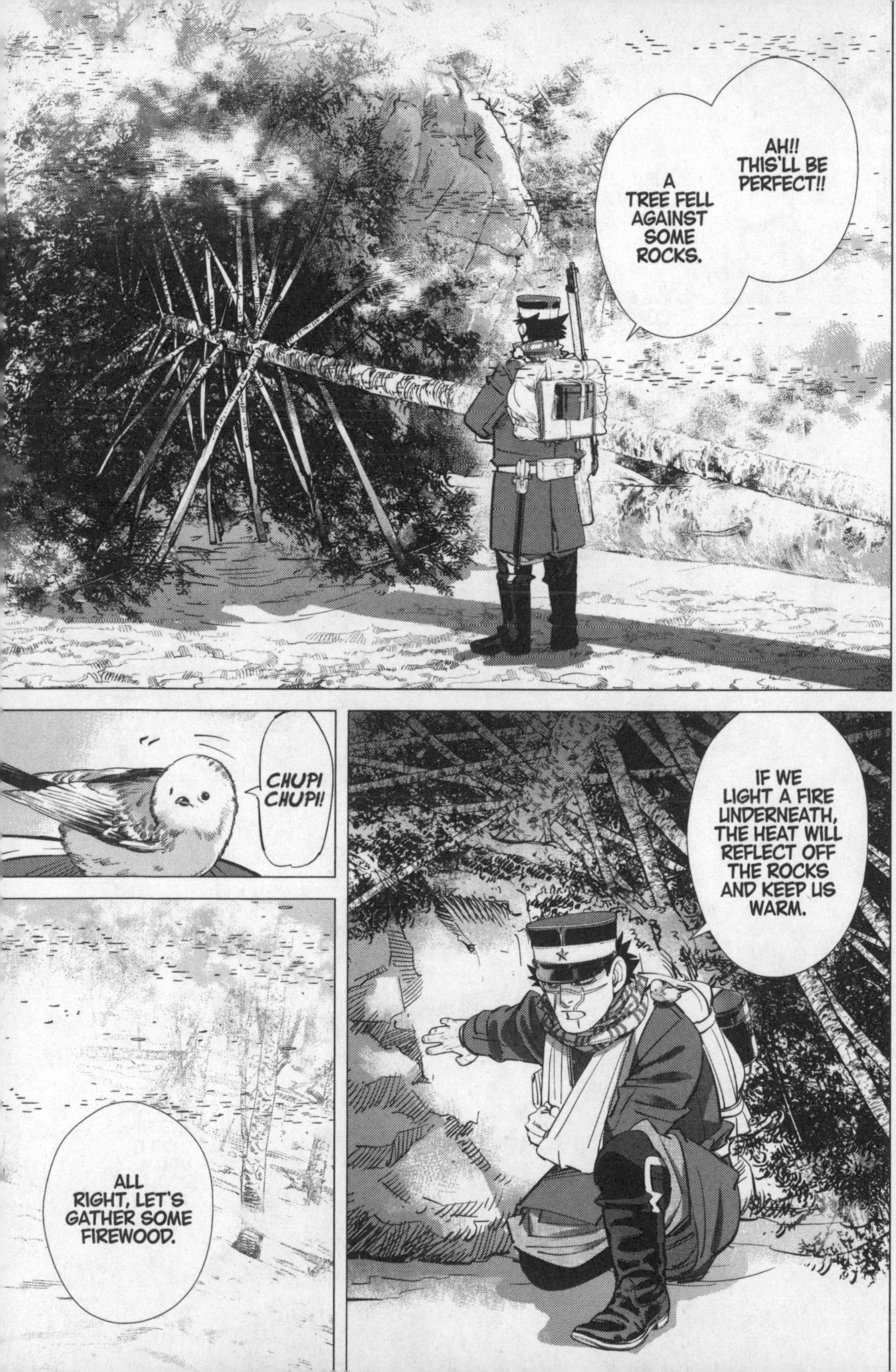
AH!! THIS'LL BE PERFECT!!
A TREE FELL AGAINST SOME ROCKS.
IF WE LIGHT A FIRE UNDERNEATH, THE HEAT WILL REFLECT OFF THE ROCKS AND KEEP US WARM.
CHUPI CHUPI!
ALL RIGHT, LET'S GATHER SOME FIREWOOD.

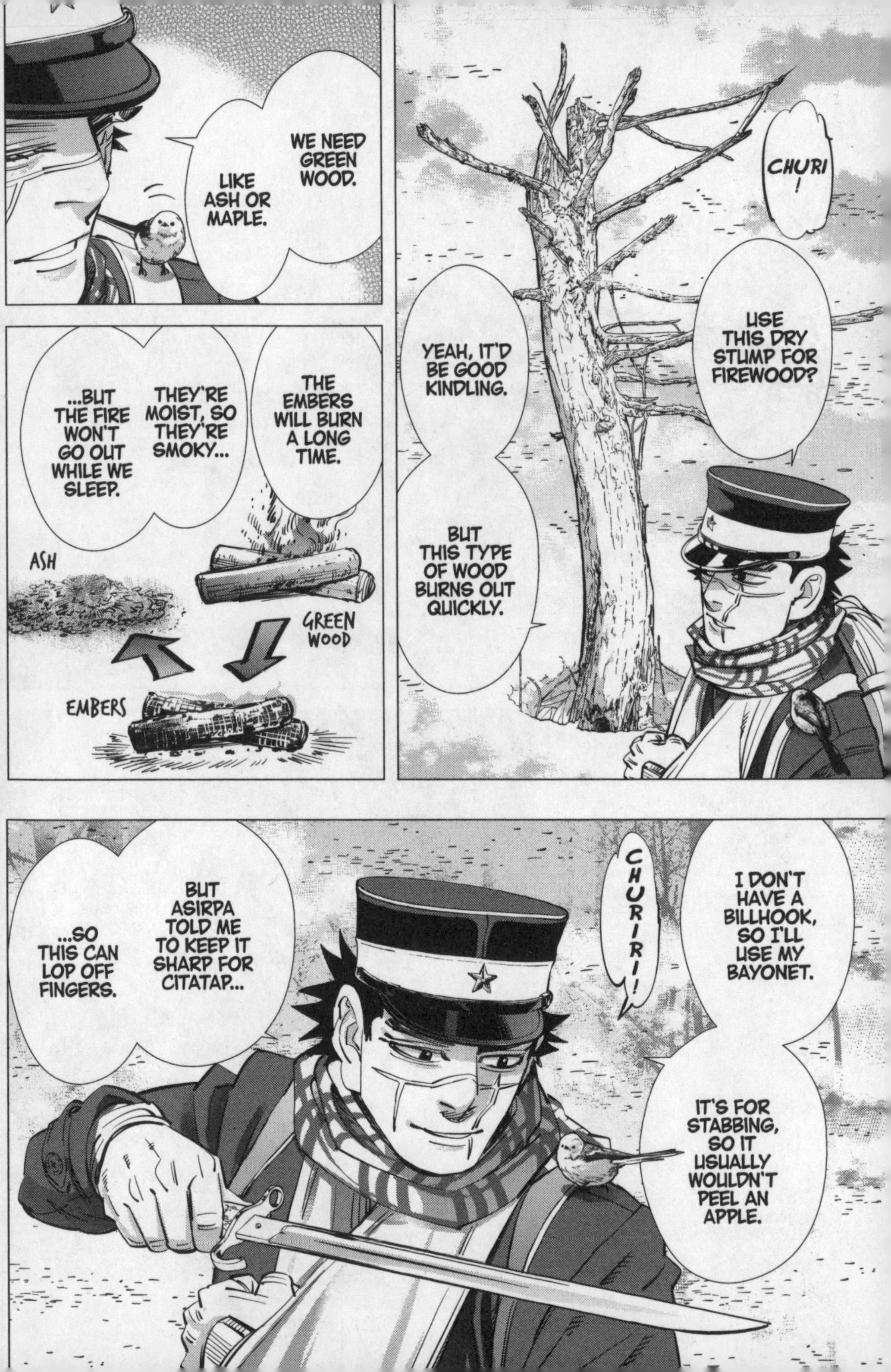
CHURI!
USE THIS DRY STUMP FOR FIREWOOD?
YEAH, IT'D BE GOOD KINDLING.
BUT THIS TYPE OF WOOD BURNS OUT QUICKLY.
WE NEED GREEN WOOD.
LIKE ASH OR MAPLE.
THE EMBERS WILL BURN A LONG TIME.
THEY'RE MOIST, SO THEY'RE SMOKY...
...BUT THE FIRE WON'T GO OUT WHILE WE SLEEP.
ASH
GREEN WOOD
EMBERS
I DON'T HAVE A BILLHOOK, SO I'LL USE MY BAYONET.
CHURIRI!
IT'S FOR STABBING, SO IT USUALLY WOULDN'T PEEL AN APPLE.
BUT ASIRPA TOLD ME TO KEEP IT SHARP FOR CITATAP...
...SO THIS CAN LOP OFF FINGERS.

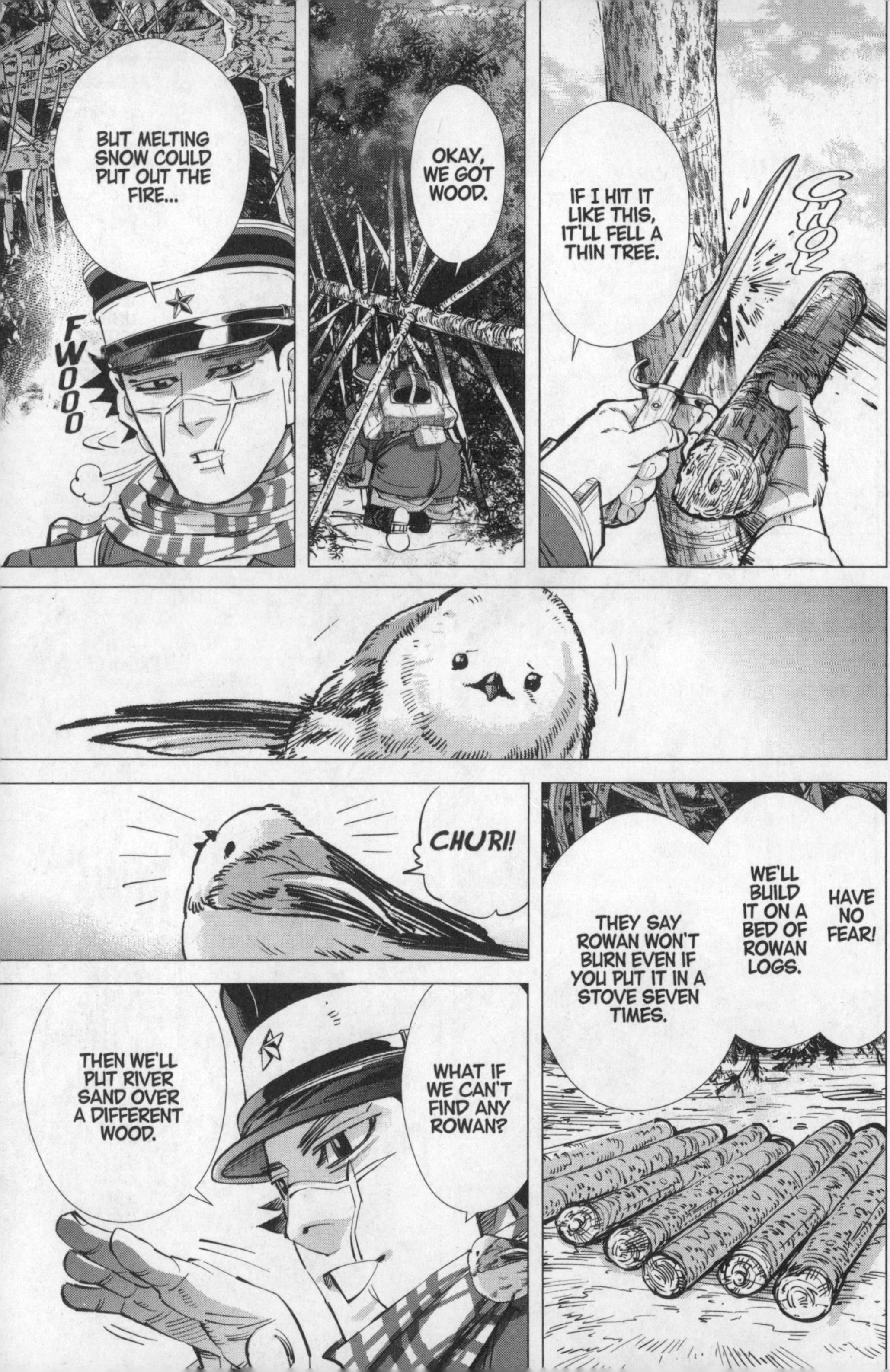
IF I HIT IT LIKE THIS, IT'LL FELL A THIN TREE.
CHOP
OKAY, WE GOT WOOD.
BUT MELTING SNOW COULD PUT OUT THE FIRE...
FWOOO
HAVE NO FEAR!
WE'LL BUILD IT ON A BED OF ROWAN LOGS.
THEY SAY ROWAN WON'T BURN EVEN IF YOU PUT IT IN A STOVE SEVEN TIMES.
CHURI!
WHAT IF WE CAN'T FIND ANY ROWAN?
THEN WE'LL PUT RIVER SAND OVER A DIFFERENT WOOD.

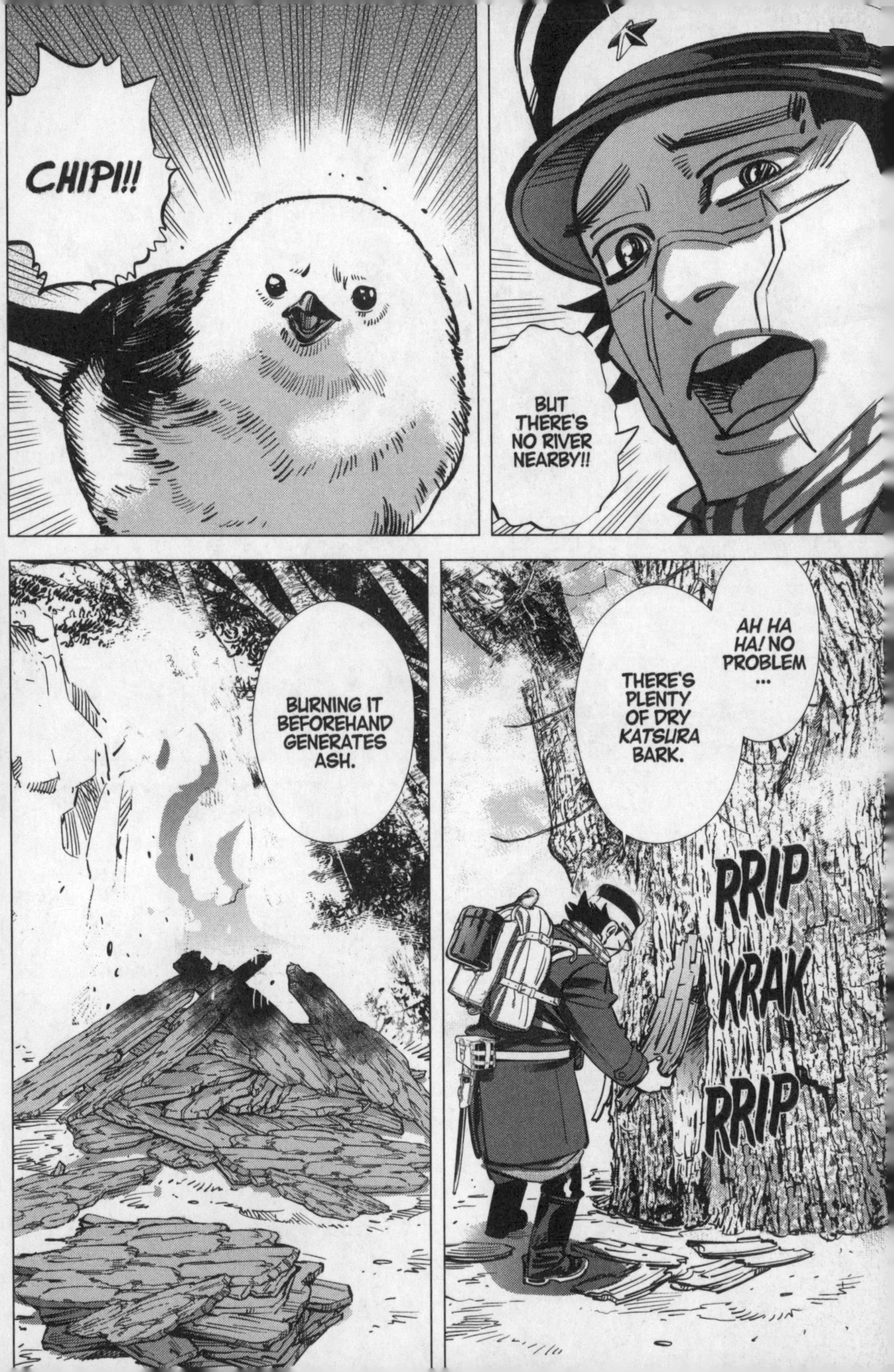
BUT THERE'S NO RIVER NEARBY!!
CHIPI!!
AH HA HA! NO PROBLEM ...
THERE'S PLENTY OF DRY KATSURA BARK.
RRIP KRAK RRIP
BURNING IT BEFOREHAND GENERATES ASH.

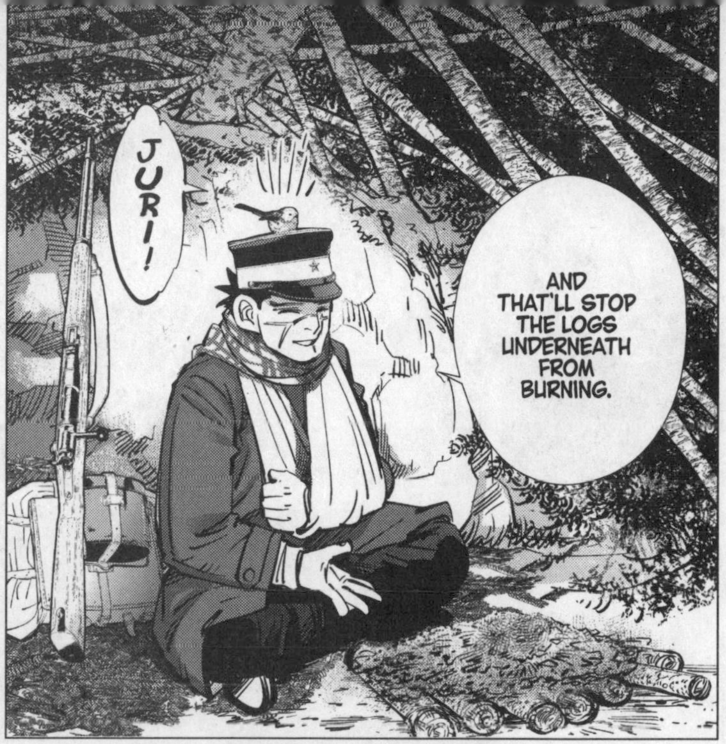
AND THAT'LL STOP THE LOGS UNDERNEATH FROM BURNING.
JURI!
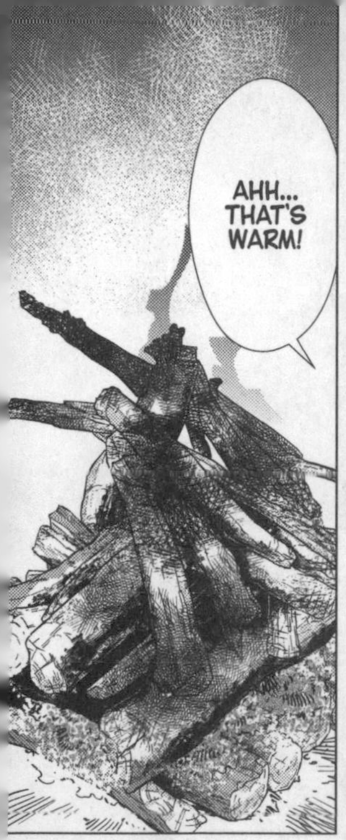
AHH... THAT'S WARM!
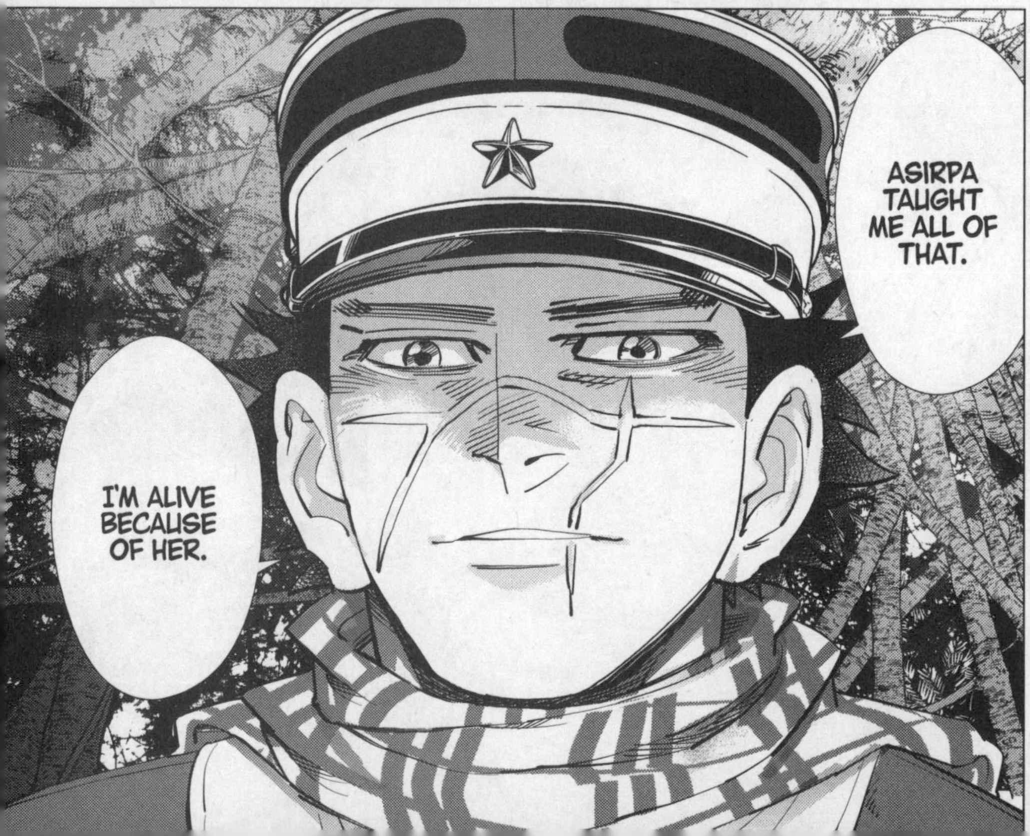
ASIRPA TAUGHT ME ALL OF THAT.
I'M ALIVE BECAUSE OF HER.

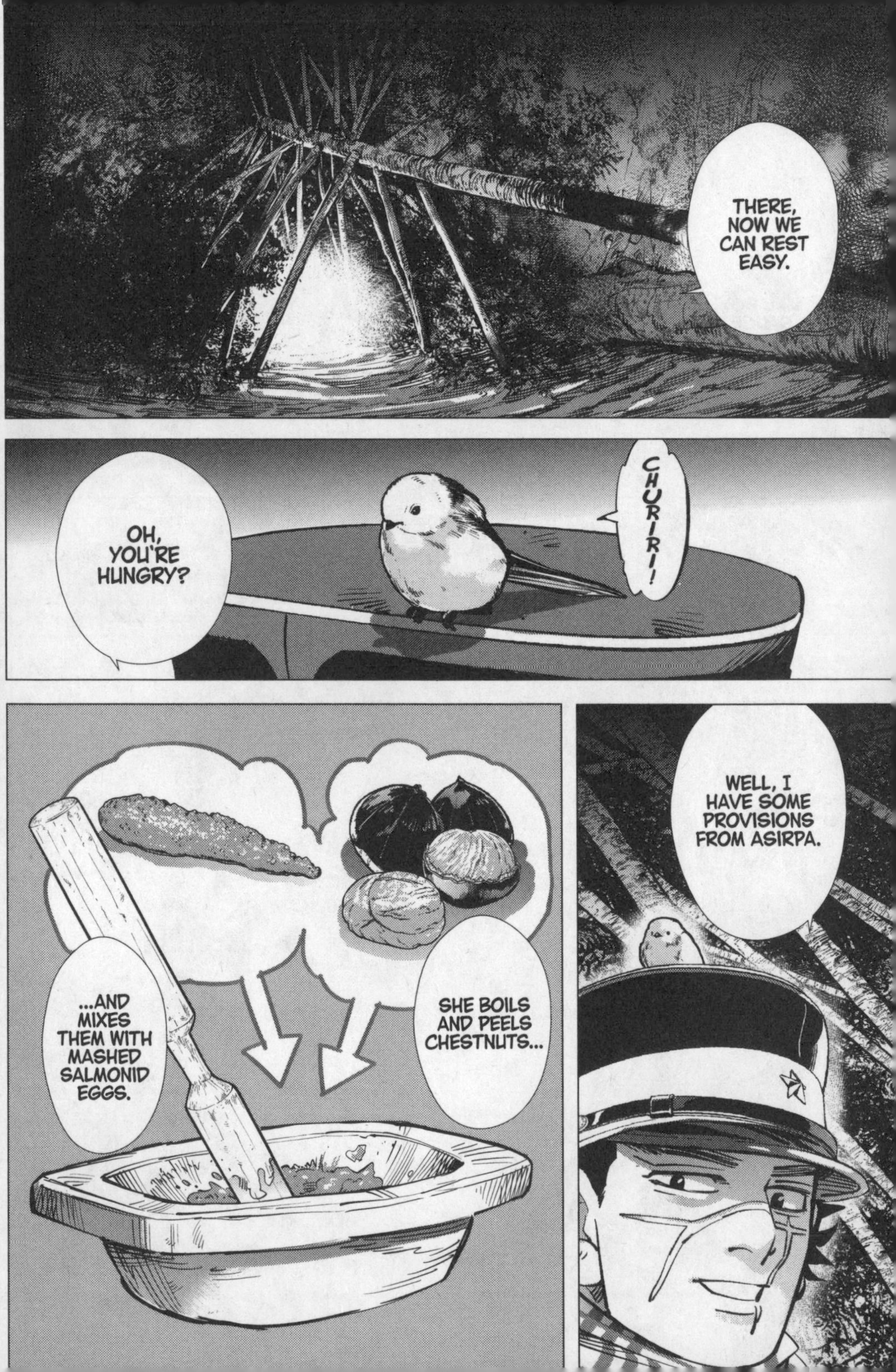
THERE, NOW WE CAN REST EASY.
CHURIRI!
OH, YOU'RE HUNGRY?
WELL, I HAVE SOME PROVISIONS FROM ASIRPA.
SHE BOILS AND PEELS CHESTNUTS...
...AND MIXES THEM WITH MASHED SALMONID EGGS.

FOR SEASONING, SHE MIXES IN ANIMAL OILS...
...FROM BEAR, EZO DEER, SEAL, WHALE, HERRING OR SHARK.
THEY MAKE IT SWEET AND MILD.
LIKE SOY SAUCE, YOU CAN PUT IT ON ANYTHING.
I CARRY IT AROUND IN DUMPLINGS...
...AND ROAST IT TO BRING OUT THE TASTE.
CHUPI CHUPI!
CHURIRIRI!
HEH HEH... DON'T GET ANTSY.

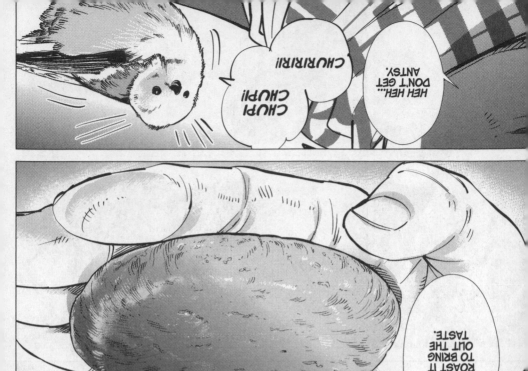

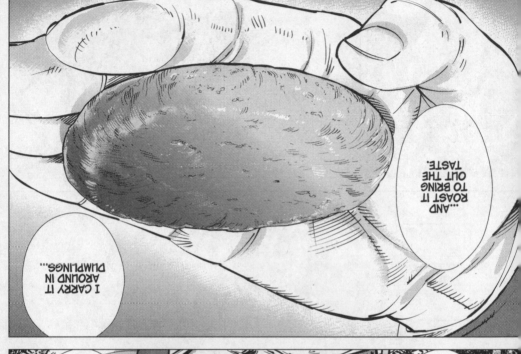

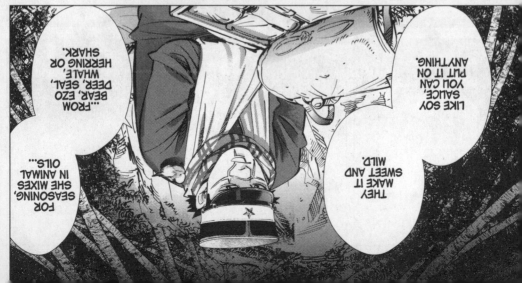

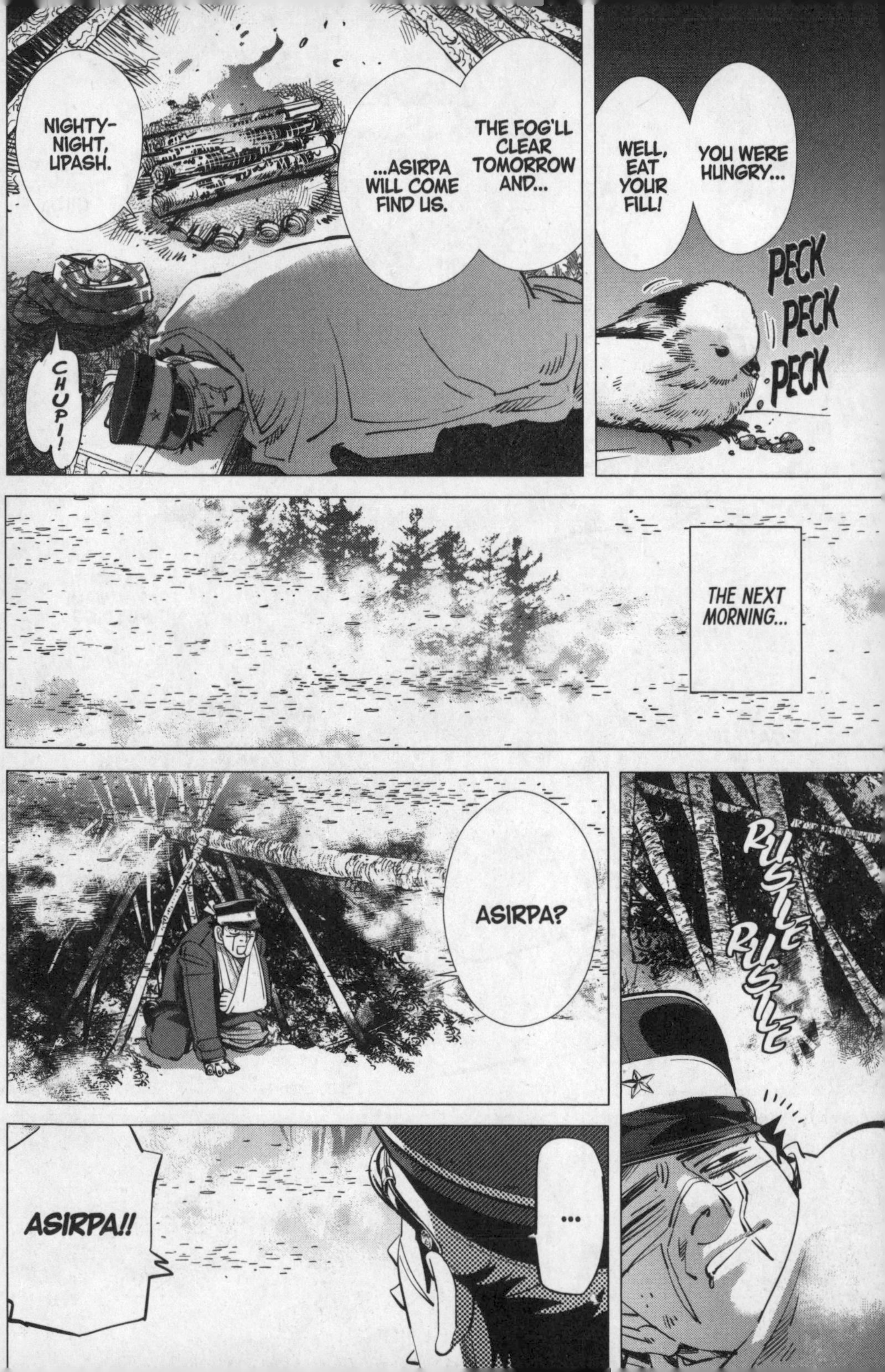
YOU WERE HUNGRY...
WELL, EAT YOUR FILL!
PECK PECK PECK
THE FOG'LL CLEAR TOMORROW AND...
...ASIRPA WILL COME FIND US.
NIGHTY-NIGHT, UPASH.
CHUPI!
THE NEXT MORNING...
RUSTLE RUSTLE
ASIRPA?
...
ASIRPA!!

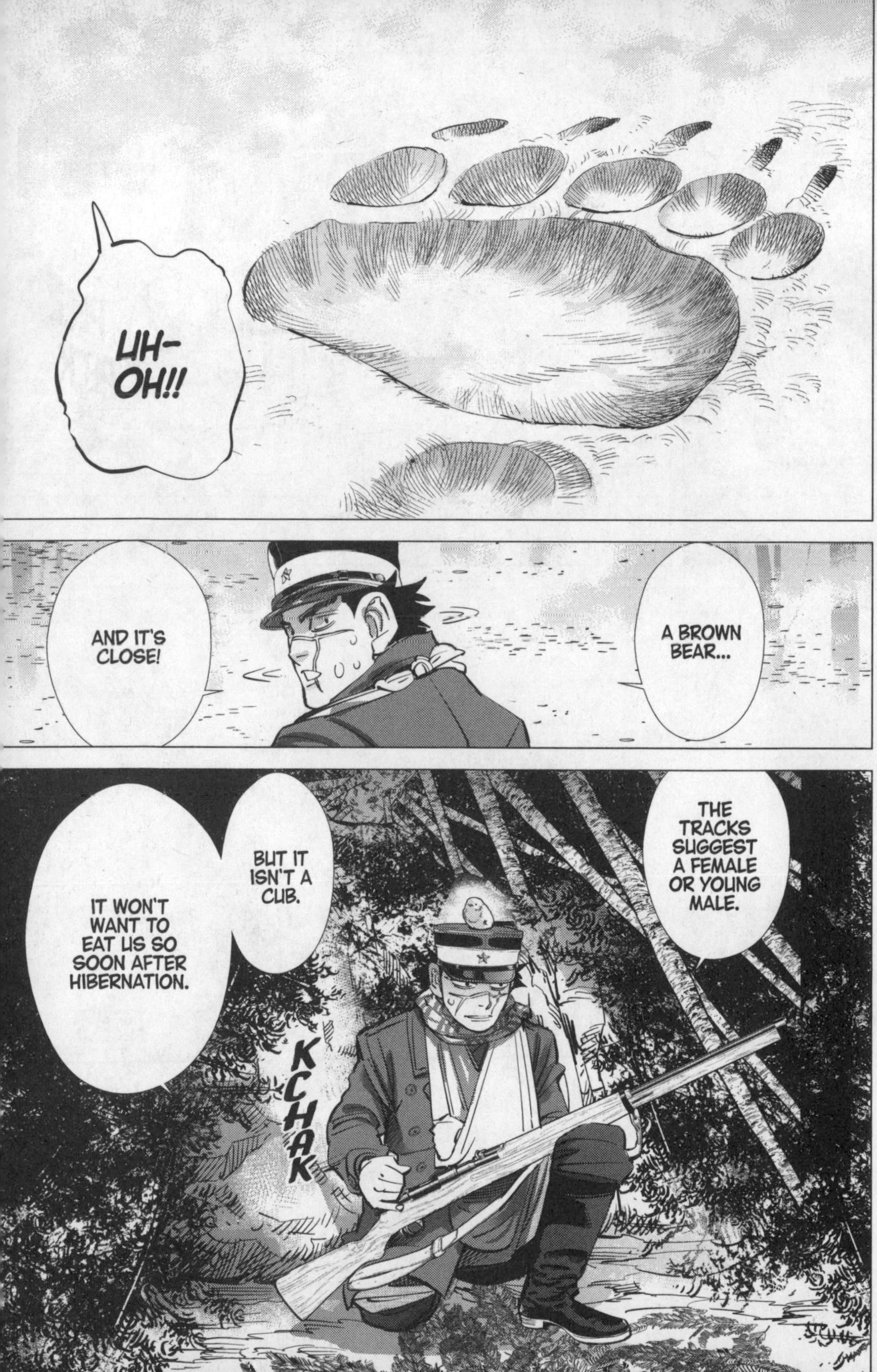
UH-OH!!
A BROWN BEAR...
AND IT'S CLOSE!
THE TRACKS SUGGEST A FEMALE OR YOUNG MALE.
BUT IT ISN'T A CUB.
IT WON'T WANT TO EAT US SO SOON AFTER HIBERNATION.
KCHAK

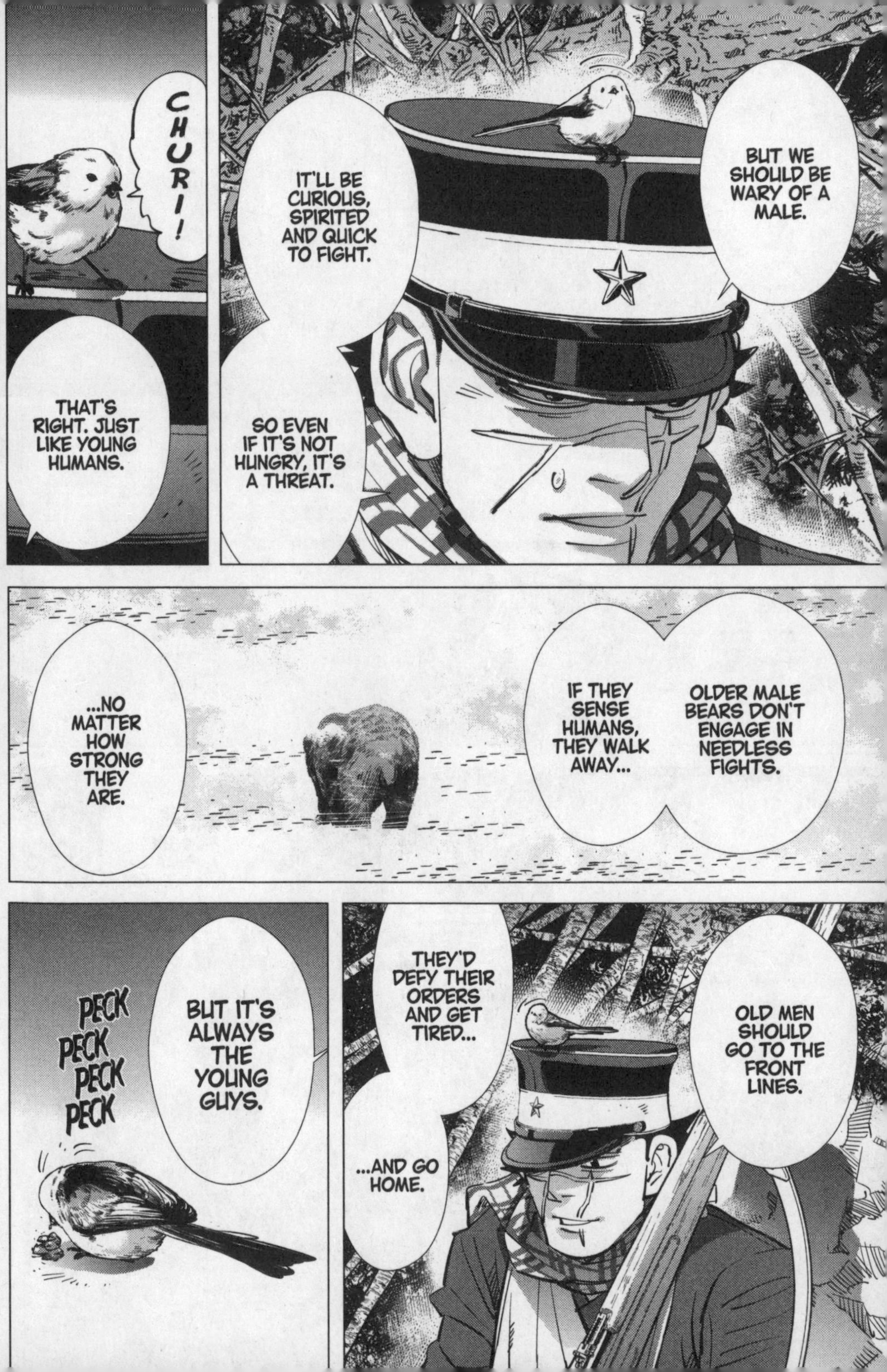
BUT WE SHOULD BE WARY OF A MALE.
IT'LL BE CURIOUS, SPIRITED AND QUICK TO FIGHT.
SO EVEN IF IT'S NOT HUNGRY, IT'S A THREAT.
CHURI!
THAT'S RIGHT. JUST LIKE YOUNG HUMANS.
OLDER MALE BEARS DON'T ENGAGE IN NEEDLESS FIGHTS.
IF THEY SENSE HUMANS, THEY WALK AWAY...
...NO MATTER HOW STRONG THEY ARE.
OLD MEN SHOULD GO TO THE FRONT LINES.
THEY'D DEFY THEIR ORDERS AND GET TIRED...
...AND GO HOME.
BUT IT'S ALWAYS THE YOUNG GUYS.
PECK PECK PECK PECK

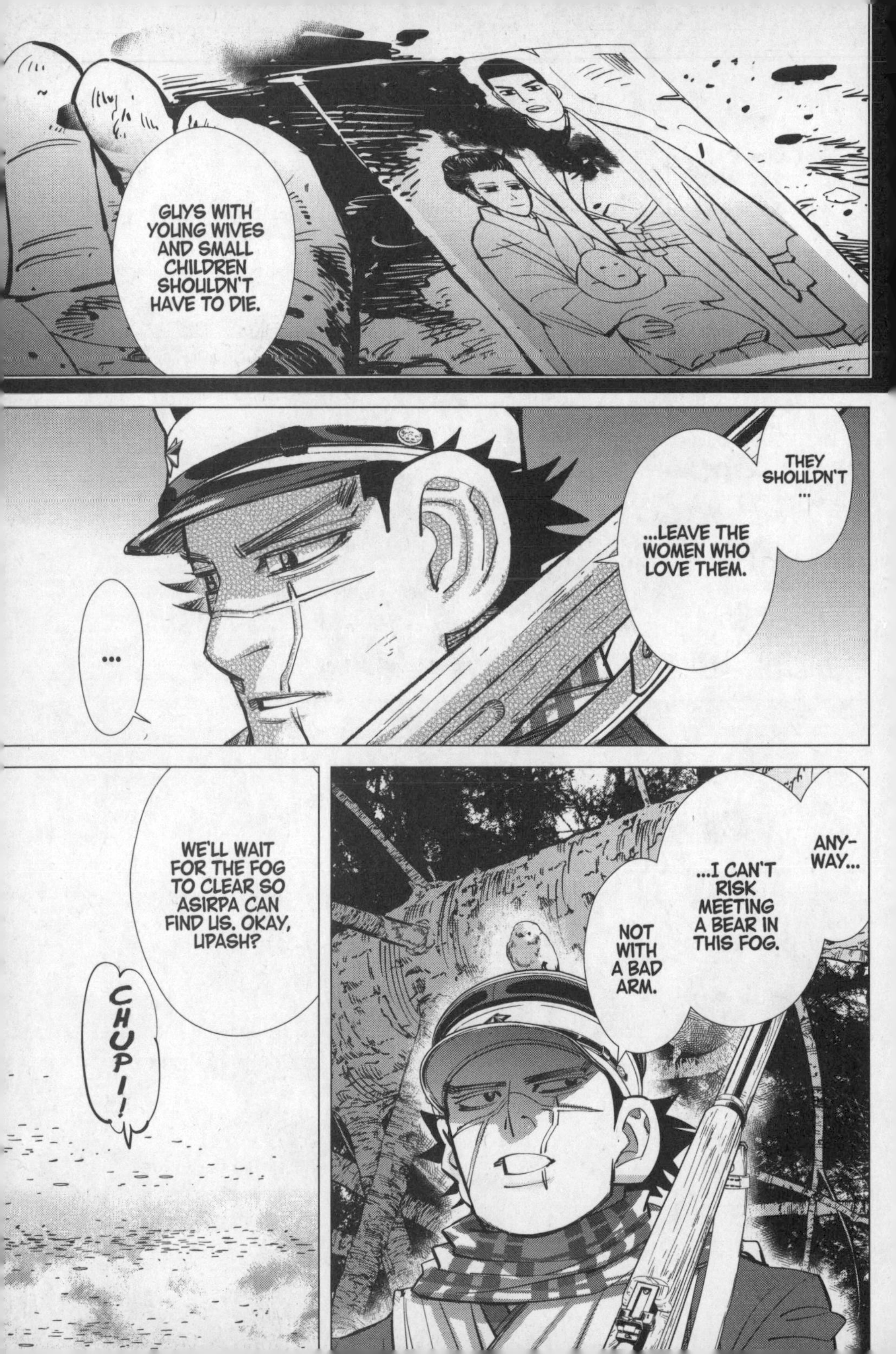
GUYS WITH YOUNG WIVES AND SMALL CHILDREN SHOULDN'T HAVE TO DIE.
THEY SHOULDN'T ...
...LEAVE THE WOMEN WHO LOVE THEM.
...
ANY-WAY...
...I CAN'T RISK MEETING A BEAR IN THIS FOG.
NOT WITH A BAD ARM.
WE'LL WAIT FOR THE FOG TO CLEAR SO ASIRPA CAN FIND US. OKAY, UPASH?
CHUPI!

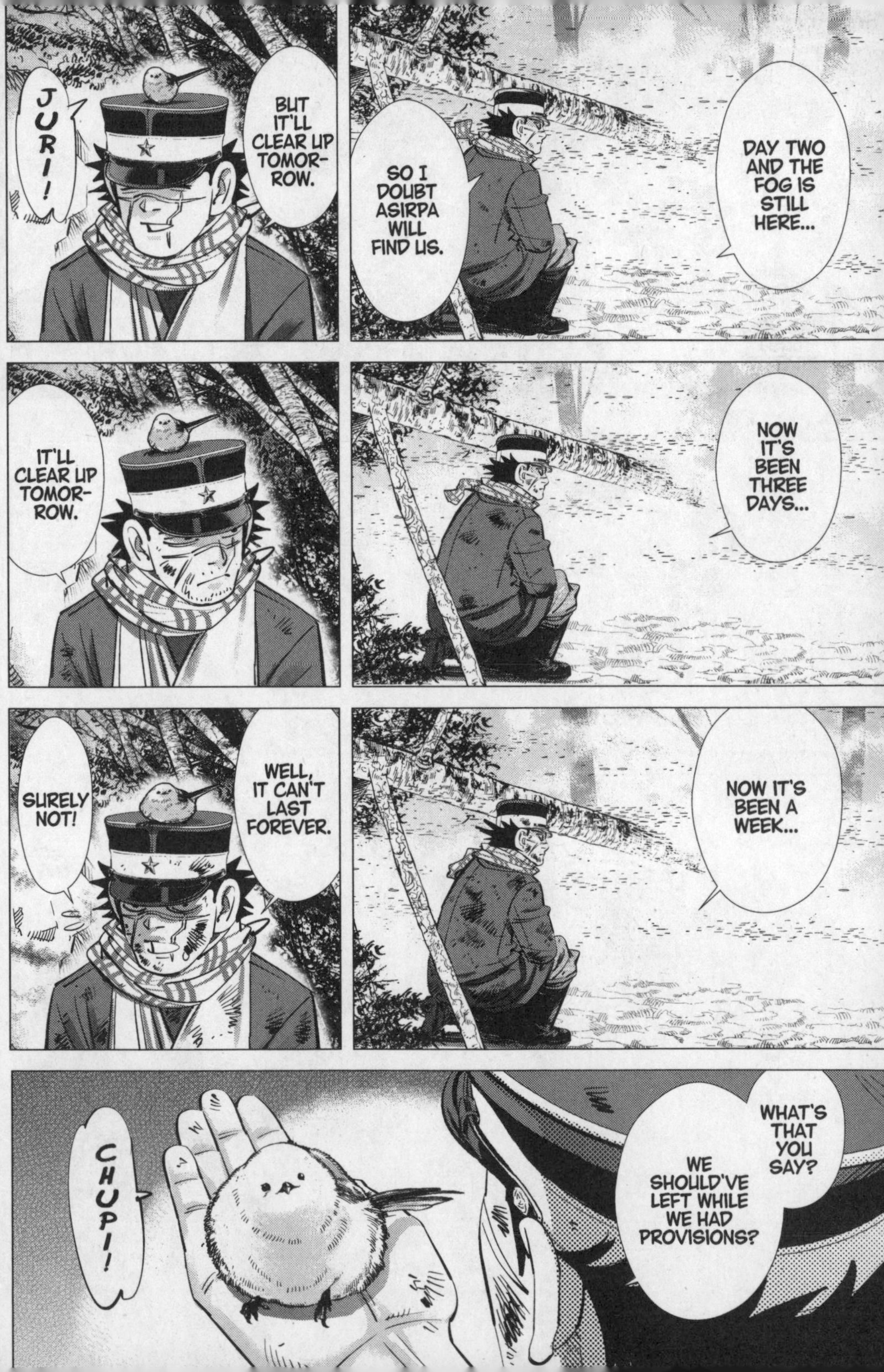
DAY TWO AND THE FOG IS STILL HERE...
SO I DOUBT ASIRPA WILL FIND US.
BUT IT'LL CLEAR UP TOMORROW.
JURI!
NOW IT'S BEEN THREE DAYS...
IT'LL CLEAR UP TOMORROW.
NOW IT'S BEEN A WEEK...
WELL, IT CAN'T LAST FOREVER.
SURELY NOT!
WHAT'S THAT YOU SAY?
WE SHOULD'VE LEFT WHILE WE HAD PROVISIONS?
CHUPI!

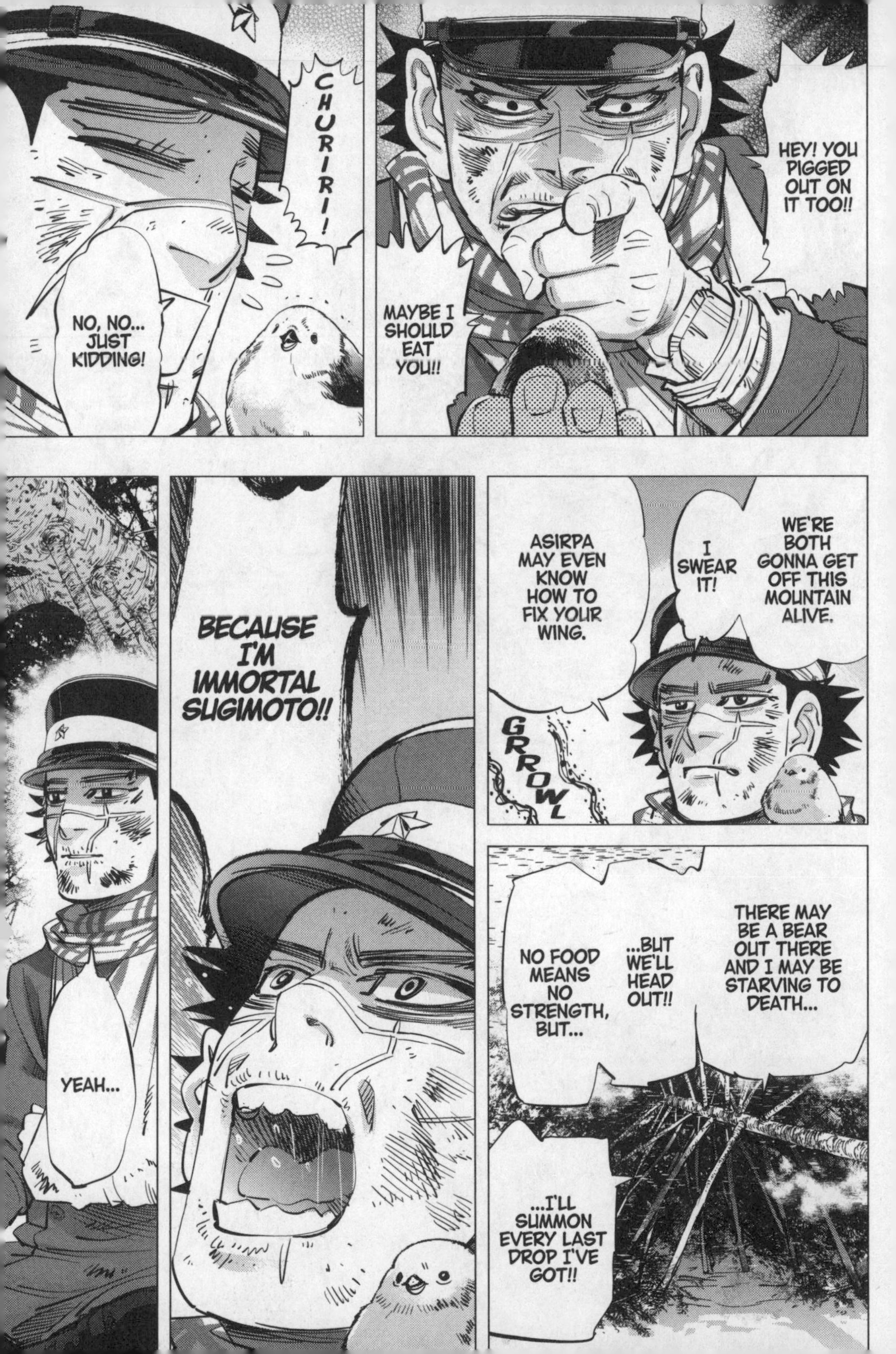
HEY! YOU PIGGED OUT ON IT TOO!!
MAYBE I SHOULD EAT YOU!!
CHURIRI!
NO, NO... JUST KIDDING!
WE'RE BOTH GONNA GET OFF THIS MOUNTAIN ALIVE.
I SWEAR IT!
ASIRPA MAY EVEN KNOW HOW TO FIX YOUR WING.
GRROWL
THERE MAY BE A BEAR OUT THERE AND I MAY BE STARVING TO DEATH...
...BUT WE'LL HEAD OUT!!
NO FOOD MEANS NO STRENGTH, BUT...
...I'LL SUMMON EVERY LAST DROP I'VE GOT!!
BECAUSE I'M IMMORTAL SUGIMOTO!!
YEAH...

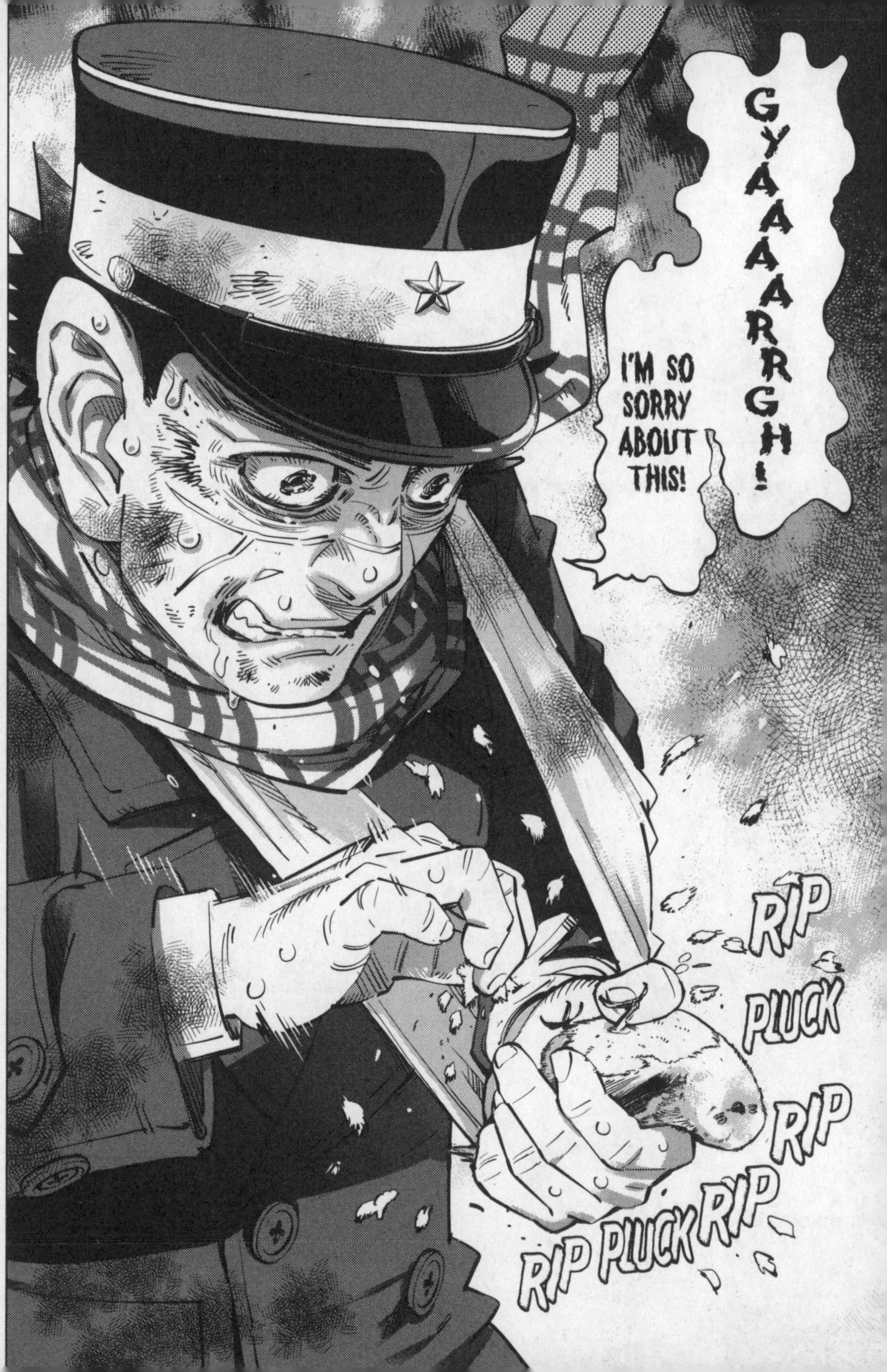
GYAAAARRGH!
I'M SO SORRY ABOUT THIS!
RIP
PLUCK
RIP
RIP PLUCK RIP

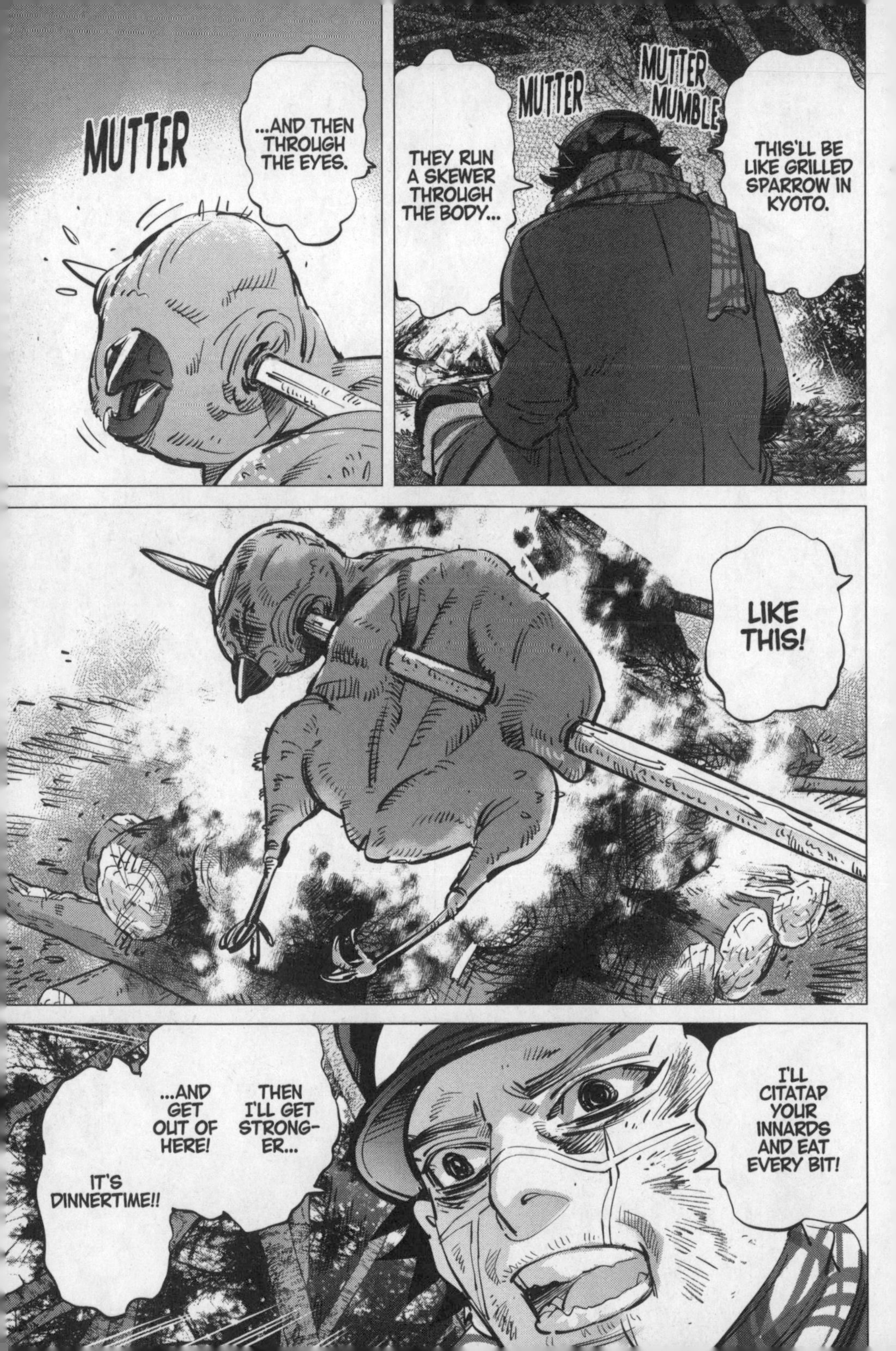
MUTTER
MUTTER MUMBLE
THIS'LL BE LIKE GRILLED SPARROW IN KYOTO.
THEY RUN A SKEWER THROUGH THE BODY...
MUTTER
...AND THEN THROUGH THE EYES.
LIKE THIS!
I'LL CITATAP YOUR INNARDS AND EAT EVERY BIT!
THEN I'LL GET STRONGER...
...AND GET OUT OF HERE!
IT'S DINNERTIME!!

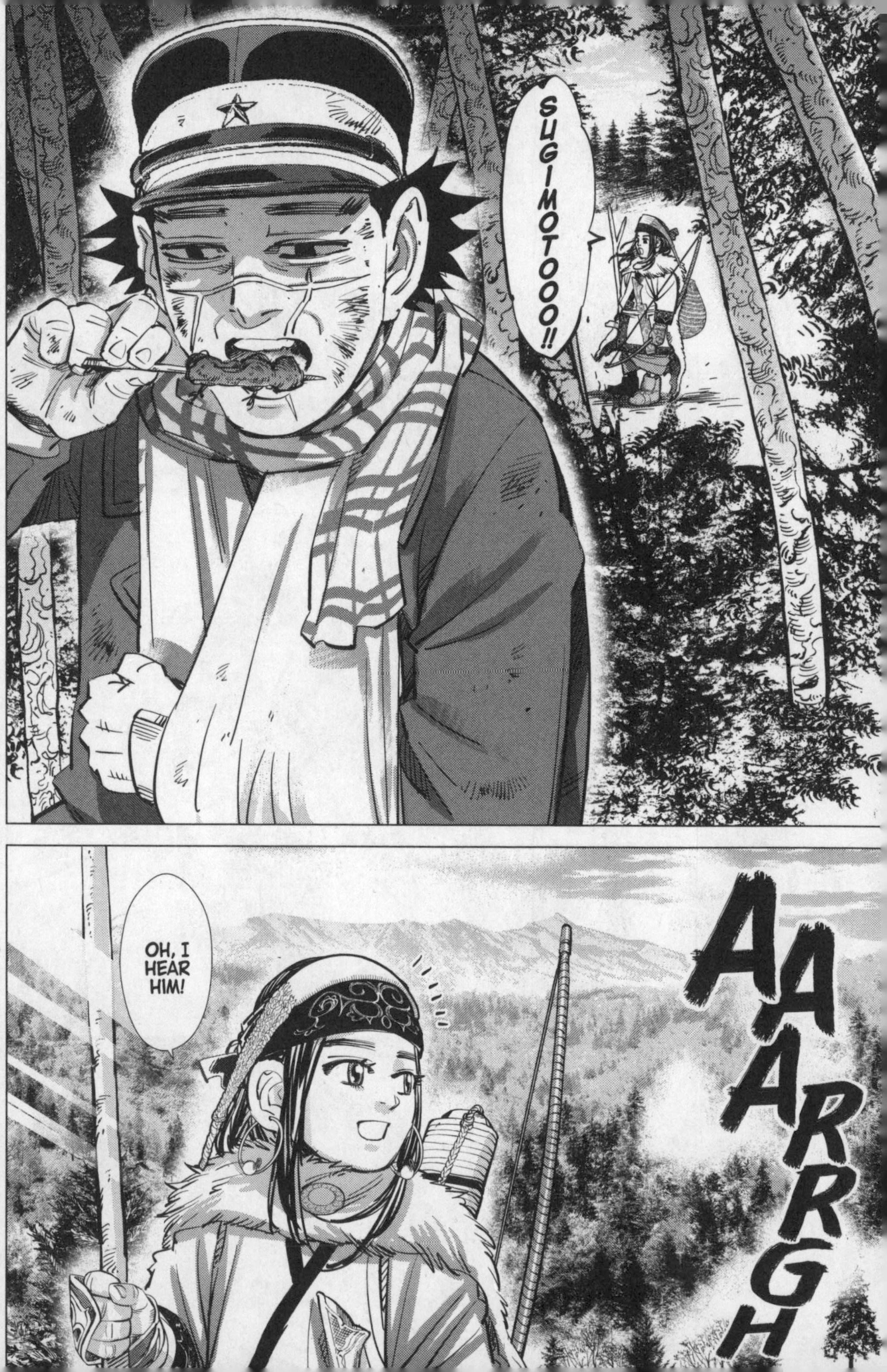
SUGIMOTOOOO!!
AAARRGH
OH, I HEAR HIM!

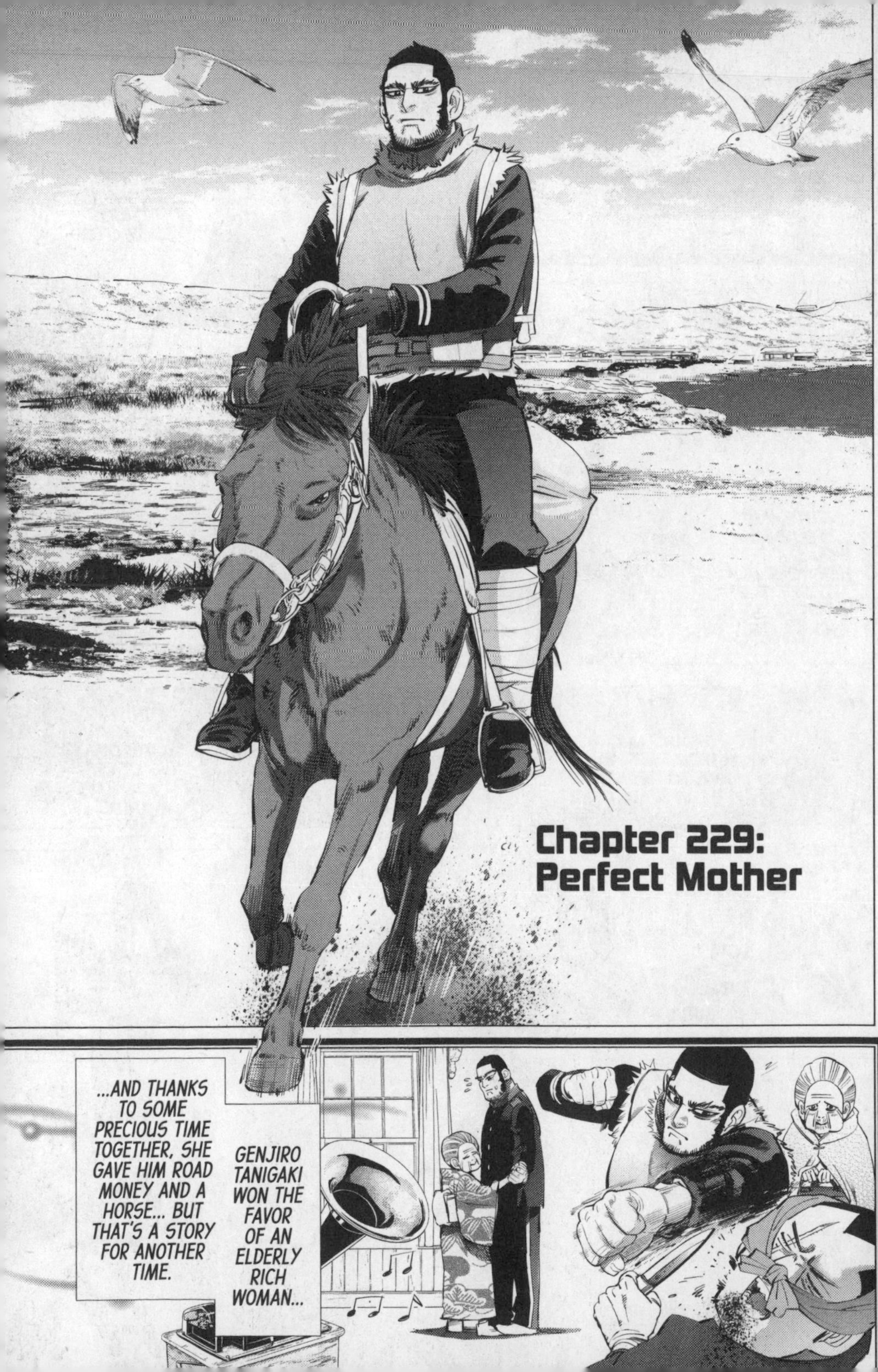
Chapter 229:
Perfect Mother
GENJIRO TANIGAKI WON THE FAVOR OF AN ELDERLY RICH WOMAN...
...AND THANKS TO SOME PRECIOUS TIME TOGETHER, SHE GAVE HIM ROAD MONEY AND A HORSE... BUT THAT'S A STORY FOR ANOTHER TIME.

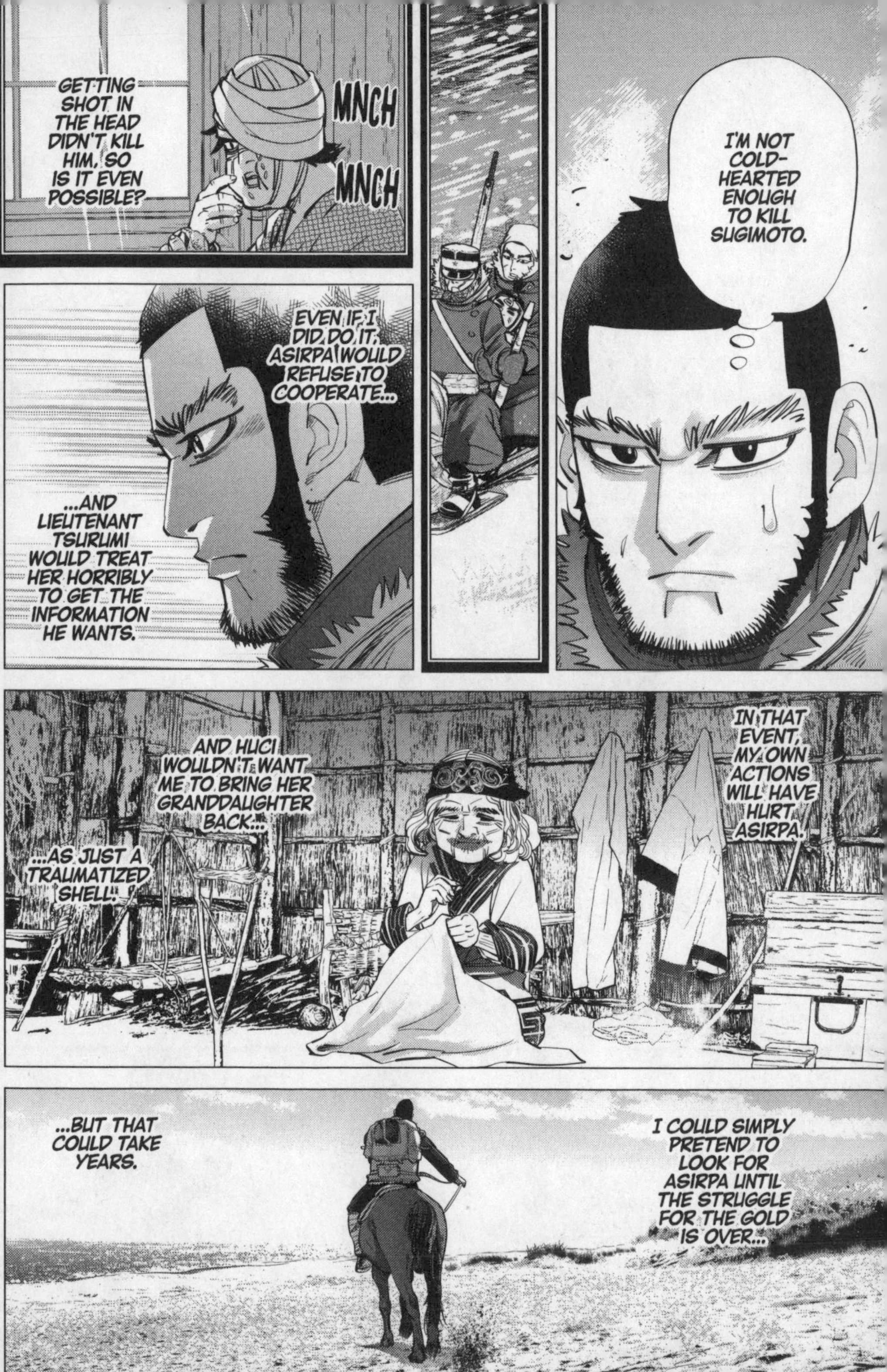
I'M NOT COLD-HEARTED ENOUGH TO KILL SUGIMOTO.
GETTING SHOT IN THE HEAD DIDN'T KILL HIM, SO IS IT EVEN POSSIBLE?
MNCH
MNCH
EVEN IF I DID DO IT, ASIRPA WOULD REFUSE TO COOPERATE...
...AND LIEUTENANT TSURUMI WOULD TREAT HER HORRIBLY TO GET THE INFORMATION HE WANTS.
IN THAT EVENT, MY OWN ACTIONS WILL HAVE HURT ASIRPA.
AND HUCI WOULDN'T WANT ME TO BRING HER GRANDDAUGHTER BACK...
...AS JUST A TRAUMATIZED SHELL.
I COULD SIMPLY PRETEND TO LOOK FOR ASIRPA UNTIL THE STRUGGLE FOR THE GOLD IS OVER...
...BUT THAT COULD TAKE YEARS.

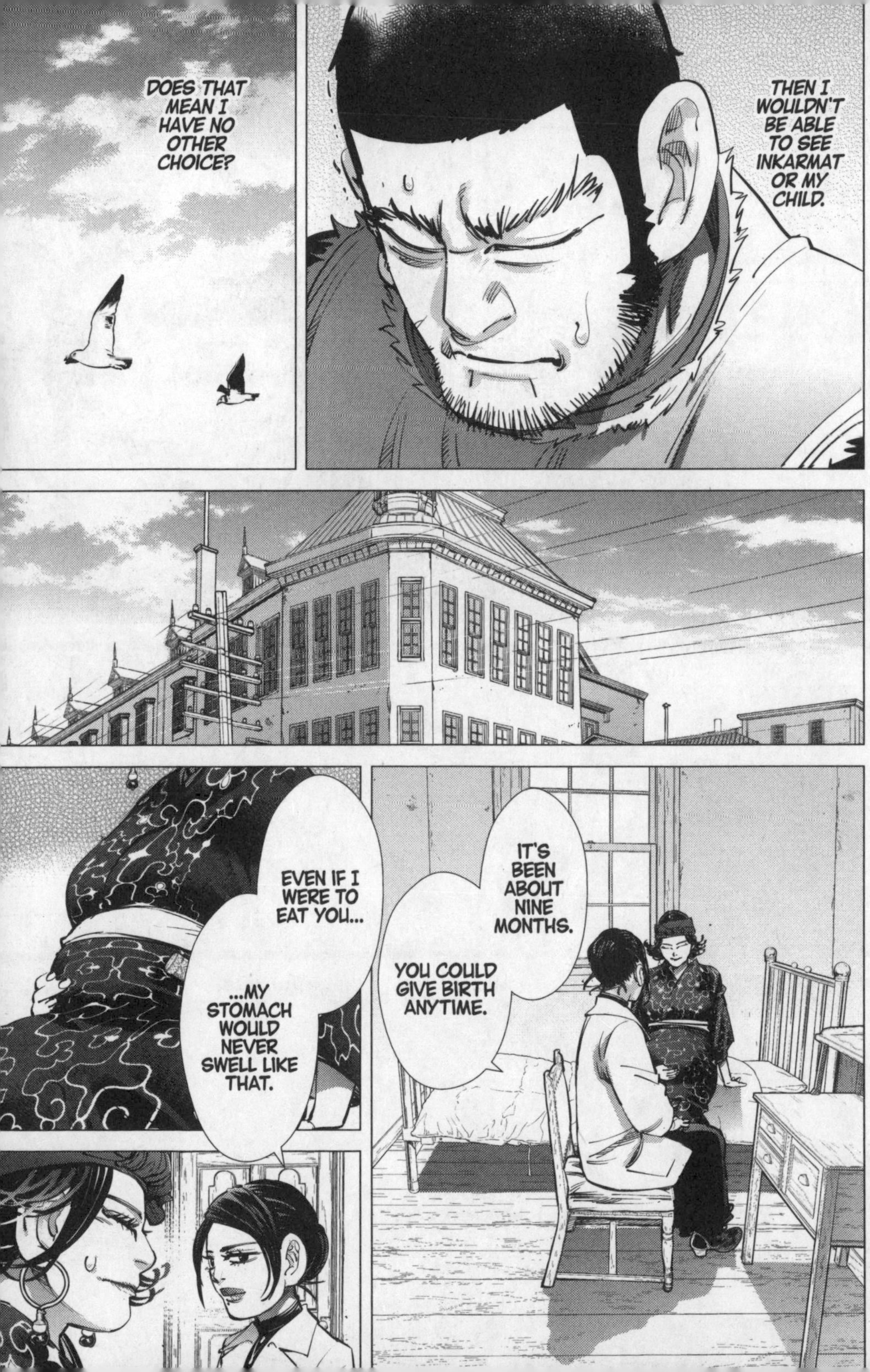
THEN I WOULDN'T BE ABLE TO SEE INKARMAT OR MY CHILD.
DOES THAT MEAN I HAVE NO OTHER CHOICE?
IT'S BEEN ABOUT NINE MONTHS.
YOU COULD GIVE BIRTH ANYTIME.
EVEN IF I WERE TO EAT YOU...
...MY STOMACH WOULD NEVER SWELL LIKE THAT.

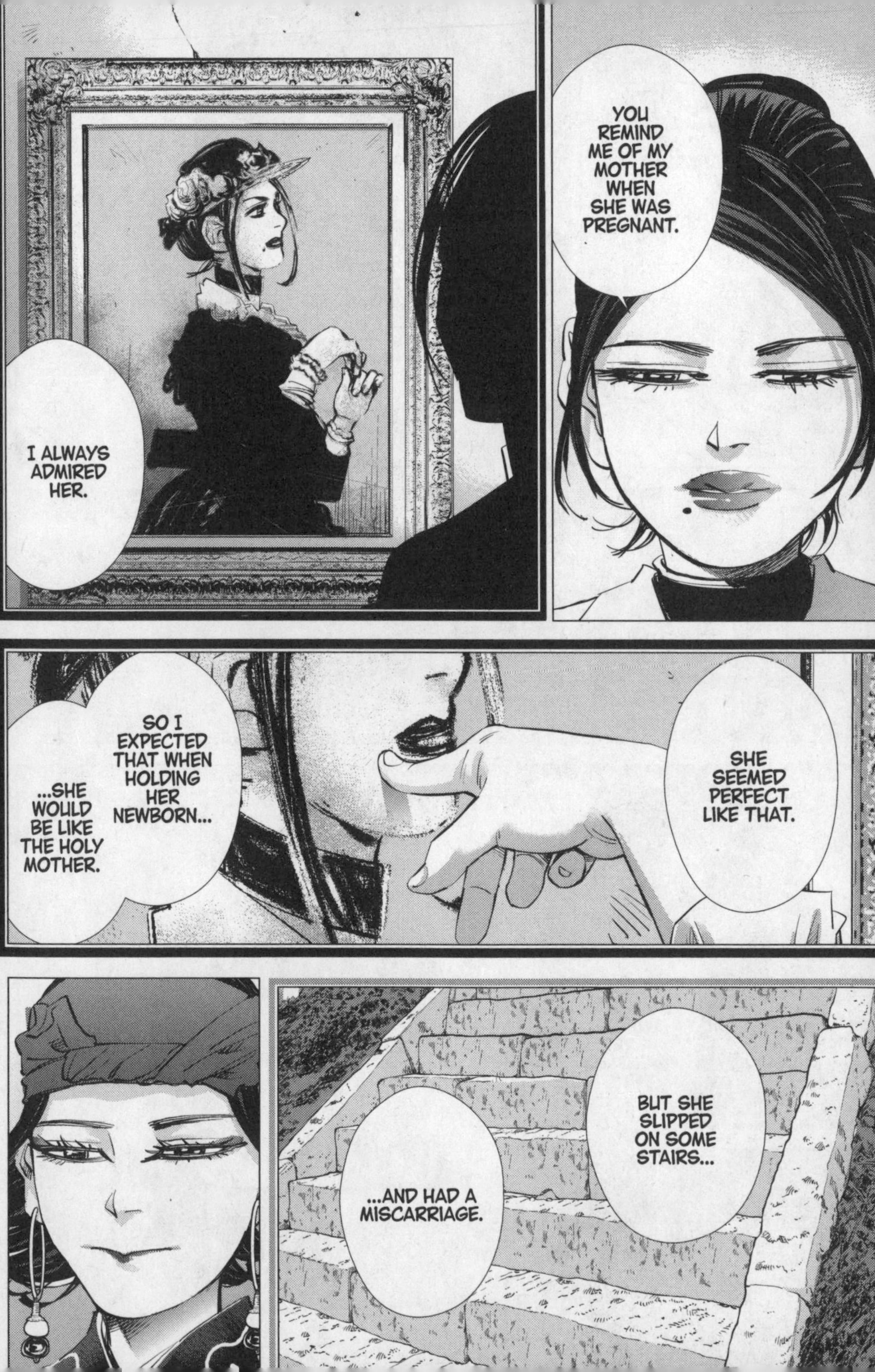
YOU REMIND ME OF MY MOTHER WHEN SHE WAS PREGNANT.
I ALWAYS ADMIRED HER.
SHE SEEMED PERFECT LIKE THAT.
SO I EXPECTED THAT WHEN HOLDING HER NEWBORN...
...SHE WOULD BE LIKE THE HOLY MOTHER.
BUT SHE SLIPPED ON SOME STAIRS...
...AND HAD A MISCARRIAGE.

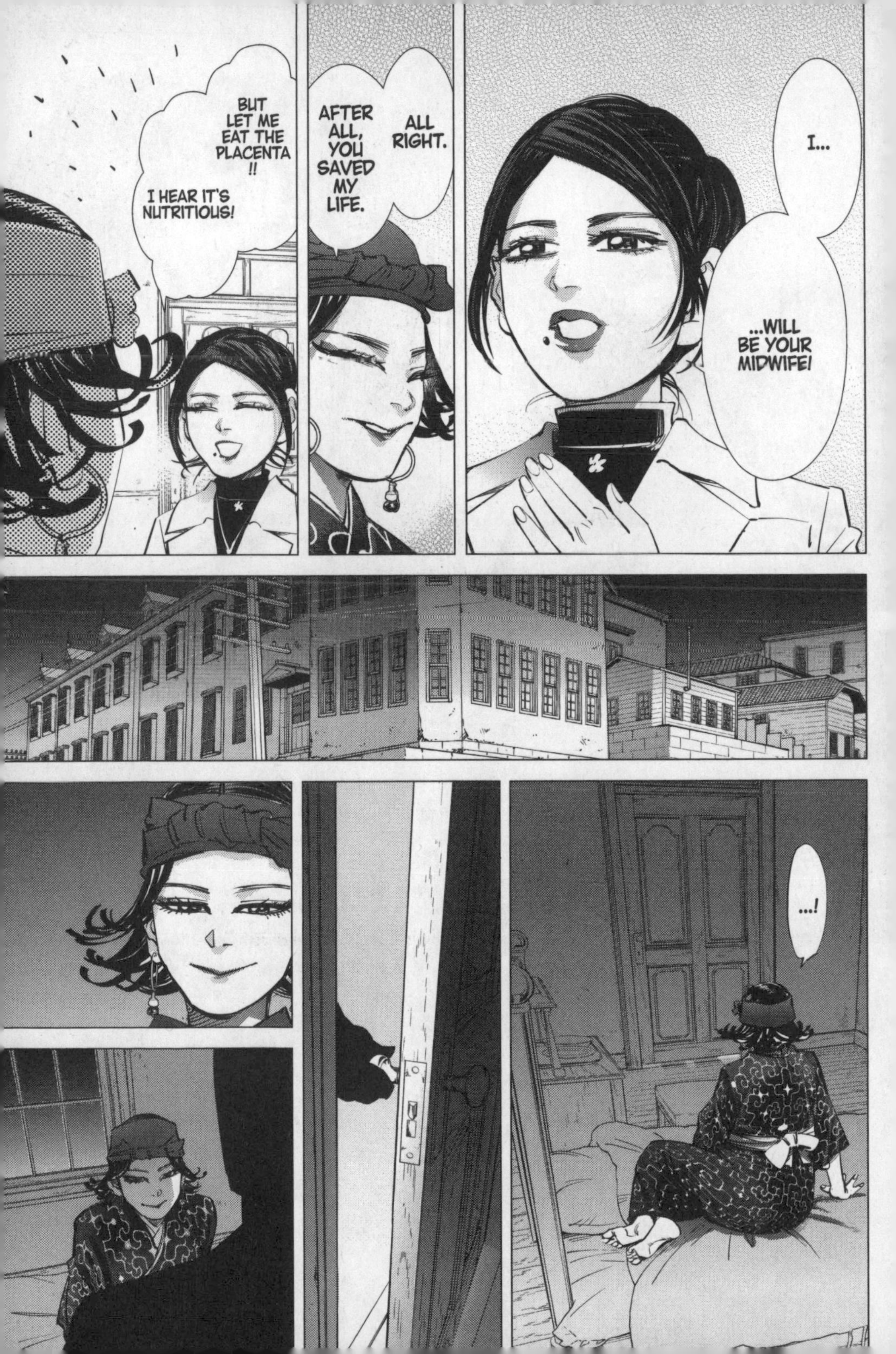
I...
...WILL BE YOUR MIDWIFE!
ALL RIGHT.
AFTER ALL, YOU SAVED MY LIFE.
BUT LET ME EAT THE PLACENTA !!
I HEAR IT'S NUTRITIOUS!
...!

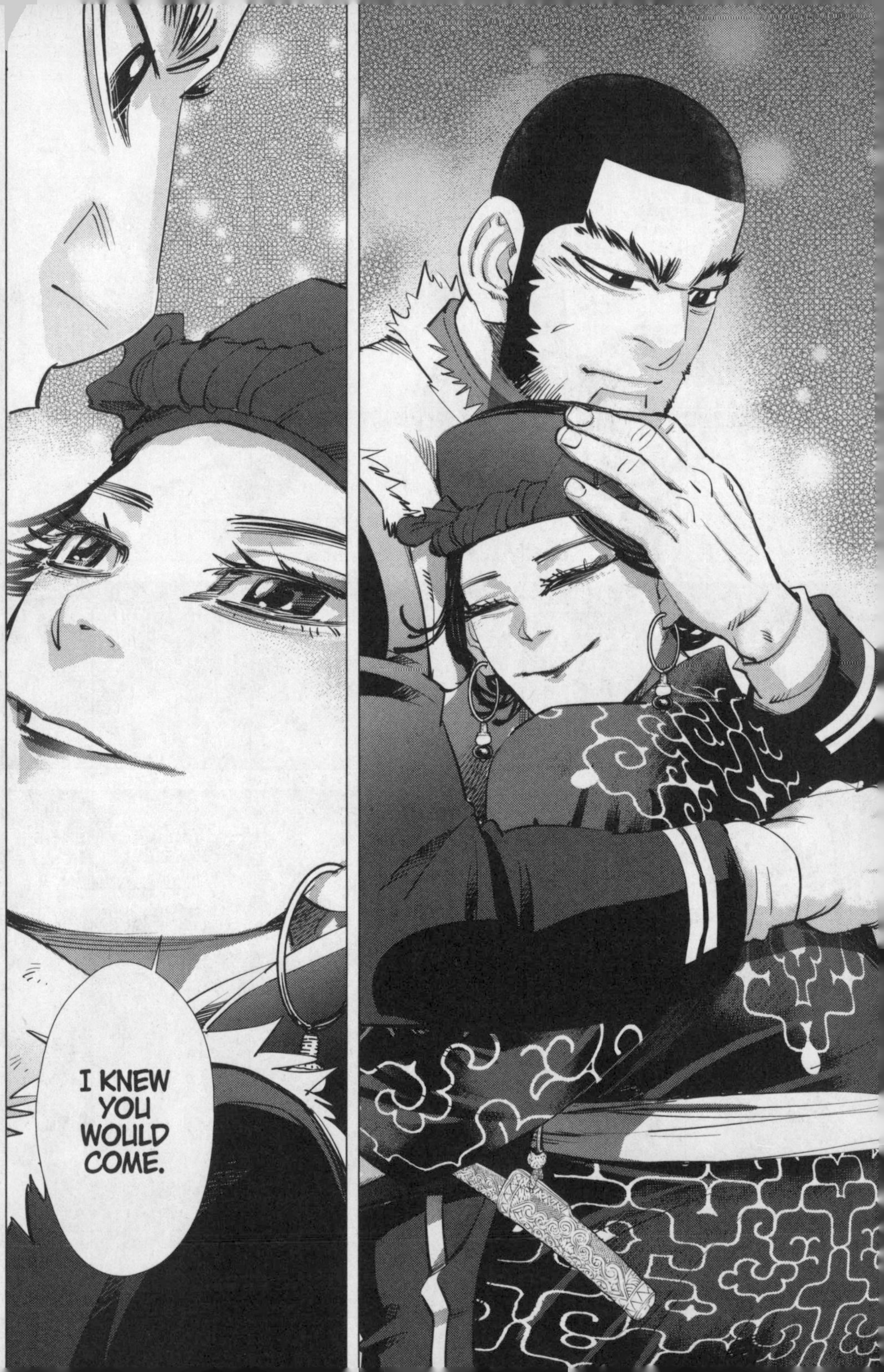
I KNEW YOU WOULD COME.

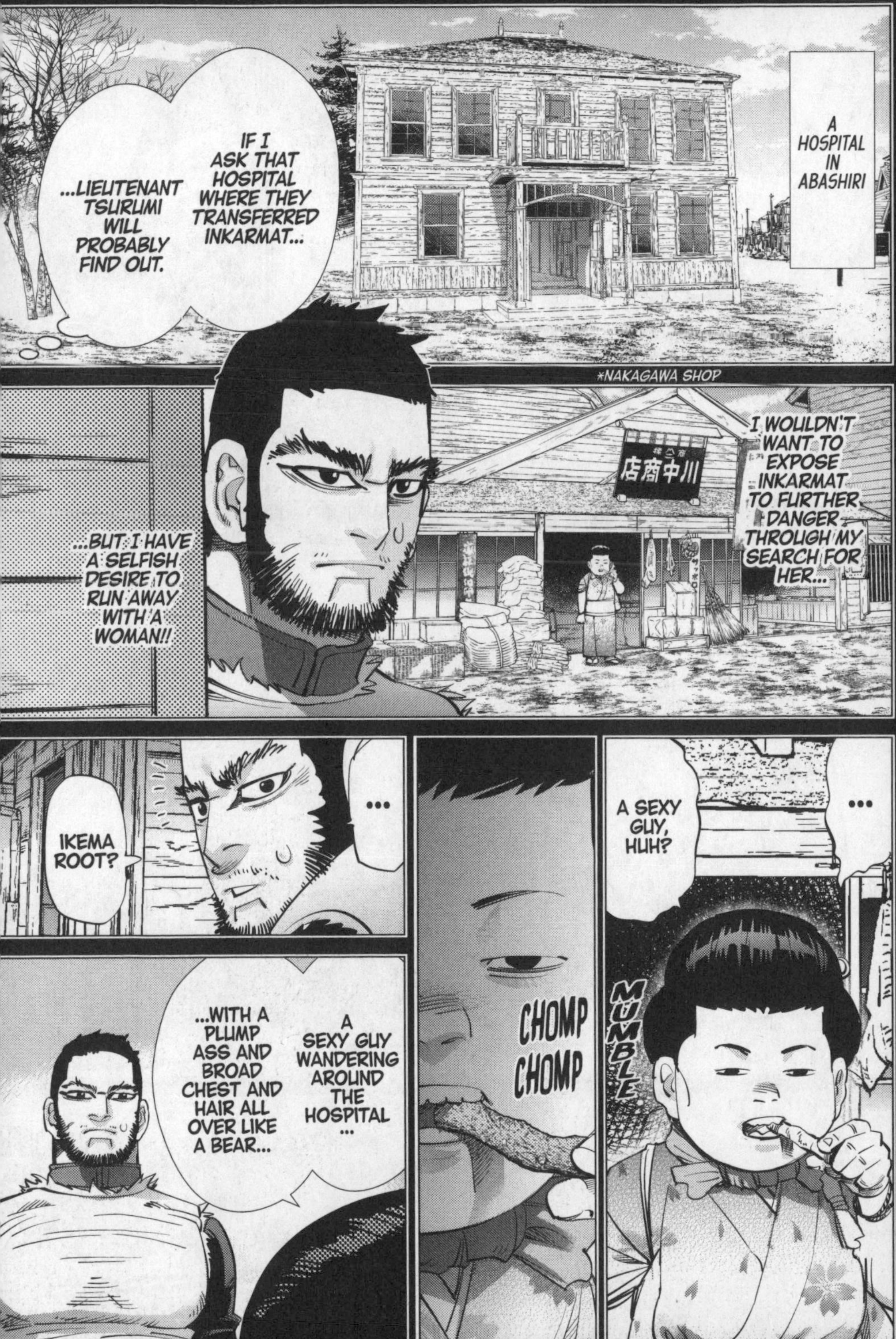
A HOSPITAL IN ABASHIRI
IF I ASK THAT HOSPITAL WHERE THEY TRANSFERRED INKARMAT...
...LIEUTENANT TSURUMI WILL PROBABLY FIND OUT.
*NAKAGAWA SHOP
店商中川
I WOULDN'T WANT TO EXPOSE INKARMAT TO FURTHER DANGER THROUGH MY SEARCH FOR HER...
...BUT I HAVE A SELFISH DESIRE TO RUN AWAY WITH A WOMAN!!
...
A SEXY GUY, HUH?
MUMBLE
CHOMP CHOMP
...
IKEMA ROOT?
A SEXY GUY WANDERING AROUND THE HOSPITAL ...
...WITH A PLUMP ASS AND BROAD CHEST AND HAIR ALL OVER LIKE A BEAR...

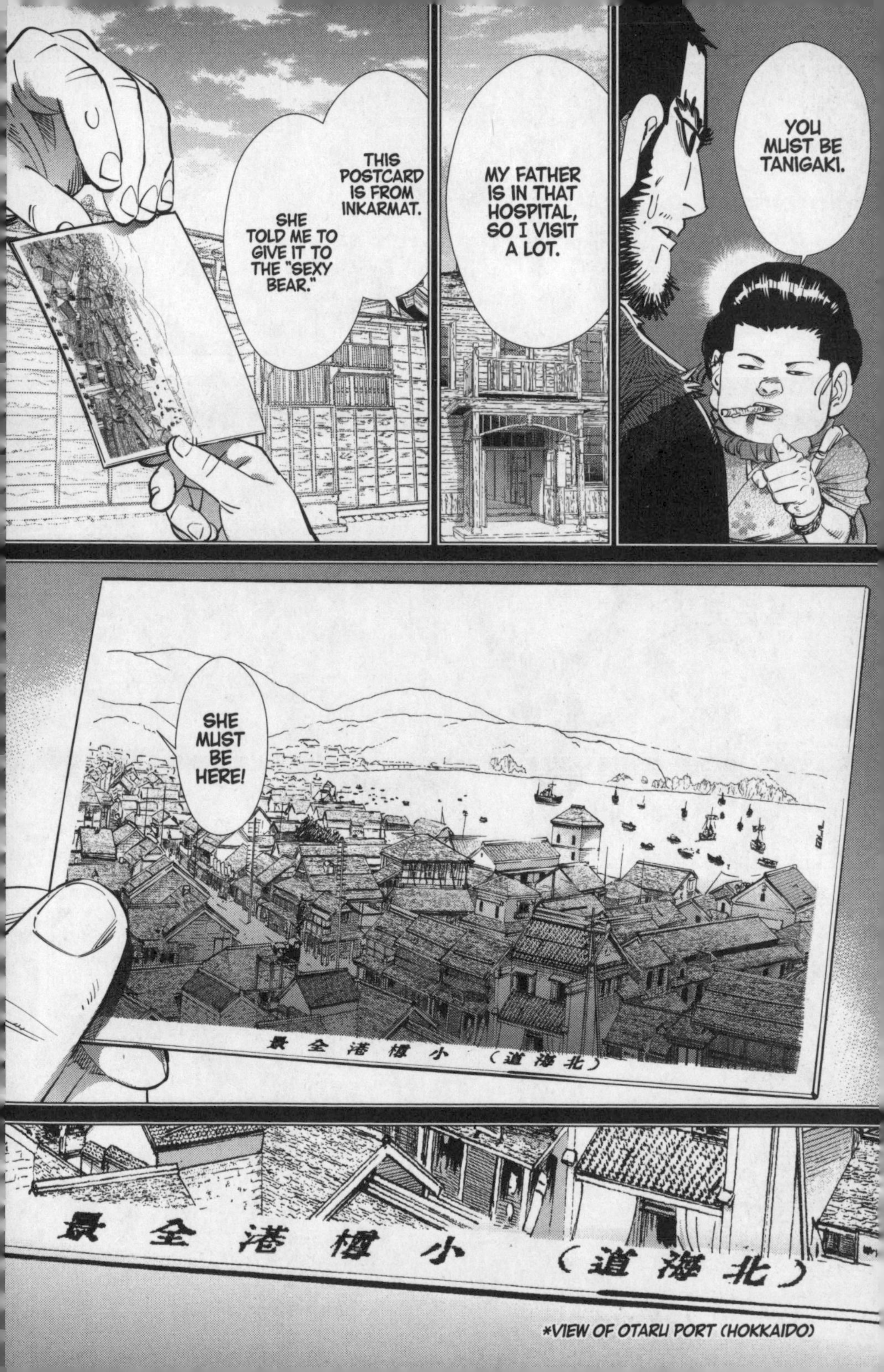
YOU MUST BE TANIGAKI.
MY FATHER IS IN THAT HOSPITAL, SO I VISIT A LOT.
THIS POSTCARD IS FROM INKARMAT.
SHE TOLD ME TO GIVE IT TO THE "SEXY BEAR."
SHE MUST BE HERE!
小樽港全景（北海道）
小樽港全景（北海道）
*VIEW OF OTARU PORT (HOKKAIDO)

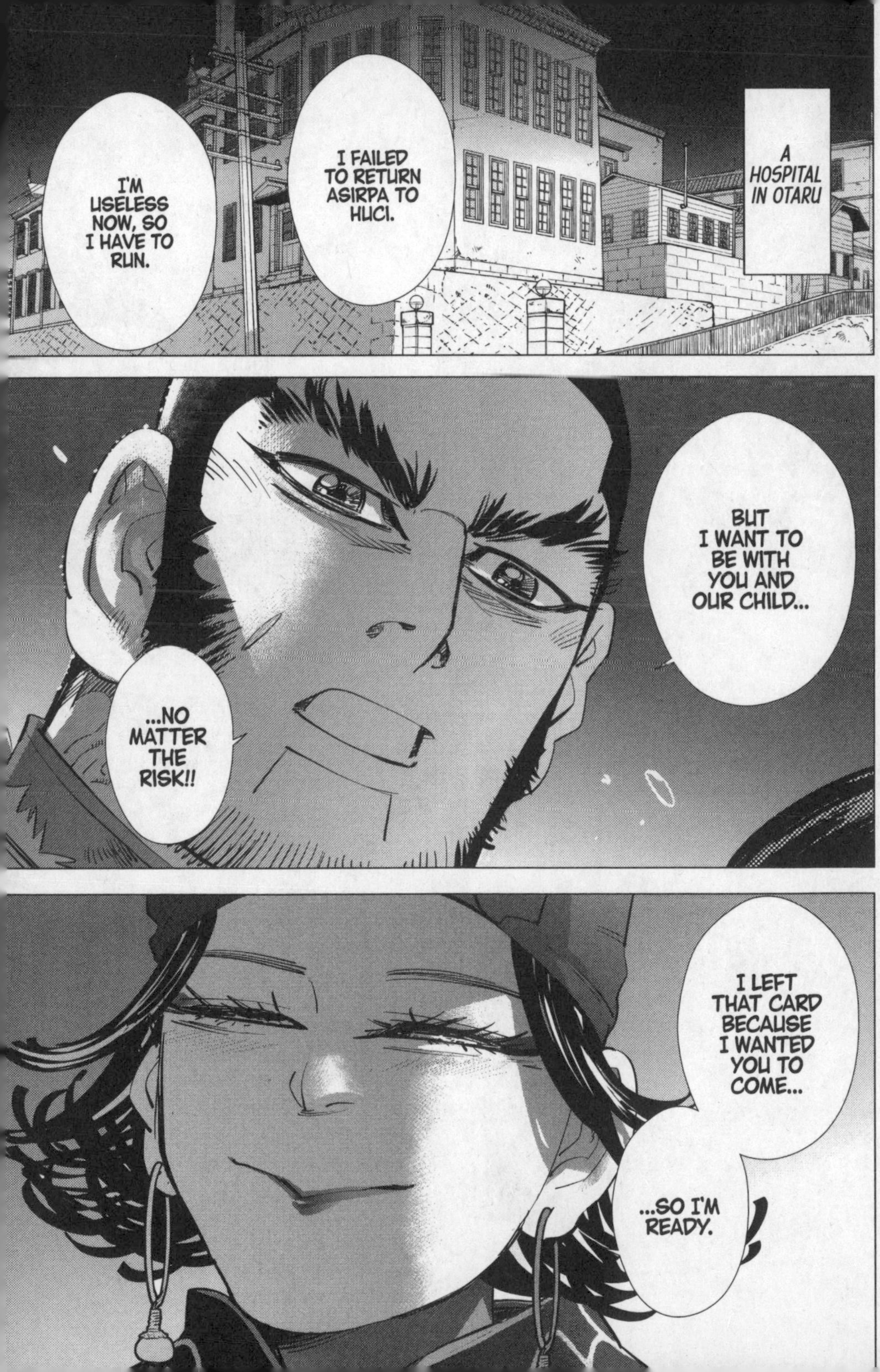
A HOSPITAL IN OTARU
I FAILED TO RETURN ASIRPA TO HUCI.
I'M USELESS NOW, SO I HAVE TO RUN.
BUT I WANT TO BE WITH YOU AND OUR CHILD...
...NO MATTER THE RISK!!
I LEFT THAT CARD BECAUSE I WANTED YOU TO COME...
...SO I'M READY.

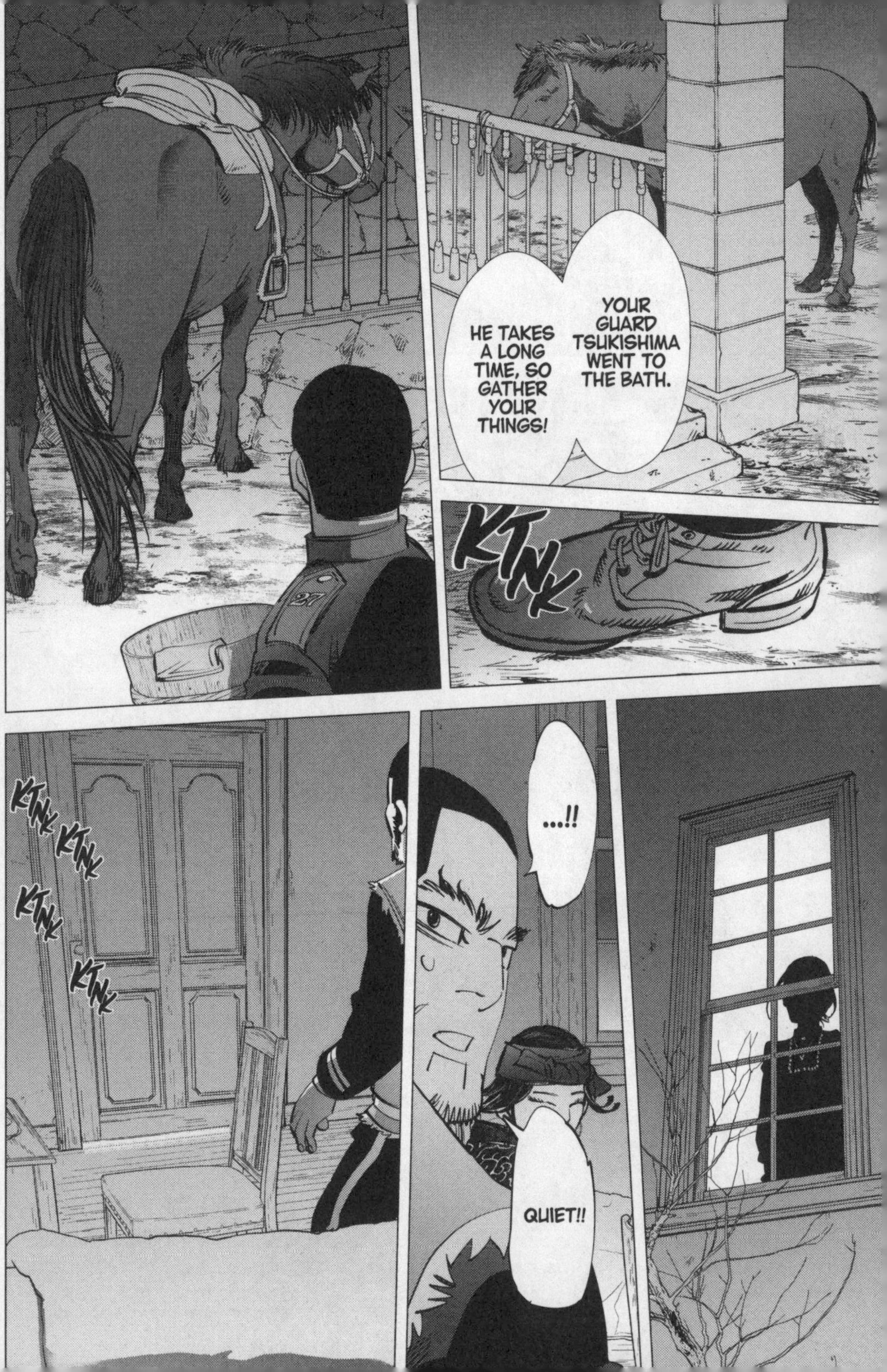
YOUR GUARD TSUKISHIMA WENT TO THE BATH.
HE TAKES A LONG TIME, SO GATHER YOUR THINGS!
KTNK
...!!
QUIET!!
KTNK KTNK KTNK KTNK

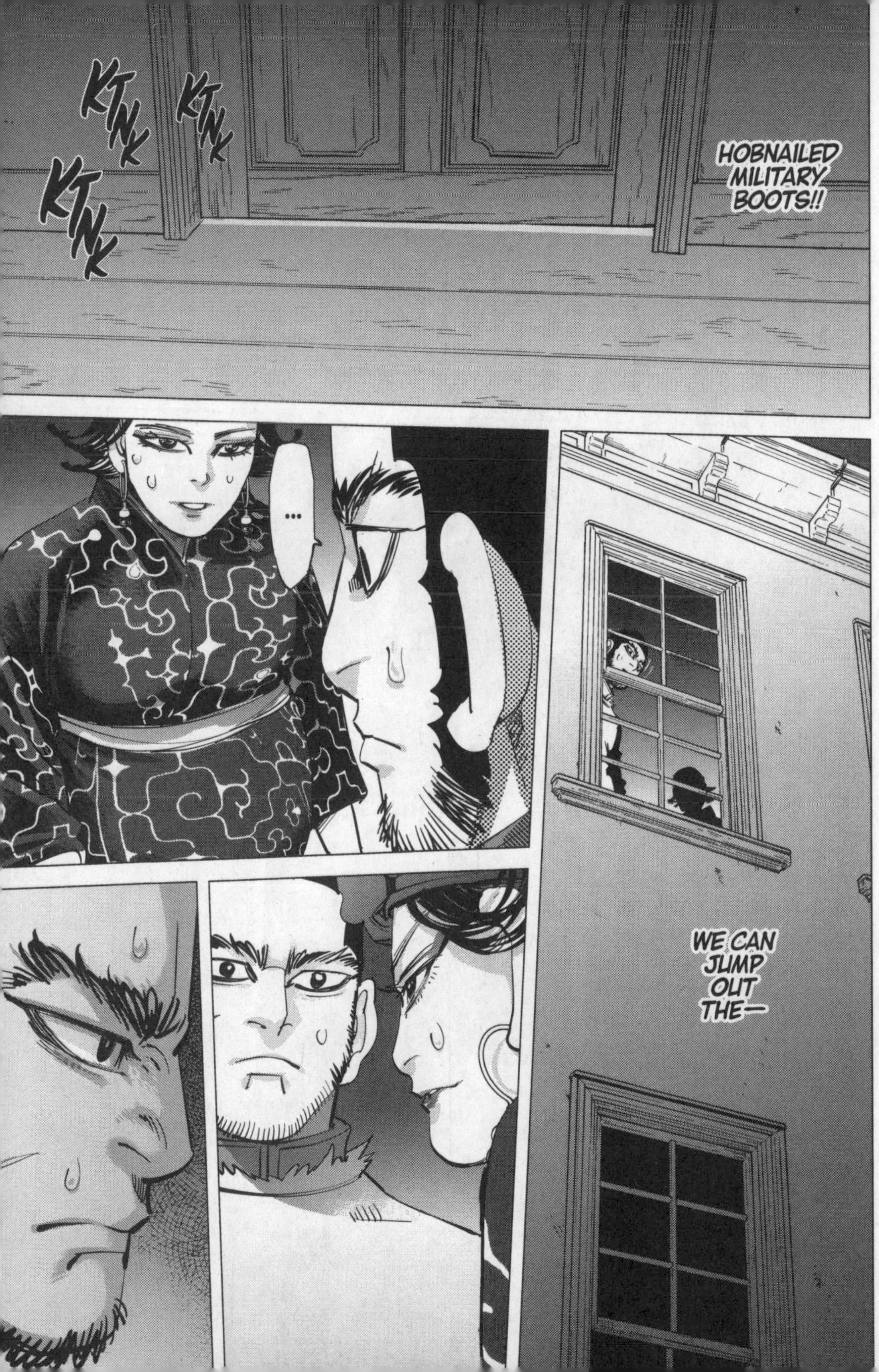
HOBNAILED MILITARY BOOTS!!
KTINK KTINK
KTINK
WE CAN JUMP OUT THE—
...

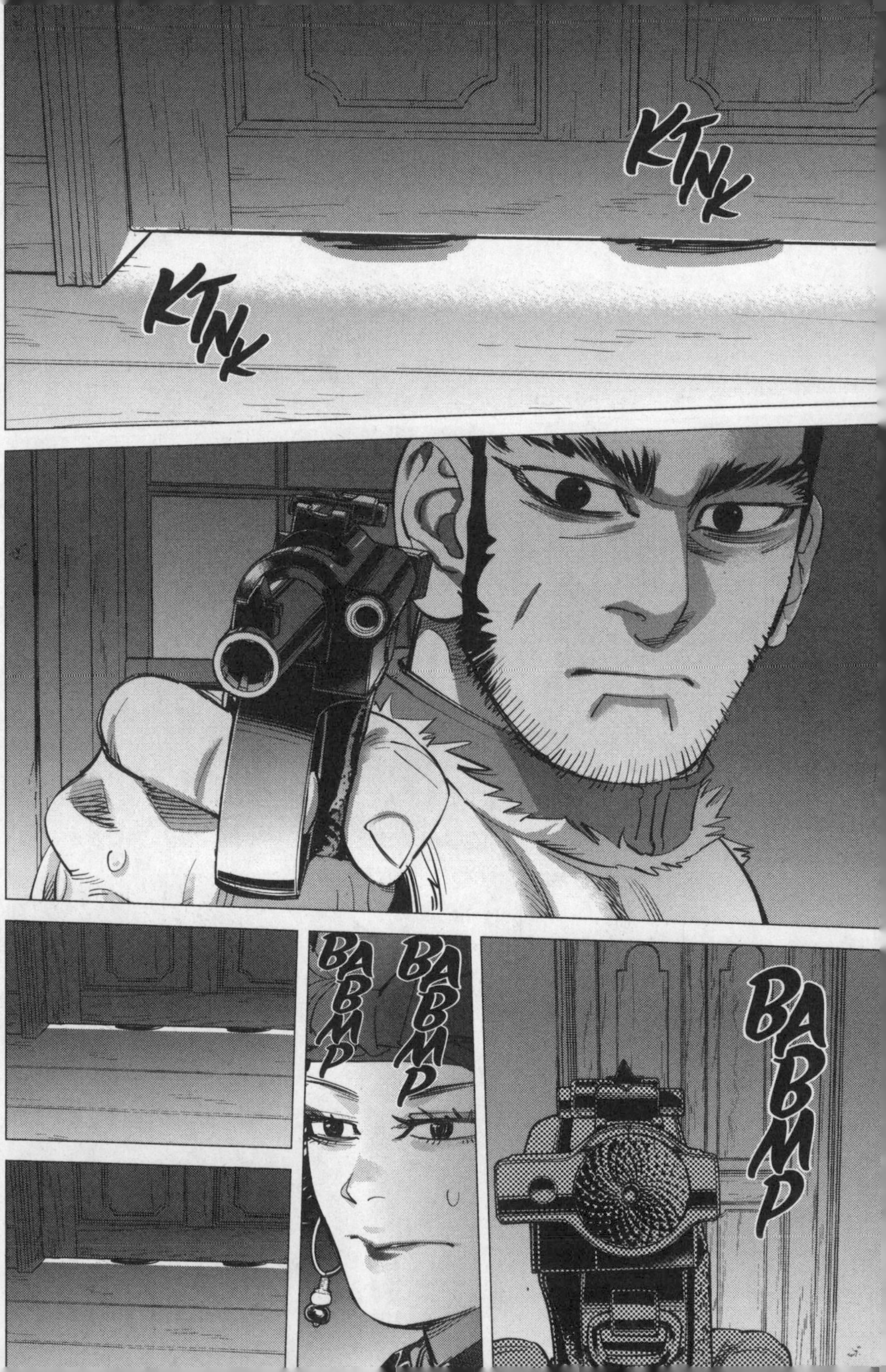
KTINK
KTINK
BABMP
BABMP
BABMP

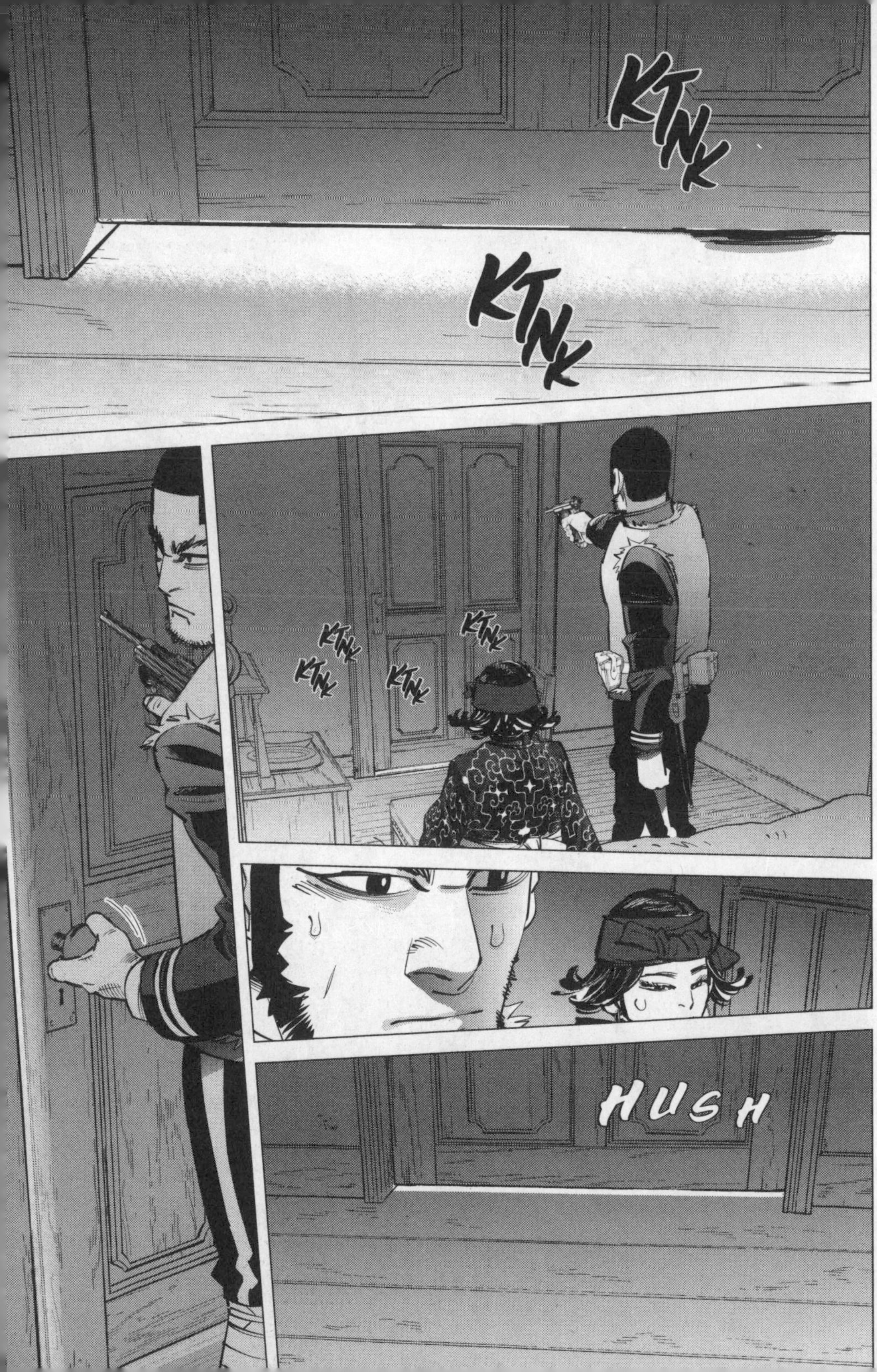
KTNK
KTNK
KTNK
KTNK
KTNK
KTNK
HUSH

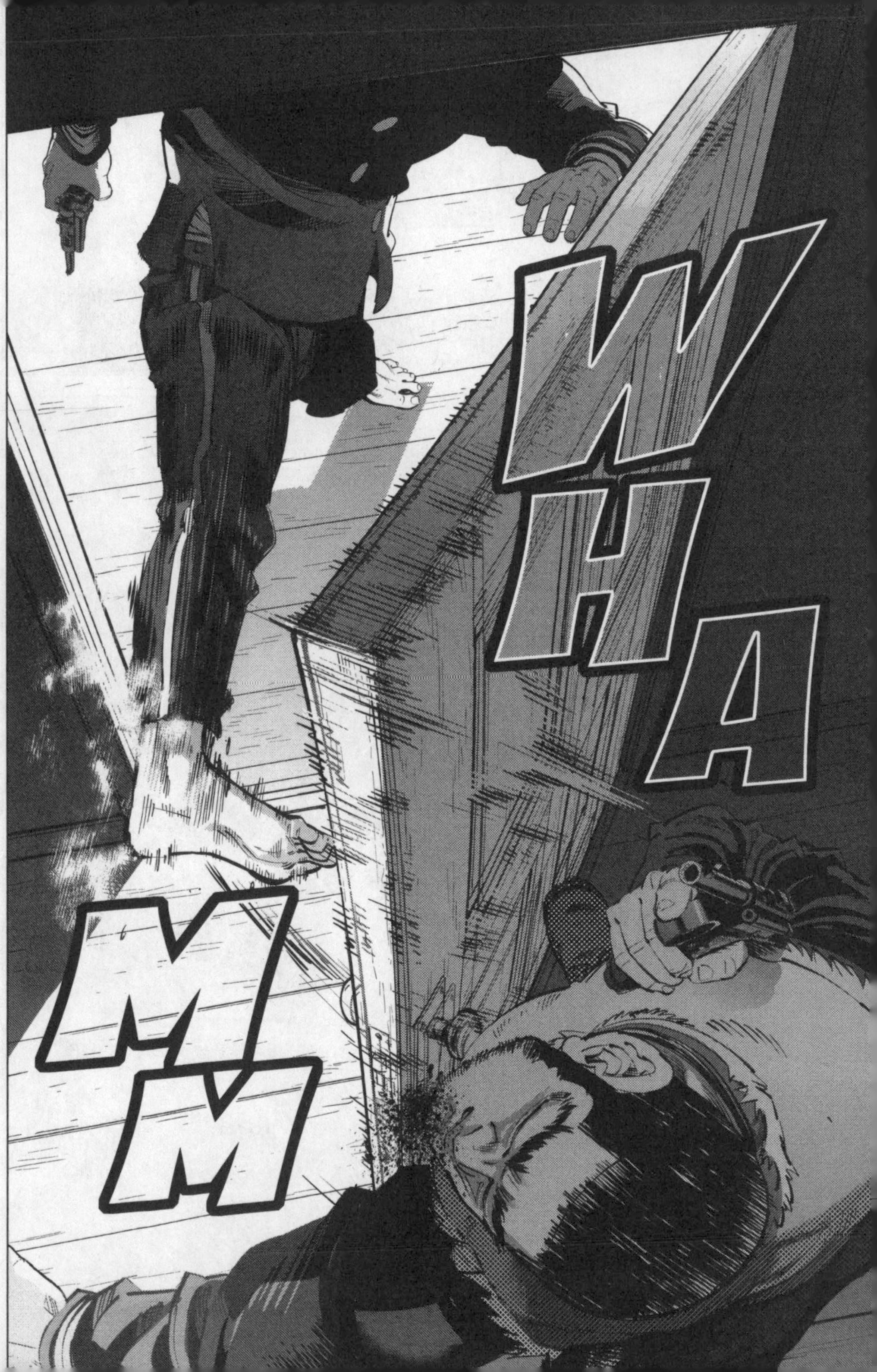
WHAMM

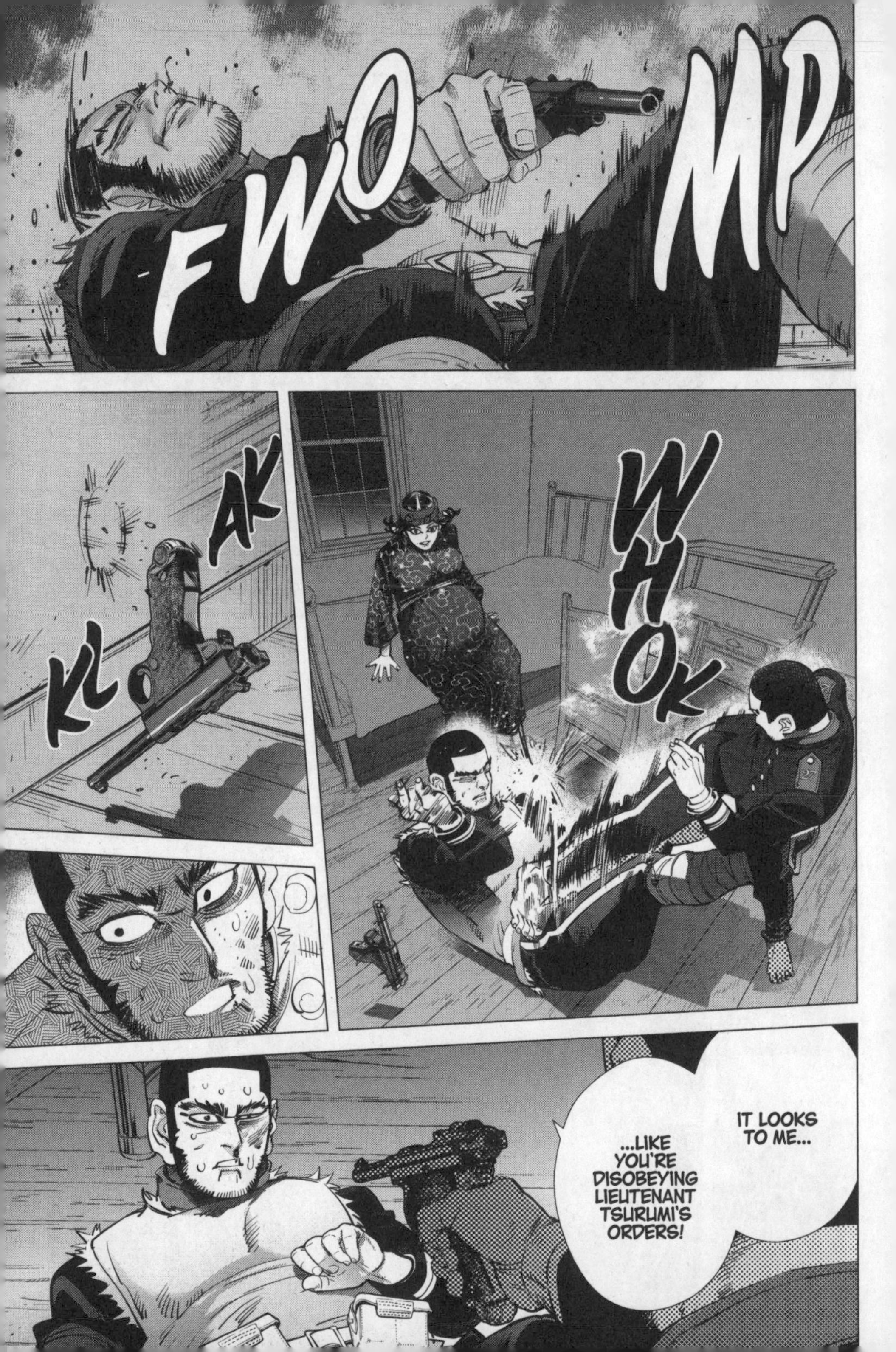
FWOMP
WHOK
KLAK
IT LOOKS TO ME...
...LIKE YOU'RE DISOBEYING LIEUTENANT TSURUMI'S ORDERS!

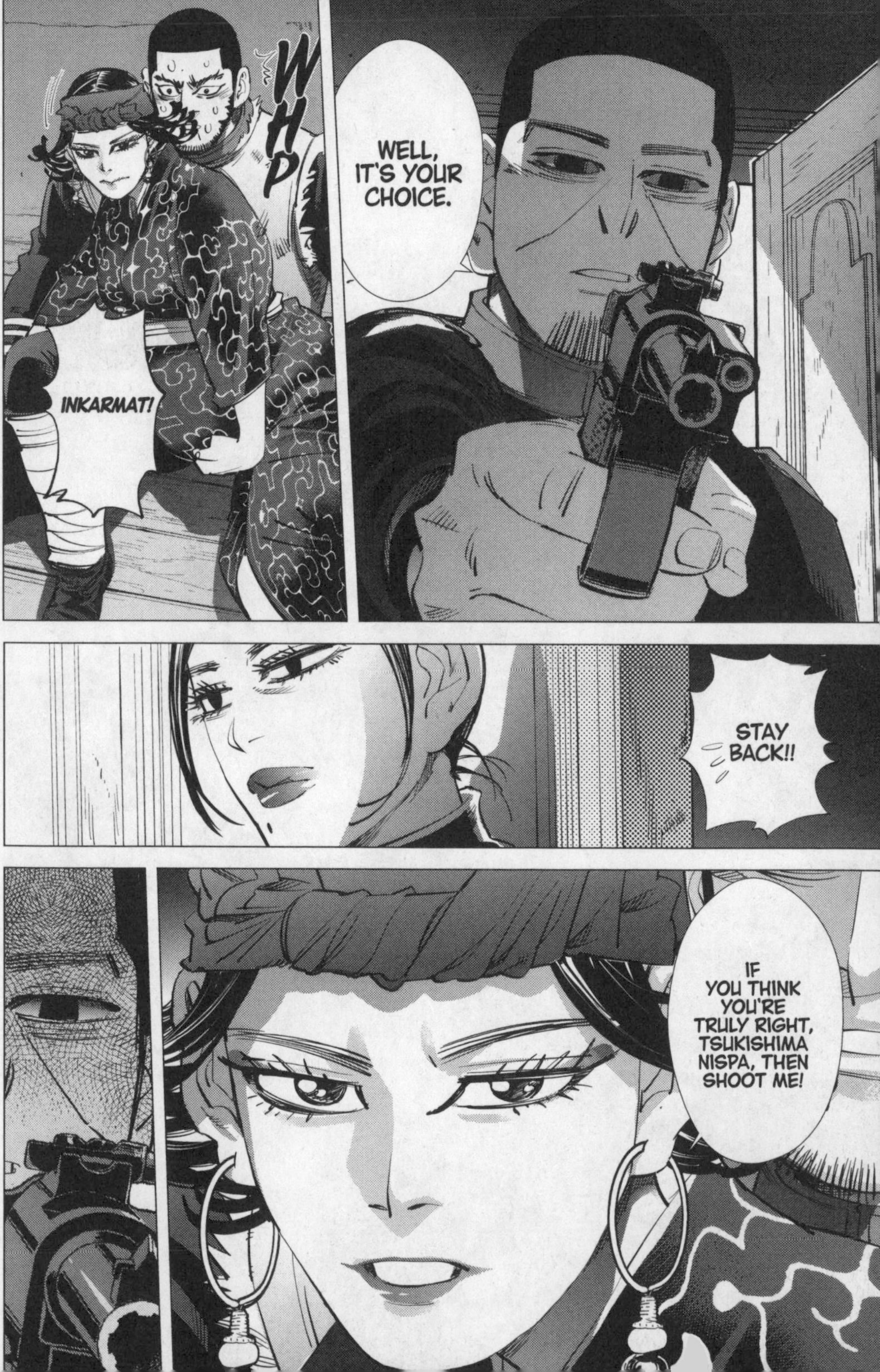
WELL, IT'S YOUR CHOICE.
WHP
INKARMAT!
STAY BACK!!
IF YOU THINK YOU'RE TRULY RIGHT, TSUKISHIMA NISPA, THEN SHOOT ME!

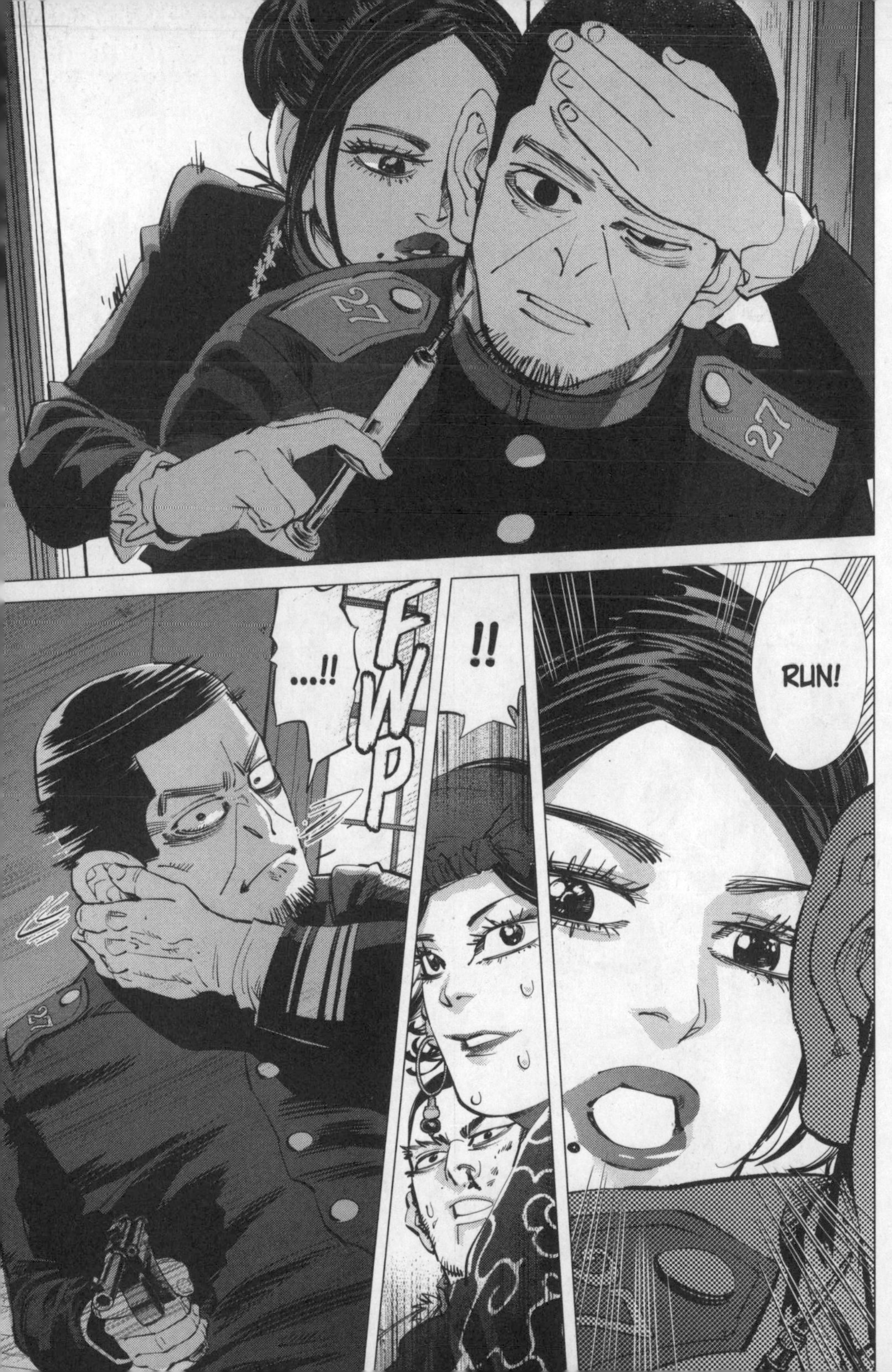
RUN!
!!
FWP
...!!

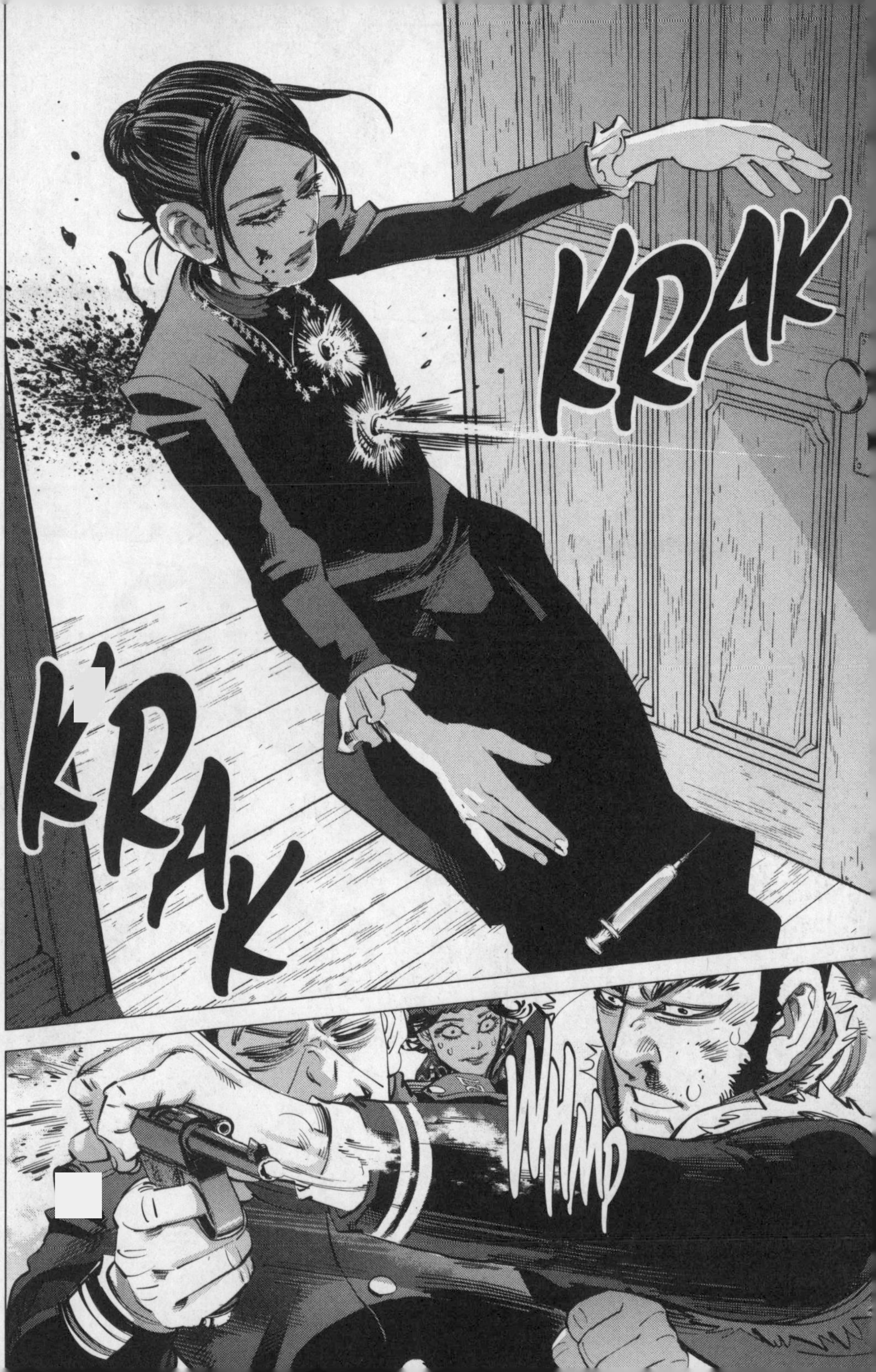
KRAK
K'RAK
WHMP

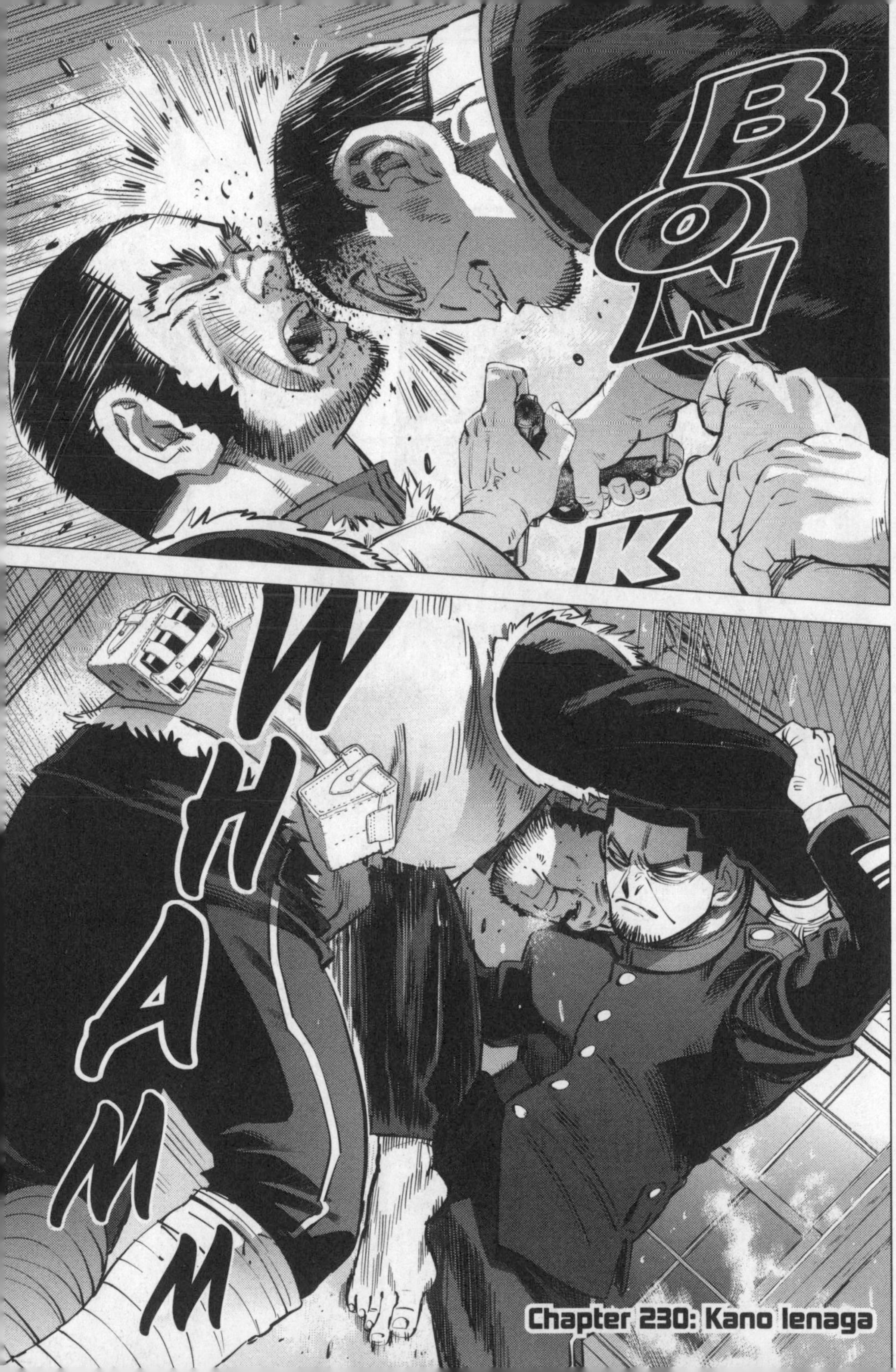
BONK
WHAMMM
Chapter 230: Kano Ienaga

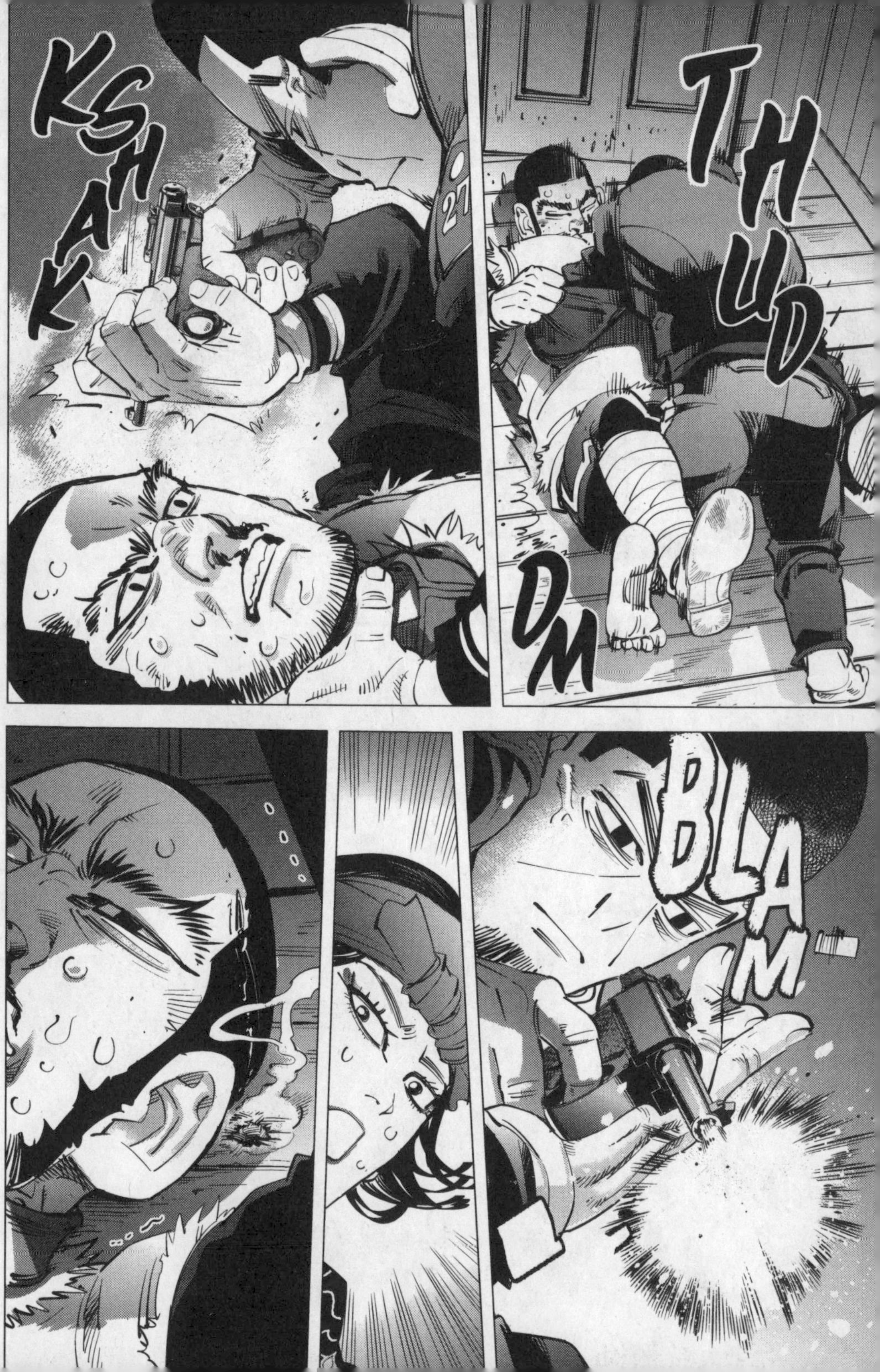
THUD
DM
KSHAK
BLAM

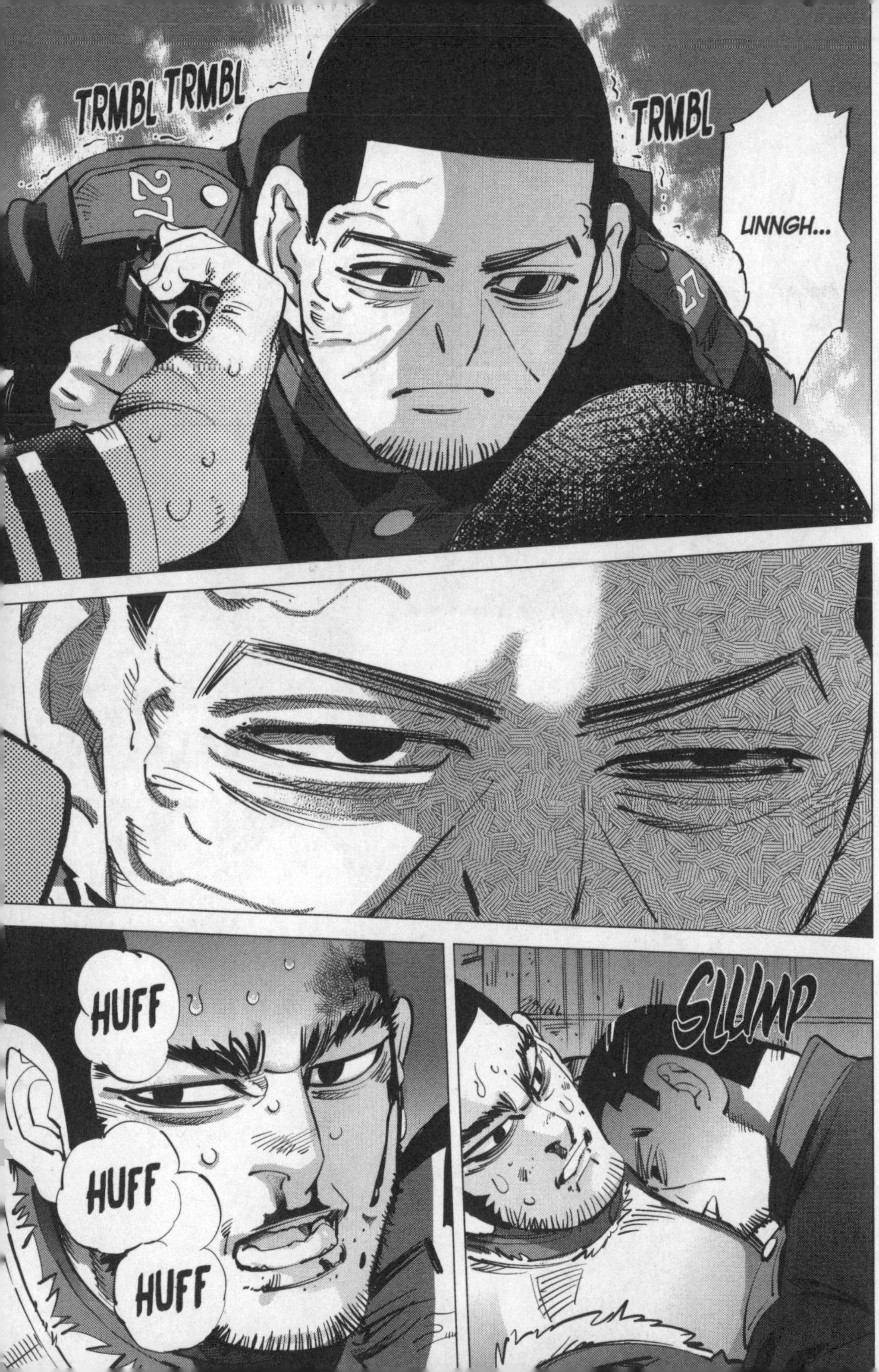
UNNGH...
TRMBL
TRMBL TRMBL
SLUMP
HUFF
HUFF
HUFF

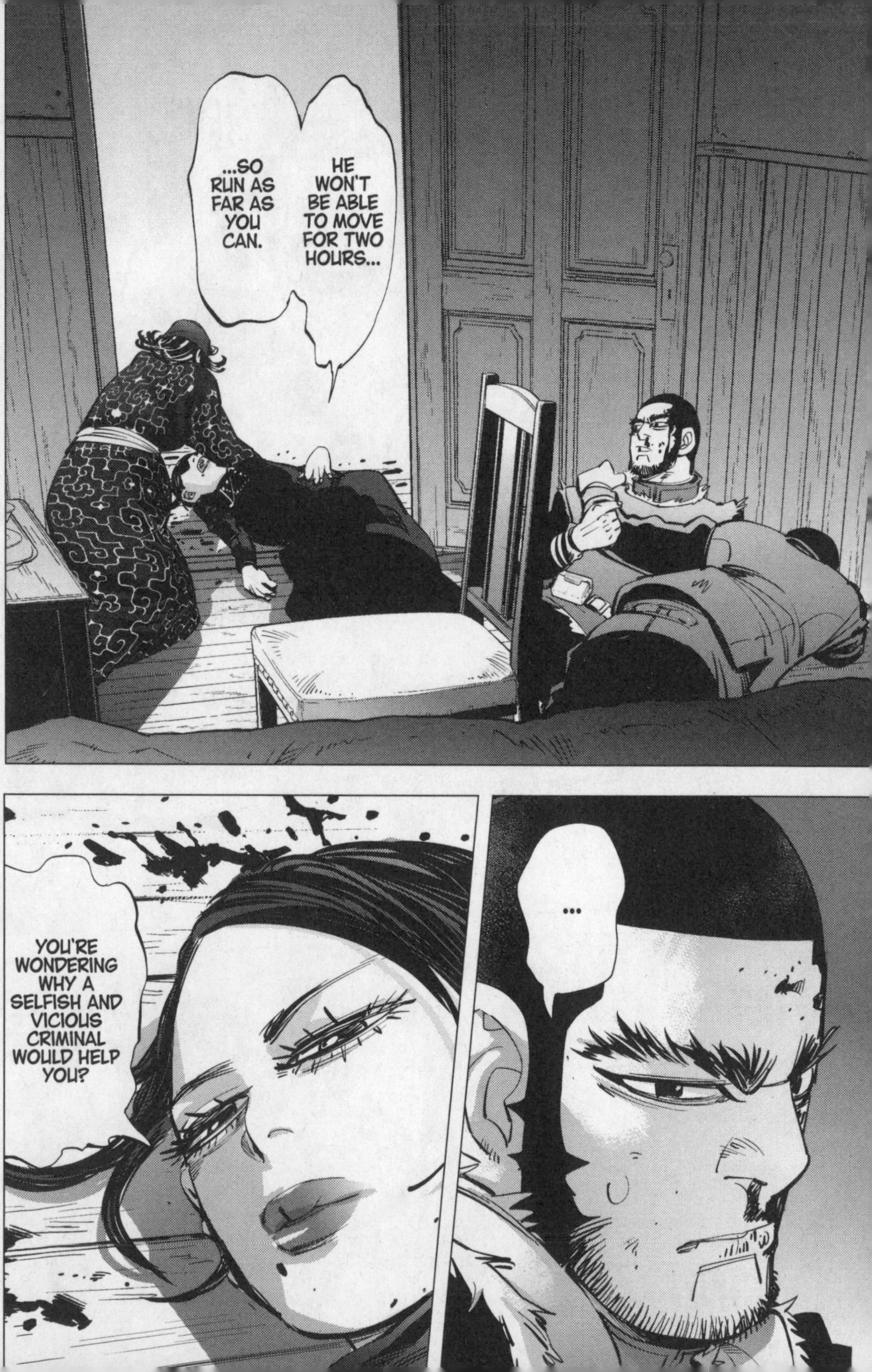
HE WON'T BE ABLE TO MOVE FOR TWO HOURS...
...SO RUN AS FAR AS YOU CAN.
...
YOU'RE WONDERING WHY A SELFISH AND VICIOUS CRIMINAL WOULD HELP YOU?

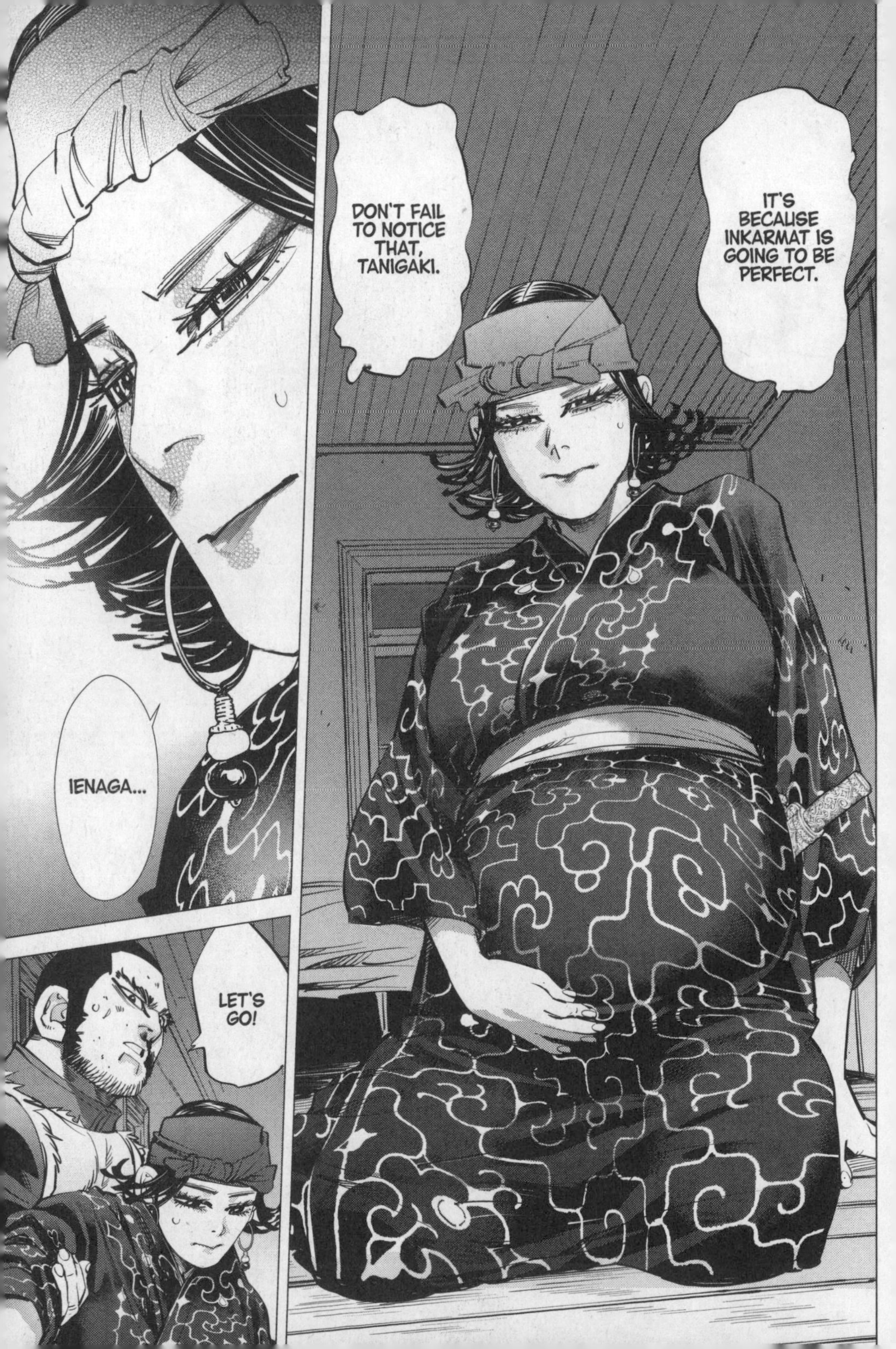
IT'S BECAUSE INKARMAT IS GOING TO BE PERFECT.
DON'T FAIL TO NOTICE THAT, TANIGAKI.
IENAGA...
LET'S GO!

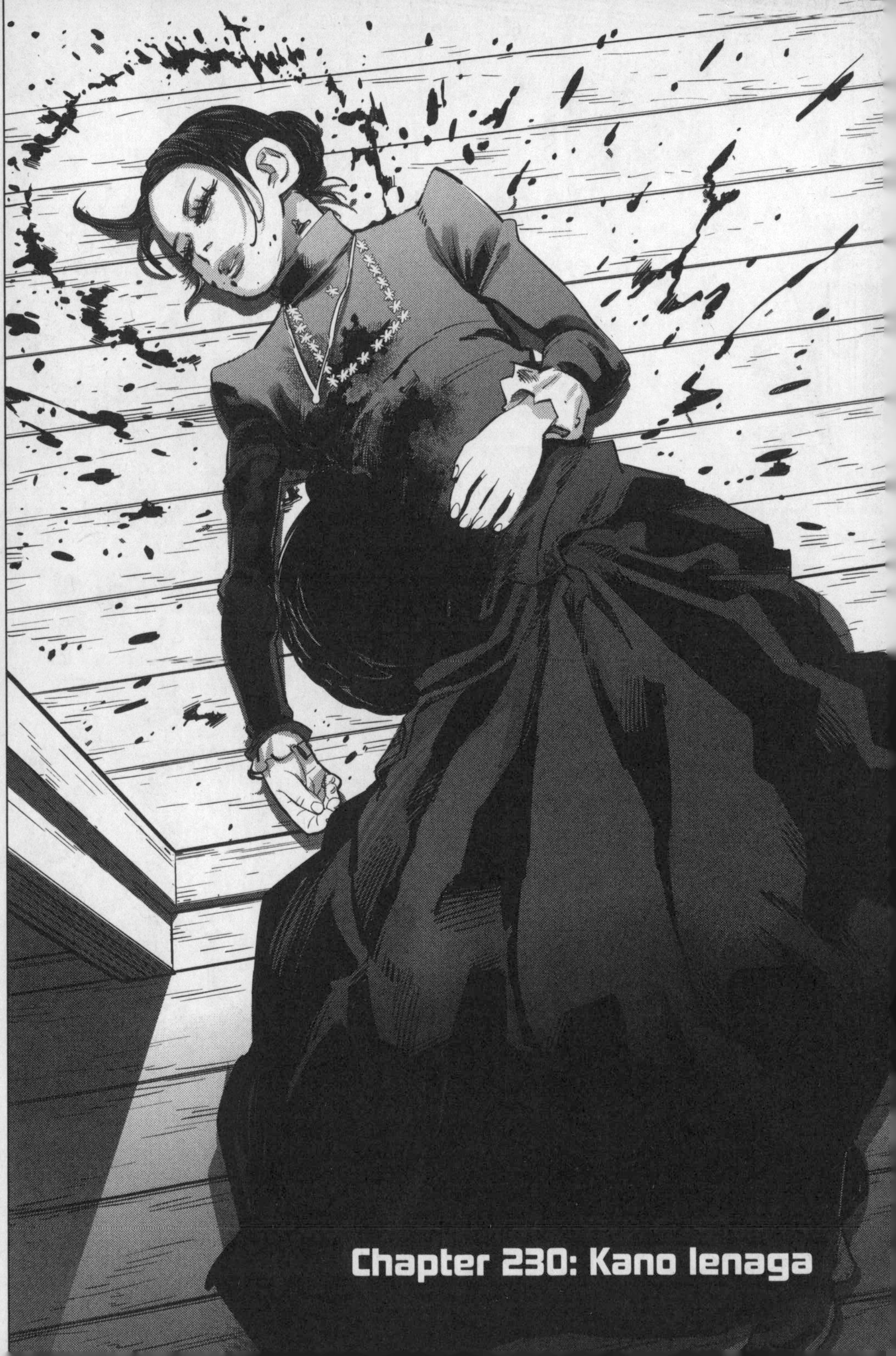
Chapter 230: Kano Ienaga

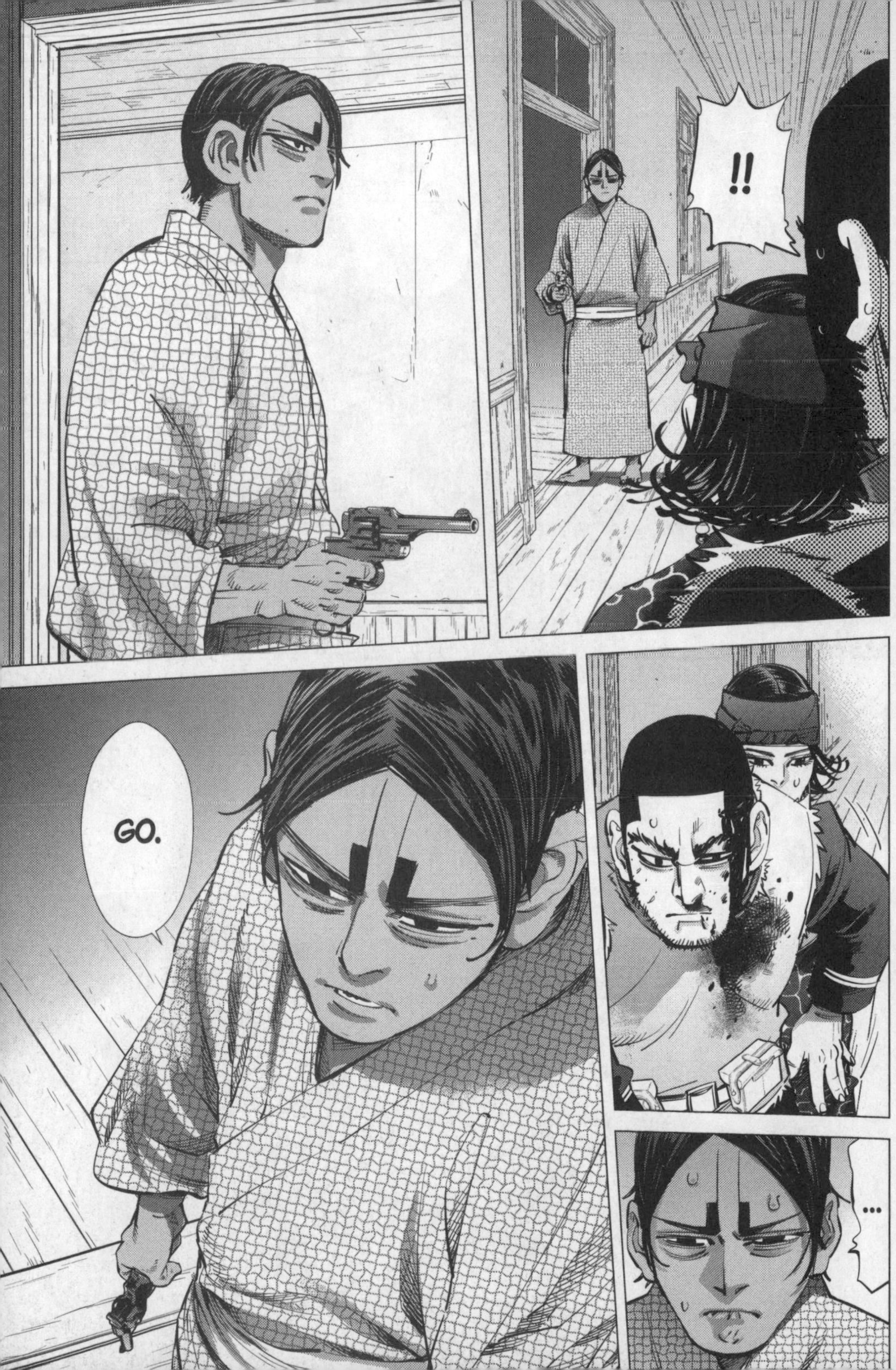
!!
...
GO.

...
TMP TMP TMP TMP
WHY WOULD HE DO THAT?
MAYBE BECAUSE I OFTEN TOLD HIS FORTUNE.
THAT WOULDN'T BE ENOUGH...
...FOR THE KOITO I KNOW.
KABLAM
ZING

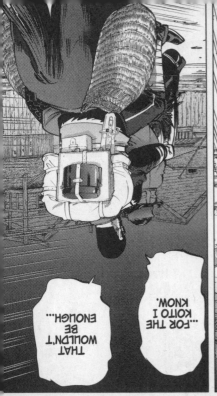

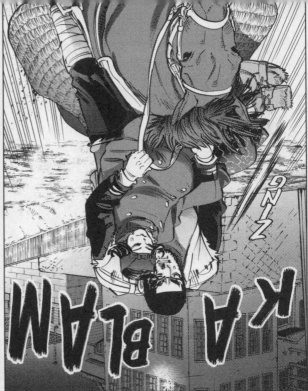

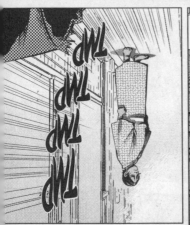

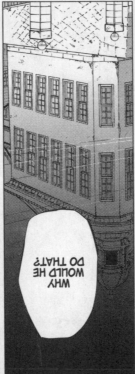

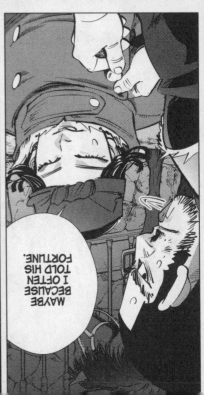

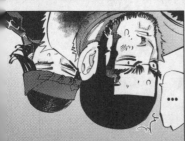

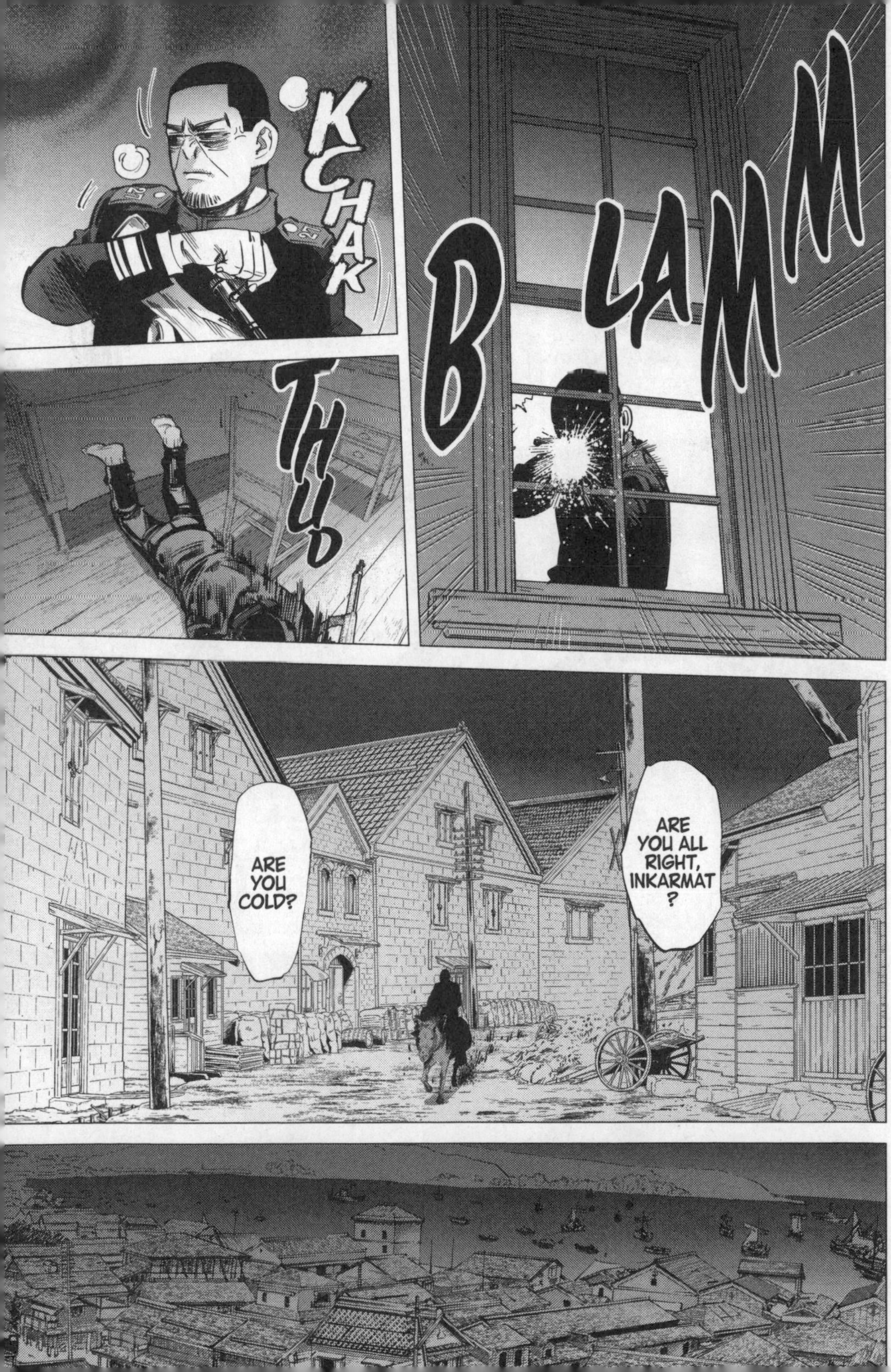
BLAMM
KCHAK
THUD
ARE YOU ALL RIGHT, INKARMAT?
ARE YOU COLD?

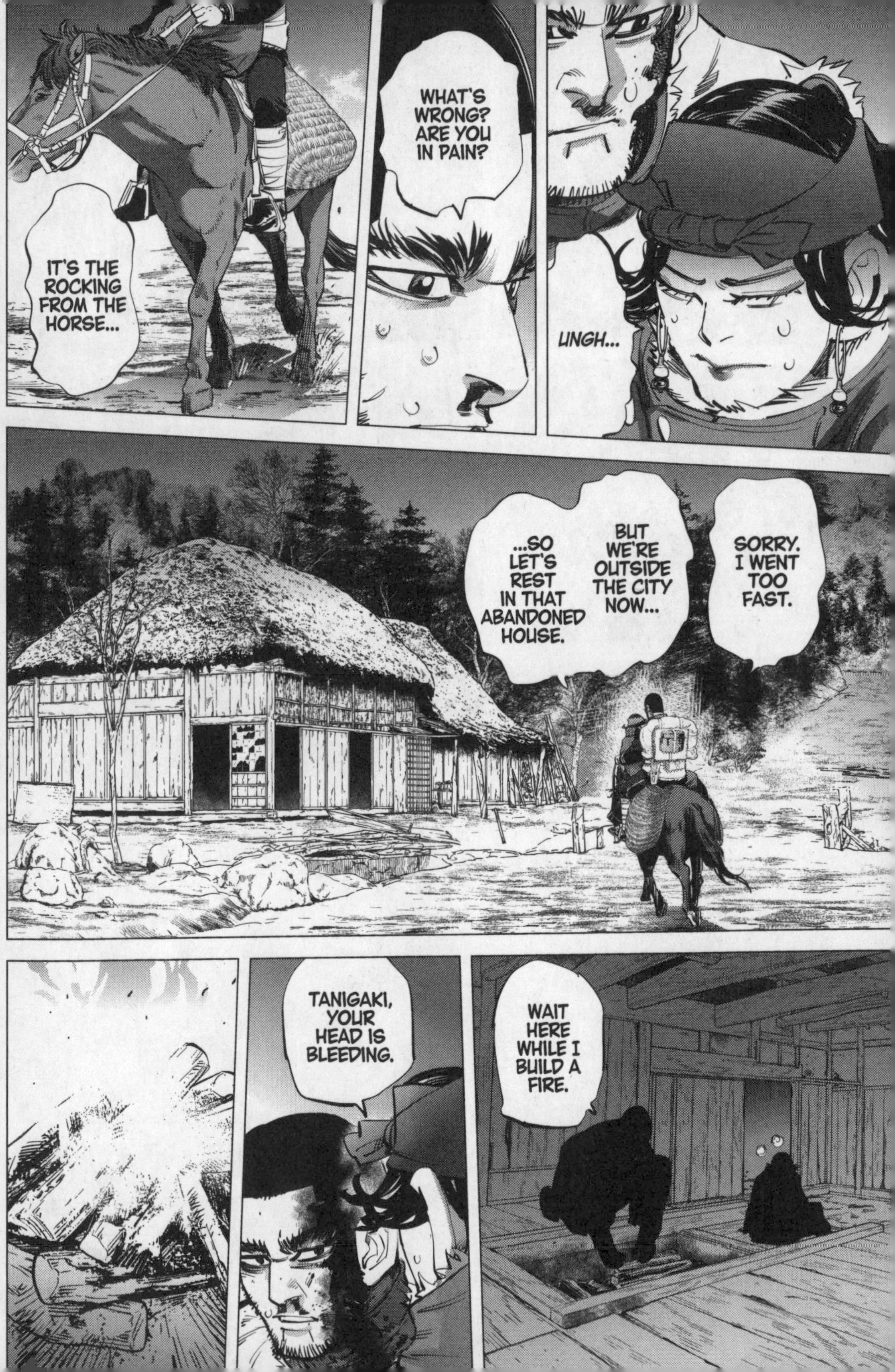
UNGH...
WHAT'S WRONG? ARE YOU IN PAIN?
IT'S THE ROCKING FROM THE HORSE...
SORRY. I WENT TOO FAST.
BUT WE'RE OUTSIDE THE CITY NOW...
...SO LET'S REST IN THAT ABANDONED HOUSE.
WAIT HERE WHILE I BUILD A FIRE.
TANIGAKI, YOUR HEAD IS BLEEDING.

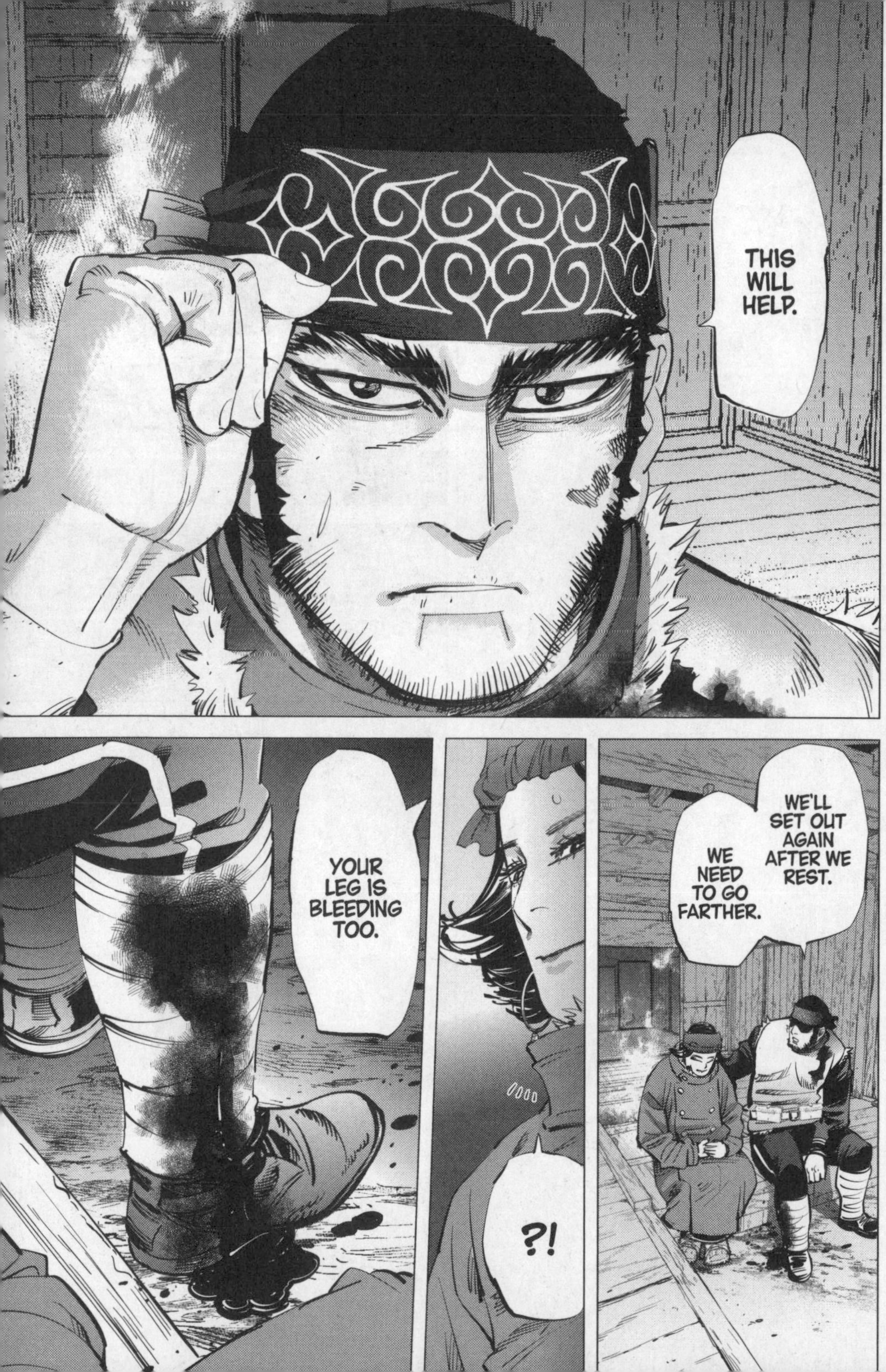
THIS WILL HELP.
WE'LL SET OUT AGAIN AFTER WE REST.
WE NEED TO GO FARTHER.
?!
YOUR LEG IS BLEEDING TOO.

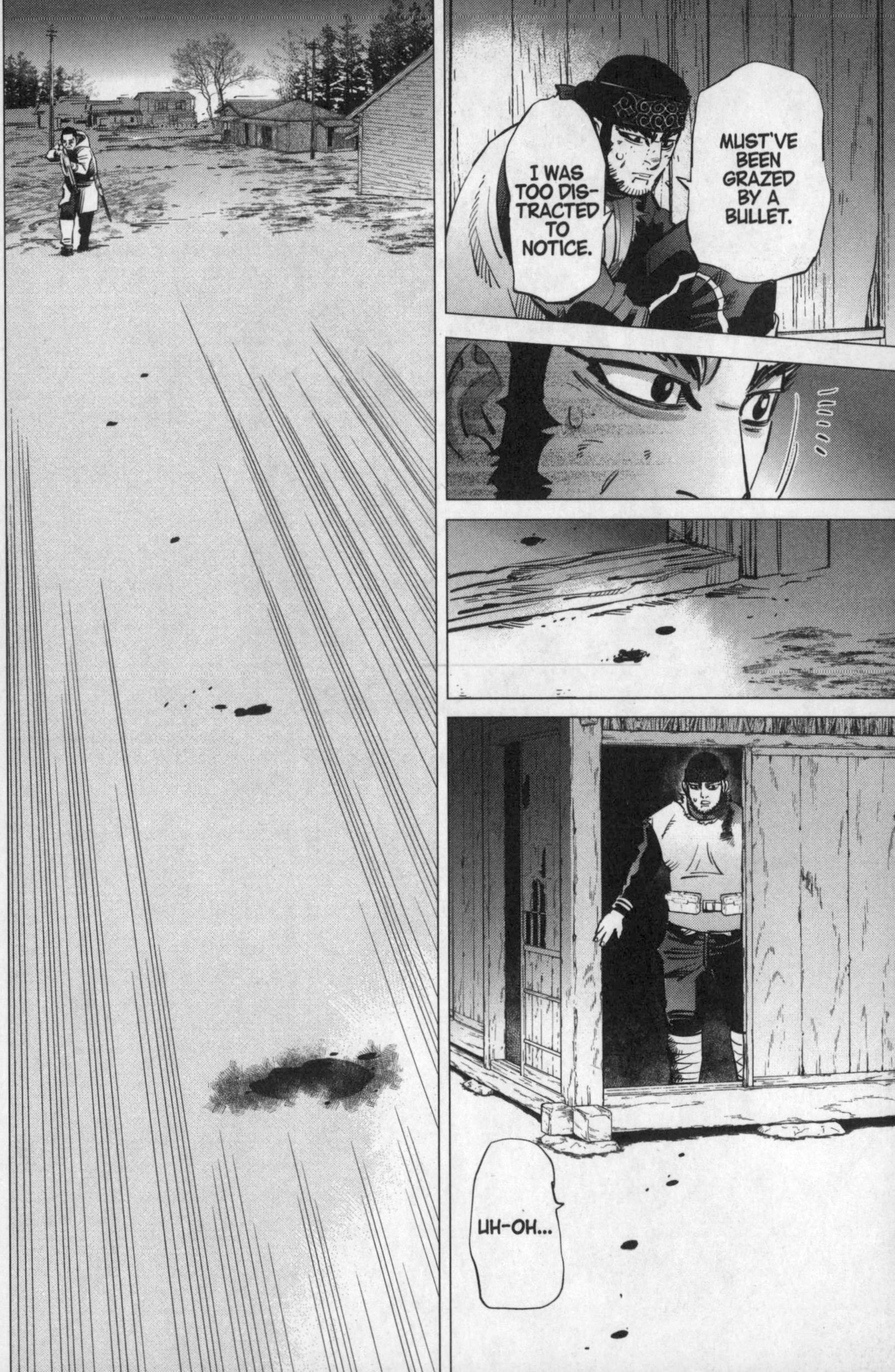
MUST'VE BEEN GRAZED BY A BULLET.
I WAS TOO DIS-TRACTED TO NOTICE.
UH-OH...

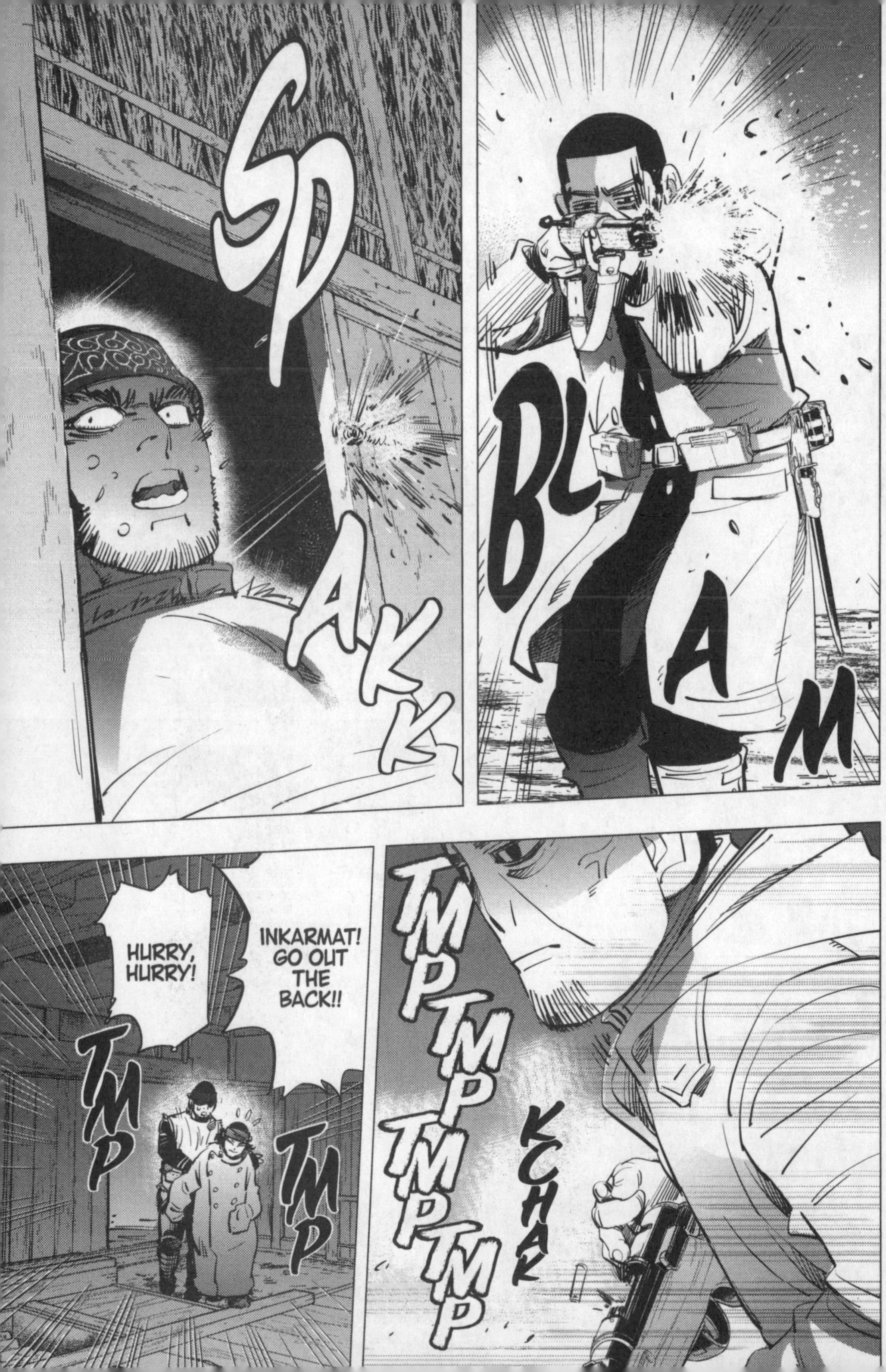
BLAM
SPAKK
TMPTMPTMPTMPTMP
KCHAK
INKARMAT! GO OUT THE BACK!!
HURRY, HURRY!
TMP
TMP

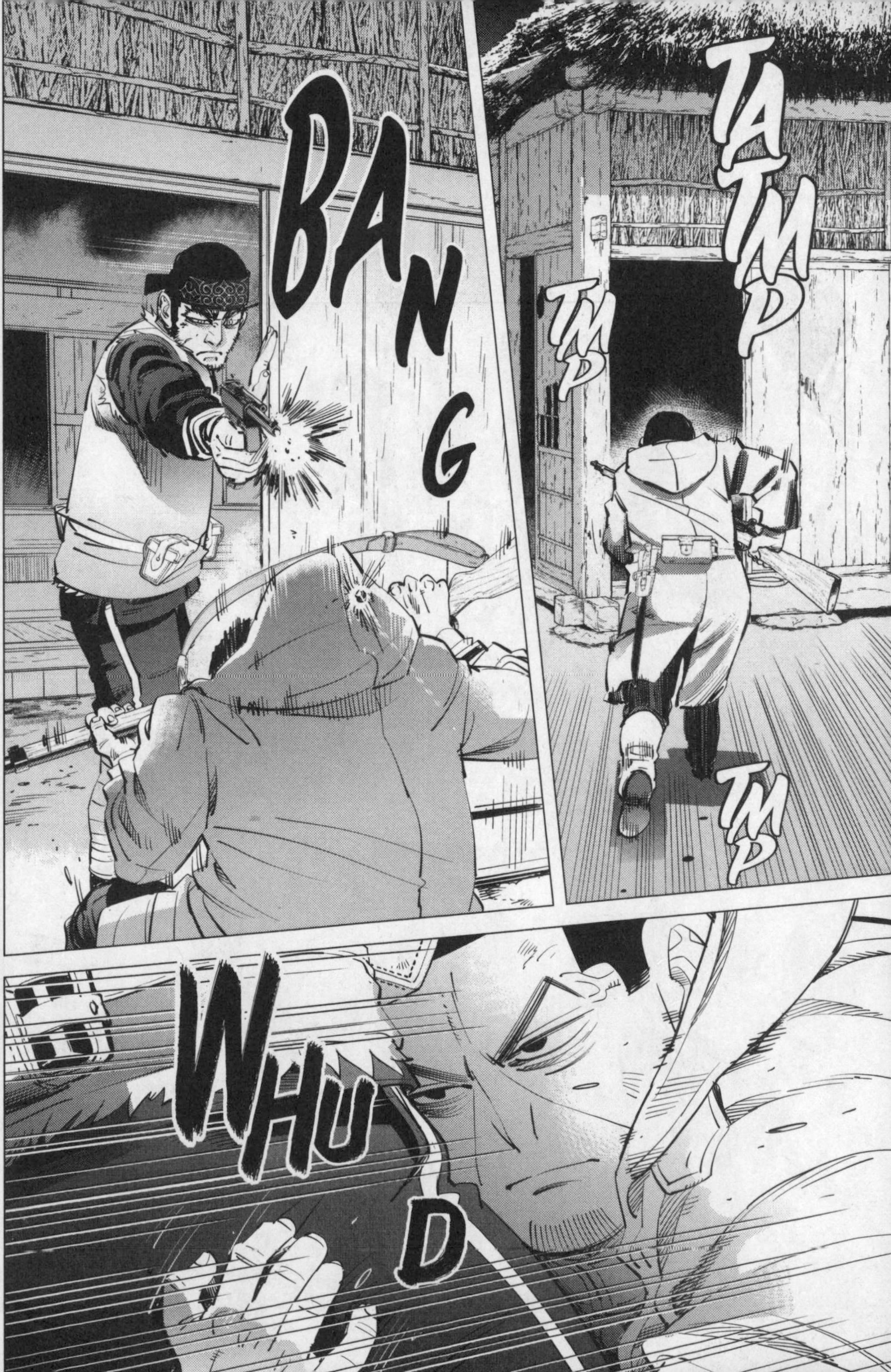
TAMP
TMP
TMP
BANG
WHUD

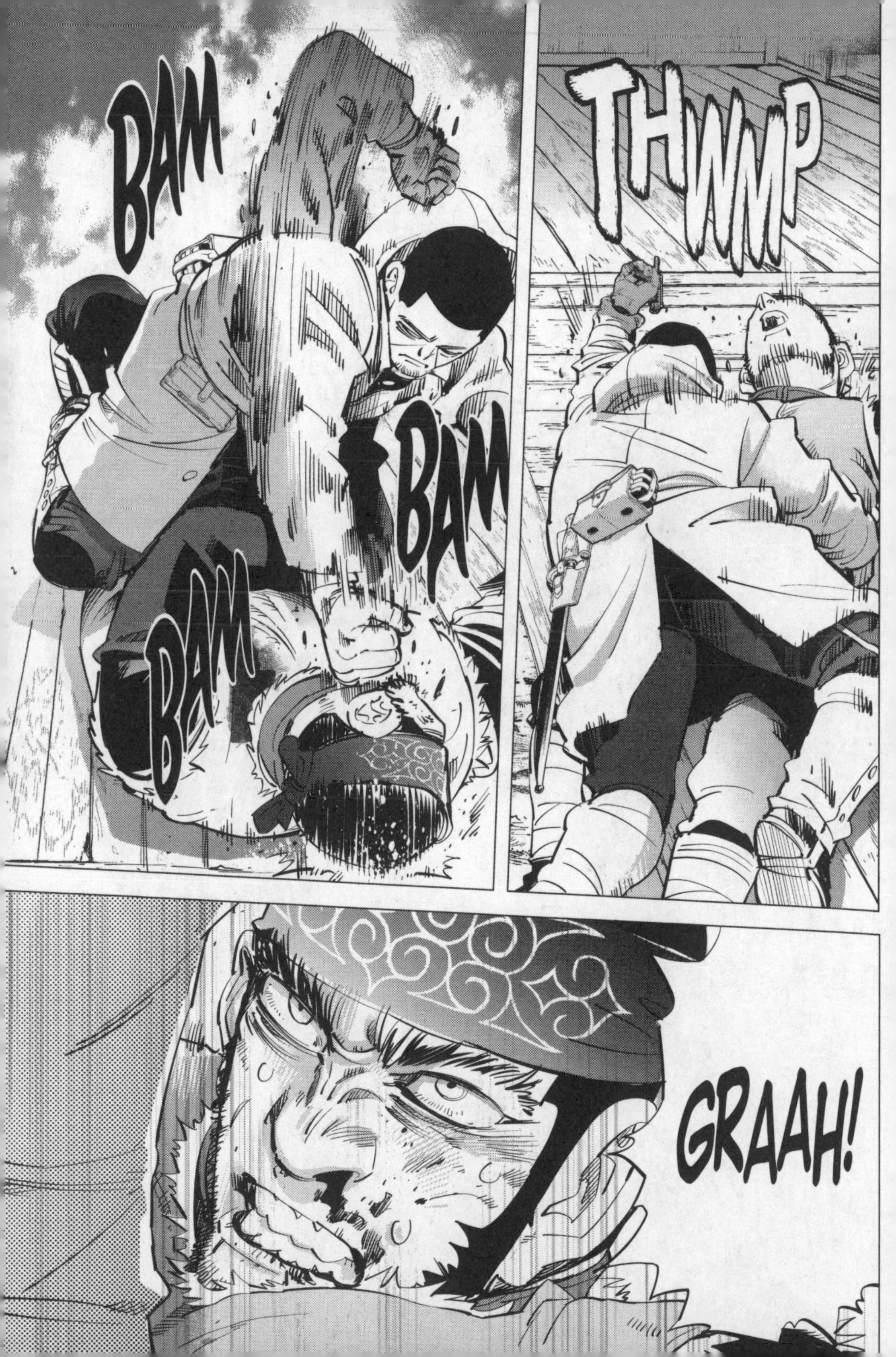
THWMP
BAM
BAM
BAM
GRAAH!

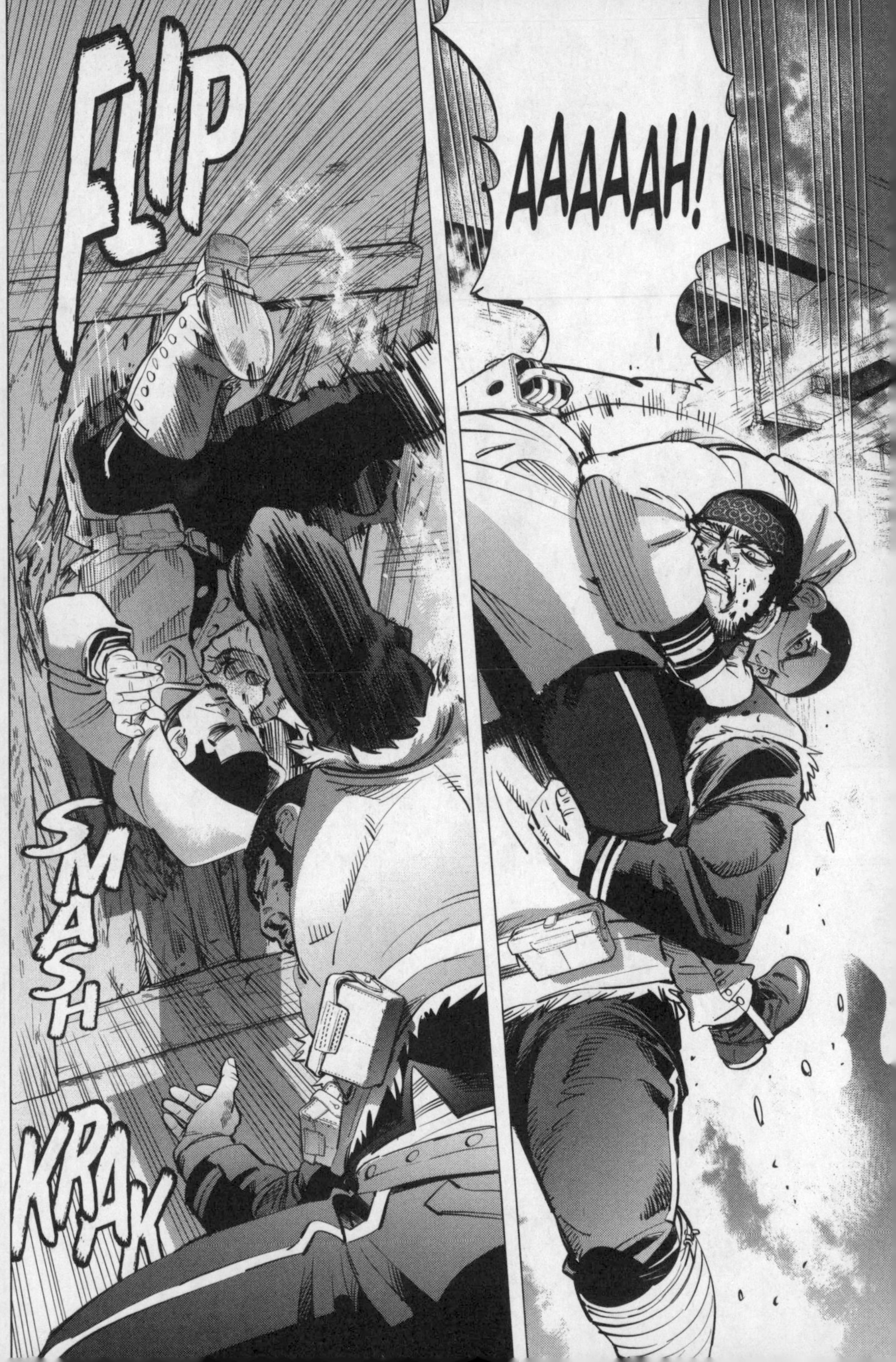
AAAAAH!
RIP
SMASH
KRAK

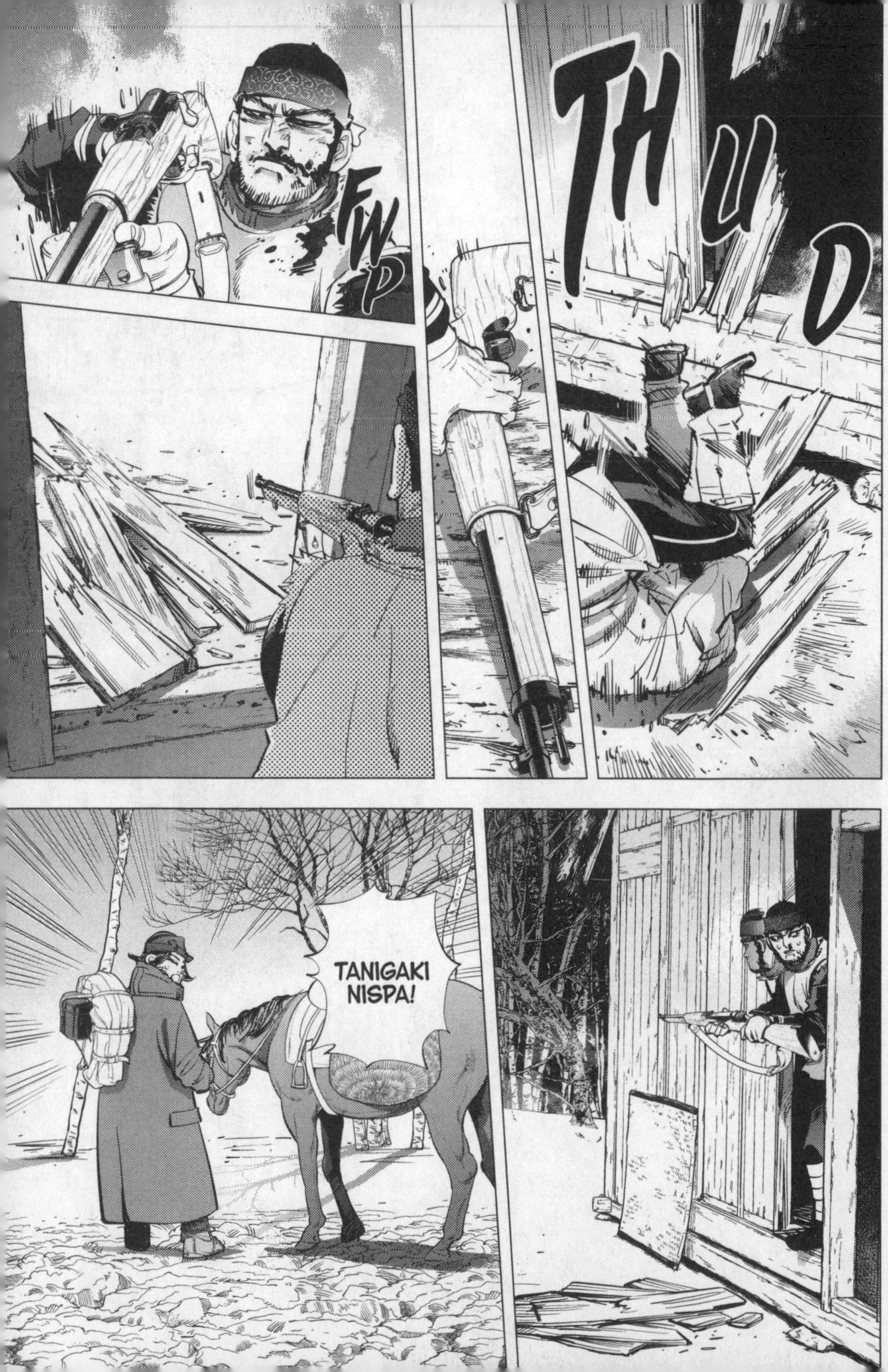
THUD
FWP
TANIGAKI NISPA!

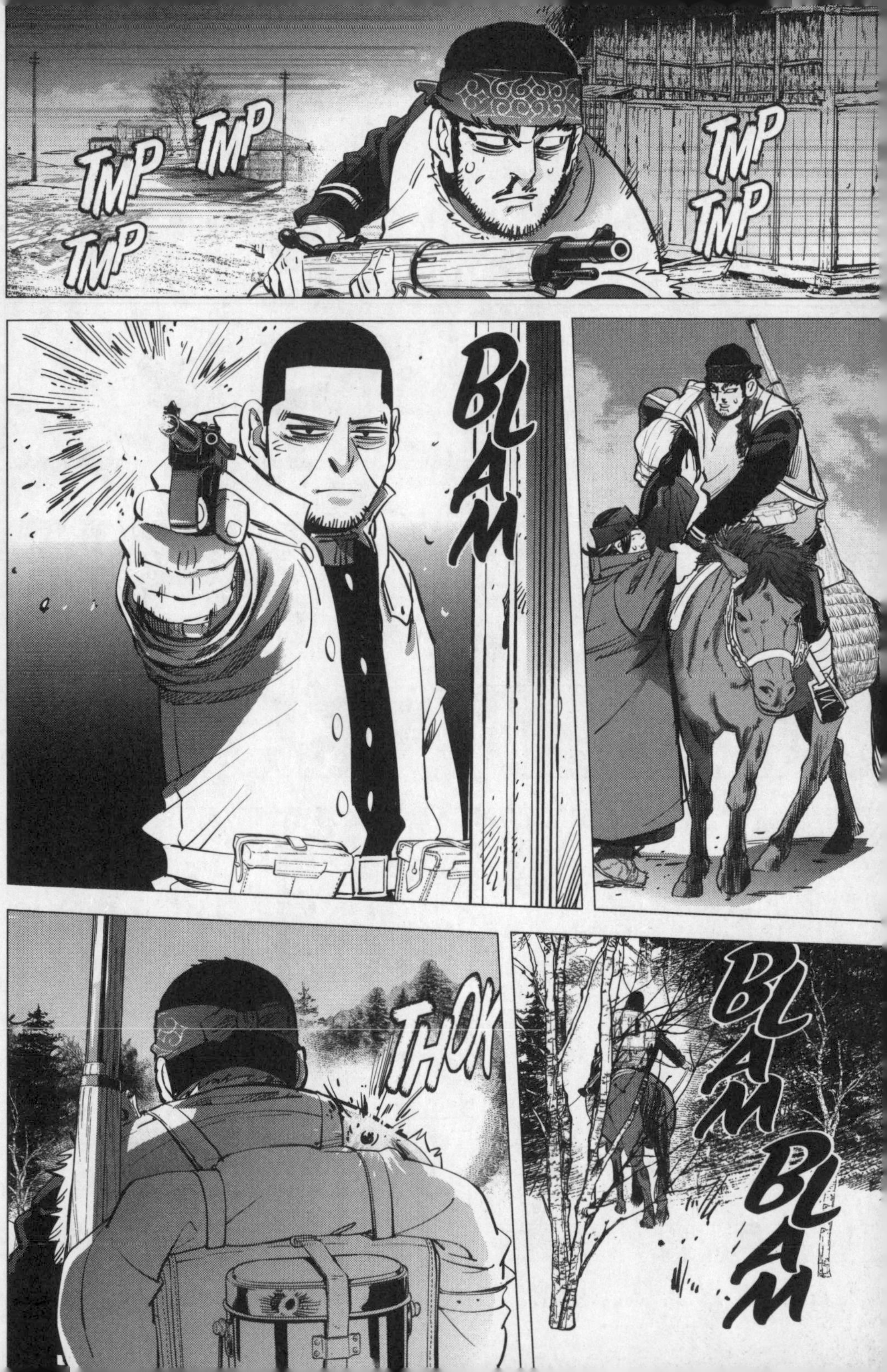
TMP
TMP
TMP TMP
TMP
BLAM
THOK
BLAM
BLAM

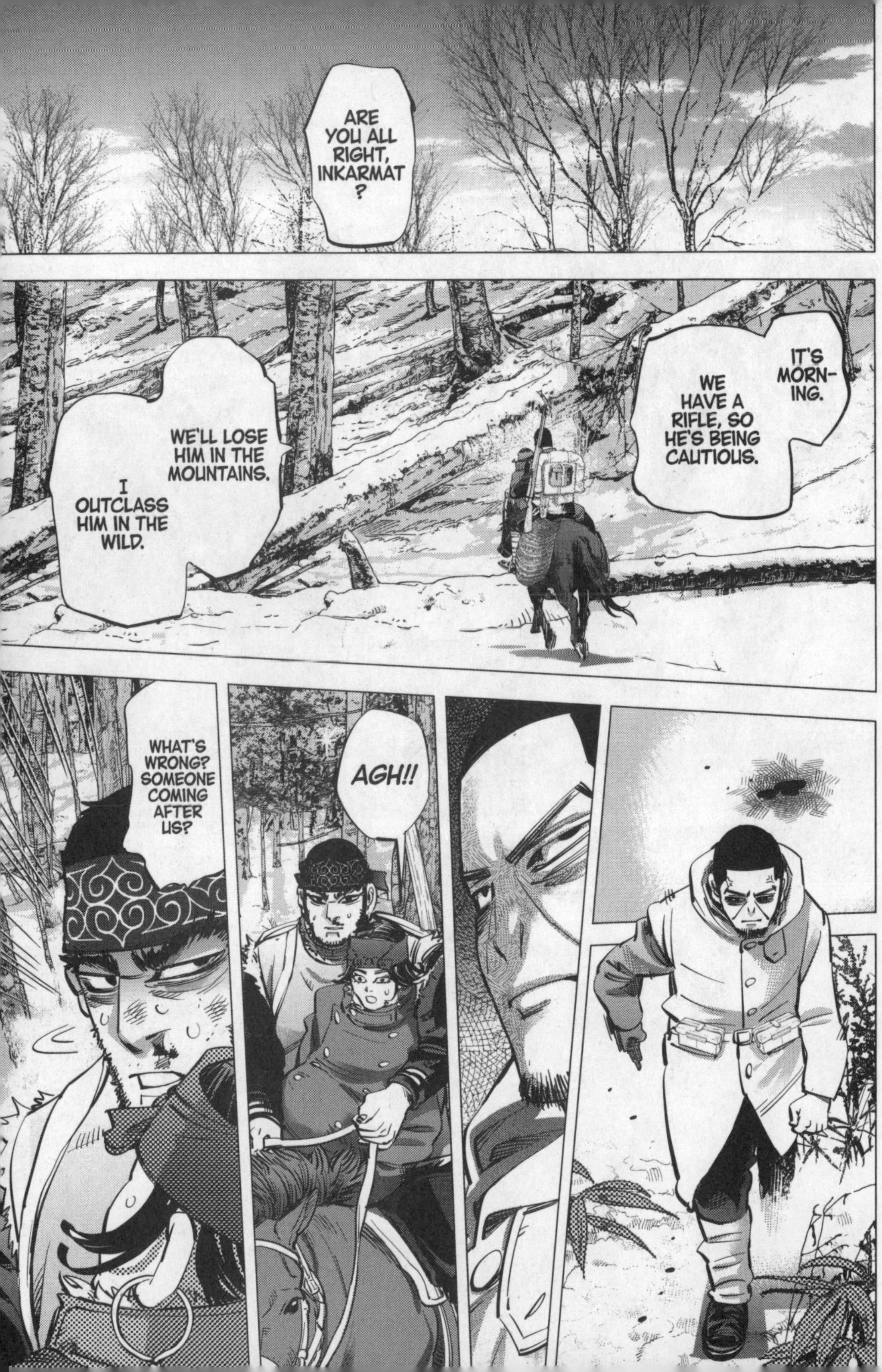
ARE YOU ALL RIGHT, INKARMAT?
IT'S MORNING.
WE HAVE A RIFLE, SO HE'S BEING CAUTIOUS.
WE'LL LOSE HIM IN THE MOUNTAINS.
I OUTCLASS HIM IN THE WILD.
AGH!!
WHAT'S WRONG? SOMEONE COMING AFTER US?

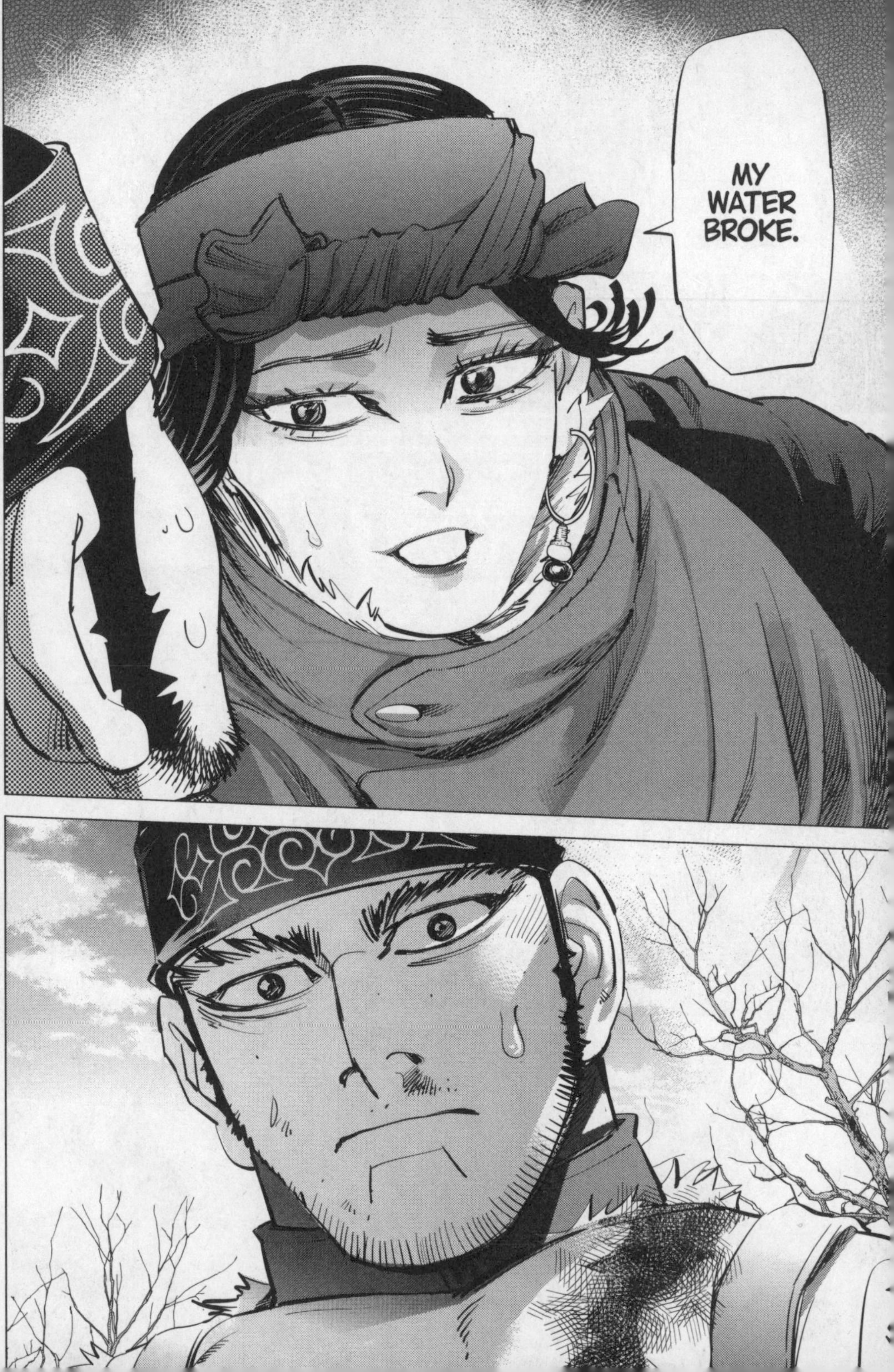
MY WATER BROKE.

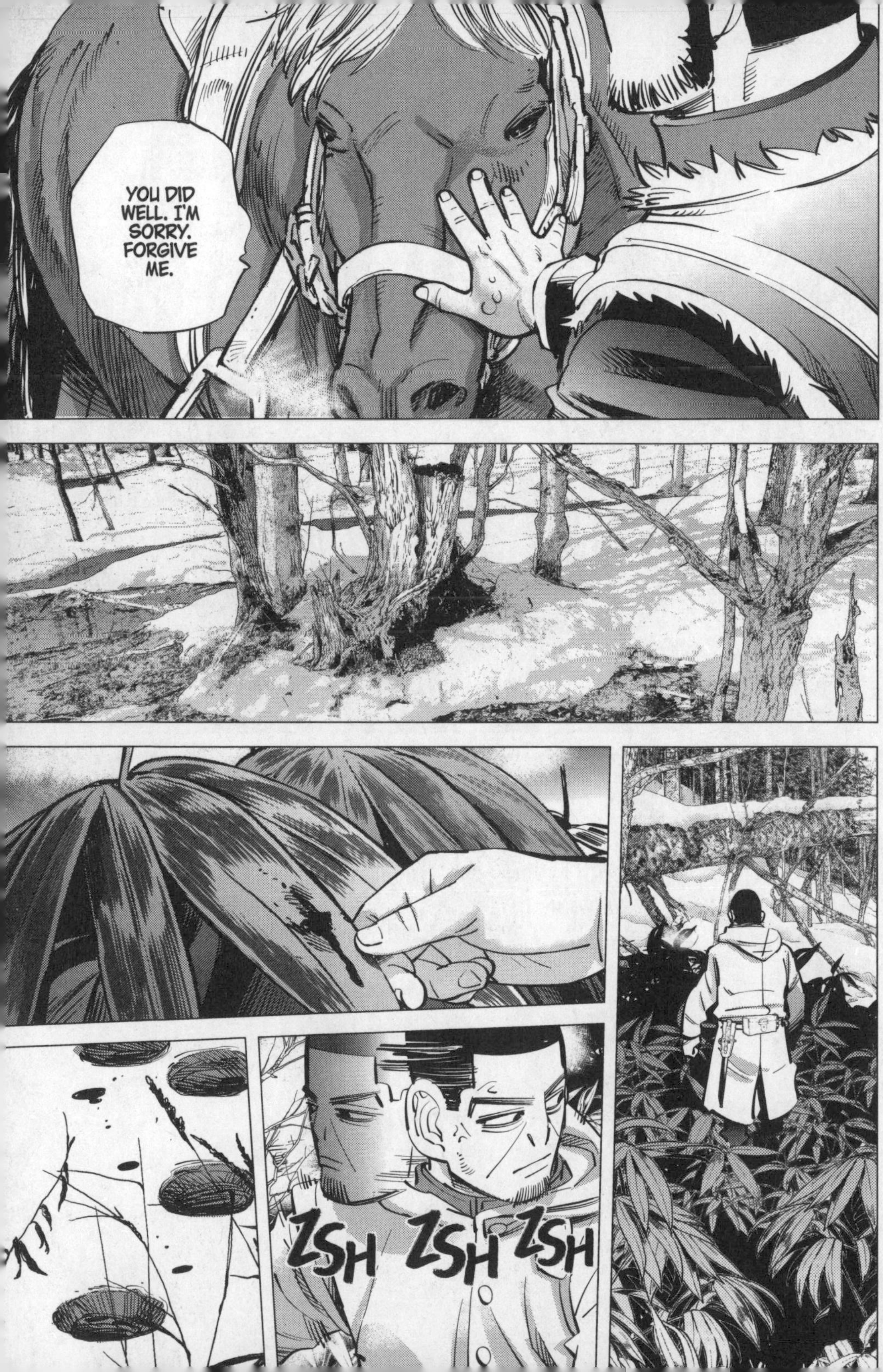
YOU DID WELL. I'M SORRY. FORGIVE ME.
ZSH ZSH ZSH

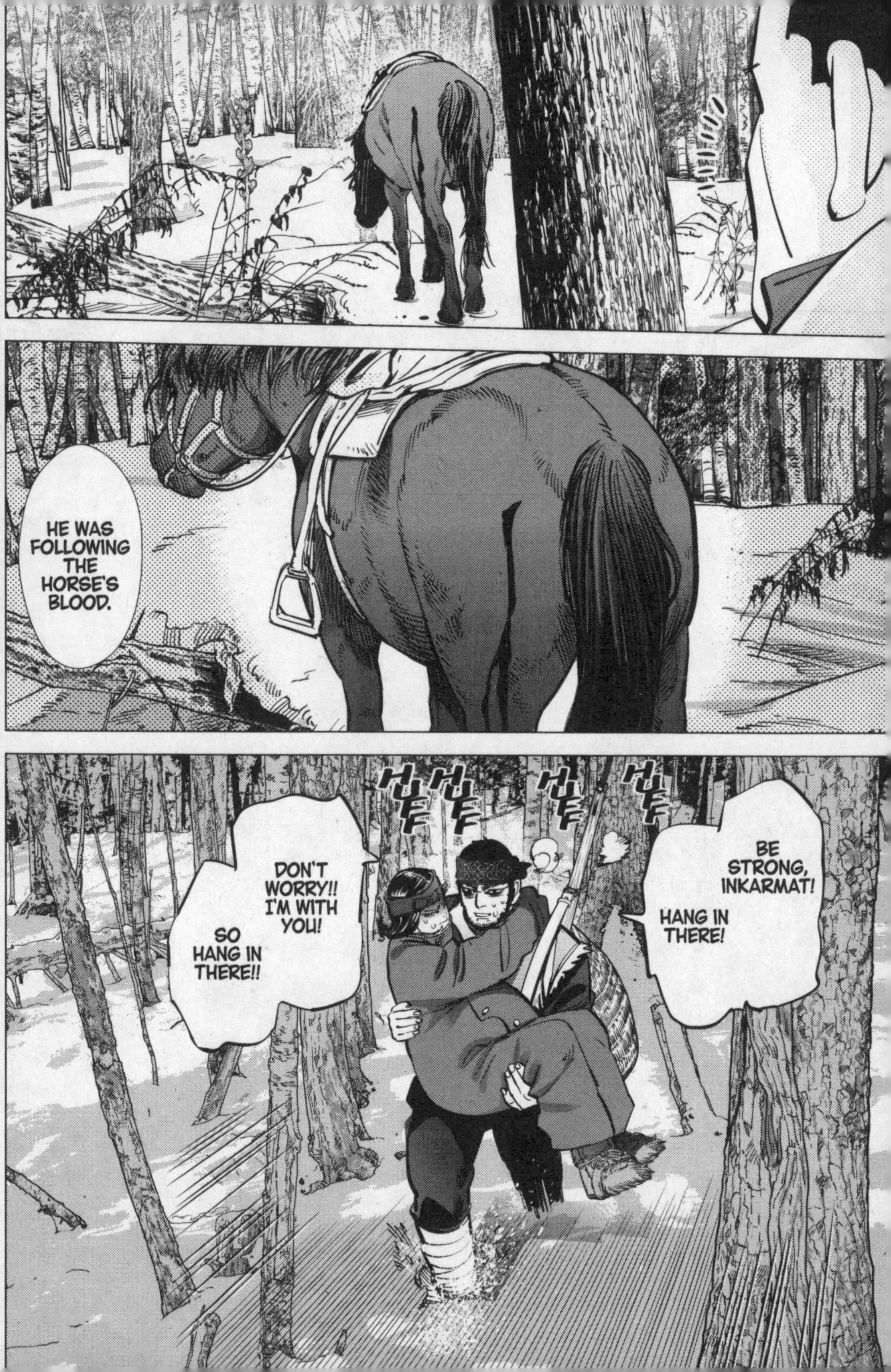
HE WAS FOLLOWING THE HORSE'S BLOOD.
HUFF HUFF HUFF HUFF
BE STRONG, INKARMAT!
HANG IN THERE!
DON'T WORRY!! I'M WITH YOU!
SO HANG IN THERE!!

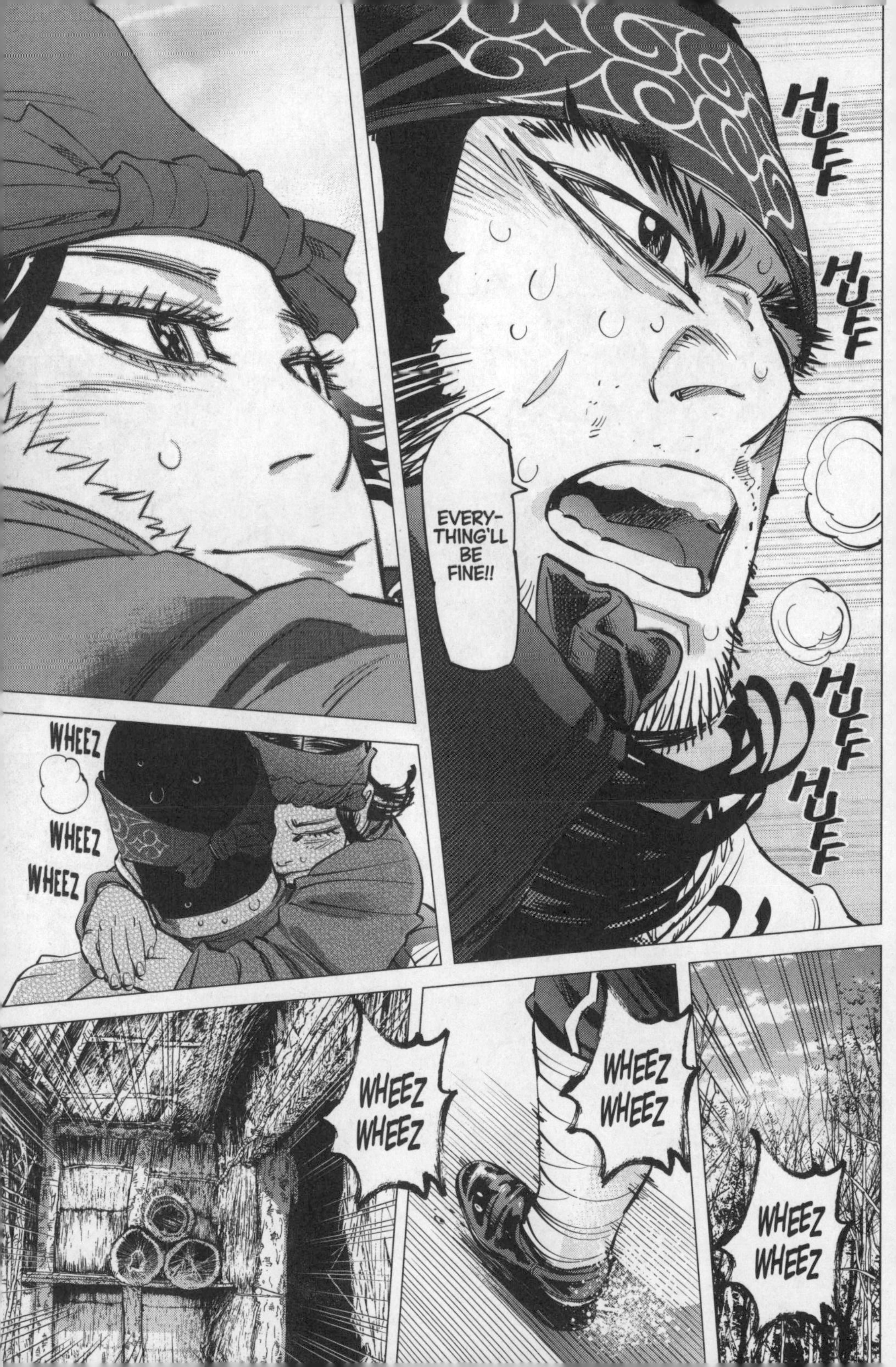
HUFF HUFF
EVERY-THING'LL BE FINE!!
HUFF HUFF
WHEEZ
WHEEZ
WHEEZ
WHEEZ WHEEZ
WHEEZ WHEEZ
WHEEZ WHEEZ

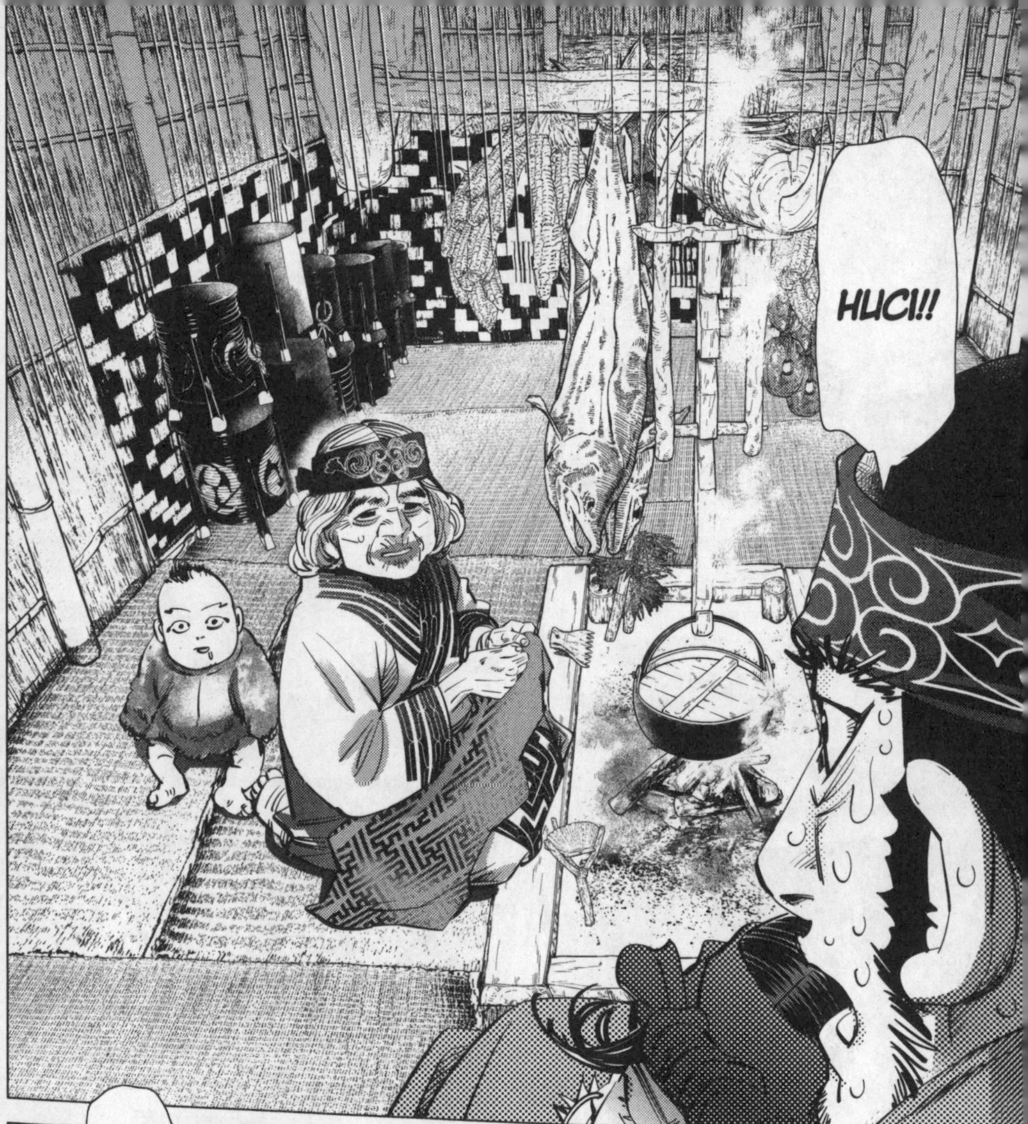
HUCI!!

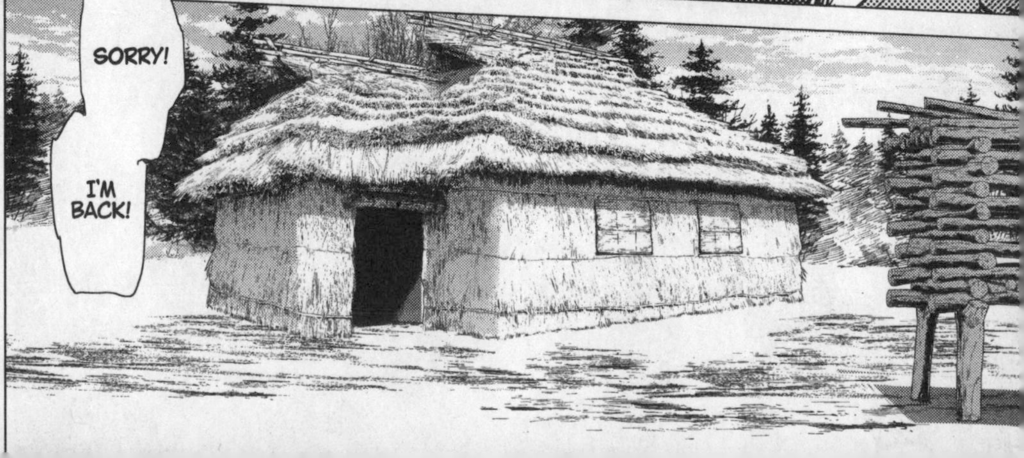
SORRY!
I'M BACK!

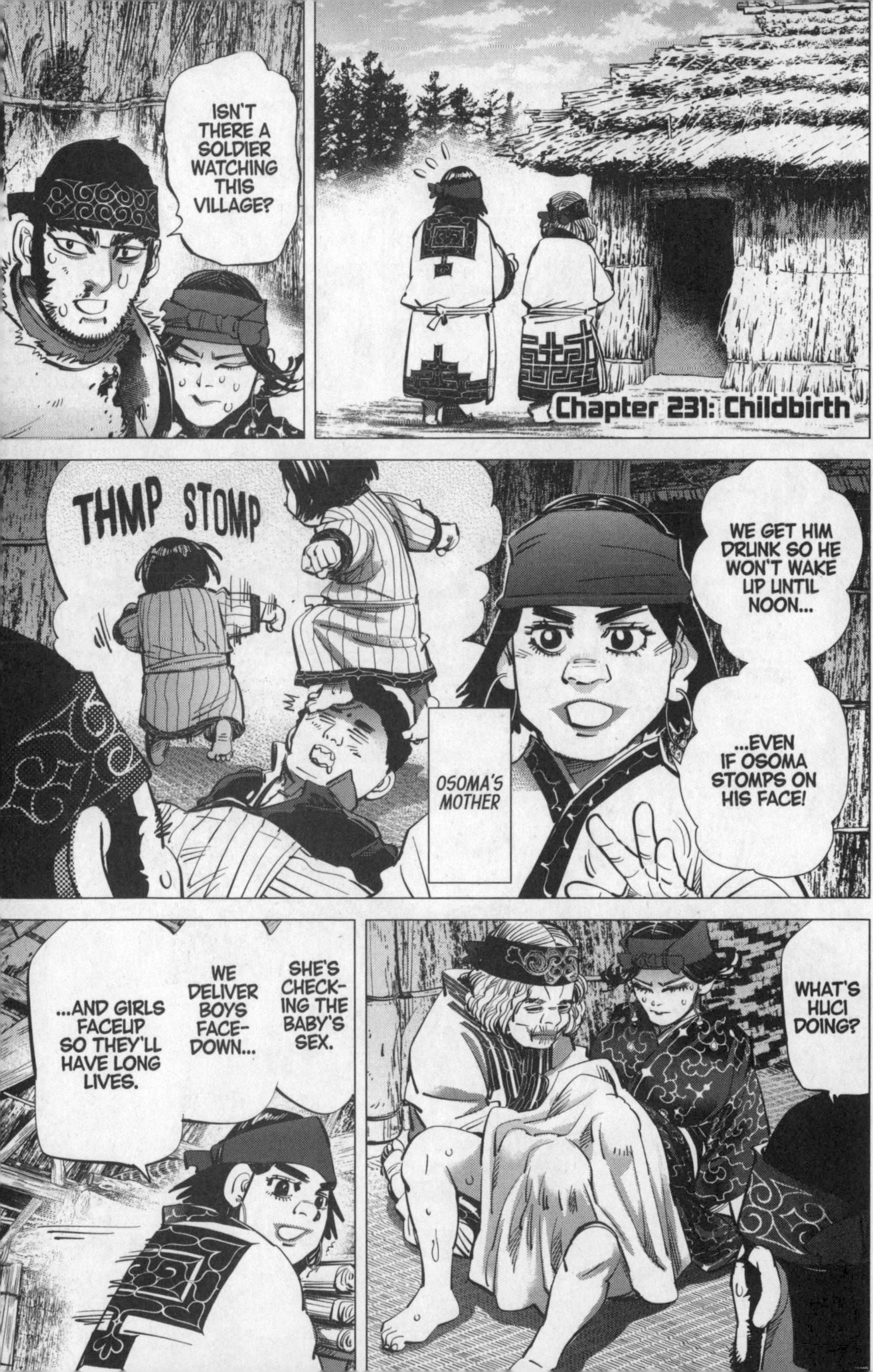
Chapter 231: Childbirth
ISN'T THERE A SOLDIER WATCHING THIS VILLAGE?
WE GET HIM DRUNK SO HE WON'T WAKE UP UNTIL NOON...
...EVEN IF OSOMA STOMPS ON HIS FACE!
OSOMA'S MOTHER
THMP STOMP
WHAT'S HUCI DOING?
SHE'S CHECKING THE BABY'S SEX.
WE DELIVER BOYS FACE-DOWN...
...AND GIRLS FACEUP SO THEY'LL HAVE LONG LIVES.

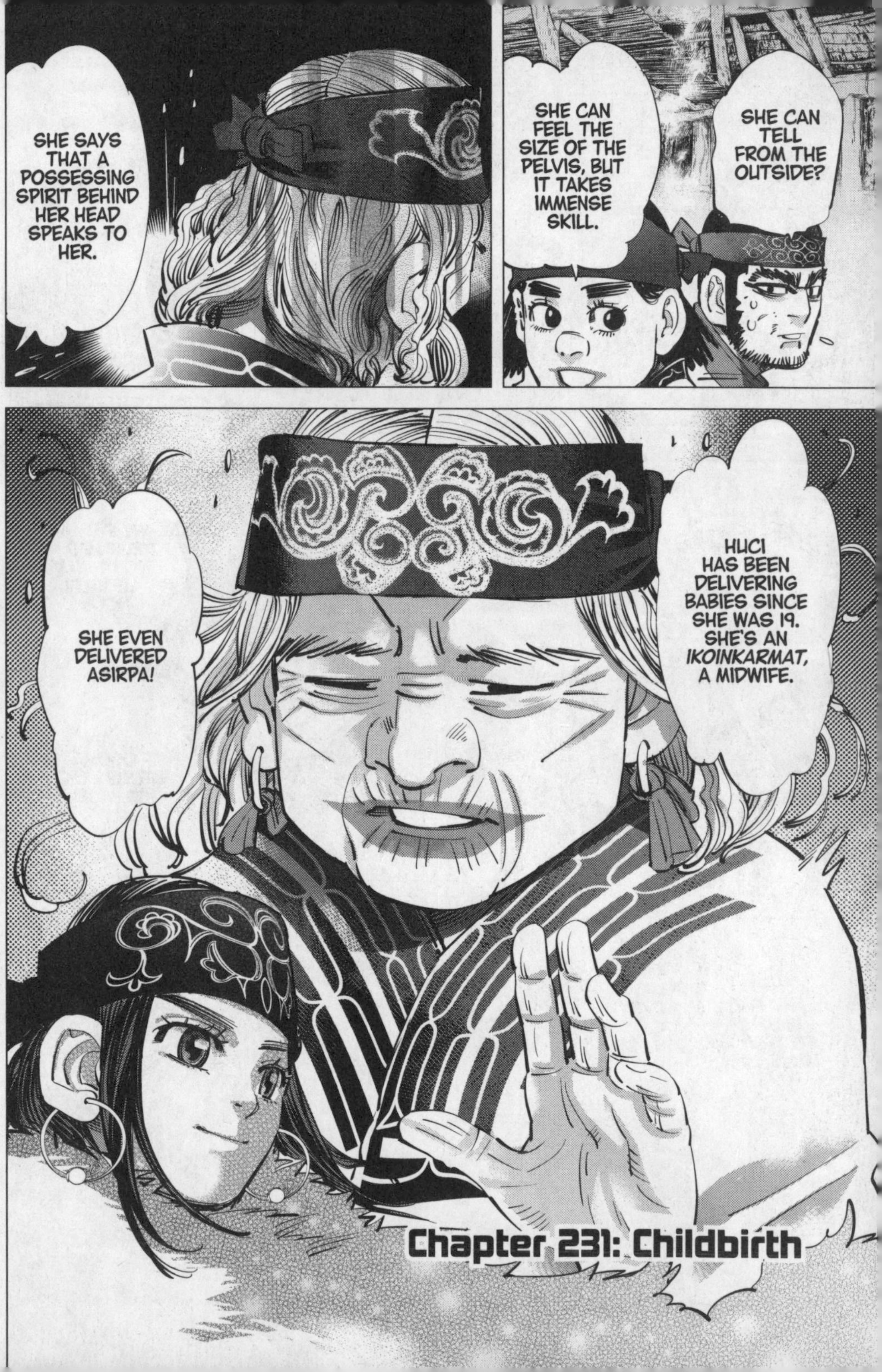
SHE CAN TELL FROM THE OUTSIDE?
SHE CAN FEEL THE SIZE OF THE PELVIS, BUT IT TAKES IMMENSE SKILL.
SHE SAYS THAT A POSSESSING SPIRIT BEHIND HER HEAD SPEAKS TO HER.
HUCI HAS BEEN DELIVERING BABIES SINCE SHE WAS 19. SHE'S AN *IKOINKARMAT*, A MIDWIFE.
SHE EVEN DELIVERED ASIRPA!
Chapter 231: Childbirth

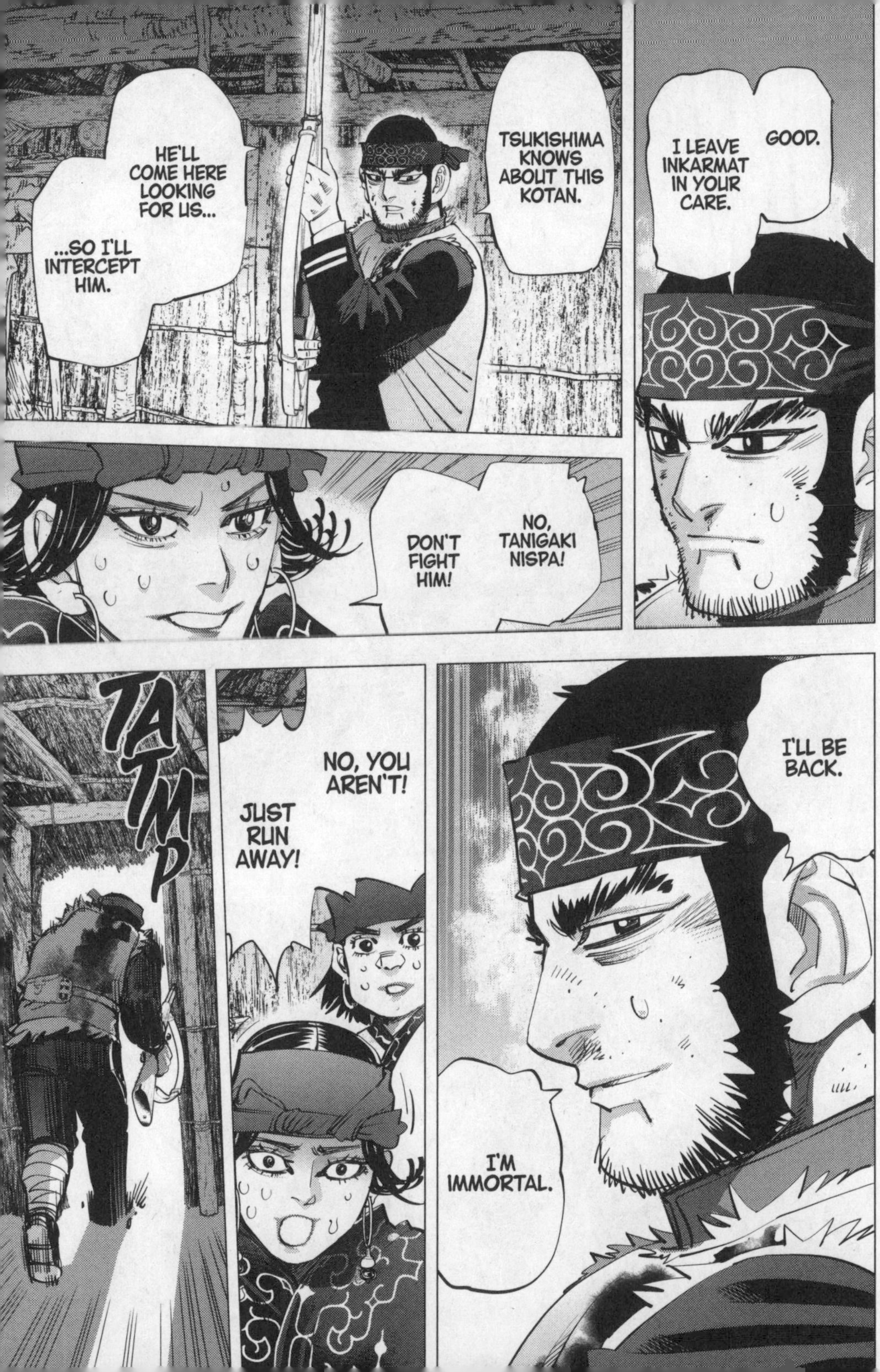
GOOD.
I LEAVE INKARMAT IN YOUR CARE.
TSUKISHIMA KNOWS ABOUT THIS KOTAN.
HE'LL COME HERE LOOKING FOR US...
...SO I'LL INTERCEPT HIM.
NO, TANIGAKI NISPA!
DON'T FIGHT HIM!
I'LL BE BACK.
I'M IMMORTAL.
NO, YOU AREN'T!
JUST RUN AWAY!
TAMP

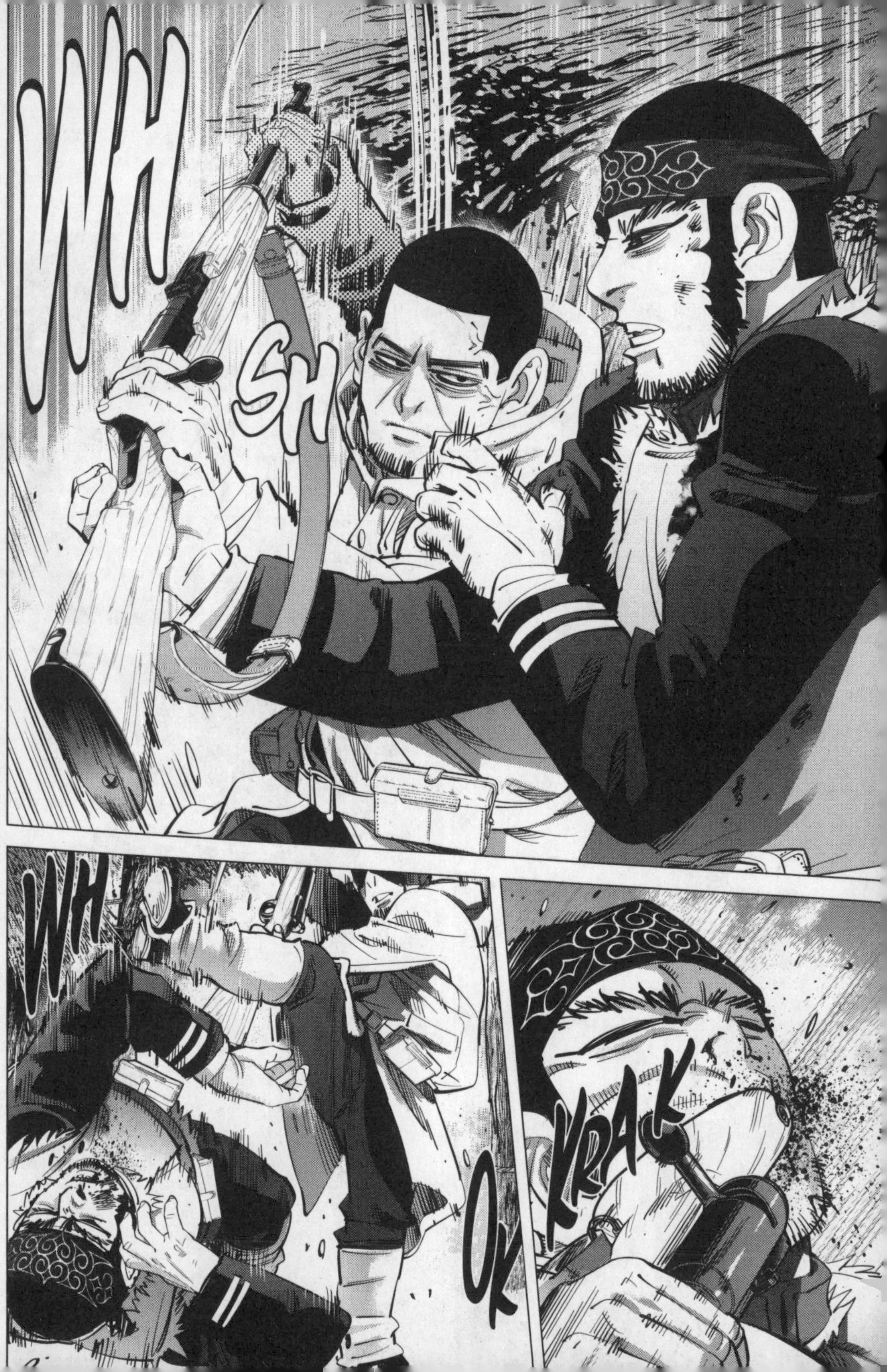
SH
WH
KRAK
OK
WH

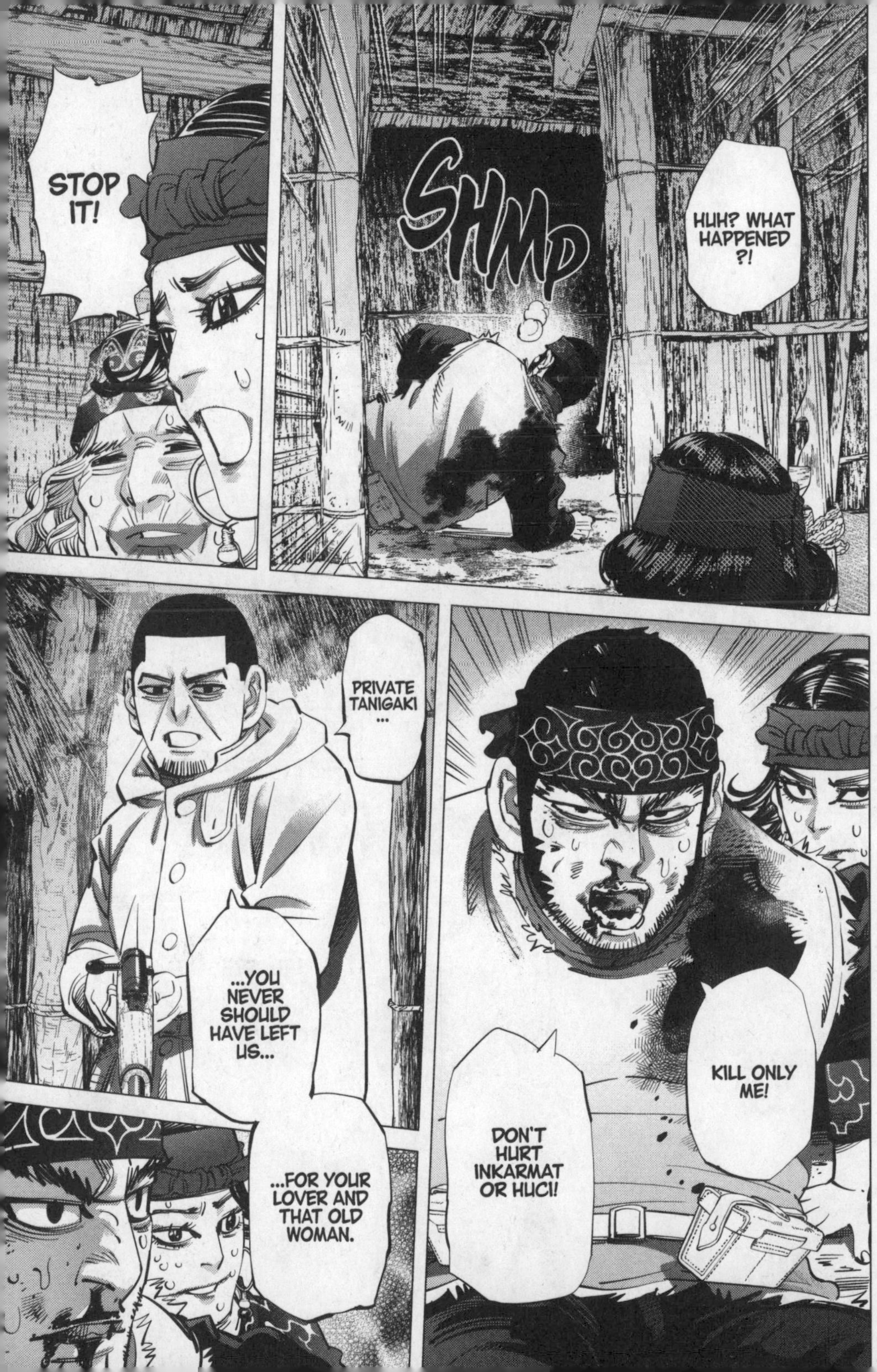
HUH? WHAT HAPPENED ?!
SHMP
STOP IT!
KILL ONLY ME!
DON'T HURT INKARMAT OR HUCI!
PRIVATE TANIGAKI ...
...YOU NEVER SHOULD HAVE LEFT US...
...FOR YOUR LOVER AND THAT OLD WOMAN.

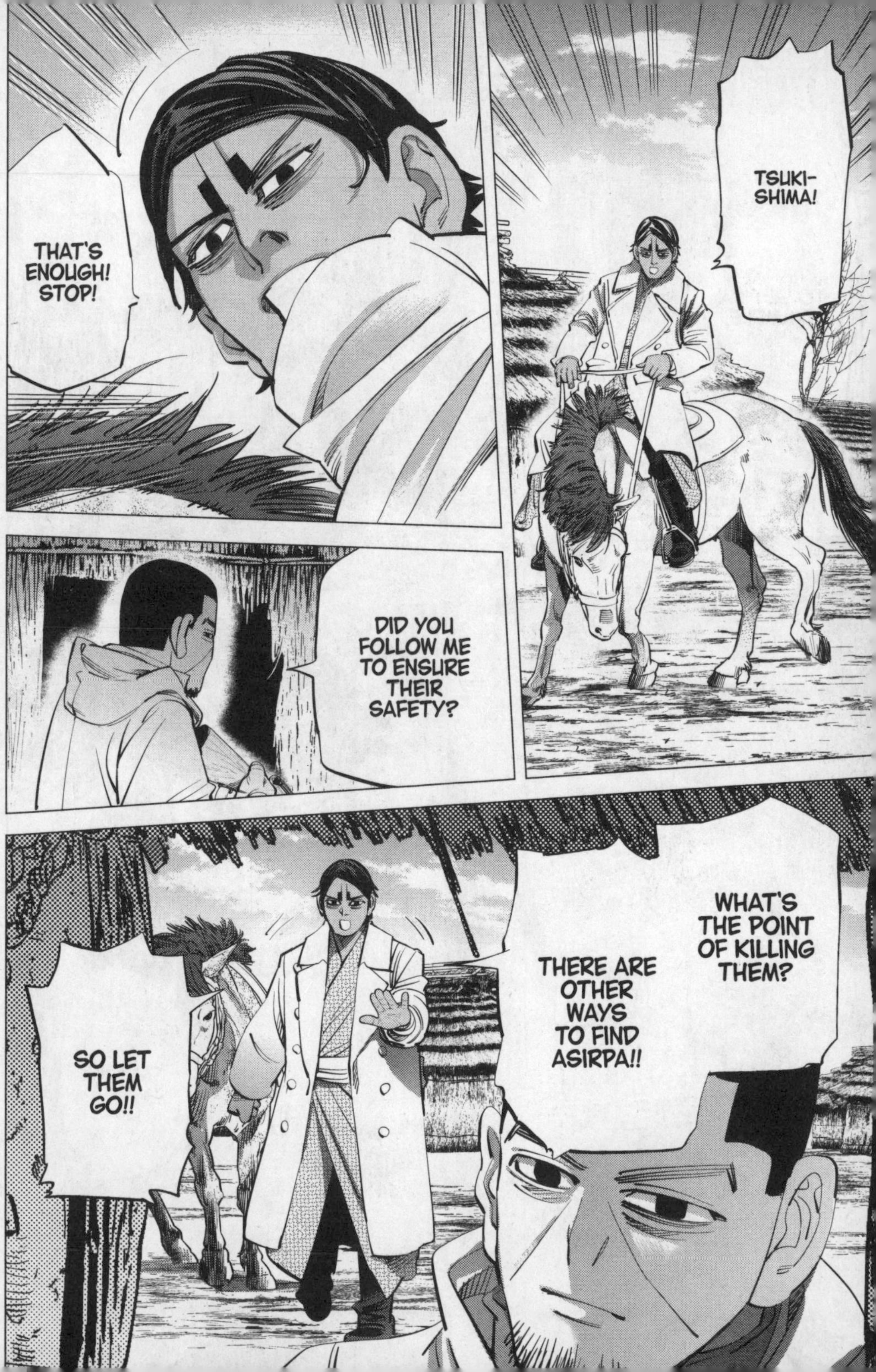
TSUKI-SHIMA!
THAT'S ENOUGH! STOP!
DID YOU FOLLOW ME TO ENSURE THEIR SAFETY?
WHAT'S THE POINT OF KILLING THEM?
THERE ARE OTHER WAYS TO FIND ASIRPA!!
SO LET THEM GO!!

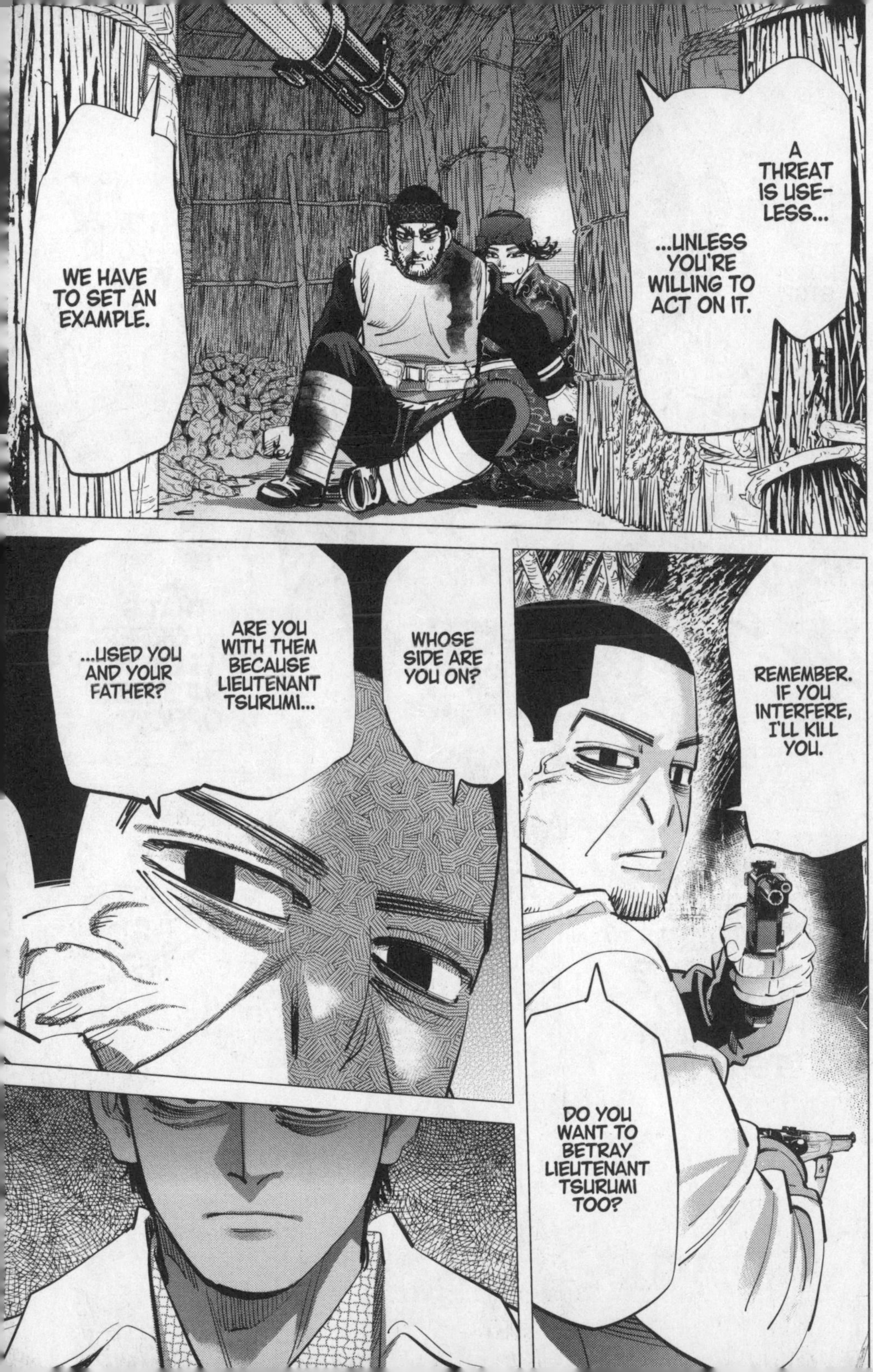
A THREAT IS USE-LESS...
...UNLESS YOU'RE WILLING TO ACT ON IT.
WE HAVE TO SET AN EXAMPLE.
REMEMBER. IF YOU INTERFERE, I'LL KILL YOU.
DO YOU WANT TO BETRAY LIEUTENANT TSURUMI TOO?
WHOSE SIDE ARE YOU ON?
ARE YOU WITH THEM BECAUSE LIEUTENANT TSURUMI...
...USED YOU AND YOUR FATHER?

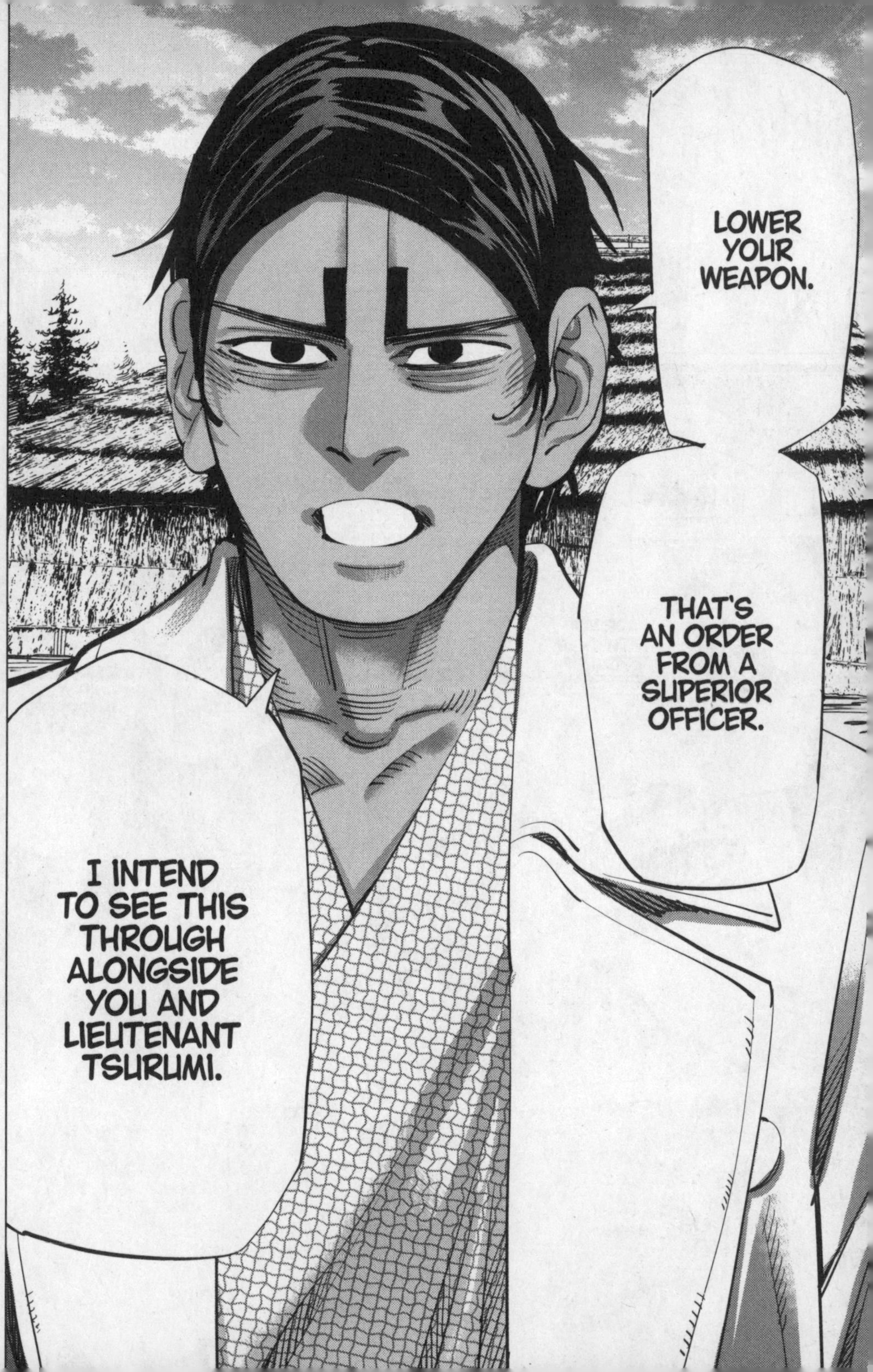
LOWER YOUR WEAPON.
THAT'S AN ORDER FROM A SUPERIOR OFFICER.
I INTEND TO SEE THIS THROUGH ALONGSIDE YOU AND LIEUTENANT TSURUMI.

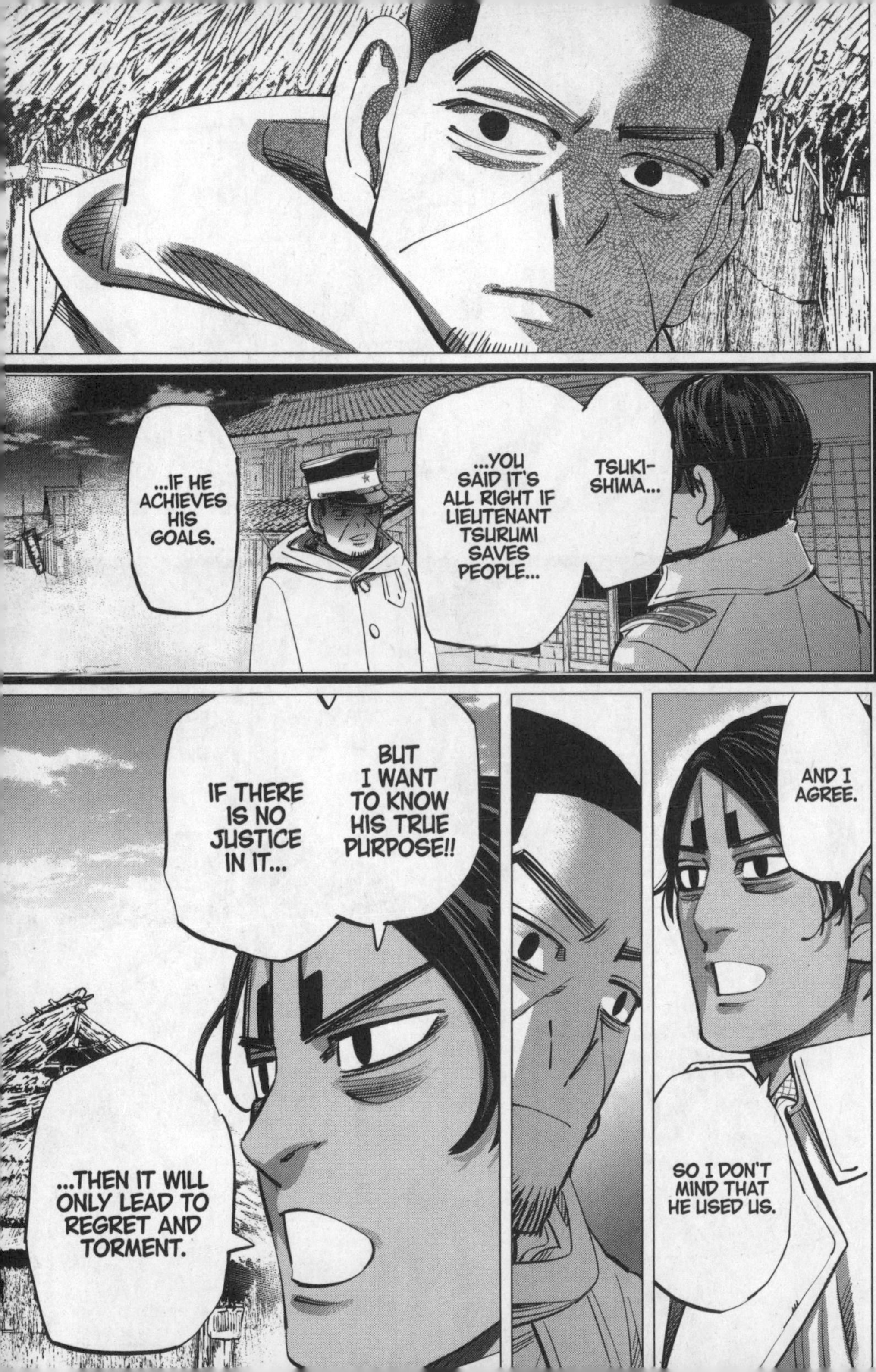
TSUKI-SHIMA...
...YOU SAID IT'S ALL RIGHT IF LIEUTENANT TSURUMI SAVES PEOPLE...
...IF HE ACHIEVES HIS GOALS.
AND I AGREE.
SO I DON'T MIND THAT HE USED US.
BUT I WANT TO KNOW HIS TRUE PURPOSE!!
IF THERE IS NO JUSTICE IN IT...
...THEN IT WILL ONLY LEAD TO REGRET AND TORMENT.

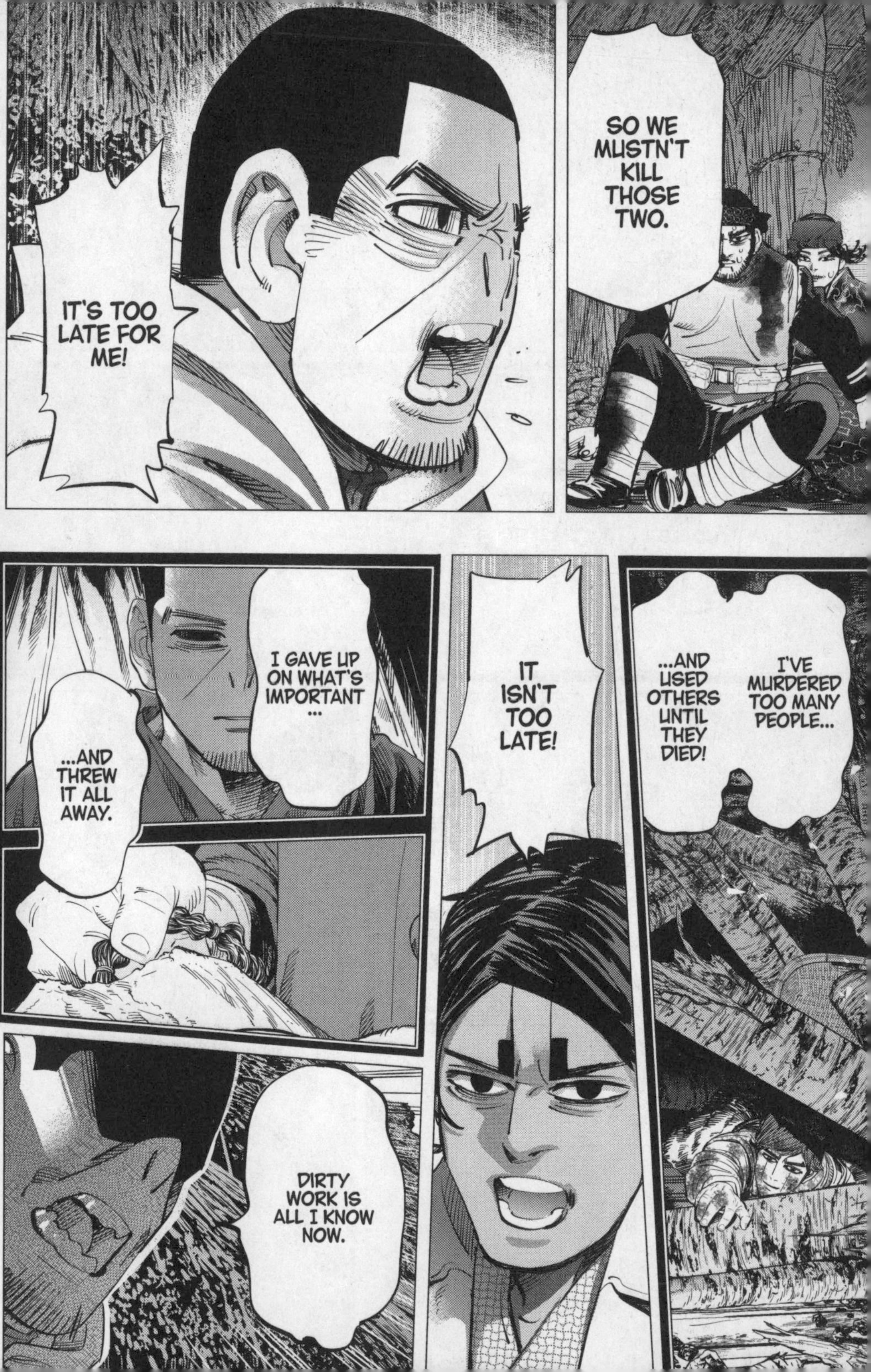
SO WE MUSTN'T KILL THOSE TWO.
IT'S TOO LATE FOR ME!
I'VE MURDERED TOO MANY PEOPLE...
...AND USED OTHERS UNTIL THEY DIED!
IT ISN'T TOO LATE!
I GAVE UP ON WHAT'S IMPORTANT ...
...AND THREW IT ALL AWAY.
DIRTY WORK IS ALL I KNOW NOW.

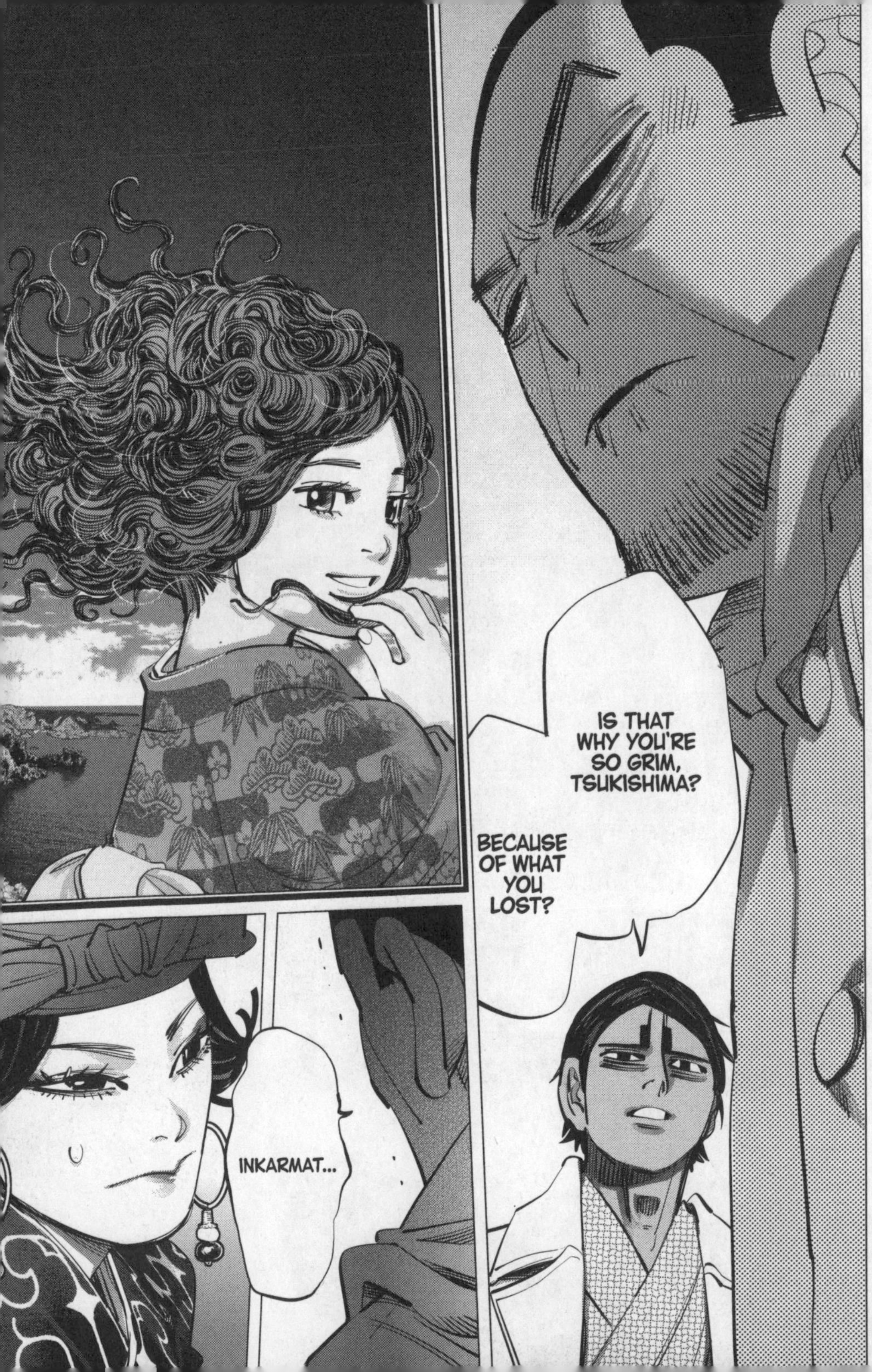
IS THAT WHY YOU'RE SO GRIM, TSUKISHIMA?
BECAUSE OF WHAT YOU LOST?
INKARMAT...

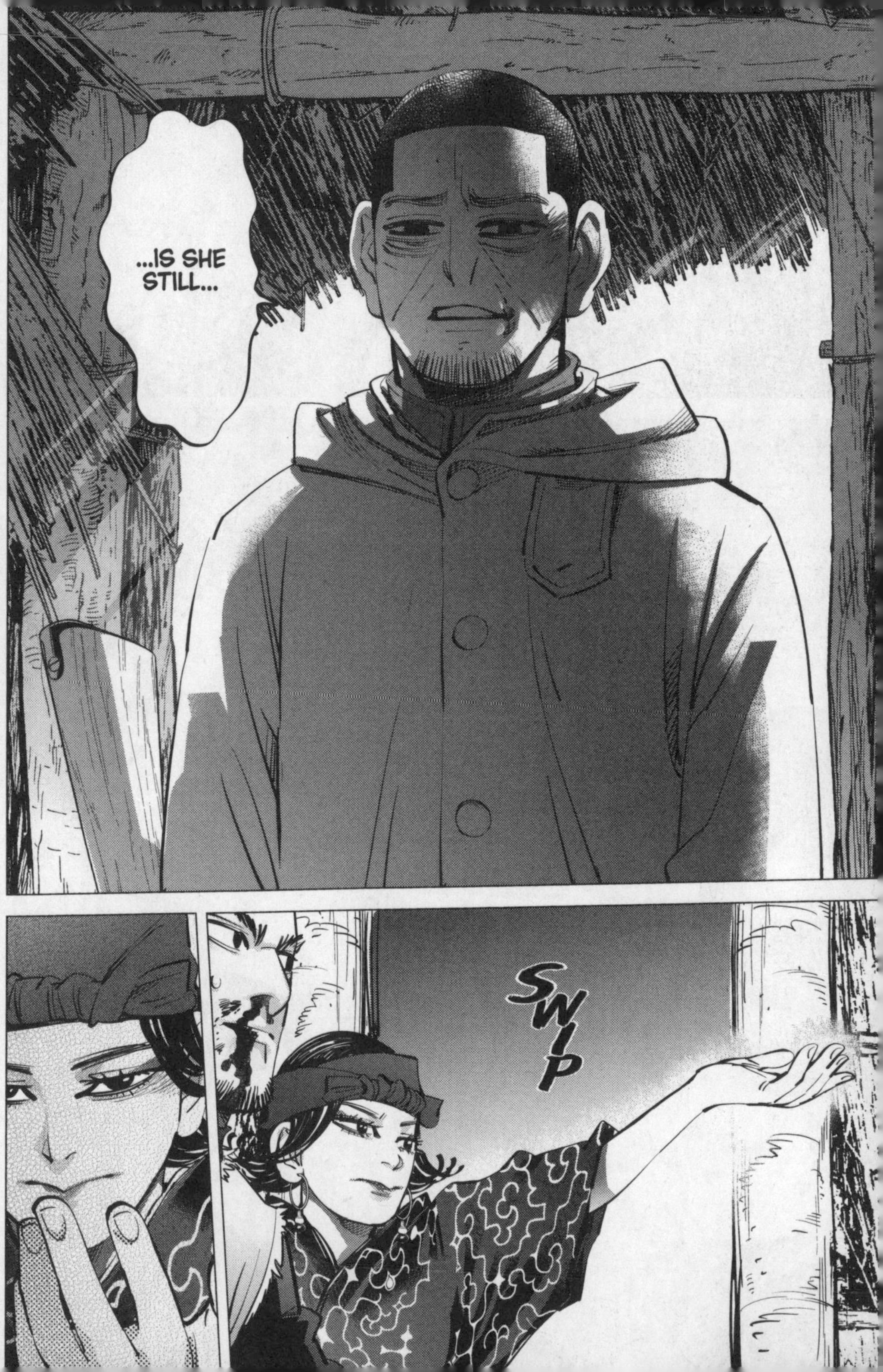
...IS SHE
STILL...
SWIP

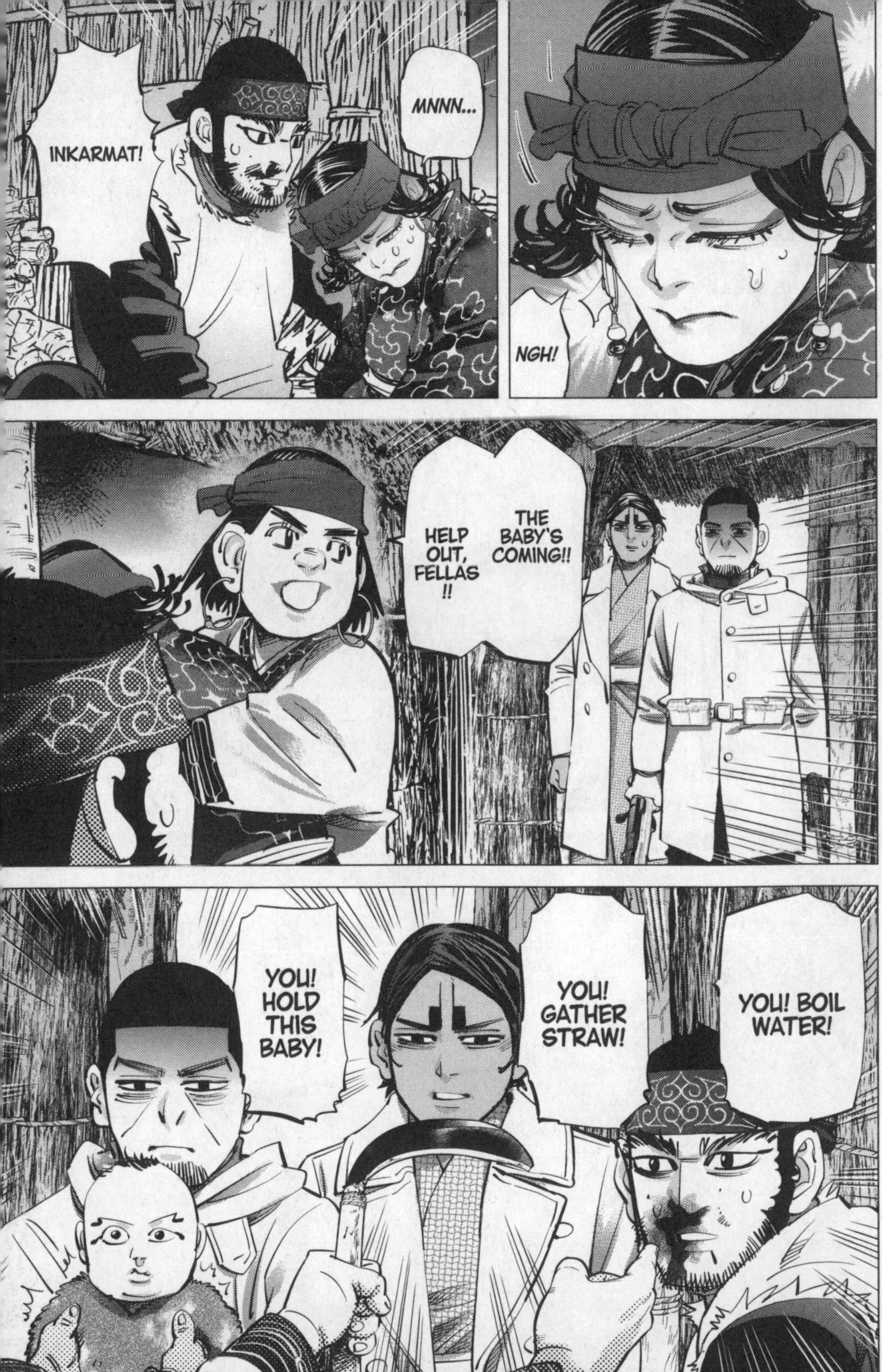
NGH!
MNNN...
INKARMAT!
THE BABY'S COMING!!
HELP OUT, FELLAS !!
YOU! BOIL WATER!
YOU! GATHER STRAW!
YOU! HOLD THIS BABY!

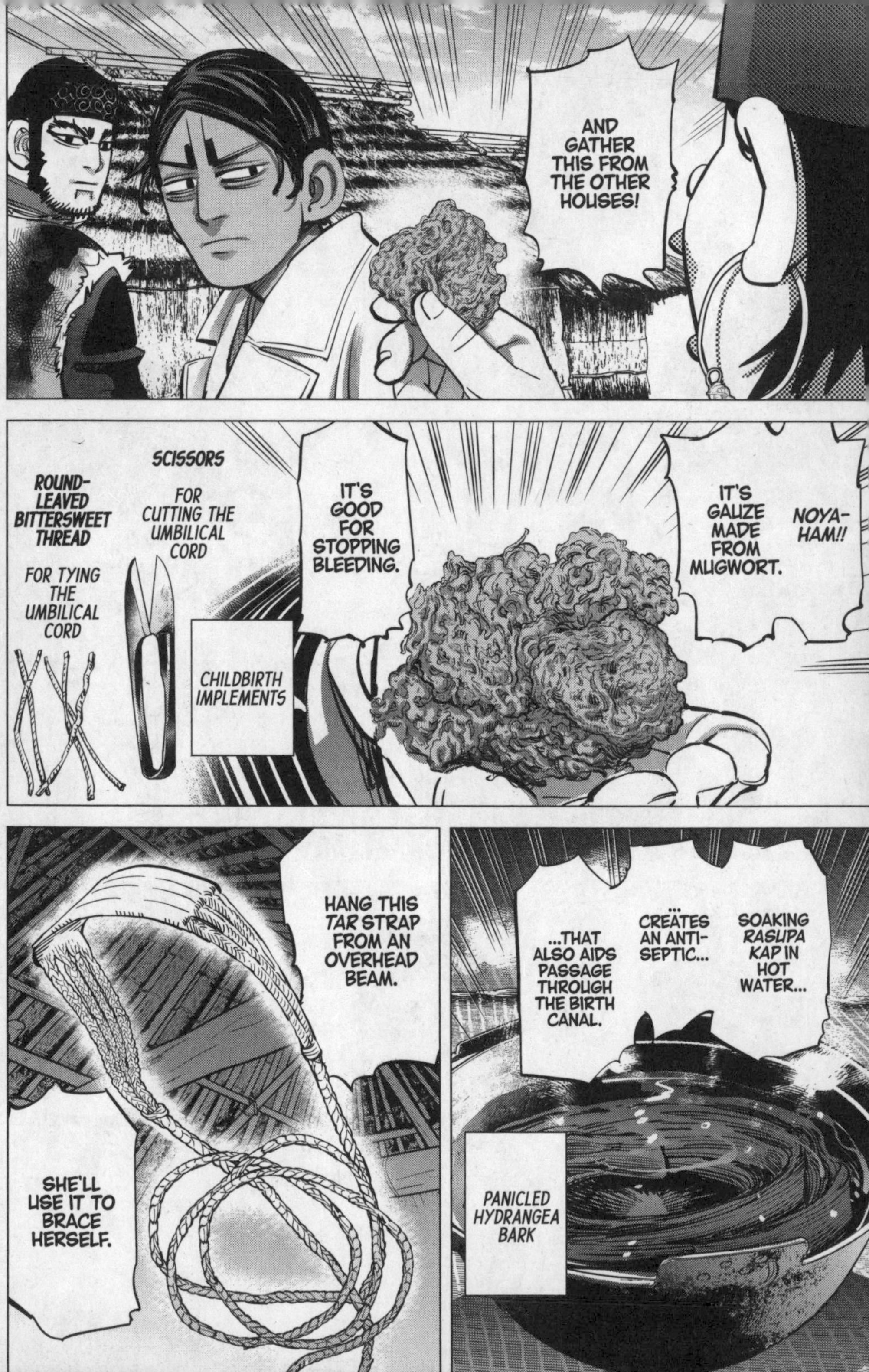
AND GATHER THIS FROM THE OTHER HOUSES!
NOYA-HAM!!
IT'S GAUZE MADE FROM MUGWORT.
IT'S GOOD FOR STOPPING BLEEDING.
CHILDBIRTH IMPLEMENTS
SCISSORS
FOR CUTTING THE UMBILICAL CORD
ROUND-LEAVED BITTERSWEET THREAD
FOR TYING THE UMBILICAL CORD
SOAKING RASUPA KAP IN HOT WATER...
...CREATES AN ANTI-SEPTIC...
...THAT ALSO AIDS PASSAGE THROUGH THE BIRTH CANAL.
PANICLED HYDRANGEA BARK
HANG THIS TAR STRAP FROM AN OVERHEAD BEAM.
SHE'LL USE IT TO BRACE HERSELF.

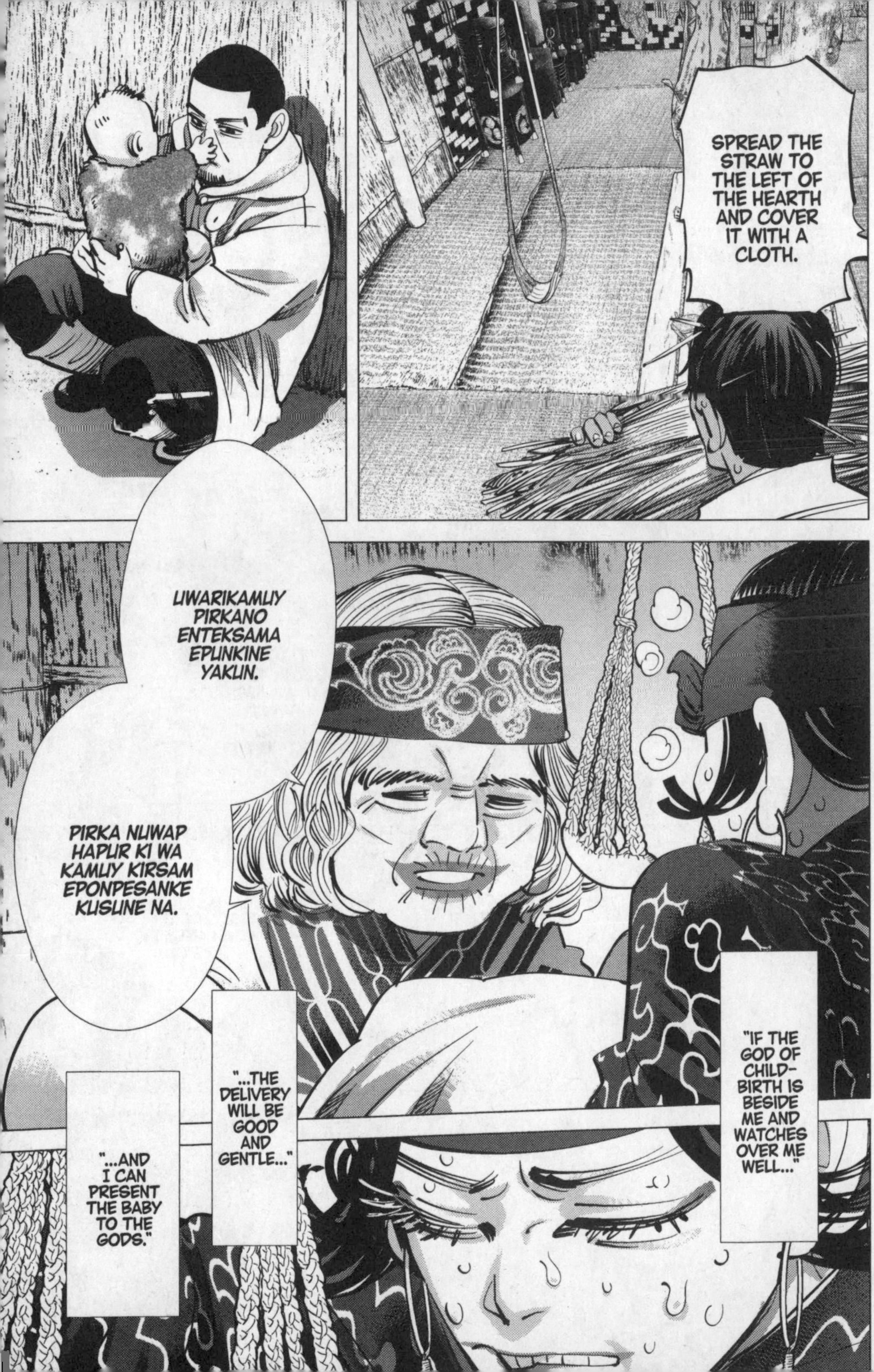
SPREAD THE STRAW TO THE LEFT OF THE HEARTH AND COVER IT WITH A CLOTH.
UWARIKAMUY PIRKANO ENTEKSAMA EPUNKINE YAKUN.
PIRKA NUWAP HAPUR KI WA KAMUY KIRSAM EPONPESANKE KUSUNE NA.
"IF THE GOD OF CHILD-BIRTH IS BESIDE ME AND WATCHES OVER ME WELL..."
"...THE DELIVERY WILL BE GOOD AND GENTLE..."
"...AND I CAN PRESENT THE BABY TO THE GODS."

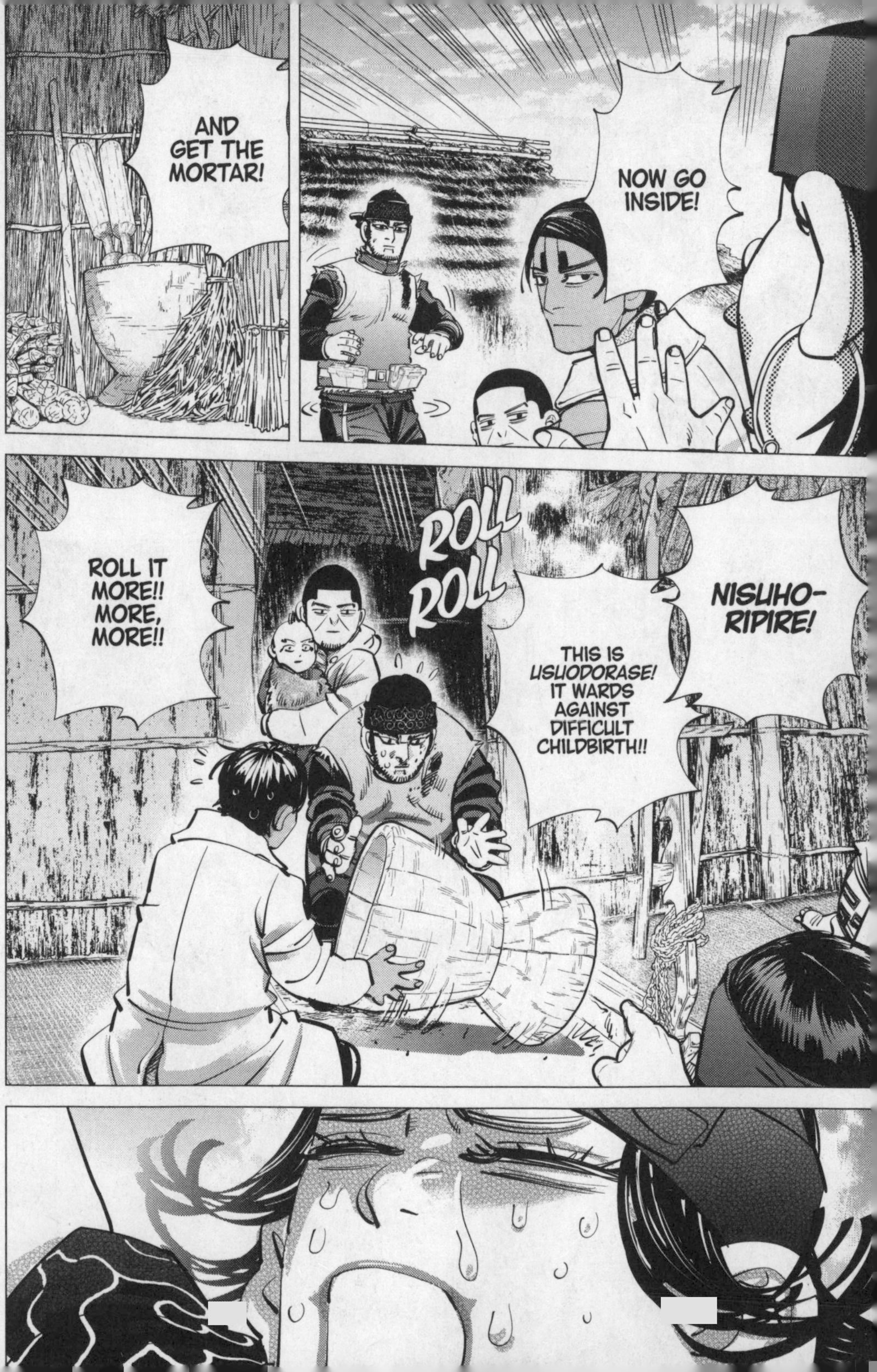
NOW GO INSIDE!
AND GET THE MORTAR!
NISUHO-RIPIRE!
THIS IS USUODORASE! IT WARDS AGAINST DIFFICULT CHILDBIRTH!!
ROLL ROLL
ROLL IT MORE!! MORE, MORE!!

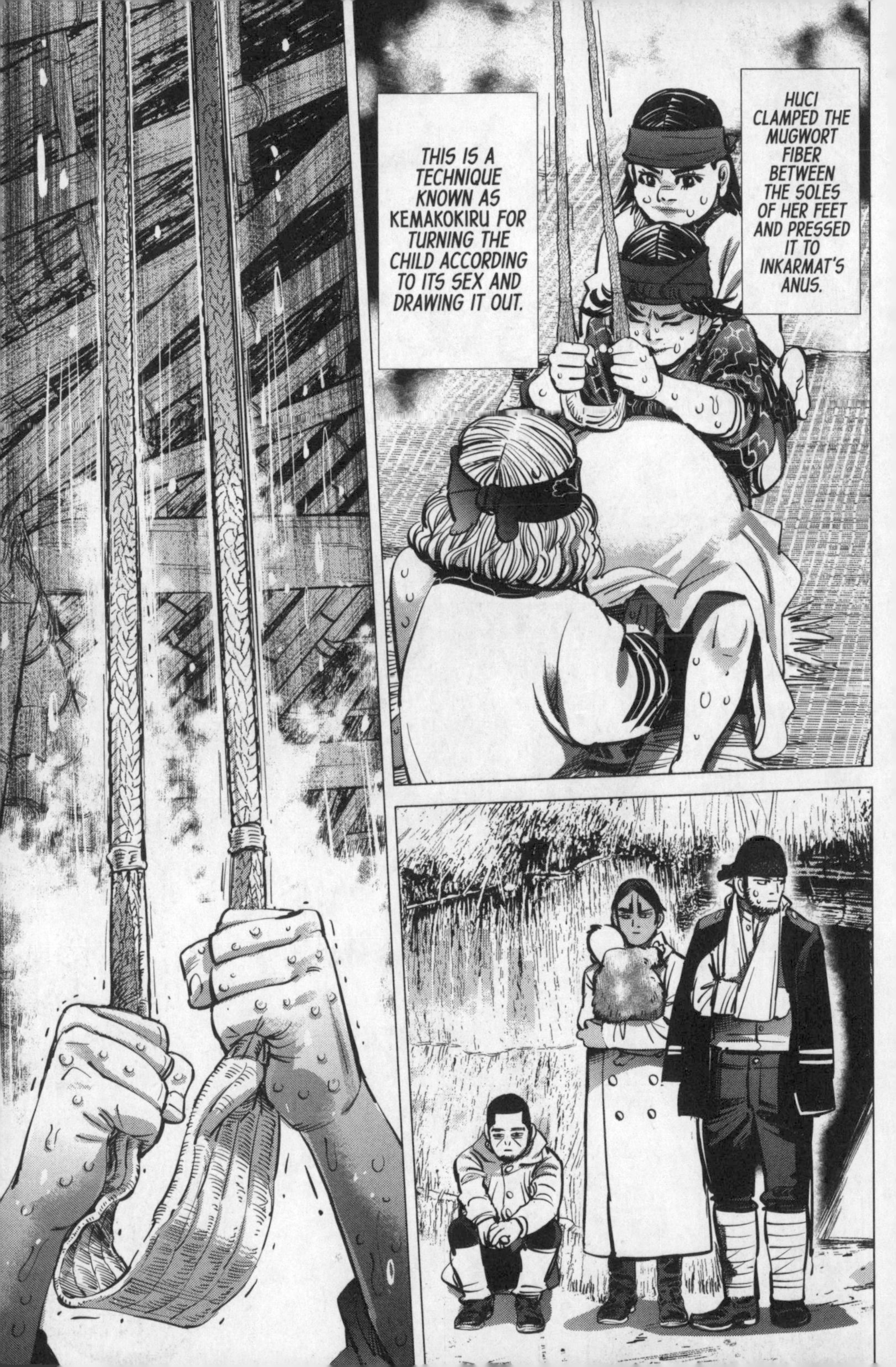
HUCI CLAMPED THE MUGWORT FIBER BETWEEN THE SOLES OF HER FEET AND PRESSED IT TO INKARMAT'S ANUS.
THIS IS A TECHNIQUE KNOWN AS KEMAKOKIRU FOR TURNING THE CHILD ACCORDING TO ITS SEX AND DRAWING IT OUT.

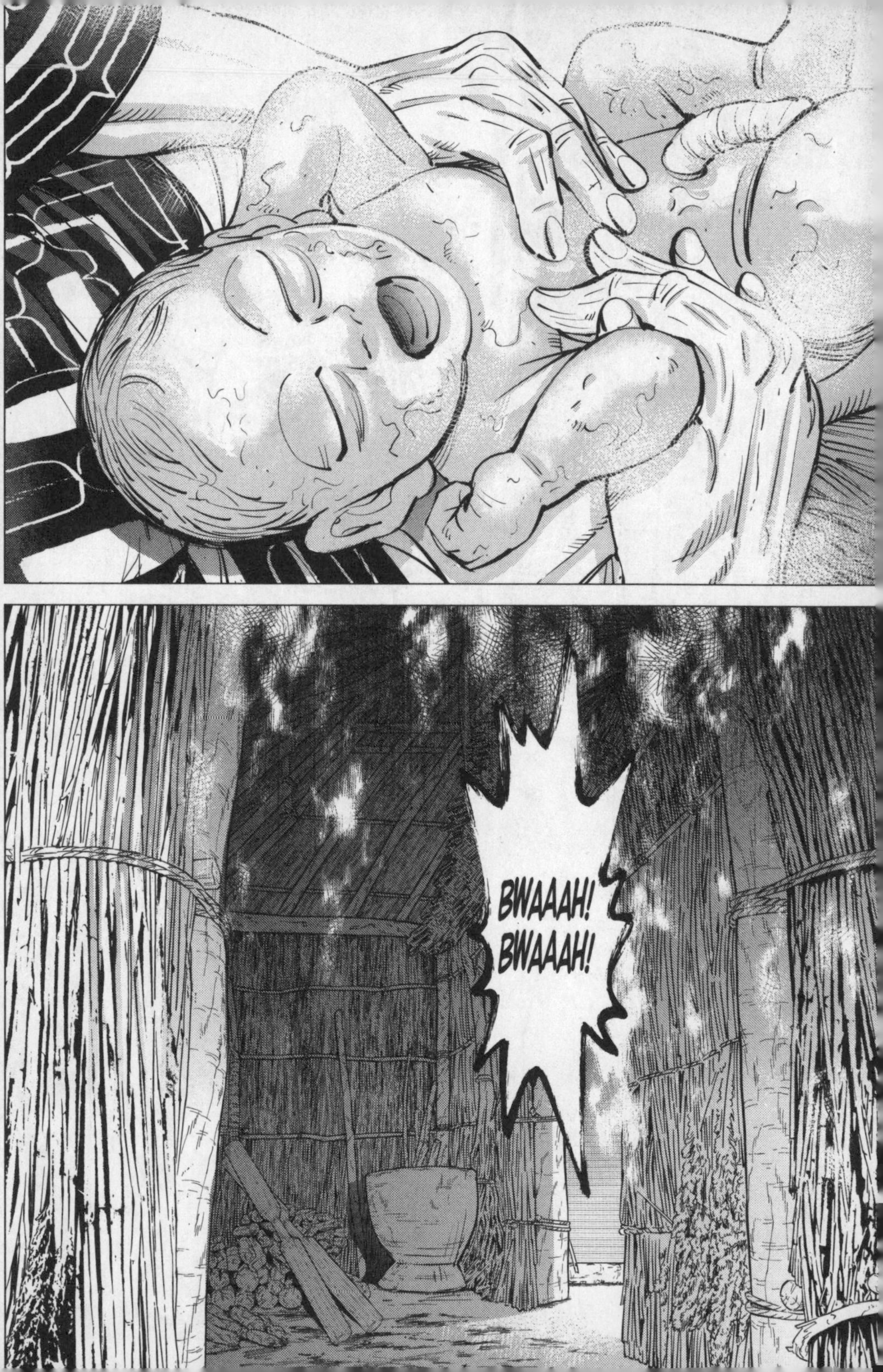
BWAAAH!
BWAAAH!

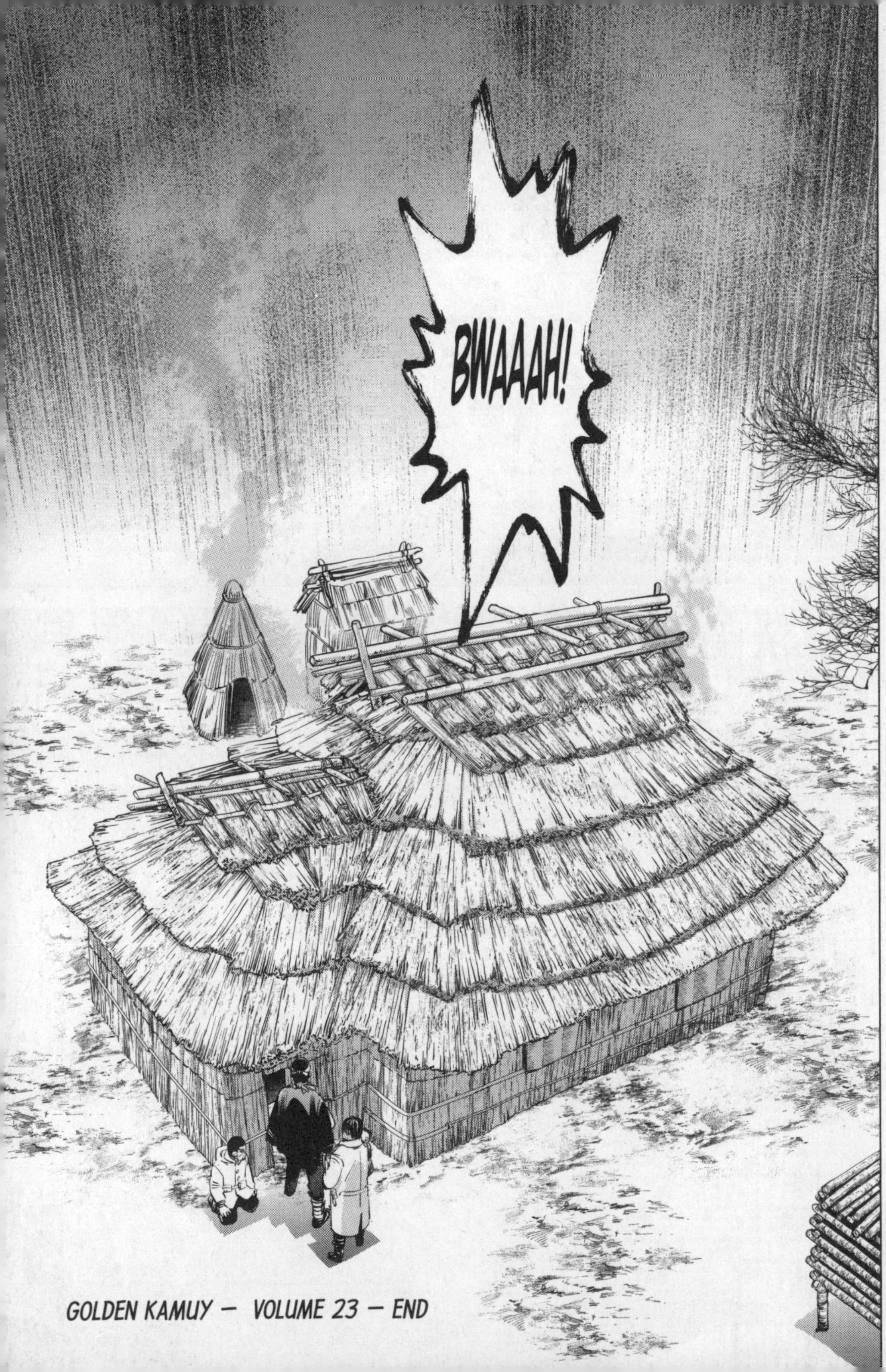
BWAAAH!

GOLDEN KAMUY – VOLUME 23 – END

Ainu Language Supervision • Hiroshi Nakagawa •
Russian Language Supervision • Eugenio Uzhinin •
Uilta Language Supervision • Yoshiko Yamada •
Satsuma Dialect Supervision • Shogo Nakamura •
Niigata Dialect Supervision • Fumiya Ito

Cooperation from • Hokkaido Ainu Association and the Abashiri Prison Museum • Otaru City General Museum • Waseda University
Aizu Museum • Kazunobu Goto, • Botanic Garden and Museum, Hokkaido University • National Museum of Ethnology • Nibutani
Ainu Culture Museum • The Ainu Museum • Moon Kabato Museum • Kushiro City Museum • Atsuyo Hisai • Tatsuhiro Tokuda •
Shigeharu Terui • All Japan Federation of Karafuto • Tokyo National Museum • Sakhalin Regional Museum • Shiraishi Hidetoshi •
Masato Tamura • Historical Village of Hokkaido • Asahikawa City Museum • Hokuchin Museum • Tomakomai City Museum

Photo Credits • Takayuki Monma Takanori Matsuda Kozo Ishikawa

Ainu Culture References

Chiri, Takanaka and Yokoyama, Takao. *Ainugo Eiri Jiten* (Ainu Language Illustrated Dictionary). Tokyo: Kagyusha, 1994

Kayano, Shigeru. *Ainu no Mingu* (Ainu Folkcrafts). Kawagoe: Suzusawa Book Store, 1978

Kayano, Shigeru. *Kayano Shigeru no Ainugo Jiten* (KayanoShigeru's Ainu Language Dictionary). Tokyo: Sanseido, 1996

Musashino Art University – The Research Institute for Culture and Cultural History. *Ainu no Mingu Jissoku Zushu* (Ainu Folkcrafts – Collection of Drawing and Figures). Biratori: Biratori-cho Council for Promoting Ainu Culture, 2014

Satouchi, Ai. *Ainu-shiki ekoroji-seikatsu: Haruzo Ekashi ni manabu shizen no chie* (Ainu Style Ecological Living: Haruzo Ekashi Teaches the Wisdom of Nature). Tokyo: Kabushiki gaisha Shogakukan, 2008

Chiri, Yukie. *Ainu Shin'yoshu* (Chiri Yukie's Ainu Epic Tales). Tokyo: Iwanami Shoten, 1978

Namikawa, Kenji. *Ainu Minzoku no Kiseki* (The Path of the Ainu People). Tokyo: Yamakawa Publishing, 2004

Mook. *Senjuumin Ainu Minzoku* (Bessatsu Taiyo) (The Ainu People (Extra Issue Taiyo). Tokyo: Heibonsha, 2004

Kinoshita, Seizo. *Shiraoikotan Kinoshita Seizo Isaku Shashin Shu* (Shiraoikotan: Kinoshita Seizo's Posthumous Photography Collection). Hokkaido Shiraoi-gun Shiraoi-cho: Shiraoi Heritage Conservation Foundation, 1988

The Ainu Museum. *Ainu no Ifuku Bunka* (The Culture of Ainu Clothing). Hokkaido Shiraoi-gun Shiraoi-cho: Shiraoi Ainu Museum, 1991

Keira, Tomoko and Kaji, Sayaka. *Ainu no Shiki* (Ainu's Four Seasons). Tokyo: Akashi Shoten, 1995

Fukuoka, Itoko and Sato, Kazuko. *Ainu Shokubutsushi* (Ainu Botanical Journal). Chiba Urayasu-Shi: Sofukan, 1995

Hayakawa, Noboru. *Ainu no Minzoku* (Ainu Folklore). Iwasaki Bijutsusha, 1983

Sunazawa, Kura. *Ku Sukuppu Orushibe* (The Memories of My Generation). Hokkaido, Sapporo-shi: Miyama Shobo, 1983

Haginaka, Miki et al. *Kikigaki Ainu no Shokuji* (Oral History of Ainu Diet). Tokyo: Rural Culture Association Japan, 1992

Nakagawa, Hiroshi. *New Express Ainu Go.* Tokyo: Hakusuisha, 2013

Nakagawa, Hiroshi. *Ainugo Chitose Hogen Jiten* (The Ainu-Japanese dictionary). Chiba Urayasu-Shi: Sofukan, 1995

Nakagawa, Hiroshi and Nakamoto, Mutsuko. *Kamuy Yukara de Ainu Go wo Manabu* (Learning Ainu with Kamuy Yukar). Tokyo: Hakusuisha, 2007

Nakagawa, Hiroshi. *Katari au Kotoba no Chikara – Kamuy tachi to Ikiru Sekai* (The Power of Spoken Words – Living in a World with Kamuy). Tokyo: Iwanami Shoten, 2010

Sarashina, Genzo and Sarashina, Hikari. *Kotan Seibutsu Ki <1 Juki / Zassou hen>* (Kotan Wildlife Vol. 1 – Trees and Weeds). Hosei University Publishing, 1992/2007

Sarashina, Genzo and Sarashina, Hikari. *Kotan Seibutsu Ki <2 Yacho / Kaijuu / Gyozoku hen>* (Kotan Wildlife Vol. 2 – Birds, Sea Creatures, and Fish). Hosei University Publishing, 1992/2007

Sarashina, Genzo and Sarashina, Hikari. *Kotan Seibutsu Ki <3 Yachou / Mizudori / Konchu hen>* (Kotan Wildlife Vol. 3 – Shorebirds, Seabirds, and Insects). Hosei University Publishing, 1992/2007

Sarashina, Genzo. *Ainu Minwashu* (Collection of Ainu Folktales). Kita Shobou, 1963

Sarashina, Genzo. *Ainu Rekishi to Minzoku* (Ainu History and Folklore). Shakai Shisousha, 1968

Kawakami Yuji. *Sarunkur Ainu Monogatari* (The Tale of Sarunkur Ainu). Kawagoe: Suzusawa Book Store, 2003/2005

Kawakami, Yuji. *Ekashi to Fuchi wo Tazunete* (Visiting Ekashi and Fuchi). Kawagoe: Suzusawa Book Store, 1991

Council for the Conservation of Ainu Culture. *Ainu Minzokushi* (Ainu People Magazine). Dai-ichi Hoki, 1970

Okamura, Kichiemon and Clancy, Judith A. *Ainu no Ishou* (The Clothes of the Ainu People). Kyoto Shoin, 1993

Hokkaido Cultural Property Protection Association. *Ainu Ifuku Chousa Houkokusho <1 Ainu Josei ga Denshou Suru Ibunka>* (The Ainu Clothing Research Report Vol. 1 - Traditional Clothing Passed Down Through Generations of Ainu Women). 1986

Yotsuji, Ichiro. Photos by Mizutani, Morio. *Ainu no Monyo* (Decorative Arts of the Ainu). Kasakura Publishing, 1981

Yoshida, Iwao. *Ainushi Shiryoshu* (Collection of Ainu Historical Documents). Hokkaido Publication Project Center, 1983

Kubodera, Itsuhiko. *Ainu no Mukashibanashi* (Old Stories of the Ainu). Miyaishoten, 1972

Kubodera, Itsuhiko (trans.). *Ainu Minzokushi* (Ainu People Magazine). Dai-ichi Hoki

Inoue, Koichi and Latyshev, Vladislav M. (coed.). *Karafuto Ainu no Mingu* (Karafuto Ainu Folkcraft). Hokkaido Publication Project Center, 2002

Russia ga Mita Ainu Bunka (Ainu Culture as Seen by Russia). The Foundation for Research and Promotion of Ainu Culture, 2013

Russia Minzokugaku Hakubutsukan Ainu Shiryoten—Russia ga Mita Shimaguni no Hitobito (Russia Museum of Ethnology Ainu Materials Exhibition—Island Peoples as Seen by Russia). The Foundation for Research and Promotion of Ainu Culture, 2005

The Foundation for Research and Promotion of Ainu Culture (ed.). *Senjima, Karafuto, Hokkaido—Ainu no Kurashi* (Ainu Life on the Kuril Islands, Karafuto and Hokkaido). The Senri Foundation, 2011

SPb-Ainu Project Group (ed.). *Russia Kagaku Academy Jinruigaku Minzokugaku Hakubutsukan Shozo Ainu Shiryo Mokuroku* (Ainu Collections of Peter the Great Museum of Anthropology and Ethnography Russian Academy of Sciences Catalogue). Sofukan, 1998

Yamamoto, Yuko. *Karafuto Ainu—Jukyo to Mingu* (Residences and Folkcraft of the Karafuto Ainu). Sagami Shobo, 1970

Yamamoto, Yuko (author and ed.). Chiri, Mashiho and Onuki, Emiko co-authors). *Karafuto Shizen Minzoku no Seikatsu* (Lifestyles of Karafuto Natural Peoples). Sagami Shobo, 1979

Chiri, Mashiho. *Chiri Mashiho Chosakushu 3 Seikatsu-shi / Minzokugaku-hen* (Mashiho Chiri Collected Works, Vol. 3: Lifestyles and Ethnology). Heibonsha, 1973

Yamamoto, Yuko. *Hoppo Shizen Minzoku Minwa Shusei* (Northern Natural Peoples Folk Tales Compilation). Sagami Shobo, 1968

Yamamoto, Yuko. *Karafuto Genshi Minzoku no Seikatsu* (Lifestyles of Karafuto Primitive Peoples). ARS, 1943

Nishitsuru, Sadaka. *Karafuto Ainu.* Miyama Shobo, 1974

Kasai, Takechiyo. *Karafuto Ainu no Minzoku* (Folklore of the Karafuto Ainu). Miyama Shobo, 1975

Tanigawa, Kenichi. Kita no Minzokushi-Sakhalin / Chishima no Minzoku (Northern Ethnography—Sakhalin / People of the Kuril Islands). San-Ichi Shobo Publishing Inc., 1997

Takabeya, Fukuhei. *Hoppoken no Ie* (Houses of the Northern Regions). Shokokusha Publishing Co., Ltd., 1943

Abashiri City Northern Folkore Cultural Preservation Society. *Uiruta no Kurashi to Mingu* (Uilta Lifestyles and Folkcraft). 1982

The Foundation for Research and Promotion of Ainu Culture (ed.). *Zaidan Hojin Ainu Bunka Fukko / Kenkyu Suishin Kiko Shuzo Mokuroku 7 (Ishida Shuzo Kyuzo Shashin)* (The Foundation for Research and Promotion of Ainu Culture Collection Catalog 7 (Ishida Collection Old Collection Photograph). The Foundation for Research and Promotion of Ainu Culture, 2012

Uilta Society Museum Steering Committee (ed.). *Shiryokan Jakka Duxuni Tenji Sakuhinshu* (Museum Jakka Duxuni Exhibition Works Collection). 2002

Bird, Isabella L. (author), Kobari, Kosai (trans.) *Meiji Shoki no Emishi Tanboki* (Report on Emishi in the Early Meiji Era). Sarorun Shobo, 1977

Munro, N.G. (author), Seligman, B.Z. (ed.), Tetsuro, Komatsu (trans.). *Ainu no Shinko to Sono Gishiki* (Ainu Creed and Cult). Kokushokankokai, 2002

Batchelor, John (author), Tetsuro, Komatsu (trans.). *Ainu no Kurashi to Densho* (Ainu Life and Lore). Hokkaido Publication Project Center, 1999

Shinmyo, Hidehito. *Ainu Fuzokuga no Kenkyu: Kinsei Hokkaido ni Okeru Ainu to Bijutsu* (Study of Ainu Genre Painting: Ainu and Art in Modern Hokkaido). Nakanishi Publishing, 2011

Aoki, Aiko (teller). Nagai, Hiroshi (recorder). Ainu O-san Baa-chan no Upashikuma Densho no Chie no Kiroku (Ainu Midwife Upaskuma: A Record of Traditional Wisdom). Jushinsha, 1998

Segawa, Kiyoko. *Ainu no Konin* (Married Ainu). Miraisha, 1998

Hitchcock, R. (author) Kitakamae, Yasuo (trans.). *Ainujin to Sono Bunka—Meiji Chuki no Ainu no Mura Kara—* (The Ainu People and Their Culture: From the Ainu Villages of the Mid-Meiji Era). Rokko Shuppan, 1990

Landor, A.S. (author). Toda, Sachiko (trans.). *Ezo-chi Isshu Hitori Tabi: Omoide no Ainu Country* (Traveling Alone Around Ezo: Ainu Country as I Remember It). Miraisha, 1985

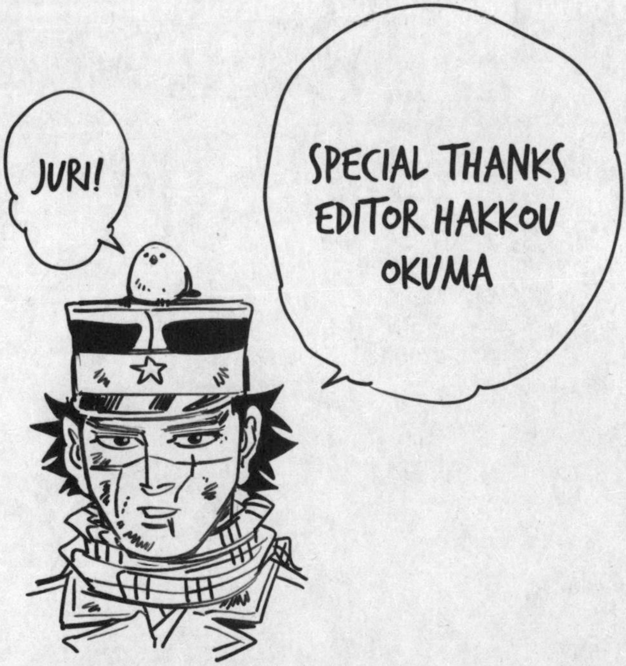
SPECIAL THANKS EDITOR HAKKOU OKUMA
JURI!

Kanto or wa yaku sak no arankep sinep ka isam.
Nothing comes from heaven without purpose. — Ainu proverb

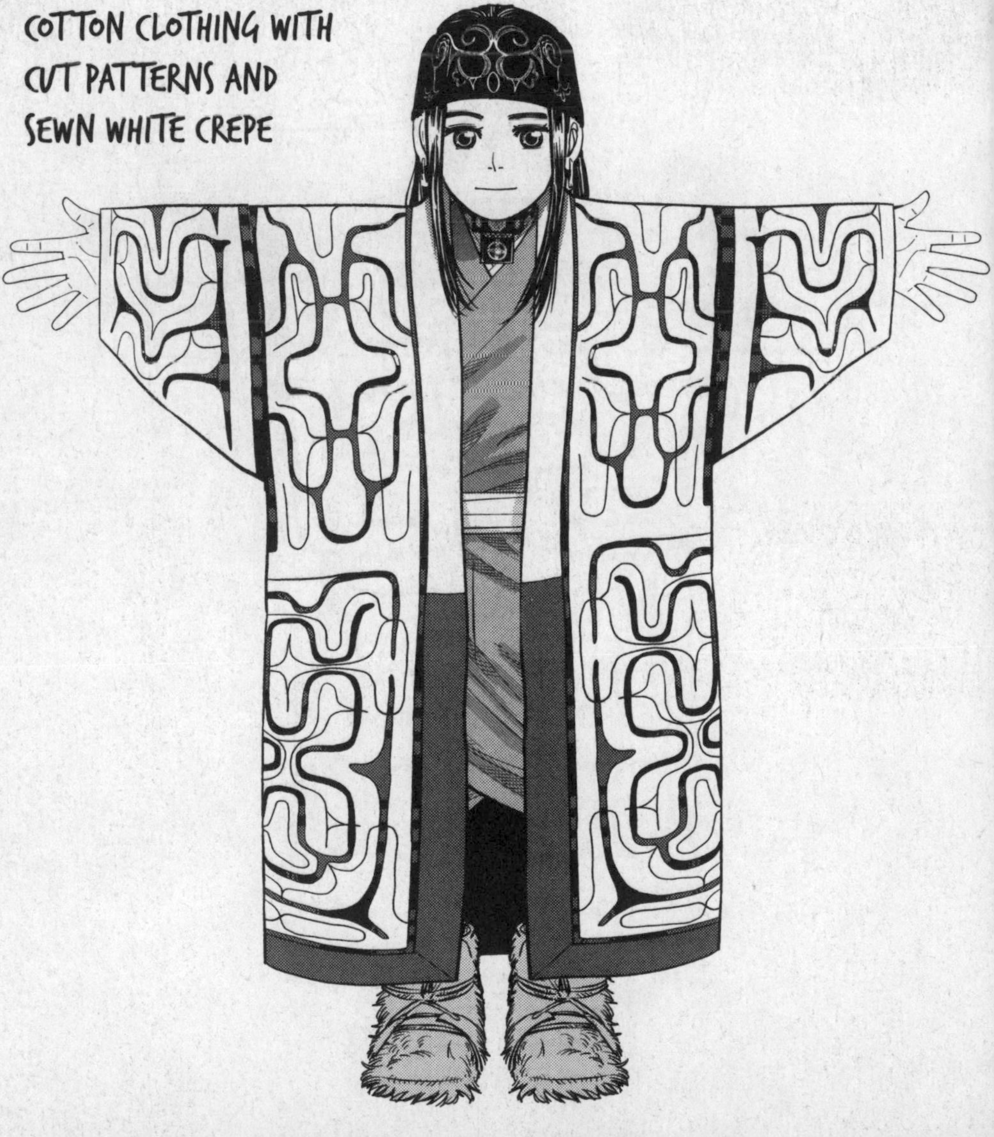
KAPARAMIPU
COTTON CLOTHING WITH
CUT PATTERNS AND
SEWN WHITE CREPE

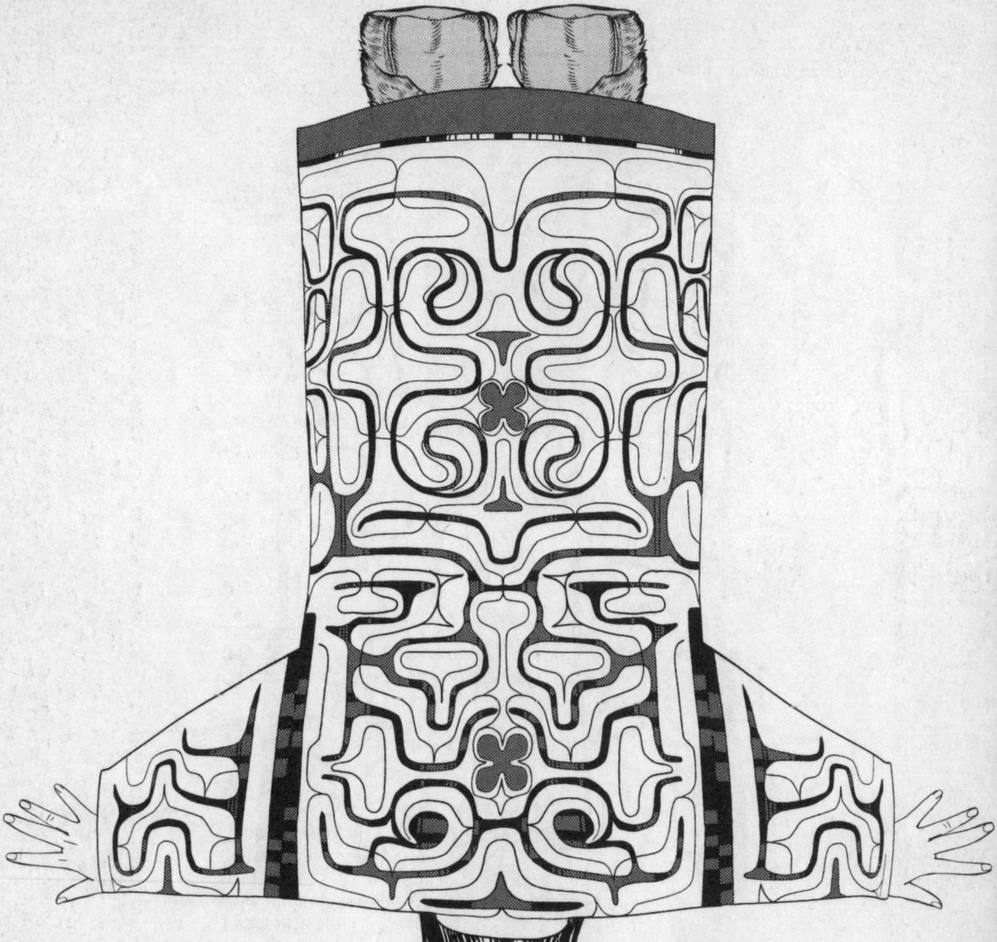

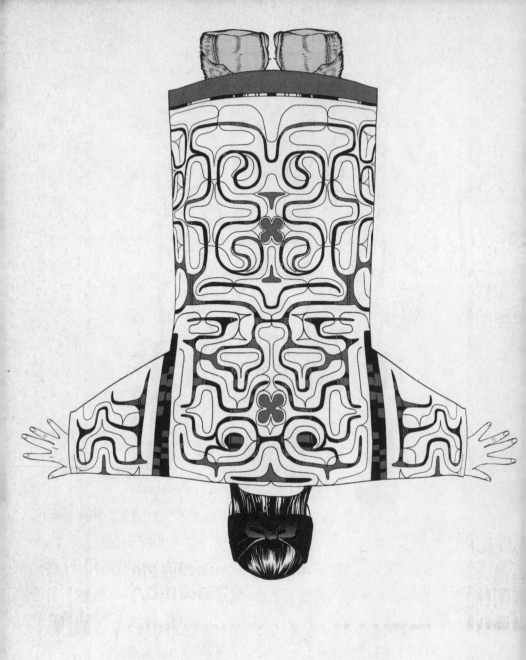

GOLDEN KAMUY

Volume 23
VIZ Signature Edition

Story/Art by **Satoru Noda**

GOLDEN KAMUY © 2014 by Satoru Noda
All rights reserved.
First published in Japan in 2014 by SHUEISHA Inc., Tokyo.
English translation rights arranged by SHUEISHA Inc.

Translation/John Werry
Touch-Up Art & Lettering/Steve Dutro
Design/Shawn Carrico
Editor/Mike Montesa

Printed in Canada

Published by VIZ Media, LLC
P.O. Box 77010
San Francisco, CA 94107

10 9 8 7 6 5 4 3 2 1
First printing, August 2021

VIZ SIGNATURE

VIZ MEDIA
viz.com

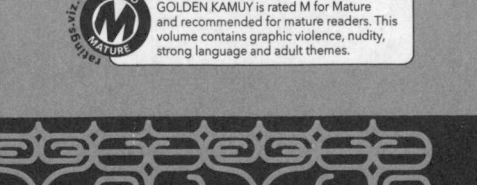

THIS IS THE LAST PAGE.

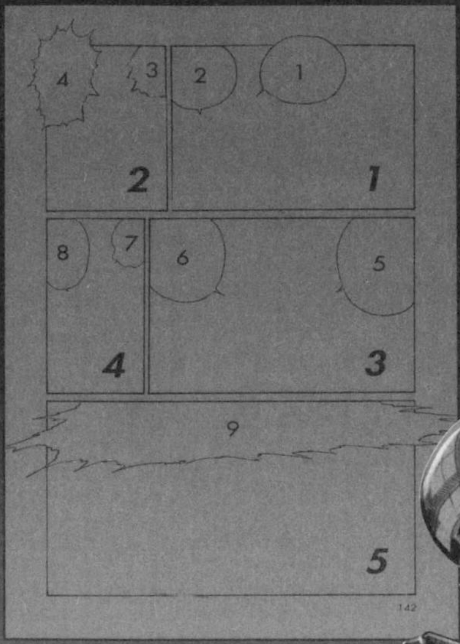

←Follow the action this way.

GOLDEN KAMUY has been printed in the original Japanese format in order to preserve the orientation of the original artwork.

Please turn it around and begin reading from right to left. Unlike English, Japanese is read right to left, so Japanese comics are read in reverse order from the way English comics are typically read. Have fun with it!

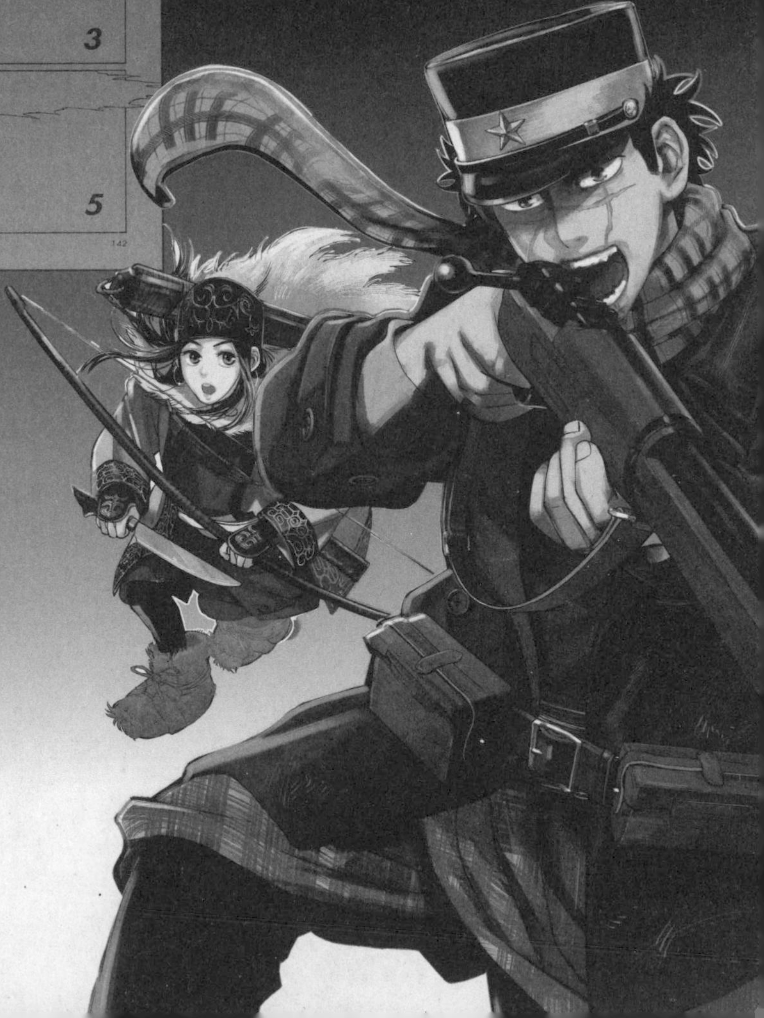